THE CLINTON HOUSE
20 NORTH SAN MATEO DRIVE, SUITE 3
SAN MATEO, CA 94401

# Effective Outpatient Treatment for Alcohol Abusers and Drinking Drivers

# Effective
# Outpatient Treatment
# for Alcohol Abusers
# and Drinking Drivers

John S. Crandell

**Lexington Books**
*D.C. Heath and Company/Lexington, Massachusetts/Toronto*

*Library of Congress Cataloging-in-Publication Data*

Crandell, John S.
  Effective outpatient treatment for alcohol abusers and drinking drivers.

  Bibliography: p.
  1. Alcoholics—Rehabilitation—United States.   2. Drunk driving—United
States.   3. Alcoholism—Treatment—United States.   I. Title.
HV5279.C73   1987        362.2'9286        86–46030
ISBN 0–669–14929–2 (alk. paper)

Published simultaneously in Canada
Printed in the United States of America
Casebound International Standard Book Number: 0–669–14929–2
Library of Congress Catalog Card Number: 86–46030

The paper used in this publication meets the minimum requirements of American National
Standard for Information Sciences—Permanence of Paper for Printed Library Materials, ANSI
Z39.48–1984. ⊗™

87 88 89 90 8 7 6 5 4 3 2 1

*To Lillian Grimes Eddy and Alger Buell Crandell*

# Contents

# Figures

# Tables

# Foreword

D rinking and driving is an emotionally charged problem that confronts contemporary society. It's hard to imagine anyone who would not support sanctions against those who drive while high on alcohol or other drugs. However, drinking and driving presents a unique social policy question in that the forces for treatment and those for punishment often clash over the appropriate responses to this problem.

Clearly, all individuals convicted of driving while intoxicated (DWI) should have some degree of legal sanction imposed against them—the punishment. However, all such offenders should also be evaluated to determine whether they have alcohol or substance abuse problems. Without a clinical assessment followed by appropriate treatment, legal action does not preclude the possibility that an offender will continue to drive while intoxicated. If alcohol abuse or alcoholism is present, the offender's drinking cannot be controlled and it is only a matter of time before driving under the influence will happen again.

For an offender with a DWI who does not have alcohol problems, the assessment can be useful to document this fact and to provide the individual with information on the signs and symptoms of alcoholism. In this way, clinical assessment can be both a clinical intervention and a preventive-educational activity.

*Effective Outpatient Treatment for the Alcohol Abuser and Drinking Driver* provides the reader with an overview of the forces that shape the debate over drunk driving. But more importantly, Dr. Crandell outlines step-by-step activities, programs, interventions, and responses to expect from the client and the therapist during treatment sessions. What are such programs like? How are they run? What will the client be doing? What types of interventions are most appropriate for whom?

The key point made by this book is that differential diagnosis is vital to the DWI assessment process. Neither a narrow examination of drinking and driving nor a broad examination of a range of problems is helpful to a client. What is necessary is a *focused assessment* that doesn't lose sight of alcohol-drug issues and their place in a broader clinical context. This focus is the strength of *Effective Outpatient Treatment for the Alcohol Abuser and Drinking Driver*.

At another level, Dr. Crandell has provided both a conceptual framework and specific intervention strategies that can serve as the core of an effective ambulatory program for alcoholism treatment. Anyone who is questioning his or her use of alcohol or other substances—or who is being confronted by others because of alcohol or substance use—could profit from participation in the types of programs and activities outlined in this book. Thus, while this book focuses on DWIs, at the same time it describes ambulatory programs for people with a wide range of substance abuse problems.

On a personal note, I can recall conversations with John Crandell in which we debated both the nature of alcoholism and the clinical complexity—or lack of it—of treating these patients. Both of us learned to argue both sides of the coin. Over the years, Dr. Crandell has gained experience and expertise in addressing the clinical context of alcoholism. He recognizes and directly confronts drinking behavior in a clinical context that can serve as a framework for devising and implementing individualized treatment.

*Effective Outpatient Treatment for the Alcohol Abuser and Drinking Driver* provides the reader with the specifics of how to treat alcohol abuse, but it also presents the way to conceptualize approaches to this problem.

—*William J. Filstead, Ph.D.*

# Acknowledgments

**M**y clients and students provided the inspiration to write this and many of the tools that I have used in treating alcohol abuse. Most of the exercises were developed by anonymous counselors and teachers. I am the beneficiary of a rich oral tradition; I hope what I have written here aids in making that tradition more accessible. To all these unnamed sources of my material, I am most grateful. Much of the unwritten tradition was conveyed to me by Glenn Paule-Carres, Ph.D., who also gave me the opportunity to work with drinking drivers.

The work was enriched by the substantive comments of John Wetsel and Charles Drake. Ruth Francis and Lynn Bolton reviewed the book and nurtured it and its author with their support and criticism.

Most of all, I am appreciative of Pia, Alethea, and Matthew Crandell for the love and patience that made the continued effort possible.

# 1
# Introduction: Toward Effective Treatment

There is a fundamental conflict in our attitude toward those with drinking problems. Complacency has given way to strong but contradictory impulses about how we should respond as individuals and as a society. On the one hand, never before has there been so much faith in treatment. The publicity surrounding the recovery of celebrities, from Betty Ford to Mary Tyler Moore to Johnny Cash, has lent a certain cachet to addiction. Successful treatment programs are available locally. Most important, it is becoming clearer which ideas and treatments effectively lead to permanent solutions to substance abuse. This means that successful programs can be developed for special populations and settings: in the workplace, in the schools, in corrections. This book shows how to develop effective outpatient programs, focusing in particular on treatment for the drunk driver.

Treatment represents a viable alternative to the old passivity and feeling of futility. But there are also strong forces coalescing that insist punishment is the appropriate response. Picture if you will the drunk sports fan in the bleachers and the futile attempts of those around him to ignore his obstreperous and unpredictable behavior. Others experience vicarious pleasure when someone yells, "Sit down and shut up," even though this does not work for more than a minute or two. Finally, there is a shared sense of relief if the drunk is ushered out of the stadium. Murmured comments confirm the contempt held for drinkers who trample on our pleasure and our values in their intoxication. All is now well—the drunk has been punished.

Anger and disparagement are a natural response when our rights have been violated; punishment does meet the needs of those who have been offended. But, unless it is followed by something more, punishment will *not* meet the needs of the alcohol abuser. Treatment is that "something more." But a climate of public outrage makes it difficult to care about the rights and needs of the problem drinker. Although treatment can be combined with punishment (as when the drunk driver is fined but given a suspended jail sentence upon completing a rehabilitation program), the prevailing attitude portrays punishment and treatment as mutually exclusive. Today, these two approaches may be on a collision course.

The polarization is especially evident in the emotional discussions about handling drinking and driving. We become deeply angry about the carnage caused by drunk drivers, who kill upwards of 20,000 people and injure 660,000 more annually in alcohol-related accidents in the United States (Podolsky, 1985a). Despite clear signs of their own danger, they keep driving—drunk. Outrage is a natural response.

Let me give a particularly pertinent example.

In May 1980 Clarence Busch killed thirteen-year-old Cari Lightner in a hit-and-run accident. He had four prior arrests for driving while intoxicated (DWI), yet he still had a license and had spent only forty-eight hours in jail. His arrogance was every bit as offensive as the lack of punishment. He told his wife after the arrest that he would have to kill four or five people before he would admit to having a drinking problem.

It was in response to this incident that Mothers Against Drunk Driving (MADD), which has effectively lobbied for tougher enforcement and punishment, was organized. Mr. Busch eventually spent two and a half years in jail and in halfway houses prior to his release in February 1985. Despite his arrest record, he was able to get a temporary driver's license. In April he ran a red light and injured nineteen-year-old Carrie Sinnott. His blood alcohol concentration (BAC) was .20—enough to have two people arrested. Mr. Busch seems intent on continuing until he does kill four or five people.

Can you feel anger? Does it make you want to do something? A local newspaper editor expressed the outrage: "Isn't that charming? Any chance the judge could lose the jail key for the next 50 years?" (Rupp, 1985, p. 4). Candy Lightner, mother of one of Busch's victims and former head of MADD, went even further:

> Alcoholism may be a disease, but drunk driving is a crime. Rehabilitation is not effective. Clarence Busch is, unfortunately, a typical alcoholic. I'm not sure there is any hope for him except to remove him from society permanently and never allow him to own or drive a car. (Farber, 1985, p. 152. Reprinted with permission from *People*.)

You can empathize with the hurt and anger. You can easily find yourself saying that there must be some greater and more suitable punishment.

But wait! Do you really believe what Mrs. Lightner said? How incredibly insulting to the millions of recovering alcoholics who have found a way to stop drinking to call Busch "a typical alcoholic." When a local hospital claims 90 percent recovery rates for clients who comply with the treatment regimen (M. Hill, personal communication, June, 1985), it is dangerously misleading to say that "rehabilitation is not effective." No matter how much sympathy I feel for her, Mrs. Lightner is distorting reality to make a political point. She would sweep you on a tide of emotion into harsh reprisals against drunk drivers, reprisals that would exclude any opportunity for treatment. Busch's lawyer asked that his client be sentenced to alcoholism treatment. Do we really want "to remove him from society permanently" before making available to him specialized treatment for his disease?

In October 1985 Mr. Busch was sentenced to four years in prison. So far as I know, no provision was made for alcoholism treatment. If you were to make a bet, would you expect him to resume drinking after his release?

## Models of Alcoholism and the Paralysis in Public Policy

We seem to cycle through advocating treatment, urging punishment, and resigning ourselves to the futility of attempts to change the problem drinker. This applies equally to our personal attitudes and our public policy. There is a long-standing tradition that regards consuming alcohol as a right and a pleasure while reviling drunkenness as a sign of weakness. Since control of consumption is taken as a measure of moral stature, this viewpoint is called the "moral model" (Rogers & McMillin, 1984). Churches call drunkenness sinful; jails have drunk tanks whose squalor reflects the contempt in which the drunk is held. This is the traditional basis for punishment as a response to alcoholism. It offers the slim hope that censure will chasten the offender into reforming.

At the end of the last century, the temperance movement developed a variation on the moral model which considered alcohol—rather than the problem drinker—to be evil. Misuse was still a moral failing, but the power of alcohol (the "devil's brew") was so overwhelming that abuse was all but certain to follow use. I remember my grandfather's pride in saying that he had never in his life had a drink of alcohol. To him abstinence was a sign of character and righteousness. The attempt to impose this perspective on the whole of American society led to the Volstead Act in 1919, which ushered in a decade in which alcohol use was prohibited. Supplies did drop, and average consumption diminished. But the goal of national abstinence was never approached. Prohibition failed, not only because drinking and alcoholism continued, but because it became glamorous to flout the law. After the repeal of Prohibition in 1933, the government gave up its attempts to control alcohol consumption—in essence, accepting the futility of intervention as public policy.

Within this vacuum of leadership, the treatment model developed, spurred by the success of the self-help fellowship of Alcoholics Anonymous (AA), which demonstrated that the problem drinker can hope for recovery. Jellinek (1960), extended by Milam (1974; Milam & Ketcham, 1981) and others, developed the idea that alcoholism is a diagnosable and treatable disease. Competing psychological, biological, and social theories of the cause and nature of the disease abound. But these theories share the common belief that education and treatment can accomplish what punishment alone cannot: the rehabilitation of the problem drinker.

There are now signs of movement, if not of progress. There is a sense that we must do something about alcohol problems in our country. Government reinvolvement is evident in recent moves to raise taxes on alcohol, to provide incentives for a standard national drinking age of twenty-one, and to develop programs for decreasing DWI deaths. But as public policy seeks to change the pattern of years of inertia, in what direction will it move? The paradox is that we have never had more effective tools for treating alcohol problems, yet the greatest emphasis seems to be on toughening penalties, in line with Mrs. Lightner's comments. We may be at the beginning of another cycle in which excessive drinking—or at least drunk driving—is regarded as a moral failing best handled through punishment and public censure.

## The Challenge of Effective Treatment for Drunk Drivers

I believe strongly that treatment is the best approach to handling the problem of driving while intoxicated. This is not to say that I reject the call for tougher penalties. The prospect of jail time or loss of license is a tremendously effective means of commanding the attention of the imbiber who had never previously questioned habitual drunken driving. But unless education or treatment is available to capitalize on this attention, powerful habits will reemerge as the memory of punishment fades:

> At first I was careful and only drank at home. But then, you know, I had
> to run to the store, and I felt all right. Pretty soon I was back at it again.

Punishment alone has only a temporary effect. Yet the philosophy behind it will not admit to this limitation. The standard response is to up the ante: "If four days in jail and three years' loss of license don't work, then give him a year in prison and take his license forever." From such a perspective, treatment can only look like coddling the criminal.

Most available treatment—at least for the drinking driver—*is* inadequate. Some examples of current approaches may illustrate this:

1. The weekend DWI school, no matter how dramatic its impact, is too brief to lead to lasting change. Where is the support for questioning old

habits? Where is the practical advice to get an alcoholic through the six weeks of edginess and irritability that come from withdrawal?

2. Required attendance at AA meetings may backfire. An unresolved negative attitude will alienate the offender from regular members. The honest sharing of recovering alcoholics, graphic in their admission of the destruction wrought by drinking, may convince the involuntary participant that "I'm not that bad." Offenders with moderate drinking problems and alcoholics denying their symptoms will simply not relate to the meetings.

3. Brief driver education courses filled with movies about the alcohol-related carnage on the highways fail in two ways. First, the personal risk is denied. After hundreds of episodes of arriving safely when grossly intoxicated, the drunk driver comes to believe that a "guardian angel" will continue to offer protection from injury. Even if a commitment is made to avoid driving while intoxicated, the promise is ignored once the person is well medicated with alcohol—a powerful antianxiety drug. The program does not teach participants how to avoid getting drunk. This failure to address the pattern of problem drinking is the second obstacle to lasting change.

If these examples typify what is available, and I believe they do, then the critics can not be blamed for dismissing treatment as a viable approach.

It is the inadequacy of most existing programs, and not the belief in treatment, that warrants attack. In an ideal world, there would be an alliance between proponents of punishment and treatment for advocating an effective response to drunk driving. The two groups would cooperate in raising public awareness so that resources would be mobilized. The most powerful appropriate therapies might then be used. Currently, few judges would mandate a month of inpatient alcohol rehabilitation followed by halfway house placement, aftercare group therapy, and AA attendance. Ideally, this might happen. But most life-threatening illnesses—and alcoholism certainly is one—are not handled in the public domain. Heroic and costly efforts to extend the life of a person suffering from degenerative heart disease are undertaken regularly by families. But they are not required by judges. We should not expect that the most expensive and extended available therapies will be routinely mandated. For the forseeable future, treatment programs will be asked to do the job of rehabilitating the drinking driver without using the most powerful tools.

The challenge is to develop effective treatment within the constraints imposed by the current climate. This means designing a comprehensive and potentially effective program that can be conducted on an outpatient basis, with weekly or twice weekly group sessions, with a total duration of less than a year. That is the challenge accepted in this book. The chapters that follow outline a tested and effective approach that works within these limits. What is presented is a set of discussions and exercises. These can be selected and organized to meet the particular needs of a program. The book also presents a model of effective treatment: the problem-solving model. This model can be used as a guide to developing alcohol education and treatment programs, even if the course does not include the specific content detailed in the following chapters. The problem-solving model—developed for use in the outpatient treatment of problem drinkers—can be applied in therapeutic, correctional, and educational settings.

## Requirements for Effective Treatment

An effective treatment program for drunk drivers must fulfill the following requirements:

1. The duration of treatment must be long enough that changes in attitude and behavior occur while the client is still in the program (Reis, 1983). Education is the beginning of effective treatment; but education without change is inadequate treatment. For the vast majority of my clients, alcohol abuse and intoxicated driving are overlearned habits: they occur automatically and without apparent intention. Alternative behavior must be practiced until it too becomes habitual if there is to be any hope that the change will be maintained. Realistically, this means a minimum treatment duration of six months. It also means that there must be evidence of behavior change (abstinence or demonstrated consistent control over alcohol consumption) for the client to complete the program successfully.

2. Effective treatment includes goals beyond avoiding future DWIs. Drunk driving is a warning sign of alcoholism. The costs of alcoholism are spread throughout the drinker's life, but nowhere is the damage greater than to the family. Impulsiveness, broken or forgotten promises, hostility, and unpredictable behavior are all traumatizing to the spouse and children. I worry about what we have done when we "succeed" in convincing the drunk driver to "do my drinking at home where I won't hurt anybody." Clients must understand the risks from alcohol abuse in all areas of their lives. A personal inventory of actual costs must be completed as a structured part of treatment. An exclusive focus on drinking and driving is counterproductive.

3. The program must be able to accommodate different types of drinkers. I help my clients distinguish three types of drinkers (see chapter 6). There are "social" drinkers (more accurately termed low-tolerance drinkers) who can succeed if they can develop alternatives to driving during their very occasional drinking periods. The second group, heavy (or high-tolerance) drinkers, will have to change the pattern and reduce the amount of their consumption to comply with the requirements of the program. They need not necessarily decide to quit drinking. The third type, the alcoholic, has only one realistic prospect for avoiding future DWIs: to become committed to lifelong abstinence. Thus, the outpatient DWI program differs from in-

patient treatment in that abstinence is not the only legitimate goal. The discrepancy between the goals will lead to confusion if those goals are not carefully linked to the diagnosis of the drinking problem. But the alternative, to represent abstinence as the only acceptable goal even for nonalcoholics, is unrealistic and an invitation to wholesale dishonesty on the part of clients.

"I'm not that bad yet," is the refrain of the majority of my clients who had not admitted an alcohol problem prior to their DWI arrest. It conveys the difficulty in reaching an honest self-evaluation. The client who is in outpatient treatment because of an alcohol-related conviction is likely to be less aware of his problem than the person enrolling for inpatient rehabilitation. This denial, often grounded in the reality that the arrest is the first recognized warning sign of a developing drinking problem, is a particular challenge in the treatment of the DWI defendant. The extent of resistance and defensiveness in such clients, in addition to the inclusion of both alcoholics and nonalcoholics, makes it unrealistic to transplant an AA-oriented inpatient model of treatment for use with the DWI offender. More effort is required to overcome denial, more emphasis is given to differential self-diagnosis, and a broader range of goals for future drinking may be appropriate in the outpatient setting. Flexibility without confusion becomes a critical requirement for effective treatment.

4. An effective program of intervention for the drunk driver must make use of other treatment resources. Because of the brief contact (two hours weekly for forty weeks is still only eighty hours, less than four days) and the variety of goals, other modalities must be used if the program is to avoid the risk of failing in a vain attempt to be all things for all people. The counselor must be able to assume the role of case manager, sending one client for therapy while helping another engage in AA. The extent to which a variety of other treatments are used by my clients becomes a sign of the program's success in motivating them to change.

5. Treatment must include training in problem-solving so that clients are prepared to handle the unanticipated challenges they encounter after concluding treatment. I tell my clients that they "will beat the DWI rap within a year, but the drinking problem is there for ever." This is obvious for the alcoholic who recognizes that his disease remains present even while he abstains. It is also true for the nonalcoholic who maintains a high tolerance even if he develops a controlled drinking pattern. Anything that disrupts his new habit carries the risk of resumed abuse. To change drinking is a lifelong process. Successful treatment requires that the client assume responsibility for self-monitoring and for seeking any needed help to deal with any future manifestations of alcohol abuse. Using resources outside of the DWI program or making plans for aftercare are important indications that the client has taken responsibility and that the treatment has succeeded.

Problem solving can be taught as a skill. It can also be modeled in the design of the treatment program. Teaching it by using it gives clients the best prospect for continued success in dealing with alcohol abuse. The following chapter describes the steps of the problem-solving process.

# The Problem-Solving Model for Intervening with Alcohol Abuse

D rinking problems have proved notably difficult to change in a lasting manner; resistance is routine, relapse is common. This is not because of some inherent limitation in the drinker's personality or because the drug is so overwhelming. Rather, major life-style changes are necessary, beginning with an altered attitude so that alcohol abuse can be faced honestly. Most problem drinkers will fail if expected to make all of the changes at once. Effective treatment presents a sequence of smaller challenges that cumulatively achieve substantial and lasting changes in drinking. This process of breaking down change into manageable and yet comprehensive steps is called the problem-solving process.

We all use the problem-solving process daily to resolve a wide range of problems in living. It is so intuitively obvious that the standard reaction when it is described is: "I know that. I use it all the time." But recognizing its logic is not the same as using it to design treatment programs that systematically apply the problem-solving process. That is the purpose of this book.

After discussing the generic problem-solving model, this chapter will detail a ten-step problem-solving process for use with the alcohol abuser.

## The Problem-Solving Model

The common elements of problem solving include:

1. Defining the problem: exploring and clarifying a difficulty to detail it in such a way that something can be done about it. Initial definitions of the problem may be abandoned or transformed by new information or by the insight developed as a result of feedback from the helper.

2. Considering effective courses of action: goals are brainstormed and then those are chosen that are likely to be effective in resolving the problem

and yet are tailored to the values and skills of the client so that he or she is motivated to attain them.

3. Developing courses of action: programs are developed and implemented which are likely to help the client achieves the goals. This includes the acquisition of any necessary knowledge and skills. Predictable obstacles to change are anticipated and discussed. Successes and failures are evaluated so that the program can be modified if necessary. A strategy is developed to maintain the program in such a way that the problem is not likely to recur.

Egan (1982) summarizes the three steps as exploration, goal setting, and action.

We have all had the experience of not really understanding an issue until we have worked on it for a while. Often action precedes insight. So the problem-solving process is really circular. The action step may lead to a new perspective on the problem that revises the goals and suggests a modified program of action. Only when the problem is comfortably and successfully being managed is the problem-solving process finished.

Although we seldom think of it as a formal process, we continuously apply the problem-solving strategy in day-to-day living. When the car doesn't start we explore the problem (is it the battery? the ignition system? and so forth); choose goals and actions that are practical and in line with our values (have it towed to the mechanic and pay him to fix it, or isolate and replace the faulty parts ourselves); and continue the process (yes, another trip to the mechanic perhaps) until the car is consistently starting. We go through the same process in changing ourselves. When we notice we have put on a few pounds (defining the problem), we decide how much we want to lose (setting the goal), consider whether we have to increase our exercise or decrease our intake of calories (choosing courses of action), and then go to it (implementing the plans). We predictably fail if we aren't specific about the goal ("Well, at least I lost a few pounds, so I can help myself to seconds"), are unrealistic about the plans or our commitment to them ("Did I really expect to run twelve miles a week?!"), or have misdiagnosed the problem ("I never considered that it might be a metabolic disturbance"). Unless we abandon the program in disgust, even our failures teach us more about what is required to succeed ultimately ("It may take longer, but I will stick with it if I can still have ice cream once in a while"). These examples are mightily oversimplified. But they should make the point that we use problem solving regularly, and we are more likely to experience success in our lives if we use the process intentionally and follow the model through step by step.

Problem solving is applicable to both simple problems and complex ones, although there are more books about the complex ones. Systematic models are available to help one choose a career (for example, Bolles, 1981, 1987) or to learn how to become an effective counselor (for example, Egan, 1982).

The twelve steps of Alcoholics Anonymous (1953, 1976) can be seen as a way of defining the problem ("admitting we were powerless over alcohol") and a course of action to stop drinking and to develop a growth-oriented sober life.

In any organized effort to change, the problem-solving model offers a number of important advantages:

1. It increases the likelihood of success by breaking change down into manageable steps. Just as a wall is built brick by brick, each step successfully accomplished brings the ultimate goal closer.

2. The client is actively involved in planning and implementing change. Counseling is bedeviled by the dependent client who passively waits for the perfect transforming intervention by the therapist. Even if the "magic bullet" worked, it would rob the client of the chance to experience the power to control his or her life. Psychotherapy with problem drinkers often bogs down as insight supplants change as the focus of treatment. Problem solving emphasizes that action is integral to change and thus avoids this classic trap for the counselor.

3. The model provides a practical guide to the treatment process. Counselors act differently at different stages in problem solving. It should not be by accident; it should be in response to the changing needs and capabilities of the client. Clients act differently as they progress through treatment: the resistant client becomes the compliant learner and then the active planner and executor of his or her own recovery. The problem-solving process can make these changing roles and relationships clear. It can also suggest when a once appropriate role is now interfering with progress (as when a rigid sponsor continues to direct the details of living for a long-recovering "pigeon," as happens from time to time in AA and in treatment programs). I teach the problem-solving model explicitly as part of treatment. It helps clients recognize where they are, where they are going, and how they and I can best collaborate in reaching their goals.

4. Once taught the model, clients can use problem solving as a strategy to cope with the inevitable unanticipated obstacles that will occur once treatment is completed. In essence, clients can be taught to be their own counselors for resolving future problems.

5. Problem solving is flexible. It describes the process of change without being overly specific about the content of each step. It provides a framework that can be individualized for each client, even in group therapy. This is crucial, since a program of change must be tailored to each client's values if he or she is expected to work it. This also honors a fundamental reality in the group treatment of drunk drivers: goals differ since some are working on abstinence while others may have a realistic prospect of controlling their drinking. The problem-solving model is equally useful for either goal.

## Applying the Problem-Solving Model to Abusive Drinking

What will be described in this book is a ten-step program of alcohol education and treatment. It is designed to guide the drunk-driving offender from a typically hostile and resistant posture at the outset to a continuing commitment to a life-style change so that drinking will not cause future problems. That is the purpose of the program I am describing. It is ambitious. It capitalizes on the problem-solving model while altering its emphasis to conform to the unique needs of the drunk driver.

### Phase 1: Laying the Groundwork

There must be an identified problem for problem solving to be used. Alcohol abusers routinely resist identifying drinking as detrimental to their lives. The first steps of treatment assist the client in accepting help to recognize the problem. Carkhuff (1973b) describes a pre-problem-solving stage in which the confusion of the client's life is empathically explored in a way that permits focusing on a specific problem as the beginning of the helping process. The DWI clients need a similar introduction to a program of change. They may expect nothing more than punishment; after all, exposure to police, judges, fines, sentences, and case officers hardly shapes the clients' expectations so that that counseling can be approached as an opportunity for positive change. Similarly, clients are unlikely to enter treatment defining their problem as one based on the pattern of drinking if the DWI arrest is regarded as bad luck or inappropriate victimization ("Officer, why are you harassing upstanding citizens because they've had a few beers instead of catching the 'real' criminals?"). These attitudes compound the problem encountered with most abusive drinkers who protect their drinking with a shield of lies and distortions.

The first task of treatment is to get the clients to define their drinking as at least a potential problem that is worth examining. A major portion of each individual's time in the treatment group typically is spent overcoming the attitudes and defenses that prevent the clients from examining their drinking. Egan (1982) notes that this is not unique: perhaps a majority of clients in "helping programs" are initially reluctant or resistant. He also suggests that this resistance is the first issue that must be addressed; it is the first problem for problem solving. The first three steps in the problem-solving progression are directed at this work. I call this the phase for "laying the groundwork."

**Step 1: Overcoming Initial Resistance.** The fundamental reality is that the DWI client is in treatment involuntarily. His shame and resentment about his arrest are compounded with anger stirred up by involvement with the criminal justice system. Police, judges, and probation officers are often gruff, impersonal, and unresponsive to the offender's attempts to justify himself. Being convicted of DWI is typically experienced as dehumanizing. The loss of self-determination is a further threat. Most people arrive at treatment expecting to be punished and with an inner conviction that they are being victimized. When the counselor invites them to discuss their experience, they may be so suspicious that they refuse. Any sharing is likely to be hostile in tone and to focus attention externally, away from the offender or his drinking. The purpose of this stage is to provide an initial experience of the counselor and group being interested in the person, his or her experience, and in the pain associated with drinking. Successful navigation of this stage is evident when the person is talking about his or her drinking.

**Step 2: Confronting Defensiveness.** The initial discussion of the offender's drinking is filled with self-justification or outright lying. A problem drinker attempts to manipulate both his own and others' attitudes so that the drinking is not seen as a problem. The DWI conviction is presented as a fluke, an isolated event unrelated to the rest of the drinking life. Perhaps the most devastating rejoinder is to have another group member respond, "I used to think that too." Observing others' distortions, testimonials and rearrest stories by veteran group members, and education/confrontation about defenses all function to impress the new participant that there are important realities about drinking that may have been overlooked. The goal at this stage is a commitment to honesty with the self, which is evident in the decision not to tell lies in group.

**Step 3: Attitude Change.** When the participants become curious about new perspectives on drinking, they become true members of the group for the first time. By listening to one another, recognizing that some are blinded by resentment while others seem to be sincerely grateful for the opportunity to change available through the program, they recognize the importance of a receptive attitude. Fear of legal consequences become secondary to concern about personal safety as they appreciate the accident risks from DWI. As some clients fail in their attempts to avoid drunk driving, all participants realize that the real issue is problem drinking. All of these represent important changes in attitude. Even if not yet convinced that they have a drinking problem, the DWI offenders have accomplished the goal of this stage when they become committed to understanding problem drinking and willing to measure their own experience in terms of this new learning.

*Phase 2: New Perspectives*

In effect, these pre-problem-solving steps have reframed the issue. Drunk driving is now seen as but one example of the multiple ways in which alcohol use can interfere with living. A new attitude of inquiry surfaces, perhaps with a sense of concern and foreboding as the imbiber becomes appropriately concerned about the negative effects of drinking. There is a feeling that something must be done. Clients are now ready to take advantage of the problem-solving process. They are open to the second phase in which they develop "new perspectives."

**Step 4: Learning.** New perspectives require new information. The goal of this stage is knowledge about alcohol and problem drinking. The easy promise "I won't drive drunk again" is discussed in terms of the effects of alcohol on judgment and an understanding of different types of drinkers. As the group comes to understand the disease concept of alcoholism, with loss of control as an integral feature, there is a growing recognition that a change in drinking habits is necessary to prevent the risk of another DWI. The effects of alcohol on health, family, finances, and job are considered. For many members this new information fosters an awareness of a much more pervasive drinking problem.

**Step 5: Self-Diagnosis.** Information must be personalized. A variety of movies and activities help the clients distinguish whether their drinking pattern is abusive or whether it is alcoholic.

**Step 6: Goal Setting.** Three goals organize the clients' efforts. First is avoiding drunk driving. The second goal, making a lasting change in drinking, must be realized if there is to be consistent success in not driving while intoxicated. The change in drinking requires that clients face the implications of their self-diagnosis. Abstinence is the only realistic goal for the alcoholic. Abusers, and some on the borderline of alcoholism, can attempt to develop controlled drinking strategies. Chances for lasting changes in drinking are enhanced when clients make progress toward a third goal: developing an altered lifestyle so that the changed drinking pattern becomes comfortable. Work toward each successive goal consolidates gains on the previous ones. Clients' efforts are most directed toward changes in drinking. The treatment program additionally seeks to assure the absense of drunk driving by helping clients become adjusted to a lifestyle that excludes heavy drinking.

*Phase III: Change*

Setting a realistic goal is not to be confused with a sustained commitment to changing the entirety of one's life-style so as to ensure that the drinking problem is managed. Resistance resurfaces when it becomes clear that action is required. Even the motivated client has to be steeled to face the likelihood of difficult weeks before the rewards start appearing. Withdrawal, loss of friends and habitual activities, and the ignorance of family and associates all tax the resolve of the DWI offender attempting to complete the third phase of problem solving, "change." The traditional models stress implementing plans and evaluating their success. As expanded for use with the problem drinker, these steps are preceded by an attempt to heighten motivation and followed by a stage in which the gains are consolidated so that they can be preserved after the treatment program has been completed.

**Step 7: Motivation.** Clients balk when action is required, especially when it involves abstinence. Defenses reappear. Obstacles to change loom. Realistic plans provide strategies, but additional exercises are needed to provide impetus. In this stage, treatment seeks to heighten awareness of intrinsic and extrinsic motivation. Exercises focus on the clients' values and aspirations, helping them to rethink the role they want alcohol to play in their lives and to focus on the future opportunities to be enjoyed if the drinking problems can be resolved. If this is insufficient, the counselor applies pressure by outlining the requisite changes for successful completion of the program. The goal is for participants to develop a commitment to change.

**Step 8: Develop and Implement Plans.** There are prescribed plans for achieving some aspects of the goals; for instance, anyone attempting to abstain should at least try to become involved in the Alcoholics Anonymous program. The prescriptive features are reviewed and discussed in group until well understood and generally accepted. But there are also enormous differences in values and life-styles among group members, leading to individualized plans and rich opportunities for comparing experiences and strategies during the planning stage. Some will need to learn new skills of assertiveness or self-discipline. Some will have to reach out for additional help beyond the program. Some will develop elaborate strategies, while others can conceive of nothing beyond the decision to stop drinking after a certain limit. The testimonials, the dialogue, and the mutual confrontation all contribute to rich give and take within the group at this stage. The counselor encourages group members to make realistic plans. But there is also recognition that sometimes the failure of an ill-conceived strategy will be necessary to motivate adequate change. This stage is being addressed when group members make sincere efforts to alter behavior.

**Step 9: Evaluation.** Successes and failures have to be discussed so that plans can be refined. If successful, can the plans be maintained? If there are failures, group feedback can help the person decide where to begin recycling through the problem-solving process. Do plans need to be supplemented? Or are there more fundamental flaws caused by an impossible goal (for example, controlled drinking for a midstage alcoholic), a self-defeating attitude (continuing rejection of the disease concept), or persistent defenses? At this stage, it becomes apparent that the problem-solving process is indeed circular (as illustrated in figure 2–1). Action fosters new awareness. These learnings must then be incorporated in revised goals and plans, which are then tested out.

**Step 10: Consolidation.** Alcoholism is not cured when it is arrested. Even for the nonalcoholic, high tolerance remains—and with it lies the potential for resumed abusive drinking. These realities mean that successful clients will be committing themselves to a continuing effort. We learn the problem-solving process explicitly so that we can use it as a model for continuing revision of plans. In this concluding stage of treatment, the group identifies the nature of the task ahead: the sources of support to replace the group,

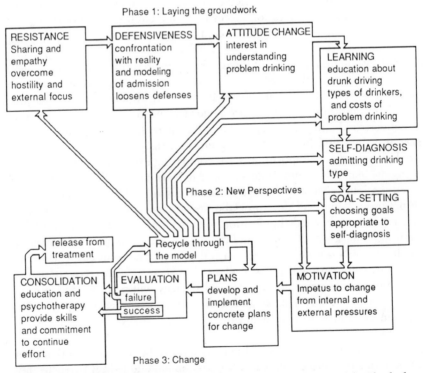

**Figure 2–1. The Problem-Solving Model for Intervening with Alcohol Abuse**

the psychotherapeutic techniques (ranging from relaxation training to communication skills) that can be included in the program or sought in other treatment, and the warning signs of a resurgent "drinker's attitude." The topics of group sessions are varied in response to the needs and initiative of members. Finally, successful plans will be reviewed with an eye to whether they have become integrated enough with the client's values and habits that they can be maintained after the client has left treatment. When the group members, now as partners of the therapist, are satisfied that this last condition has been met, the problem-solving process is complete, and the client is released.

This problem-solving process does not work for all clients. Their progress may be incomplete. Despite the counselor's efforts to help them navigate through each of the stages, they may be blocked by the resistance engendered by involuntary therapy, the defensiveness that is integral to alcohol abuse, or a stubborn refusal to change. A client who has not completed the ten stages is unlikely to have satisfactorily dealt with the drinking problem. The promise to begin AA after release from treatment is a classic example of the incomplete implementation of plans. Yet most programs operate under a time limit that cannot be extended to accommodate the participant making slow progress. In addition, successful completion of the ten steps does not guarantee that clients will continue to use the model. They fail to adapt plans to changing pressures, or they simply stop working the program.

Although failure or relapse are inevitable for some group members, risks can be minimized if the treatment program is designed so that clients have a reasonable opportunity to master the tasks of each stage of the problem-solving model. Toward the development of such programs, this book compiles discussions and exercises that have proved useful in helping alcohol abusers move through the problem-solving process. Each of the ten stages of the model is the focus of a specific chapter.

This material is specifically addressed to those conducting treatment for drinking drivers. Yet the flexibility of the problem-solving model assures that this book can be profitably used by others disseminating information about alcohol abuse. I have used these discussions and exercises in family and individual therapy, in training helpers to be more sophisticated in their understanding of alcohol problems, with groups of codependents, and so forth. If you follow the logic of the problem-solving model, you can tailor your own program to the unique needs of your setting. You can choose among the exercises in the following chapters and supplement them with new activities and with the new information that is constantly emerging in this field. This book not only gives exercises for each stage of the problem-solving model, but it also invites you to be actively involved in tailoring its application to your setting. With this invitation in hand, let us examine techniques for overcoming the initial resistance of the client entering the treatment program.

# 3
# Handling Initial Resistance

**B**y the time they arrive for treatment, drunk driving offenders have been through one of the most humiliating experiences of their lives. They will have been frightened or angered by a criminal justice process that, from arrest to mandatory intake with a probation officer, repeatedly drives home the reality that others control important aspects of their lives. The threat to their license and their freedom may evoke defiance or passive compliance. But they will almost certainly feel resentful at the intrusion in their lives. When they arrive at my office they are usually prepared to tolerate passively or negativistically punishment by what they see to be an unfair system.

This attitude is antithetical to that needed for effective problem solving. DWI offenders must be engaged in a process that encourages them to take responsibility for their actions, to become active rather than reactive, and to focus on themselves rather than on the system that compelled them to seek treatment. Handling the resistance contributes to the problem-solving process by:

1. *Distinguishing treatment from punishment.* By treating the new client with respect, with interest in his or her experience, and with empathy for the negative feelings, the counselor relates to the client as a potential ally rather than as an adversary (Malfetti & Winter, 1980). Cooperation becomes possible.

2. *Defusing hostility.* The opportunity to ventilate the strong feelings that had to be held in check previously provides a tremendous release. Initial vituperation clears the air and makes the client more comfortable and receptive to learning later.

3. *Creating active involvement.* Having been conditioned to be passive with the arresting officer and the judge, clients arrive at treatment expecting to "put in time." The flexible combination of interest, empathy, and provocation used by the counselor and group all serve to draw clients out. When they are expressing ideas, feelings, and attitudes, they are active and potentially able to change.

4. *Focusing on self.* The power to change is primarily power for self-change. No matter how defensively it is done, discussion of the arrest and its consequences puts the self back on center stage.

5. *Facing a problem.* A recognized problem must exist for problem solving to take place. Counseling gradually shapes this orientation. The initial motivation is to avoid the pain of rearrest or reengagement with the court. By offering the tools to "beat the rap," treatment elicits active involvement in problem solving. Beating whatever drinking problem contributed to the rap will emerge as a theme later as part of the solution in avoiding further legal troubles. By joining the clients in working on their initial area of concern, counseling begins to help them move from a posture of ducking responsibility to one of facing the issues.

**Counseling Skills** The key skills that the counselor must be able to demonstrate in handling initial resistance are empathy and reality orientation. Empathy is the ability to communicate nonjudgmental understanding of the client's experience. It helps the DWI offender to share, access suppressed feelings, and own responsibility. It helps the counselor avoid being pinned in the role of defending the system. If the client is bitterly complaining about the heavy-handed way in which he was arrested, the counselor can give one of several responses:

Sympathy encourages more focus on the felt victimization.

Defending the police invites a debate in which the counselor is pitted *against* the client. Whoever wins the argument, both lose the chance to work as a team.

Challenging elements of the story forces the client to defend himself and to become more entrenched in hostile resistance.

Empathy with the underlying anger and sense of betrayal respectfully focuses discussion on the client's feelings and actions, which are, after all, what we are interested in.

There has already been enough evaluation and judgment of the DWI's actions. What is needed now is an accepting environment in which learning from the experience is encouraged.

Readers who would like to upgrade their skills at empathy can find excellent practical guides in Carkhuff's *Art of Helping* (1973a) and Egan's *Skilled Helper* (1982).

Yet the client's experience must accommodate the world as it is. The counselor must be able to say, in effect, "Whether we like it or not, this is how things stand. So what are you going to do about it?" This is what is meant by reality orientation. It is not an attack on the client's feelings but rather a reminder of what is out there to be dealt with. The realities of the immediate situation are that the client has been apprehended for drunk driving, that there are consequences to be faced now, that there will be further consequences if a rearrest occurs, and that the client's attitude largely determines how many and how painful the consequences will be. If the group is fleeing from the task at hand—and groups in the resistant phase will readily focus on society's culpability for their crime—the leader must be securely tethered to reality so that they can be brought back to earth: "But what are you going to do so that you are not rearrested?" Humor is permissable. For example, after one group lost itself in a lament about roadhouses and liquor store hours that forced them to drive, I slapped my knee in the shock of sudden insight and exclaimed, "I've got the solution. Why don't we outlaw cars." Perhaps that type of humor should not be permitted. But it did help the group members to refocus on what they could change in their lives. Not all realities have to be confronted at once. But the counselor must emphasize two crucial ones: only the client can change, and change is the only way to avoid the pain of another DWI.

**Counseling Attitudes** The counselor must have personally resolved two related issues: in what way does he or she fit as part of "the system," and how should he or she respond to the clients' predictable initial hostility.

I see myself as a bridge between the court and the client. I do not work as an employee of the court, and I use this distance to avoid being seen as a partisan. I do not feel compelled to defend the criminal justice system when it is attacked by clients. Most important, my goal is rehabilitation rather than punishment. I try to collaborate with the clients to resolve whatever drinking problem led to the DWI, and I constantly remind them not to mistake "beating the rap" for "beating the problem." I am not on the court's side when it comes to revealing confidential information that is unrelated to the DWI (for example, use of illicit drugs). Nor will I take responsibility for the court's decisions that bear on my clients, as when a probation violation leads to the removal of an offender who has been doing well in treatment. This degree of independence is reassuring to the clients, as is occasionally demonstrated when one returns for a refresher course after being released from the program and from probation. But neither am I willing to take the clients' side against the system. If it becomes clear that an offender will not alter drinking patterns in a way necessary to avoid driving under the influence, I will clearly indicate this to the court and will return the person for judicial disposition, no matter how close a relationship has been developed in our work together. My overriding commitment to assuring that the client will not be an immediate risk for a further DWI prevents me from being seen as a partisan for the people referred to me. With an awareness of both perspectives, with a foot on both sides, I can best help the client to reduce the distance between his or her attitude and the law.

There may be partiality to the criminal justice system, especially when it pays the bills. Yet even to those counselors who are employed directly by the court I would suggest that they seek enough independence in their work that they can be seen as interpreters rather than as agents of the legal system.

The counselor's performance at this initial stage of problem solving is also affected by his or her understanding of the hostility that is likely to be directed at him or her by the beginning client. The key is to remember not to take it personally, even when there is a direct verbal attack. To do so almost inevitably leads to a counterproductive reaction. Responding in kind (with sarcasm, criticism, or defense of the system against the client's perspective) heightens defensiveness and confirms the client in the role of victim (see chapter 4). But absorbing the hostility is stressful. It contributes to ulcers, withdrawal into artificial professional distance, resentments displaced onto friends outside of treatment, and to all the other ills that accompany "burnout." Hostility from clients has a less noxious impact when it is understood dispassionately. Hostility is normal at this stage of treatment. There is certainly nothing wrong with the client for feeling it. Indeed, to express it is the most healthy means of getting past it: ventilating it helps the client to relate genuinely with the counselor and to engage in the problem-solving process.

**Related Exercises** The hostility will predictably continue for five to ten weeks for most clients. It is impractical to remain at the first problem-solving stage until resolution is complete. Subsequent exercises can be prefaced with an acknowledgment of how their meaning will be altered depending on the client's attitude. For instance, I introduce the alcoholism screening questionnaires (chapter 7) by explaining that the cutoff score is not absolute, but rather floats up for the self-critical and down for those who give themselves a break on every question. Resolution of the hostility may never occur. But even entrenched resentment will often collapse when there is pertinent learning about the effects of alcohol use on important aspects of the drinker's life (chapter 6), or when self-evaluation may lead the client to recognize how inadequate the change has been to date (chapter 11). The attitude change, the particular focus of the first three stages, is a continuing process lasting the duration of the program.

Resistance can also recur at any point. Whenever progress reports (see chapter 11) are prepared, hostility may be revived by the documentation of differences in the way the counselor and client evaluate change. Step 8, motivation, will likely generate resistance to the degree that coercion is used to change drinking behavior. Any point of confrontation, or any point at which the client believes the counselor is acting primarily out of allegiance to the courts, renews the initial attitudes dealt with in this step. I once told a group about a client who had been given a ninety-day jail term after dropping out of treatment. The group confronted me about my apparent delight at her pain. In fact, I was pleased that the rather attractive and flirtatious young woman had not been able to con the judge. I felt vindicated in my assessment. The group had to question me closely after I owned up to these feelings to accept that I could still be "for them" while wanting to see the negative consequences meted out to those who fail to change. The rapport built on empathy and the honest representation of the reality facing each DWI offender are the counselor's tools for bridging between the experience of the client and the society that demands change. To the extent that initial resistance can be faced and resolved in this first step of problem solving, a model is set for working through the subsequent hostility engendered by changing old and important ways of acting.

# Introductory Lecture

*This lecture was developed by Glenn Paule-Carres, Ph.D. The presentation lasts sixty minutes and requires a chalkboard.*

**Rationale.** In the setting in which I work, clients have been prescreened by the court system. Based on the arresting officer's report, prior court involvement, and an interview that includes an assessment of drinking, those judged to have a drinking problem are referred to me for education and treatment. They arrive for their first visit to complete the requisite paperwork and be assigned to the group with which they will be working for the duration of their treatment. This lecture is given during the introductory session, prior to assignment and in the company of other new intakes. One of its purposes is to orient the client to the program.

The goal of the lecture is to engage the new client in the problem-solving process. An invitation is issued to let go of some of the resentment that typically remains from the contact with the enforcement and judicial systems. By stressing that treatment is independent of the criminal justice system, I help the clients distinguish therapy from punishment. A new beginning, with new attitudes, is possible. Second, the lecture underlines the client's responsibility and personal choice as the keys to success in the program. Third, an introduction is given to some of the new perspectives offered on drinking in the program.

**Content.** I write my name on the board and introduce myself as a psychologist, noting that most people who work with me have sought treatment voluntarily by making an appointment to talk. When I rhetorically ask who is there voluntarily and am met with knowing smiles, I acknowledge their experience of coercion. We label and discuss the mix of anger, fear, and resentment typical after being arrested and convicted for drunk driving. Giving some time to ventilate conveys the interest in their perspective and feelings that was missing in their contact with the judicial system. It underscores the difference between treatment and punishment. But I note that they must get past anger if they are to change. I usually emphasize this by asking how much success they have had in trying to get their point of view across to someone who was steaming mad.

We then trace the chain of events: you + car + alcohol → police → judge → probation officer → alcohol education and treatment. After the choice to drive (which may be so overdetermined as to seem to have been compelled) there have been no "real choices" until beginning treatment. Resisting arrest, fleeing the jurisdiction, or accepting loss of license and the full jail sentence exemplify the "false choices" that are unattractive to participants, but are real options for people with less going for them. This contrast implicitly recognizes their attempt to reassert control over their lives, and the involvement in treatment as as the vehicle for doing so. I list what they have to gain by successfully completing the therapy program, dividing their answers into two columns:

| | |
|---|---|
| Freedom | New Learning |
| Job | Changed drinking |
| License | Avoiding future DWIs |
| Money | Greater self-respect |

The first column is then labeled "beating the rap," while the second is "beating the problem." Most clients will comply enough to complete treatment and avoid the worst sanctions of the court. But fewer will invest themselves in the program enough to avoid further drinking problems—the announced goal of the program.

A common variation on the lecture at this point is to ask if any of the clients have been through a DWI program previously. I draw them out on their (typically transitory or inadequate) efforts to change their drinking and driving. Most recognize their poor attitude: "I have no one to blame but myself." They usually model the intention to "beat the problem" this time, while cautioning against the naive and self-satisfied belief that "it will never happen to me again." Here is introduced the indispensable element of the client's choice. I usually emphasize it by saying, "You will see what you want to see, hear what you want to hear, and get what you want to get." I now explicitly invite them to make the "real choice" to work the program in a way that resolves any underlying drinking problem.

The evidence of the drinking problem is briefly presented. Each of the clients shows tolerance since each drove with toxic amounts of alcohol in his or her body. Each showed a loss of control of his or her drinking or behavior prior to arrest. Each is clearly aware that his or her drinking caused painful problems on at least this one occasion. I confront them with these facts to underscore the need for them to take an honest look at the role of drinking in their lives. Education about the symptoms of alcoholism and the opportunity for self-diagnosis will come later. My goal now is to suggest that there are alternative perspectives that will be more useful to them than continued resentment of the system.

I then present the procedures and requirements of the program. Questions about fees, attendance, and the duration of treatment need to be answered fully. I explain that weekly attendance of an Alcoholics Anonymous meeting is expected. As a rationale, I suggest that even those without drinking problems benefit by a fuller understanding of the risks of excessive drinking and by exposure to people committed to change. AAs also offer the perspective of long-term recovery, a perspective that is otherwise lacking in a program where no participant could have more than a year of sobriety. Clients are told that they will not be permitted to remain for the session if they attend group with drugs or alcohol in their systems. If queried, it is adequate to remind them of times when they tried to make a point to someone who was drunk.

I reiterate that the goals of the program are to learn and to change. In this, I anticipate a fuller description of the problem-solving process that will come later. If questioned, I will explain that there is no assumption that all are alcoholic or that abstinence is the only appropriate goal. These are decisions that they must make as they move through the treatment. What is crucial is that the clients be honest with themselves and be open to new information from the counselor and other group members. I invite them to make the "real choice" to "beat the problem" and to begin by being honest in completing the intake forms that are then distributed.

**Variations.** In my program, clients are assigned to ongoing groups. No effort is made to introduce those in the intake session to one another since they will not be working together in the future. It is possible to have intake structured as the initial meeting of a continuing group. If members will be working together throughout the program, then there is a greater need to introduce them to each other and to draw out the initial self-disclosure that helps to create an initial identity within the group. Every counselor has a store of icebreaker activities that encourage initial participation.

I use the "name game." In its simplest form, the member simply states his or her first name. To add an element of sharing, clients may be asked to come up with an alliterative adjective to describe themselves: Hardheaded Harry or Cautious Karen, for example. The challenge of the activity develops as introductions continue around the group circle. Members repeat the names of all who have gone before and then add their own name. The challenge is considerable when the tenth person's turn is reached, so the group usually joins in celebrating success. It is always all right to forget a name as long as help is requested and corrections are offered. This simple activity guarantees that names are learned as well as setting norms for humor, attention, direct interaction between members, and seeking assistance from one another.

An alternative means of encouraging initial sharing is to intersperse questions and empathic listening throughout the intake. When discussing feelings engendered by involvement with the criminal justice system, it is a natural step to ask who is angry or who is ashamed and then engage in dialogue briefly about the feeling. As was mentioned earlier, the repeat offender is often ready to share the difference between the current attitude and the one at the time of the previous arrest. This natural self-disclosure can be developed out of the presentation so that each member has said something personal, setting the important norm of active participation.

Spouses or significant others are always invited to group sessions and may be specifically required to attend to assist the client who is illiterate or has a hearing problem. A potentially powerful variation is to invite their attendance at a separate orientation that seeks their active cooperation in treatment. Content would include discussion of codependency, resources for help (including AlAnon), and how to stop enabling. Discussion and brief role-playing would help them anticipate resistance from the offender to their attending sessions and to their providing honest evaluation of the drinker's progress. My experience indicates that clients who are willing to bring a significant other to sessions are more likely to discuss and personalize the material presented, to be honest about changes, to be more committed to maintaining their problem-solving plan, and to return for help if they slip after discharge. Additionally, the spouse, adult offspring, and friend of the DWI are themselves at high risk for drinking problems. Encouraging the active involvement of significant others constitutes effective prevention or early intervention for them, as well as a variation in program structure which heightens its impact on the DWI (see McCrady et al., 1986).

# *Arrest Report*

*This activity serves to introduce each new member to the group. It is a question-and-answer session that typically lasts about fifteen minutes.*

**Rationale.** The primary purpose of the exercise is to get the new person speaking, setting the norm for active participation. The exercise aids in handling the initial resistance by permitting the ventilation of previously unexpressed anger about the arrest process. Exposure to a group whose norms have developed beyond resentment simultaneously challenges the new member to move on to more positive attitudes. Secondarily, the self-disclosure provides the opportunity for the counselor to evaluate further the degree of the drinking problem, the person's awareness of the problem, and the extent and type of defenses used in response to questions from the group. The exercise also reaffirms the norm of member-to-member interaction in the group.

**Content.** The leader notes the presence of the new member and explains that there is a ritual introduction in which questions will be asked about his or her life, drinking patterns, and the arrest. The person then shares in response to these deliberately vague instructions. Good insight and sharing is reinforced by supportive comments from the group or leader. Countersharing and commenting is encouraged by the rest of the group. If the discussion falters, the group members are invited to ask questions. While the content of the questions differs with each introduction, the leader continues the process until the following areas are covered:

1. The drinking occasion that lead to the arrest or accident (this is the "twelve hours before arrest" exercise that has been part of DWI treatment from the beginning; see Malfetti & Winters, 1980)
2. Feelings about the arrest and involvement in the criminal justice system
3. Concerns about driving under the influence and general concerns about drinking or drugging
4. Attempts to change since the arrest, and history of previous efforts to change drinking patterns
5. Personal goals for change while in the group

**Variations.** The introduction provides a good opportunity to restate the confidentiality rule or other norms of the group that the leader would like to make explicit. This may be an opportune time for the "name game," especially if several new members are joining.

Depending on the initiative taken by group members, questions may arise spontaneously or the leader may structure the session so that each veteran asks a question as we go around the circle. I will often seek to make the sharing more mutual by asking that the veterans share their own responses to the question asked of the newcomer. The newcomer is always given the opportunity to ask questions of the leader or of experienced participants before the exercise ends.

Introductions begin sessions because they often set themes for further discussion. In-depth sharing in response to an issue raised in the questioning is encouraged. There are often opportunities to do some pertinent teaching, especially about laws, accident risk, blood alcohol content, or tolerance. At times the new member's attitudes mobilize the latent resentment in the entire group. Then there will be energetic discussion of the ways members felt victimized by one or another part of the system. Although I will confront this as a defense in a group that does it routinely, it is more typical for me to keep quiet. The ventilation usually leads to the paradoxical result that some participant expresses a growing sense of personal responsibility for the arrest. Failing this, there is often a shift to a balanced discussion of the difficulty in dealing with a drinking problem in a society in which everyone seems intent on glamorizing drinking while criticizing the problem drinker.

# DWI Laws: *What You Need to Know before You Drink and Drive*

*This presentation and discussion takes twenty to forty minutes and requires a blackboard.*

**Rationale.** Even the most resistant clients share an underlying goal of the treatment: they want to avoid the legal consequences of rearrest for DWI. Their fear of punishment can be focused and directed in order to provide the initial motivation for change. By highlighting the elements of their suspended sentence, the counselor reminds them that they want to comply with the program to "beat the rap." Hearing fellow group members describe the stiffer penalties for rearrest provides clients with incentive to "beat the problem," at least by avoiding further drunk driving. The foregoing exercises have focused more on encouraging involvement by empathizing with the client's perspective. This discussion provides the balancing emphasis on the reality that the DWI faces: drunk driving is unacceptable to society and costly to the perpetrator.

**Content.** I first review the current laws pertinent to drunk driving. Included below are the ones that apply in Virginia in 1987. Copies of the law in other states can be readily obtained from the Department of Motor Vehicles, the Alcohol Safety Action Program, or from local judges or attorneys involved with drinking drivers.

A blood or breath test is part of the evidence considered by the court. A .10 blood alcohol content (BAC) gives rise to a presumption of guilt. Nearly everyone at this level or above is convicted of DWI. For the future discussions in the program, being drunk means having a BAC higher than .10. It does not refer to feelings of intoxication (high-tolerance drinkers often feel unaffected at .10); it does not imply staggering or slurred speech; it does not entail uncontrolled emotion or behavior. This is important to understand because testimony that the client is acting or feeling sober is unlikely to rebut the presumption of intoxication. If the BAC is .05–.09, there is no presumption of drunkenness, but other evidence of intoxication or sobriety will be considered—including the arresting officer's testimony—which may be sufficient to convict the accused. Since the judge will be aware of prior convictions for DWI, which is likely to undermine the repeat offender's credibility as a witness, I urge that my clients never drive after having more than two standard drinks or with what they estimate to be a .05 BAC.

The law applies to all intoxicating chemicals, including prescription and street drugs. Since there is no dose below which a client is presumed to be unimpaired, the arresting officer's testimony, combined with the presence of any trace of a drug, can be enough to lead to a conviction. Clients must avoid driving with any intoxicants in their system. The law gives the police the prerogative to decide between a blood or breath test. A DWI conviction is possible, even in the absence of measurable quantities of alcohol, if the blood test reveals the presence of marijuana or other drugs.

I also review the Implied Consent Law, which makes it a separate crime to refuse to provide a blood or breath sample when requested. Conviction for this offense carries with it a license suspension for an additional three to six months. The refusing driver can still be convicted for a DWI based on testimony about impairment, even in the absence of a sample. I caution against refusal because of the experience of past clients who have been repeatedly stopped on the roads. A BAC of less than .05 precludes arrest for driving under the influence of alcohol. So, the breathalyzer can protect the driver.

The DWI law applies to all motor vehicles operated on the public highway or on property open to the public. Mentioning this in group usually occasions stories about the guy caught driving his tractor or lawn mower to the corner store for another case of beer. I also stress that this law applies to mopeds, even though there is no state law requiring a license to drive them. Other traffic laws in Virginia extend the rules to other means of conveyance used on the roads: bicycles, skateboards, and even horses. I then pull out a weathered newspaper clipping about a man returning drunk from a trail ride who was arrested after crisscrossing a busy highway on horseback. The arresting officer was frustrated, however, by the difficulty of hitching a saddlehorse to a tow truck.

We then review the fines, jail terms, and license suspensions resulting from a DWI conviction, as listed in table 3–1. I supply the range and the mandatory minimum punishments, and the group members share their sentences. I highlight the suspended portions of the sanctions as an indirect reminder of consequences if they fail to complete treatment successfully. There is usually direct sharing and comparing of experience at this point. The discussion notes the increasing sanctions with rearrest, the supposed ineligibility for treatment on a third or subsequent conviction (although local judges may offer the treatment option and second-offender sentences to those who have not had previous alcohol education), and the pain associated with a prolonged loss of license. I then discuss the Habitual Offender Act, which can lead to separate proceedings and to a ten-year license revocation for the two- or three-time loser, and which contains a provision for a mandatory one-year prison sentence for a subsequent felony conviction of driving after license revocation. Clients usually are chastened and eager to avoid further legal consequences.

**Variations.** The discussion may continue with a consideration of the likelihood of the clients' being rearrested. I stress that any subsequent offense

Table 3–1
**Legal Consequences in Virginia for DWI Convictions**

| Number of Convictions | Range | Typical if Treated | Without Treatment |
|---|---|---|---|
| First | $0–1000<br>0–1 year<br>0–6 months | Fine suspended<br>No jail time<br>No license suspension | $250 fine<br>0–30 days jail<br>6 months loss[a] |
| Second | $200–1000<br>48 hours–1 year<br>1–3 years | $500 fine<br>72 hours jail<br>6 months license loss[a] | $500 fine<br>90 days jail<br>2–3 years[a] |
| Third | $500–1000<br>10 days–1 year<br>Indefinite | | $500–1000<br>3–6 months jail<br>3–10 years license revocation |

[a]The judge may permit restricted driving at work and to treatment.

within a ten-year period will count as a repeat offense and ask if their plan to avoid drinking and driving is strong enough to stand that test of time. Because of their recent experience, DWI clients tend to feel that there is a high probability of rearrest if they drive under the influence. When I survey the class, I am routinely told they face odds of 1:3 to 1:20. These odds vary from the research estimates of 1:200 to 1:2,000 (Beitel, Sharp, & Glauz, 1975; Borkenstein, 1976; Jones & Joscelyn, 1978) and make fear of rearrest a very powerful deterrent (Ross, 1984). I translate these odds to suggest that the clients are saying they would probably be rearrested if they slipped up no more often than once in six months. Someone usually states, "If you keep doing it, they'll get you sooner or later."

If a number of group members seem to respect the rationale for the DWI laws, as distinct from having a general fear of the law, I may invite the group to role-play being legislators and to design their own DWI laws before reviewing the actual laws. There is usually a good discussion, with self-appointed "bleeding hearts" ribbing the "hanging judges" in the group. Every time I have done this, the group has settled on sanctions that are at least as tough as those in the prevailing laws. Attitudes toward a treatment option are usually mixed, with some clients decrying the escape from "fair punishment for everyone," while others emphasize the need for corrective education and treatment for problem drinkers. This role reversal provides a good opportunity for the group to break out of the unhealthy antisystem, antitreatment norm and to express the underlying urgency to change. I'll never forget the surprised expression on the face of a rebellious young client who heard himself conclude this discussion by stating, "I'm glad I got caught before it got any worse."

# 4
# Meeting Defenses

In addition to overcoming resentment toward coerced treatment (the *external* obstacle that was discussed in the last chapter), drinkers must overcome *internal* obstacles to examining their drinking. Operative in each of us are defense mechanisms that distort our experience to protect our self-esteem and our sense of security. The price paid is that we are not fully facing reality, and at some point that means that we will not cope effectively. To have driven under the influence shows a disregard for safety risks; to have been arrested for DWI indicates a misreading of the risks of apprehension. Each drinker has a history of enjoyable experiences with alcohol that has led to some degree of dependence—the drink that aids relaxed initial socializing at a party or permits uninhibited dancing. Recognizing the costs of drinking would lead to a painful choice of accepting pain or renouncing the pleasures alcohol has afforded. It is easier to avoid the difficult decision by denying that any problem exists. Without treatment, the tendency is to cling ever more tightly to the comforting distortions rather than face painful facts. So the alcoholic may interpret the repetitive arguments with loved ones about drinking as signs of their craziness rather than his or her own. The goal of the exercises that follow is for the drinker to let go of the distortions more quickly so that whatever drinking problem exists can be recognized and resolved.

Defense mechanisms operate automatically and out of the awareness of the person using them. If effective, defenses keep the person from knowing that he is lying to himself or to others. This is why they are notoriously hard to see or to change without outside help. Defenses block psychological pain, whether from anxiety, guilt, regret, or other sources. Because they serve this protective function for self-esteem, they are difficult to relinquish even when recognized.

Our concern is somewhat broader, encompassing any process that contributes to avoiding open awareness of drinking and its personal consequences. This certainly includes the formal defense mechanisms that operate unconsciously. But there are three other sources of distortion that must also be considered. First there are the intentional and entirely conscious manipulations used to "get off the hot seat." These include lying, excusing, changing the subject, and other manipulations that are used to keep others from knowing painful facts about the drinker's use. A lie may succeed in deflecting another's anger, but the prevaricator must live with the guilt from both the past event and the lie. If the defense mechanism of repression comes into play, the drinker would truly be unable to remember the alleged transgression and would believe himself or herself to be blameless. Not surprisingly, the conscious manipulations that serve when the drinker is on the spot are often subsequently reworked with defense mechanisms so that the incident is forgotten. Second, there is a whole range of generally accepted myths that make drinking look glamorous. Advertising intentionally gives a distorted view of alcohol use in which the good times are overemphasized and the bad times barely acknowledged at all. That the myth is shared with just about everyone else doesn't alter the fact that reality is being distorted in a way that is dangerous to the drinking driver. Third, there is ignorance. Even without defense or distortion, wise decisions are unlikely when information is insufficient. Especially when it comes to drunk driving, what you don't know can kill you. Once the other defensive functions are reduced, ignorance will give way to the influence of education.

Problem solving cannot progress without a problem that the client is willing to work on. The following activities contribute to the process by reducing the gap between the drinker's experience and consensual reality. Defense mechanisms, conscious manipulation, myths, and ignorance are all challenged through a mixture of education and therapeutic confrontation. When defenses are diminished, the drinker has a fuller appreciation of the price paid for drinking and the awareness that others have a different and potentially more accurate perspective on the problem. These changes are the foundation for a subsequent attitude shift, an openness to learning, and a commitment to resolve the drinking problem. Diminished defensiveness is evident in the client's willingness to talk about drinking honestly and personally.

**Helpful Attitudes for Dealing with Defenses.** Never forget that defenses serve to protect self-esteem. They must be stripped away for an honest appraisal of drinking costs to take place. But this need not be done in a brutal and attacking way. Some people have an outdated image of treatment for substance abuse, that it inevitably requires a relentless psychological assault by the group, which tries to overwhelm the defenses of the hapless member on the hot seat. This is like forcing the members to strip off all their clothes on a frigid winter day. Not surprisingly, such an approach is met with considerable resistance. I much prefer to work in a supportive rather than attacking manner. By maintaining a tone of empathy, the leader can reinforce those who model efforts to be psychologically open. Defenses are identified and talked about, with acknowledgment that it may be temporarily painful to drop them. But it is important to stress that life gets better when reality is faced honestly, when there is no underlying worry that what was hidden will surface at an inconvenient moment. This is immediately apparent to any drinker who has tried to ask indirectly if anything bad happened during a blackout. I contrast the "false pride" that can be maintained only through bluster and hiding doubts with the "real pride" that is felt when you truly know yourself. This way of teasing off the defenses is like pointing out that there is a cool breeze but a warm sun, that there is more freedom of move-ment when the confining winter coat is removed, and that one can see others moving about comfortably without layers of insulation. The counselor tries to be an ally of the drinker's self-esteem, working in a way that preserves the pride and suggests alternatives for increasing it.

Challenges to defenses are inevitably distressing for they ask the person challenged to drop his or her own worldview to take on an outsider's per-spective. Egan (1976) notes that the right to challenge is earned. I try to build a base of influence by treating clients respectfully, by being empathic to their perspective, by being humorous and not taking myself too seriously, and above all by being psychologically open and nondefensive myself. I try similarly to empower other group members by reinforcing them for acting in similar manner.

The best confrontation is self-confrontation. When someone is talking nondefensively about drinking, I make sure that the group remains suppor-tively attentive. The most powerful inducement to a client to lower defenses is to watch another's relief and pride when he or she is accepted after sharing past problems honestly in the group. At some point during the program someone notes that he sees his drinking very differently from the way he did months ago. I will encourage that person to explore the how and why of this. It is almost a given that self-disclosure includes the discovery of a new and much more durable sense of pride as the client recognizes and deals with the drinking problem. Because such sharing is the most effective way to acknowledge and defuse defensiveness by others in the group, such discus-sion takes priority over any other group activity. It is effective modeling. It also puts that member in a position to confront another's defenses without being seen as "one up."

The second-best confrontation comes from peers. I constantly invite and support one member's giving honest feedback to another. The resulting tone is usually one of caring rather than attacking. The challenge, especially when it comes from a participant other than the leader, is likely to be accepted as an attempt to help.

I have all participants in the program attend weekly meetings of Alco-holics Anonymous, where there is usually a well-developed norm of nondefensive sharing, self-confrontation, and caring challenge of defenses by peers. I work to set similar norms in my own groups. This usually means that I have to model confrontation. If the challenge is mild or easy to accept, I do it in front of the group. But my respect for my client's self-esteem takes priority. Major confrontations, which are likely to provoke defensiveness or strong emotion, are done one-on-one so that the member does not lose face.

I try to respect the purpose behind the defenses even while challenging them. For example, I tell groups that I know people will lie in the sessions. People like to drink; change is hard; and facing a drinking problem is a lifetime task. From that perspective, whether it is this week or ten weeks from now that the attempt to be honest begins is really not that important. It is unfortunate that there will be little learning in the interim. But my experience is that people who don't end up becoming honest will eventually be rearrested and will return to group later, perhaps becoming more receptive at that time. This talk has several purposes. It attempts to shift the attitude toward the group con artists from one of envy (they probably are avoiding the hot seat) to concern and pity. It reminds me not to be personally offended or angry when someone's lie has surfaced. It also defines my role realistically: I will help those who become receptive to cooperating, but I will not play the intrusive parent who pursues them to catch them in their lies. Working on an outpatient basis, it is impossible to check up on what reportedly happens during the extensive time when group is not in session. So I do not try to catch participants in their lies. Without the hunter, the chase dies. My gambit is to engage their appropriate concerns: "You can lie to me, but not to yourself (or to the disease)."

Not pursuing is not to be confused with playing patsy. I will tell a person if he or she is clearly lying, and I will use the power I do have to stop that person from benefiting from lying. One of the clearest ways that the alcoholics among my clients get "caught" by their disease is when they come to the group under the influence. If I smell alcohol I will give an opportunity for sharing but will be sure to bring out the breathalizer to check who has been drinking. I drop clients who repeatedly attend with alcohol or drugs in their systems. Ultimately, I will discontinue treating anyone whose defenses are so pathological or unyielding that outpatient therapy is inappropriate. The choice between inpatient rehabilitation and a return to court for judicial disposition is probably the strongest confrontation I can generate. My goal is to be flexible enough to adapt my style to the needs of various people. I always begin by trying to build an alliance so that I am clearly "for them" even as I challenge their defenses. But being for them is not the same as being for their defenses or maladaptive behaviors. I will not continue to accept distortion just because that is what is easiest for the clients to offer.

There is a spectrum of responses to typical defensiveness, ranging from confrontation to temporary acceptance. Whatever strategy the counselor uses to help clients relinquish the distortion of reality caused by defense mechanisms, that conselor should remember that the presence of those defenses is an attempt on the part of the client to protect self-esteem and is not simply resistance.

**Rationale for Discussing Controlled Drinking.** The following exercise is the first in the book that implicitly or explicitly teaches clients how to drink. This may seem controversial, particularly for those whose experience has been in abstinence-oriented settings. I share the concern. Drink-counting strategies will fail for those who are impulsive or immature, or whose alcoholism makes control unreliable. Yet there are a number of reasons to discuss continued drinking in an outpatient curriculum. First, many clients may be able to drink without further trouble. Malfetti and Winter (1980) note research that suggests that only one of three DWI offenders is alcoholic. Second, many clients who will eventually quit will be drinking at the outset of treatment. To insist on sobriety without a persuasive rationale sets up massive resistance. Until that rationale can be developed and linked to personal experience, it is helpful to accept clients where they are. While supporting those who have decided to quit, the counselor must be prepared to work with those who are still using. Third, discussing safe drinking practices sets boundaries that may begin to alter drinking practices. Success in preliminary change encourages attempts at more substantive change later. Fourth, ignorance can no longer be used as an excuse for improper drinking when there has been education about alternatives. Fifth, the initial focus of education is on how to avoid drunk driving and the attendant risk of arrest. This goal is shared by everyone in the group. Education should be directed at helping clients meet this goal from the outset. It will prevent accidents and save lives. It will set up a powerful confrontation for those who find themselves continuing to drive under the influence. It is not only a program goal that is violated by continued drunk driving; it is also a personal goal that has been publicly stated in group, making it very difficult for that person to ignore defensively the conflict between intention and action. Many clients report that failure to adhere to a plan to avoid drunk driving forced them to acknowledge the drinking problem that they had previously denied. Education undermines defensiveness.

# How the Body Handles Alcohol

*This lecture takes about thirty minutes, including discussion. A chalkboard is needed for the presentation. If the movie,* Drink, Drive, Rationalize, *is shown and discussed, the total presentation will last about ninety minutes.*

**Rationale.** Low-tolerance drinkers can judge their degree of intoxication from their feeling of drunkenness (Huber, Karlin, & Nathan, 1976). The same *cannot* be said for high-tolerance drinkers. Perhaps because the same degree of intoxication has resulted from different quantities of absolute alcohol over the years, the internal cues cannot be used to determine when such persons are legally under the influence (Nathan, 1982; Silverstein, Nathan, & Taylor, 1974). High-tolerance drinkers must learn techniques using external information to calculate their blood alcohol concentration (BAC). Practically, this means using a breathalizer or learning to count drinks.

Ignorance is not an acceptable excuse in courts of law. Yet it is common for high-tolerance drinkers to believe sincerely that they were legal drivers because they felt fine, despite a BAC of .15 or higher. I believe that this is not simply a matter of impaired judgment. The ability of these high-tolerance drinkers to handle alcohol has reached the point that they feel normal with levels of intoxication that would leave most people on the verge of passing out. This does not imply that they are safe drivers (see chapter 5). An initial treatment goal is to educate clients about how the body handles alcohol so that they can learn to estimate their BAC. This lecture provides two of the elements needed to do so: learning what constitutes a standard dose of alcohol, and learning how the body metabolizes it.

**Content.**

*The Standard Drink.* On the chalkboard I draw a shot, a wine glass, and a can of beer. I then ask the group which will contain the most alcohol. We clarify that the percentage of alcohol is exactly one-half of the proof. So 80° whiskey is 40 percent and 130° moonshine is 65 percent alcohol. Then I demonstrate (using table 4–1) that there is a comparable amount of alcohol in a twelve ounce beer, five ounces of wine, or in one and a half ounces of liquor.

It does not matter what is the favorite type of drink; all contain the same dose. Despite the possible differences in felt effects, the same BAC will result from the same number of standard drinks, whichever type of beverage is consumed.

### Table 4–1
### Standard Drinks Contain Comparable Amounts of Alcohol

| Type | Liquor | Wine | Beer |
|---|---|---|---|
| Quantity (ounces) | 3/2 | 5 | 12 |
| Alcohol concentration | .40 | .12 | .05 |
| Absolute alcohol (ounces) | .6 | .6 | .6 |

Not all beverages contain a standard dose of alcohol. Fortified wines, overstrength liquors, "oobie doobie" (grain alcohol cut with fruit juice), and moonshine deliver higher quantities of alcohol per drink, making it difficult to keep track of consumption. Clients drinking martinis or zombies are combining different types of alcoholic beverages. Those who drink beer in enormous mugs or free-pour bourbon into a tumbler before adding an ounce of cola as a topper may get several standard drinks in one glass. The bartender "doing a favor" for a friend or angling for a big tip may be pouring doubles without having been asked. Any of these practices make calculating the BAC difficult or impossible.

*Practical Hint 1:* Always use a shot glass in mixing drinks.

*Practical Hint 2:* Order bottled beer or ask for standard drinks when tracking the BAC.

*Drink, Drive, Rationalize.* This movie, produced by the AAA Foundation for Traffic Safety in 1973, remains an effective means for debunking myths underlying drinking and driving. It is also a good introduction to a discussion of alcohol metabolism. Best of all, it is fun. The ten scenarios cover common myths underlying unsafe drinking practices for the driver:

1. Eating: food slows absorption of alcohol and so decreases feelings of intoxication but does not prevent excessive BACs. The alcohol may take longer to reach peak concentration (up to an hour longer than typical on an empty stomach), and this may occur just when the diner leaves the table and begins driving.

2. Sweating: only an insignificant 1 or 2 percent of the alcohol in the body is excreted by sweating. It is the fluid that ends up in perspiration, not the alcohol.

3. Sweet drinks: pineapple juice and syrups may hide the bite of the alcohol, enough that several doses of alcohol may lace a "lady's drink."

4. Experienced drinkers: they will probably have as high a BAC per drink as a novice, but they just won't feel as impaired or, accordingly, try to avoid driving.

5. Trusting feelings to "know my limit": this won't work for high-tolerance drinkers.

6. Small people: they may develop a "whole lot of capacity" and yet have a higher BAC per dose than large people simply because there is less fluid in their bodies in which the alcohol can diffuse. This accounts for the tremendous tolerance sometimes found among women who try to go drink for drink with husbands or boyfriends who are twice their weight.

7. Waiting after drinking: this works beautifully, but only if it is understood that it takes more than an hour per standard drink to metabolize the alcohol. Waiting an hour, or even sleeping it off in the car for three or four hours, will only delude the heavy drinker into believing that he or she is sober.
8. Coffee: it makes for a wide-awake drunk but not an unimpaired one.
9. Punch: it may hide the bite of liquor and make it impossible to guess the dose of alcohol consumed.
10. Near beer: it can still get you drunk if you drink enough of it.

Most group members are surprised to find that a cherished strategy they have relied on never worked. Not only does the education debunk the specific myth that contributed to unintentional drunk driving, it highlights that there may be important facts about drinking that they do not know. Naive self-confidence begins to give way to a new openness to learning.

*Alcohol Metabolism.* The first fact to be considered is that alcohol does not have to be digested. Absorption begins in the mouth, and 20 percent of the alcohol may have been absorbed before it leaves the stomach (Chafetz, 1982). The remainder is quickly absorbed in the small intestine. Peak BACs are reached fifteen to thirty minutes after ingestion on an empty stomach. Food slows absorption by trapping alcohol in the stomach while the food is digested. BACs will be reached sooner with warm drinks, carbonated mixers, concentrated doses, and an empty stomach.

How drunk you feel is only partially related to how high a BAC you have. Tolerance, state of health, mood, and tiredness all influence the psychological impact of a given dose. Other things being equal, you will feel more drunk while your BAC is rising and if it is rising quickly instead of slowly. People often report getting more drunk on liquor than on a comparable dose of alcohol in beer. The more concentrated solution means that the liquor will hit the system faster and lead to a stronger surge in BAC, resulting in greater feelings of intoxication although the peak BACs may be comparable. The more gradual rise in blood alcohol level with beer allows continuous drinking, which explains why a disproportionate number of DWI offenders with BACs above .20 have been drinking beer (Waller, 1982). Again, how drunk you feel may not be the same as how drunk you are.

I ask the group members how they think alcohol is eliminated from the system and list their answers before sharing with them the percent of the dose handled through each channel, as is shown in table 4–2. People usually overestimate the importance of the secondary pathways, although there is usually someone who notes that time (which I translate as liver metabolism) is the only surefire cure.

Table 4–2
How Alcohol Is Removed from the Body

| Means of Removal | Percentage Removed |
|---|---|
| Sweat | 1 |
| Urine | 1 |
| Breath | 5 |
| Liver | 93 |

Sources: National Safety Council, 1972; Tewari and Carson, 1982.

You can't hyperventilate or exercise your way out of a drunk. All those trips to the bathroom show that the alcohol is irritating the kidneys. But all that is being removed is the liquid, not the alcohol. Time indeed is the only way to get straight.

The liver will preferentially detoxify alcohol. This means that the liver is not doing its other work (removing other toxins, purifying the blood, aiding in the storing of energy, and so forth) as long as alcohol is present. This accounts for the risk of overdose when other sedative drugs are in the system and are not removed with the usual efficiency.

The liver will work at a consistent pace, through cycles of rest and activity. *The alcohol in about three-quarters of a standard drink will be metabolized in an hour by a healthy liver.* Because of the strain imposed by chronic alcohol abuse, liver function may be compromised. I had one client who swore he had drunk nothing that day and yet had the equivalent of one and a half beers in his system at ten o'clock one evening. When confronted he confirmed he had drunk two beers the previous midnight. His girlfriend confirmed that he wasn't lying. It had taken his liver twenty-two hours to detoxify the alcohol that it should have removed in forty minutes. It was confirmed that the man was suffering from cirrhosis—the scarring of the liver that severely compromises its functioning. Fatty liver and hepatitis may also interfere with liver functioning (see chapter 6).

The only exception to the rate of detoxification occurs when tremendous quantities of alcohol are consumed. Occasionally a client will be puzzled that he had a BAC of "only .20" after quickly consuming a fifth of liquor. In the presence of extremely high concentrations, the liver has backup pathways for metabolizing potentially lethal doses of alcohol. These pathways may eliminate up to 80 percent of the alcohol, but the price for the increased efficiency is that use of unintended pathways is more likely to result in liver damage (Korsten & Lieber, 1985).

*Practical Hint 3:* Since the liver eliminates less than a drink an hour, limit yourself to less than a standard drink per hour if you will be driving.

Since most alcohol abusers fail to follow this advice, they struggle with the question of how long they must wait for the liver to catch up with the overload. Most underestimate the time required, even if they sleep it off. They awake feeling sober (indeed we feel less intoxicated with a falling BAC) and make the ultimate mistake of trusting their feelings when it comes to drinking and driving.

*Practical Hint 4:* Count your drinks and wait one hour (from the time you commenced) for each standard drink consumed before driving.

This means that the case consumed beginning at 6:00 P.M. Friday should keep the drinker off the road at least into Saturday evening. (This is usually a moment of truth for those daily drinkers who realize that they have not been alcohol-free for years. Their stories become the focus of the group's attention if they begin to share appropriate concern.)

There are qualifications to this guideline: (1) Women on the pill or at points in their cycle with high estrogen levels may eliminate alcohol at a slower pace. They may want to wait two hours for each standard drink. (2) People who weigh less than 150 pounds will get higher BACs per standard drink and will want to extend their waiting period proportionally. (3) Anyone with liver damage cannot trust these guidelines and should probably not be drinking at all. (4) Anyone who cannot control his or her drinking or cannot maintain the presence of mind to keep count should not be drinking. I remind clients that there is no health risk and no possibility of another DWI if they abstain.

The process of alcohol detoxification in the liver is then described. Alcohol is converted to acetaldehyde, which is subsequently broken down into acetic acid, and then into carbon dioxide and water. Calories are released in the process, making it likely that the drinker will feel a surge of energy and that the heavy drinker will skip meals.

**Variations.** Detoxification may be examined in depth, since acetaldehyde is a very toxic chemical with far-reaching consequences. There are three variations.

First, we can discuss antabuse therapy. Antabuse, or disulfiram, stops the liver from metabolizing acetaldehyde. A toxic accumulation results in symptoms of nausea, cramping, vomiting, headache, flushing, falling blood pressure, pounding heart, dizziness, weakness, and anxiety (Ewing, 1982). Antabuse has been prescribed to provide additional incentive for those intent on quitting drinking. In essence, it reverses the usual pleasure-pain sequence for drinking. Few people would drink if the hangover preceded the high. It helps some clients to take a pill first thing in the morning and know that their decision has already been made long before they may be tempted to drink at the day's end. Once antabuse is in the system, it may take up to two weeks before the client can consume alcohol without side effects. This time allows the client to reconsider a decision to resume drinking.

This direction is indicated if a client appears to need antabuse to stay sober. It also effectively demonstrates the toxicity of acetaldehyde. Antabuse adds no poisons to the body; it simply allows the drinker to experience the full effects of the toxins present in alcohol.

The second tack is to explore the possible role of acetaldehyde in explaining tolerance and loss of control. I do this if the group is ready to understand alcoholism as a physical disease. Acetaldehyde has stimulant properties. Many drinkers are familiar with the jitters or shakes with which they awake early the "morning after," when the depressant effects of the alcohol have worn off. This stimulation is caused in part by acetaldehyde, and it will last for several hours after the direct effects of the alcohol have disappeared. After several hours of drinking, the stimulant effects of acetaldehyde may offset the depressant effects of alcohol so that the drinker will not pass out, even after developing a very high BAC. The body must adapt to the accumulated toxins, which results in permanent changes in cell membranes and consequently in tolerance for high doses of alcohol. But as the alcohol concentration rises, so does the acetaldehyde level. To avoid the nervous irritability that is symptomatic of an acetaldehyde overdose, the drinker must counter it with another dose of depressant: alcohol. This is the vicious cycle of alcoholism. Once high-tolerance drinkers begin, they will face a physical imperative to continue drinking until they can either sleep it off or find the fortitude to face the acetaldehyde edginess. For some, the vicious cycle continues: the discomfort from the previous night's imbibing is countered with the morning drink that temporarily quiets the nerves but sets up another cycle of self-medication (sometimes called maintenance drinking). The group notes that there is no reference to will power in this account of tolerance and loss of control—the central symptoms of alcoholism. This account of the disease is traced to liver metabolism. Research suggests that there may be an inherited tendency for alcoholics and even for their light-drinking offspring to be inefficient at metabolizing acetaldehyde (Lieber, 1976; Schuckit, 1980; Schuckit & Rayses, 1979).

The third variant, and the most theoretical, considers the effect of acetaldehyde on neurotransmitters in the brain. The blood/brain barrier is intended to insulate the central nervous system from disruptive chemicals circulating through the body. Yet animals that otherwise avoid alcohol will drink to intoxication if acetaldehyde metabolites are introduced directly into the brain (Duncan & Dietrich, 1980; Myers, McCaleb, & Rowe, 1982; Myers & Melchior, 1977). Other research documents that acetaldehyde combines with naturally occuring neurotransmitters to form chemicals that have opiatelike effects on the pleasure centers of the brain (Berger, French, Siggins, Shier, & Bloom, 1982; Davis, & Walsh, 1970; Myers & Critcher, 1982). There is a paradox here: acetaldehyde may be destroying the body while the brain is registering "this is great." It may be that cravings begin when, after repeated high doses of acetaldehyde, the blood/brain barrier is breached (Milam, & Ketcham, 1981; Myers, 1978). Moreover, this may be the unifying concept explaining addiction to other drugs. Psychoactive chemicals identical to those resulting when acetaldehyde combines with brain neurotransmitters have been found to occur naturally in marijuana, the opium poppy, and hallucinogenic plants (Fluharty, 1987). While this account is the subject of considerable research, and remains controversial, it offers a provocative explanation of alcoholism as a primarily physical disease resulting from acetaldehyde metabolism.

The metabolism discussion, whether it continues in the variations just described, is intended to relate responsible drinking practices to the body's limits in processing alcohol. But clients need to have a fuller understanding of BACs before they can have a realistic prospect of remaining within legal limits. The next exercise should be taken up in the following session to complete the education.

# Calculating Blood Alcohol Concentrations: Confronting the Temptation to Lie

*The discussion takes approximately thirty minutes and requires a chalkboard. If the group is tested for alcohol, sampling requires a breath analyzer and takes an additional fifteen minutes.*

**Rationale.** There are three interrelated purposes to this exercise. First, this exercise is a continuation of the previous discussion of alcohol metabolism, the purpose of which is to teach clients to estimate their BAC at any given level of consumption and to know for how long it will be illegal for them to drive. Second, the exercise presents an opportunity to check the peak BAC resulting from a sample dose of alcohol. Third, the breath analysis provides the evidence to confront any client who comes to group under the influence. It is not only the individual's conning that is challenged. The whole group learns that attending class under the influence has negative consequences and that defensiveness or dishonesty will eventually be discovered. For this reason, breath analysis is done during the group session, and everyone present is sampled.

**Content.** The breathalizer is brought out whenever the leader smells alcohol. Sampling may also be done periodically (perhaps after fifteen weeks without testing) or during the first session after holidays, even if there is no evidence in class of drinking. There should be a clear norm, which should be restated at this time, that no one in group is to have even a trace of alcohol in his or her system during class. It is easy for the group to appreciate the impossibility of one's learning while drunk. Most participants can also accept the idea that it is rude to be blowing fumes in the face of a neighbor who may be trying to quit. Before sampling begins, the leader should ask if anyone will test positive. If any admit that they may, the leader ascertain their estimated BACs, the quantity drunk and the time they began drinking, their reasons for drinking, and why they believe they ended up violating the prohibition against coming to class with alcohol in their systems. It may also be appropriate to praise their candor. There is often an animated discussion at this point. There is often admission of loss of control over drinking and recognition of previously denied alcoholism. Excuses may be offered and challenged by the group. In short, defenses surface for discussion even before the sampling is begun.

All group members are tested, and any positive BACs are written on the chalkboard. Some who admitted drinking may be surprised that they are clean. The embarrassment of unnecessary disclosure provides incentive to learn how to calculate the BAC accurately, assuring close attention for the remainder of the session. Someone else may test positive after having kept quiet previously. Those who have admitted drinking are justifiably annoyed with the individual. The group usually confronts the typically more entrenched defensiveness aggressively. One Tuesday night client summed it up: "If you must, you can drink Wednesday night, Thursday night, Friday night, Saturday night, Sunday night, or Monday night. But if you drink Tuesday night, you've got a problem." The leader tries to help the client hear the comments and makes sure that the drinking episode is thoroughly discussed. In some instances clients have driven to group under the influence or are grossly intoxicated. These clients may be asked to leave class for the session, they may be sent to a detoxification facility, and relatives may be summoned to retrieve their vehicles. I make clear my sense of responsibility to prevent anyone from driving home under the influence. If a participant responds to the group confrontation with threats to leave, I promise to call the law if he or she drives. A client's repeated attendance at group with alcohol in the system or gross drunkenness constitutes grounds for the client's being dropped from outpatient treatment and returned to face an angry judge. I recommend delaying this decision until the offender is sober and can be seen in private. But the client's response to the group session provides the leader an opportunity to decide whether adjunct therapy, inpatient rehabilitation, or other treatment should be required as a condition for the client's remaining in the program.

A client's being caught attending under the influence is a crisis, for the individual and the group. If clear norms have been set, no excuse or rationalization can effectively cover the transgression. Nor is lying effective in the presence of a breathalizer. Defenses are revealed and confronted, usually with active participation by peers in the group. The ad hoc intervention can powerfully change the client's perception of his or her drinking because defenses are disabled and consequences become immediate. Clients routinely report that being caught in group forced them to drop their initial hostility and get serious about facing their drinking problem. The group as a whole leaves with a recognition of the power and danger of defensiveness.

Education here also handles ignorance about how long alcohol remains in the system. An 150-pound man will *average .02 peak BAC from a standard drink*. A healthy *liver will detoxify .015 BAC per hour*. The metabolism of alcohol appears to be relatively constant regardless of the weight of the person. In contrast, the larger the person the more body fluids in which the alcohol is diluted. The average peak BAC will vary in proportion to the individual's size. A 100-pound person would expect to get a .03 BAC per standard drink, while at 200 pounds a .015 BAC would be typical, and at 300 pounds .01 BAC would be the average. Using these figures, it is possible to estimate the BAC resulting from any amount of consumption over any period of time.

The second level of challenging defenses is to use the client's report of drinking to check whether it squares with the residual BAC. At 7:00 P.M. a client with a .04 BAC reports having drunk two beers beginning at 4:30 in the afternoon and ending at 5:30. The estimated BAC is:

2 beers × .02 = .04 peak BAC; from which is subtracted
2 hours × .015 = .03 BAC (Note: thirty minutes is subtracted from the elapsed time to give the alcohol time to get into the system);
.04 − .03 = .01

The estimated and actual BACs do not match closely. When presented with this fact, the client "remembers" the third beer.

A client with .033 BAC at 10:00 A.M. denies any drinking that morning but admits drinking an unspecified but "moderate" amount the previous evening between 6:00 P.M. and midnight. Estimating his BAC:

10 hours × .015 = .15 BAC eliminated since midnight, or
16 hours × .015 = .23 BAC eliminated since 6:00 P.M.
.23 + .033 remaining = .263 BAC in system since 6:00 P.M.;
.263 / .02 per drink = 13 standard drinks the previous evening.

The client protests that he could not have had more than three or four mixed drinks since his friend was drunker than he, and they didn't quite finish a fifth between them. The group might tease him about having hogged the bottle and skimping on the mixer. If the denial persists, I might dramatize the situation like this:

> There are two explanations that come to mind. You might be lying or minimizing how much you drank. I really hope this is the case. Because the other possibility is that your liver is damaged so that your body is unable to get rid of the alcohol you have drunk. Let's test your BAC again in an hour, when it should drop to .018 (.033 − .015). If it hasn't gone down, you need to make an immediate appointment with a doctor.

The BAC usually declines at an approximately normal rate, and the drinker is again confronted with the distortion about how much he has drunk.

The breathalizer provides accurate feedback about how much alcohol the person has consumed. It is hard to dispute the accuracy of a positive reading when the rest of the group is clean. The drinker must then acknowledge that the lie has surfaced or that he or she truly couldn't remember or control the amount consumed. There are a number of explanations for attending group under the influence. Ignorance is resolved the first time this presentation is made. Active resistance or a "don't give a damn" attitude can be brought to the surface and challenged. The indirect cry for help or the unintentional loss of control can both be identified as symptoms of alcoholism, and the treatment contract can be updated with the group's help. In each instance, there is a new awareness and openness about the client's drinking problem. Even when clients sullenly reject the opportunity to explain the positive BAC, future conning is undermined since they know they have been "caught." As defenses are interpreted or disabled, clients take a more active role in dealing with their drinking problem.

If there are no positive BACs, the group uses the opportunity to review and practice calculating BACs. At the most elementary level, the leader asks how many drinks in an hour before the average 150-pound man reaches a .10 BAC? (Five). How many hours would it take before a man with a .20 BAC could legally drive with no more than .05 BAC? (Ten hours if his liver is functioning).

*Practical Note 5:* The group should agree to use .05 BAC as the target because it is the level at which rearrest is possible and because it provides a margin for error before .10 is reached.

Clients are invited to describe a typical evening's drinking and get the group's assistance in estimating peak BAC and the waiting period necessary before a .05 BAC is reached and driving is again legal. The leader may also provide some cautionary scenarios, including the implications of heavy drinking. A BAC of .35 is lethal to 1 percent of the population, although it is not likely to be deadly for the high-tolerance drinkers who compose the group. A BAC of .50 is deadly to 50 percent of the people (Favazza, 1982; Rogers & McMillin, 1984). With this in mind, the group looks at the implications of drinking a case of beer between 5:00 P.M. Friday and 2:00 A.M. Saturday. The twenty-four standard drinks would provide a peak BAC of .48 if the liver were not working. If it is functioning properly, it could still have eliminated only .135 (9 hours × .015 per hour), leaving an estimated .345 BAC at 2:00 A.M. At 8:00 A.M., there would be .09 less (6 hours × .015) but still a .255 BAC, even if there was no morning beer. The group usually figures the drinker would not venture forth until noon, at which time the BAC would be .195. At 5:00 P.M. on Saturday, twenty-four hours after imbibing began, the estimated BAC is .12. It is 10:00 P.M. before the driver is again legal on the road and 1:00 A.M. Sunday before the body is again alcohol free. There is awed recognition in the group of how much unintentional DWI driving was done after "sleeping it off." A bit of calculation also shows that it takes twenty-four hours to eliminate eighteen standard drinks. This means that anyone drinking this amount on a daily basis is never giving his or her body time to recuperate from the toxic effects of the drug.

These scenarios provide practice at the calculations as well as cautionary tales. Check your accuracy. Clients who are slow with math recognize the added obligation to maintain moderate consumption and stick to the drink-an-hour rule.

**Variations.** This mental arithmetic is enough of a challenge for most groups. I may spare the complications that follow. But there are important qualifications to the weight/BAC ratio, in addition to the ones specified in the previous exercise. Individuals who intend to continue drinking and have proved themselves able to control it need to learn their personal peak BAC.

The .02 BAC is an average. As with height, IQ, ring size, and any other measurable human characteristic, the figure will vary from one person to another. I once worked with a 140-pound man whose BAC peaked at .045 from a standard drink. Somewhere there is another person of the same weight who would have gotten no more than .01 BAC from the same dose. If they were all assuming they were average, they might limit themselves to four drinks in an hour and expect to be below the .10 cutoff for drunk driving. The average person would indeed go no higher than a .08 (4 × .02), while one companion would be clearly illegal at .18 (4 × .045) and the other would be legally untouchable at .04 (4 × .01). It is important to clarify that this is unrelated to tolerance. The person with the highest BAC might appear the least intoxicated.

I will occasionally share a personal anecdote in group to illustrate this. For example, my associate and I got clearance from our wives to spend an evening researching the singles scene with a common friend, also an alcoholism counselor. Because to be arrested on a DWI charge would not have contributed to our job security (and because we needed a conversation piece to compensate for our dated lines), we took along the breathalizer. We started out after lunch with no alcohol in our systems. We each downed a twelve-ounce beer. Presumably, I would have had a higher BAC than my partner, who outweighed me by ten pounds. But thirty minutes later his BAC was .023, and mine registered .013. After joining our colleague an hour later and consuming a sixteen-ounce "tall boy," his .038 was almost twice my .021. After another hour, and a three-way split of a forty-eight-ounce pitcher of draft beer, my partner had a .048, and I had a .028 BAC. For those who are calculating, my level was about what would be expected for 3.3 drinks in two hours and thirty minutes. But how do you explain the elevated readings on my associate, who had consumed the same quantity of alcohol? Despite some teasing about the condition of his liver (which could not have explained the first reading in any case, and which was demonstrated to be fine, since his levels dropped normally at the end of the evening), we realized that there are idiosyncratic differences between us. For some inexplicable biochemical reason, he gets a much higher BAC out of comparable quantities of alcohol than I do. We stopped matching drinks at that point. At the end of the evening, which was early (we work hard) and uneventful (we're happily married), we again compared BACs. He looked uneffected while I felt a bit tipsy. Yet his BAC was .13 while mine was .03. Again, feelings of drunkenness are not directly related to peak BAC levels.

Group participants are often eager to be tested with a standard drink in their system. I will accommodate this wish if they have first demonstrated that they can control their drinking (see chapter 7) and the group assents. The client is asked to drink a twelve-ounce beer ten minutes before group. His BAC is then monitored at ten-minute intervals throughout the session. (This test would be misleading for women, whose peak BAC may fluctuate throughout their menstrual cycle.) This gives the drinker evidence about his peak BAC and the efficiency of his alcohol metabolism which will make it possible for him to calculate his BAC much more precisely than would be possible with the common dose/weight charts based on averages.

# Mass Media Myths

*This discussion takes from fifteen to forty-five minutes and requires no props.*

**Rationale.** Americans are constantly bombarded with messages glamorizing drinking. This discussion seeks to sensitize them to the distortions embedded in commercials, to counteract the "brainwashing."

The discussion often begins when someone accuses the treatment of overemphasizing the negatives about drinking. I counter by saying that it is not I who have been brainwashing the clients but the mass media that they have been tuning in since they were toddlers. In the United States, 15 percent of the population consumes 74 percent of the alcohol sold (Mandell, 1982). On broadcasts $750 million is spent, and over $1 billion is spent on all media alcohol advertising (American Medical Association, 1986; Jacobson, Macker, & Atkins, 1983); and it is obvious that the advertising is not aimed at the occasional drinker. Despite the disclaimers from the liquor industry, the goal is to encourage heavy drinking and to influence the brand preference of the alcohol abuser. To understand this removes some of the power of the advertising.

Clients often complain that they experience cravings when a beer commercial comes on in the middle of a football game on television or when glamorous people start boozing again in the middle of one of the prime time soaps. Studies over the last decade have shown that commercial television averages more than eight drinking episodes per hour (Wallack, Breed, & Cruz, 1987; Waller, 1983), most emphasizing the positive effects of alcohol even though it is often an inappropriate drinking occasion (often a response to a crisis), and most of the drinking is being done by the "good guys" with whom we are to identify (Breed & Defoe, 1981). TV creates a false norm of problematic drinking. Those who watch more television have been found to drink more and to be at higher risk for driving under the influence (Atkin & Block, 1981). Clients need help to counteract the mass media influence. By teaching them to analyze the underlying message, counselors can give clients a mental activity that supports their control and distracts them from any craving elicited.

**Content.** First, we go round the group and each person volunteers an adjective that describes the image of drinking created by the mass media. The leader may write them on a chalkboard: fun, relaxing, sexy, heroic, successful, glamorous, a way to get beautiful women, friendly, and so on. It is then easy to discuss how imbalanced a perspective this is, how the negatives experienced by group members are seldom if ever confirmed on TV. We may then discuss how this unbalanced portrayal adds to their guilt and isolation for the problems they have encountered. But the goal is reached if they recognize that the mass media is encouraging a distorted perspective.

Second, we analyze group members' favorite commercials, noting the focus on heavy drinking and the subtle celebration of psychological dependence. The leader usually offers several examples to demonstrate. My favorite examples come from Strohs' commercials; their excellent humor permits them to be more obvious in their message. When a young professional athlete invites his childhood friends to have a poolside drink and the pool is entirely filled with iced beer, we are not seeing social drinking modeled. In another commercial, when the bandits are in hot pursuit and the stagecoach riders have to jettison part of the load to gain speed, the girl goes and the beer is kept on board. The group may laugh at the recounting and endorse the decision, but they recognize the implicit priority by which drinking is considered more important than relationships. When a grizzly bear steals the beer from three campers, one of them risks his life to rescue two cases. Is it really worth fighting a grizzly to protect the alcohol supply? Do three guys, presumably on a weekend trip, really need two cases of beer to enjoy themselves? Abusive drinking is the implicit norm here. An old Miller series likewise ends with a compelling image in which not one but several beers are thrust toward the camera, as if to invite the viewer to drink heavily to catch up with the party in progress. Michelob had a long-running campaign to glamorize the product as the beer of successful people celebrating their weekends. But then the message changed: first it was "put a little weekend in your week," and then it became "the night belongs to Michelob." Not only is a switch in brand allegiance encouraged, but also a troubling intimation of loss of control. I would prefer that my nights belong to me and not to some brand of beer.

The group goes through several predictable reactions: enjoyment of the descriptions of commercials gives way to skeptical comments about how "psychologists read something into everything." This is usually followed by fascination as they find the interpretation interesting. Lastly, some begin their own attempt to decipher a few commercials. Once we have progressed to this point, the exercise is stopped. The goal is to leave it somewhat unfinished so that the next commercial will provide group members with an opportunity to practice analyzing the implicit endorsement of heavy drinking.

**Variations.** Two additional activities are suggested by this discussion. First, group members could be asked to do some research. To the following class they could bring print advertising or their interpretations of commercials or scenarios from the week's television fare. The discussion could continue. Second, a creative group might be invited to craft a commercial that shows the negative side of drinking. This would provide an outlet for the energy often generated by the foregoing discussion as well as a nonthreatening way to acknowledge nondefensively the problems experienced with drinking.

This activity is appropriate at other points in the problem-solving process. Sharing the personal drinking history (chapter 6) often begins with a discussion of the attitudes toward alcohol use that preceded personal drinking experience. This discussion can serve as an icebreaker that will prepare the group for individual sharing. In discussing how to avoid relapsing (chapter 10), this discussion is often a useful tool in helping clients to cope with the craving brought on by their inability to escape the mass media portrayal of drinking as part of the good life.

# Victim, Rescuer, Persecutor

*This is a fifteen-minute presentation and discussion that usually occurs spontaneously in response to excessive defensiveness by a group member. A chalkboard is helpful.*

**Rationale.** This discussion is based on an adaptation of the game "Alcoholic" described by Eric Berne (1964). The goal is to block a specific participant from maintaining a posture of being the innocent victim. It challenges that participant's failure to assume responsibility for actions and decisions. It also brings to the surface a pathological relationship pattern for examination and possible change.

I often introduce this discussion at a time when I find myself getting angry at a passive-aggressive client. Instead of becoming punitive, I use the presentation to help the group understand the underlying dynamic.

**Content.** First, I draw an equilateral triangle on the board and label the respective corners "Victim," "Rescuer," and "Persecutor." Each term is defined, and the obvious differences among them are noted. The white hat of the rescuer is contrasted with the black hat worn by the persecutor to symbolize further the polarities (and to separate both from the victim, the maiden tied to the tracks). These characterizations belie the underlying similarity and interchangeability of the roles which eventually become clear.

The game is illustrated by describing the argument between a husband and his wife when he arrives home, late and drunk. The group is invited to contribute the dialogue and usually is readily able to recognize the pattern:

*Wife (as Persecutor):* Where have you been? You're drunk again. You're disgusting!

*Husband (as Rescuer):* Now, now dear, don't worry. I just stopped off for a couple of drinks.

*Wife (as Victim):* I was worried. You might have been in an accident or arrested again. (As Persecutor): Why do you do this to me? I can't stand it! No self-respecting man would keep putting his wife through it, especially after he promised . . .

*Husband (as Victim):* I wouldn't if I could just get a little peace and understanding at home. (As Persecutor): You are such a shrew!

The ensuing uproar continues with his raging (Persecutor), placating (Rescuer), but eventually settling into the Victim role. Her transactions show complementary shifts among the roles of complaining (Victim), threatening (Persecutor), and eventually feeling guilty about her harsh words or upset by the coldness between them and so trying to patch things up (Rescuer). The dialogue changes each time as the group volunteers it, often with the Victim's delight at caricaturing the wife. The dialogue continues until it is clear that the group understands that the roles are interchangeable and the game is interminable. The group clearly recognizes that there is no true good guy or bad guy beneath the posturing.

All the roles show a similar inability to take responsibility for self. Though the Rescuer appears healthiest, the role's satisfaction depends entirely on the Victim's getting better. The Rescuer is, in fact, dependent on the Victim, who holds the real power in the game. No wonder the drinker tends to prefer that role. Effective control of the relationship is masked by powerlessness, which eliminates the need for guilt or apology as surely as it prevents honest sharing.

The group next discusses how to get out of the game. I help the clients realize that switching roles is not to be confused with ending the game. The solution lies in assuming responsibility for the self. It is evident when accusatory "you statements" (as in "If only you would . . .") are replaced with "I statements." The payoff in ending the game is gaining a sense of power over the course of one's life, at least to the extent of having a more honest perspective.

The discussion concludes by turning back to the interaction that led to the presentation. Typically this means that a member has issued an invitation to play the game by overplaying his or her victimization or portraying the group leader as persecutor. For example, I was recently taken to task for failing to rescue a client who had a number of "good excuses" for missing appointments with his probation officer. Though I clearly had the power to intervene (and so could be seen as Rescuer) but refused to use it (and so could be Persecutor), I chose instead to stick by our previously agreed-on contract that makes group members responsible for their relationship with the criminal justice system. The invitation was for the client to assume adult responsibility for his actions and the resulting consequences. Studying the game helped the group to confront the member appropriately instead of lapsing into collective self-pity.

**Variations.** This discussion can also be productive when a participant blames marital conflict for continued drinking or, more rarely, when the drinker and the accompanying spouse begin to argue in group.

# Rearrest Stories

*This sharing, often spontaneously initiated by a group member, lasts indefinitely and requires no props.*

**Rationale** The client who has been rearrested failed to learn from previous treatment or punishment. Any sharing about prior attitudes and efforts presents warnings of what is to be avoided. By recounting the risks of a negative attitude and, usually, by modeling more appropriate concern the second time around, the repeat offender encourages the entire group to be less defensive.

The sharing is often spontaneous, sometimes prompted by a defensive comment that triggers the repeat offender's recollection of having made similar remarks. The leader may also initiate the discussion to help an individual or the group face defenses. This may be needed when the group is actively resistant. More optimally, sharing will be encouraged when the group is struggling about how open to be.

**Content.** There are two types of rearrest stories: those from clients rearrested while in the group, and those who from people who had completed treatment and were apprehended for DWI some time later. The second group, with greater distance from the first arrest, is more likely to be comfortable discussing attitudes contributing to the rearrest.

The leader elicits sharing with such questions as: "Why did you fail to change?" "Why didn't the changes last?" "What was your attitude like the last time through?" To get the repeat offender to comment on another's defenses, watch for nonverbal indications of discomfort from the repeater and then ask: "Does that remind you of your own attitude?" or "Does anyone here remind you of the way you used to be?" Such questions often generate a discussion of how defenses prevent adequate change. Most clients who have been rearrested are serious about dealing with the drinking problem this time through treatment. They can share previous mistakes without loss of self-esteem. But the leader should emphasize their efforts and reinforce their pride by ending with a focus on positive efforts. This may begin with: "How is your attitude different, how are you doing things differently this time?" Group discussion expands on these issues.

When a client is rearrested while in the initial course of treatment, the discussion is even more powerful for the group because of the immediacy of the crisis. The fear of legal sanctions and the cost of the lawyer's expenses to avert them remind the group of similar experiences that were starting to fade. All participants also experience an unspoken sense of responsibility. The rearrest shows that the client was, at a minimum, unable to ask for group time to discuss continued drunk driving. Usually there was evidence of conning or defensiveness that the group permitted to pass unchallenged. This awareness typically leads to a spontaneous discussion by the group of the need to help one another with caring confrontation. The sympathy for the rearrested group member is expressed in tandem with criticism for failure to be honest in group. The rearrest is discussed both to offer practical advice to the client and to heighten the group's recognition of the risks associated with unresolved defensiveness.

**Variations.** Modeling of nondefensive attitudes can come from those who have been through rehabilitation, those active in twelve-step programs like AA, and from responsible veterans in the group. Each can affirm the importance of recognizing and countering defenses. Although the person who failed to change in previous drunk driver treatment "qualifies" best to warn about a poor attitude, anyone who has undergone the changed perspective resulting from a commitment to self-honesty can help group members contrast defensive and nondefensive attitudes toward drinking problems.

# Identifying Defenses

*The initial presentation and discussion of defenses takes about thirty minutes. Use of any of the movies increases the time to about seventy-five minutes.*

**Rationale.** The psychological defense mechanisms operating in the individuals and in the group are taught. After an invitation is issued to acknowledge those defenses that are recognized as personally operative, the group is challenged to confront defenses whenever they appear in the group. This gives group members practice at what must be a lifelong process of observing and challenging their own distortions, so that they can prevent a recurrence of the attitudes that block honest self-appraisal and increase the risk of a return to abusive drinking. Self-honesty is generally seen as a key part of recovery from alcoholism (Alcoholics Anonymous, 1976; Johnson, 1973; Milam & Ketcham, 1981) as well as a requisite for effective problem solving.

Such self-confrontation is a high-level skill, requiring motivation and a good cognitive grasp of the material. There is a graduated process for teaching how to challenge defenses: learn them, see them demonstrated, identify them when present in ongoing conversation, engage in self-confrontation, and finally confront other members in the group.

This discussion is often planned at a time when the group has made enough of a commitment to self-honesty that such education will consolidate gains. The timing may be influenced by the need to confront an entire group that is avoiding effective work.

**Content.** Begin by defining defenses as unconscious and unintentional, as attempts to maintain self-esteem or to avoid threatening or painful truths, as a distortion of reality, as impediments to an accurate evaluation of the extent of the drinking problem, and as an obstacle to effective problem solving. They can be seen operating in all people to some degree. Rogers and McMillin (1984) point out that no one could live in most of California without the ability to deny the imminence of what geologists see as a certain major earthquake. But comforting illusions prevent change, and drinking problems must be faced without blinders if further problems are to be avoided. This is particularly so since alcohol is such an effective antianxiety agent, which further undermines motivation to change.

List, define, and give examples of five or six of the following defense mechanisms that are most relevant to the group:

1. *Denial:* Maintaining that something is not so when it is in order to avoid facing it by ignoring it. "I do not have a drinking problem," or "The machine is wrong; I couldn't have a BAC because I haven't been drinking at all."

2. *Minimizing:* Acknowledging the situation but downplaying its importance. "I only drank a couple" (despite a BAC of .15), or "Going to jail isn't that big a problem."

3. *Rationalization:* Logical-sounding explanations of illogical behavior. "Anyone would have gotten drunk if he had the kind of pressure on him that I do." Rationalization requires that the person believes the explanation. Closely related is "alibiing," an excuse that may satisfy another even though its creator knows that it is not true. "I didn't go drinking. I'm late because I stopped off to see Tony."

4. *Intellectualization:* Losing the emotional and personal relevance in a fog of analysis or argumentation. "I wasn't really driving drunk. You see, to be drunk you have to be slurring your speech, or emotionally out of control, or . . ."

5. *Projection:* Recognizing one's own undesirable thoughts or characteristics only in others. "I can't get anything from AA when people are so cold and unfriendly." "You don't give a damn about me, so why should I tell you anything." The world is distorted into such a dangerous, hostile place that help is impossible and isolation is justified. This is particularly damaging to family relationships: "I wouldn't drink so much if you weren't so angry all the time."

6. *Externalization:* Focusing on outside causes of behaviors or feelings to avoid taking responsibility for them. "All of my friends drink, so what do you expect?" "Their nagging got me so mad I had to drink to calm down."

7. *Diversion:* Changing the subject to avoid a sensitive area. "You wouldn't believe how much the police drink." Humor and stories about past drinking, though potentially appropriate, can be used to avoid the task at hand.

8. *Hostility:* Becoming angry and threatening when personally sensitive issues are raised. "We're here to learn not to drive drunk. Don't you *ever* talk about my marriage in here."

9. *Negativism:* Actively or passively resisting change. It ranges from playing helpless, to procrastinating, to willful noncompliance. "I couldn't find the AA meeting," or "I was too busy to go." "I know I'm quiet in here, but I don't have anything to say."

10. *Undoing:* Thinking the slate has been wiped clean because unacceptable behavior has been atoned for: for example, bringing flowers to the wife after a drunken rage and expecting others to "forgive and forget."

11. *Regression:* Acting immature as a way to handle stress: throwing a temper tantrum, for example, or getting drunk after a period of sobriety because the counselor wouldn't offer early release from the program.

12. *Fantasy:* Distracting oneself through daydreaming when something painful is being discussed.

There are also a number of roles in group that a client can use to avoid personal responsibility for change:

13. *Dependency:* Acting helpless so that the leader does all the work. "I don't think we can put together a good plan for avoiding driving. After all, we all got caught. What would you do, doctor?"

14. *Rescuing:* Excessive preoccupation with others' progress, to the point that personal work is not completed. This is a particular risk for codependents—those who grew up or live with someone who is disabled or addicted. "I'm OK, but I'm worried about Laura."

15. *Pairing:* Building alliances or romantic liaisons as a means of handling anxiety and avoiding work.

16. *Complaining:* A variant on externalization in which the situation is always found to preclude learning. The counselor may notice the following trap: "You don't understand me because you're not an alcoholic," and yet "I can't learn anything from the people in the group. If they had the answers, they wouldn't be here."

17. *Boredom:* Showing an obvious lack of interest in the group process, without taking responsibility to make the process more personally relevant.

Good discussions of defenses are available for counselors who would like to go deeper. Rogers and McMillin (1984) discuss group defenses common in alcohol treatment settings. Egan (1976) and Corey and Corey (1982) describe the defenses typical at different stages in the development of a group. Johnson (1973) elegantly details the distortions in thinking that maintain drinking problems.

John Wallace (1978b) talks about using the "preferred defense" of the client to foster change. In this approach, the defense is not confronted but coopted for therapeutic purposes. For example, denial is often used to make recovery look more attractive: "If you just stop drinking, everything will work out fine." I concur that it is more important to challenge defenses when they interfere with treatment. I may not immediately confront the undoing evident when a client participates unusually well the week after being caught with a positive BAC. In the long run, though, lowered defensiveness is the goal. Appropriate problem solving requires that plans be made for the challenges of recovery, and so even the "pink cloud" that makes many newly recovering alcoholics overly enthusiastic about being dry can act as a setup for later discouragement and relapse. The long-range goal is to replace defenses with more effective coping techniques (see chapter 12). The immediate goal of this exercise is learning to recognize the various defenses when they are evident in group.

Having reviewed the most relevant of these defense mechanisms, I challenge the group to identify their presence in a sample. I usually show a movie at this point. I may also drop the discussion at this point and ask that during the next week they try to recognize defenses operating in their day-to-day life. Having access to a handout listing the common defenses will help in this work.

A number of movies exist that can be used effectively to demonstrate defense mechanisms. *How to Sabotage Your Treatment* emphasizes the roles assumed in groups which discourage openness. This movie can be followed by an attempt to identify which of the modeled defenses best characterizes each group member. *Denial: The Inside Story* uses a number of different scenarios, not all immediately linked to alcohol abuse, to demonstrate the pervasiveness of this defense.

My personal favorite is *A Slight Drinking Problem*. This movie, which can also be used to discuss the effect of alcohol abuse on family relationships, has the virtue of showing that the whole family uses defenses to avoid dealing with the drinking problem. In the first instance, the drinker's transparent alibi is accepted with relief by his wife, who clearly would prefer to rationalize his embarrassing absence from a celebration. As the marriage deteriorates into recriminations, denial and externalization are readily apparent in remarks like "I don't have a drinking problem—I have a wife problem." As the wife learns to stop playing "Victim, Rescuer, Persecutor," the drinker comes to face his problem, but only partially. The group can see the minimizing in his concluding comment: "Maybe I have a drinking problem. In fact, it's probably true. I probably have a slight drinking problem."

I often stop the projector and ask the group to identify each defense mechanism as it is demonstrated. Alternatively, I will poll the group after the movie about whether they expect the drinker to seek help or to make a lasting change in his drinking. The resulting discussion usually notes the threat of residual defensiveness—precisely the issue the group needs to face.

The group is now able to recognize defenses. It still may not be motivated to do so, especially if confrontation violates a group norm. I shape the response through as many of the three following steps as necessary. First, identify the defenses group members observe in day-to-day life. Since this process is often unrelated to drinking or to group, such sharing is nonthreatening. Second, identify the defenses that are most important personally. It may help to start in the past: "What defenses did you use before you got caught?" Or, "Which were typical for you when you first began the program?" This step should include an attempt to identify the defense mechanisms that are most important at present. If a client asks for feedback from the group, the third step is painlessly achieved: group members engage in confronting one another about any emerging defensive distortion.

If the movie is used, or if the group is too threatened to proceed quickly, I will often stretch the exercise out over two sessions. In this case, members are invited to get feedback from their families or to do some private soul searching before beginning the sharing of personal defenses and the confrontation of others. These last two steps begin the following session. Because this is difficult work, it is important to review ideas and prompt the group for several weeks if the confrontation of defenses is to become a norm.

**Variations.** The recognition and confrontation of unconscious defenses is a demanding task, one that may be beyond the capacity of the group at this early stage of the problem-solving process. The entire presentation may be delayed until the last two steps of problem solving, when the group is better prepared to cooperate. Because the self-confrontation of resurgent defenses is a continuing task for the client hoping for enduring recovery, the defenses should be reviewed before treatment ends.

# 5
# Attitude Change

C lients give evidence of attitude change when they become active participants in the program, volunteering their experience, trying to understand the perspective of others, and gradually becoming receptive to education about alcohol and alcohol-related problems. The resistance to new learning is overcome. In part, this is because the initial learning relates to avoiding further drunk driving, an area of vital concern to group members. By beginning with what they want to learn, they begin to develop an interest that generalizes to other areas of education. Since the initial learning proves valuable, they gain the motivation to continue. The desired attitude is not always passive. A good demonstration of attitude change may include a feisty willingness to disagree with the counselor when the teaching does not match personal experience. Active involvement indicates that this step in the problem-solving process has been successfully taken.

There is more initiative from clients at this stage. For the first time, they allude to television programs and begin to bring in clippings from the newspaper. There is more direct sharing of "war stories," which should continue to take precedence over planned activities since it is the best modeling of improved attitudes as well as the best confirmation of the attitude change of the person sharing. There will be more discussion of ideas presented, including a willingness to bring up controversial ideas.

Attitude change is a process of reframing the problem so that drunk driving is no longer the only issue. It may now be seen as a symptom of a broader problem with drinking. Clients come to see that long-term success in avoiding rearrest requires an understanding of the extent of their problem and a willingness to alter their drinking. When this reframing has been accomplished, participants will be ready for new perspectives, which consist of the information and self-evaluation covered in chapters 6 through 8.

Several interrelated goals are accomplished through the exercises in this chapter. First, there is an interest in new learning. Some opportunities are provided, to learn not only about avoiding drunk driving but also about problem drinking. Second, the learning includes education about remaining obstacles to developing a positive attitude (for example, the discussion of alcohol and anxiety). Third, a challenge is issued for the clients to examine personal attitudes and to assume responsibility for making appropriate changes so that they can maximally benefit from the learning to come (see the discussion of self-talk). Fourth, a direct attempt is made to alter prevailing myths in order to destigmatize alcoholism (models of alcoholism and the diabetes analogy). This permits clients to enter the self-evaluation phase with less emotional reaction to the label, *alcoholism,* so that they can more accurately evaluate the extent of their own drinking problem. Finally, this stage begins to model problem solving. While the model is not yet formally introduced, its logic is applied in developing drinking while intoxicated (DWI) avoidance strategies, and its stages are modeled in the symptoms → diagnosis → treatment discussion. Each of these goals helps the client make a more complete investment in benefiting from the remainder of the program. At the minimum, participants will "make the best of it" and "get my money's worth." For most, there is a commitment to apply the new learning actively to their own lives, with an underlying appreciation that they are getting the information that they have always needed to understand their drinking.

**The Counselor's Attitudes.** I have found it useful to remind myself and my clients that they are in charge of their learning. They can now begin to assume the responsibility for making this a positive experience. I still encourage the reticent to join in, but I am less likely to accept ventilation of negative feelings. (In fact, I will use them as an opportunity for confrontation about changing to a more productive attitude, as in the discussion of self-talk.) I am more likely to take the approach of being available to help those who are receptive. I act as though most are intending to cooperate—which they probably are as we discuss DWI avoidance—while I provide information about how to develop appropriate attitudes. In sum, the work is positively focused. The preceding chapter was more involved with obstacles; the following material is more concerned with opportunities. In the group I respond to evidence of attitude change with warmth and praise. When I remind someone of his or her initial hostility, it is in the context of commenting on how much better that person seems to be feeling now.

There are times when I will be conned by a client who is "talking the talk." But it is harder to maintain spurious interest and involvement than it is to lie in reporting on the week's drinking. In time a negative attitude will surface, even if I don't set traps. I am less likely to act like a detective and more inclined to be a friend and a teacher. By this point, many clients have accepted me as an ally, even if they are unprepared to change their drinking yet. I build on this base of influence with them, knowing that there will come a time when they may need my influence to develop the motivation to make difficult changes.

The attitude a client develops is the most reliable indicator I have of his or her prognosis for changing during treatment and beyond. I am confident that a receptive client will find the education persuasive and will attempt to change. I am confident that problem solving will prove useful for those who actively apply it. So I watch for receptiveness and activity. There is an exception to this general strategy for evaluating client progress. It is not uncommon for some clients to try to quit drinking at this point, precisely because they have a good attitude toward treatment. Yet they may run into withdrawal that leaves them irritable or withdrawn. I may anticipate this by doing some early education about withdrawal symptoms (see chapter 6). I try to check out unexpected negativism, often in a private minute during break before I conclude that a client has been faking it or backsliding. My concern and validation of an altered attitude is often helpful to a client. In turn, there may be a crisis or a difficult effort at change which the client can share.

This section of the course challenges the counselor to reevaluate his or her attitude toward alcoholism. It is surprising how many workers in this field have an underlying attitude that an alcoholic is bad or weak. This attitude comes through to clients, who often will then confirm those negative expectations by remaining guarded and uncooperative. The presentation of the disease concept and the review of the models of alcoholism are opportunities for the counselor to do some attitude adjustment, just as they are for clients. Attending meetings of Alcoholics Anonymous, where there is such evident work at recovery, may be a good reminder of the courage and determination to recover shown by many alcoholics. Milam and Ketcham's (1981) *Under the Influence* will also help destigmatize alcoholism through its clear depiction of a physiological disease process underlying the often frustrating behavior of the drinker.

**Related Exercises.** Attitude change is a continuing process. While this section specifically seeks to create active involvement, comparable changes are a by-product of subsequent education that hits home, of compelling sharing by a participant, and of successes and failures in changing drinking. Problem solving is a circular process. Clients will often reevaluate their attitude later in treatment. For these reasons, I will use the following exercises out of sequence, at any point in the program when they might be helpful.

The issue of attitude is likely to resurface at step 8—motivation. Behavior change that has been postponed until it must be coerced will likely bring to the surface an underlying negative attitude. It may be particularly appropriate to present one of the exercises from this chapter at that stage of treatment. Conversely, this may be a good time to insert an activity designed to heighten motivation.

# Safety Risks of Drinking and Driving

*This discussion takes thirty to sixty minutes and requires a chalkboard. It is usually accompanied by a thirty-minute movie.*

**Rationale.** The goal of this and the following two exercises is to effect a permanent change in attitude and behavior so that there will be no more drinking and driving.

For change to endure beyond the end of treatment, internalization of new standards must take place. Internalization means that the clients accept as their own the values taught by the program. This can be contrasted with compliance, where behavior is temporarily brought into line with expectations, usually out of fear of punishment. Such coerced change is likely to be resented and temporary. Internalization requires that new attitudes be adopted by the clients so that the change in behavior is seen as personally desirable (Kelman, 1958).

This exercise explicitly invites attitude change and provides education about the safety risks of drinking and driving to underscore the need for change.

**Content.**

*Fear versus Respect for the Law.* I ask the group if they understand the difference between fear of the law and respect for the underlying goals the law is trying to accomplish. The initial compliance out of fear of the consequences of rearrest will probably not endure. I share my experience that between six months and two years after the end of treatment, fear will lose its power. It is human nature to forget the bad times. It is characteristic of drinkers not to think about the negative consequences possible while imbibing. Most of all, once the rap is behind them, once they have graduated from treatment, clients will have no reminder of their commitment to change. They are likely to adopt the dangerous goal of avoiding arrest rather than of avoiding drunk driving. Fear does not lead to lasting change if clients convince themselves that the feared consequence can be avoided.

Enduring change requires a different attitude, one based on respect for the purpose embedded in the law. The laws against drunk driving are an attempt to safeguard lives since driving under the influence of alcohol or drugs is dangerous. If the group members become convinced of the personal relevance of the accident risks, they may make a lasting decision to avoid breaking the law.

I illustrate this with a digression about my own speeding. I learned to drive 70 miles per hour and feel comfortable doing so on the highway. I will break the speed limit as long as I think I can get away with it. I will slow down if I see a patrol car or pass a likely speed trap. This is compliance out of fear. Once I feel reasonably safe from detection, I resume speeding. I contrast this with my driving within city limits. Here I will not go more than the posted 25 or 35 miles per hour limit. Even in the small country towns where I know there will be no patrol cars, I obey the law. Why? Because I have seen children and pets dart into the road, and I have been hit by cross traffic that failed to yield. My concern for safety will keep me from speeding in town. Since it is my choice, based on reasons that are important to me, no outside enforcement is needed. I respect the law here. This is adhering to the law because it matches my internalized values.

The group readily understands the contrast between fear and respect, and can understand why lasting change is probable only when there is respect. We then move on to discuss the reasons why group members should have appropriate respect for the risk of accident when driving under the influence.

Driving is a complex skill involving alertness, quick reactions, coordination, and judgment. Alcohol has detrimental effects on each of these (National Safety Council, 1972). Reaction time begins to slow with a blood alcohol content (BAC) of .02. Alcohol has pervasive and detrimental effects on eye movements and thus on vision (Stapleton, Guthrie & Linnoila, 1986). At .03 eye convergence (controlling depth perception) begins to suffer, and by .10 the reflex controlling dilation of the pupil (and the ability to see after passing the headlights of an oncoming car) is grossly impaired. Functionally, the driver may be blind for up to fifteen seconds (*Until I Get Caught*, 1980). By .05 the ability to execute complex tasks begins to suffer, even in high-tolerance drinkers. Although alcohol gives a false sense of enhanced skills, a 25 percent overall decrease in driving skills occurs by .05 BAC. Attention has declined 75 percent by the time .10 BAC has been reached (National Safety Council, 1972). The drunk driver is aiming the car but not truly driving. He or she has little ability to respond to the unexpected.

*Under the Influence.* The group is asked to watch for evidence of these effects as they view the movie *Under the Influence*. In this film, high-tolerance drinkers are observed as they are trained to maximize their driving skills on a police test track. Once their BAC is raised to .10, there is a universal loss of skill. Poor judgment is evident as they take curves at constant acceleration rather than at constant speed and in the expressed desire to "really honk it on." Poor coordination and reaction time is shown in an accident simulation when drivers overcompensate for a late decision by oversteering and throwing the car into a fishtail. The desired change in attitude is modeled, as drivers express surprise and distress at their poor performance. The message is made more compelling because the reference group is composed of high-tolerance drinkers, comparable to those in the DWI class.

This movie powerfully suggests the difference between feeling as if one is unimpaired and actual driving safety. We may discuss the effects of alcohol on judgment and skill in self-observation. Most people have witnessed or experienced being the obviously intoxicated person who insists that he or she will drive home because "I am doing just fine." This discussion further undermines the minimizing of dangers inherent in the old attitude.

*Accident Curve.* Automobile accidents are the fourth leading cause of death in the United States and are the greatest single risk for those between the ages of one and forty (Waller, 1982; Zobeck, Williams & Bertolucci, 1986). In 1985 there were 43,555 automobile fatalities. Up to 85 percent may have involved some drinking, and 40–50 percent involved a driver with a BAC above .10 (Richman, 1985; Waller, 1982). The more serious the accident, the greater the likelihood that alcohol contributed. Some drinking is involved in 17 percent of all traffic accidents (McIntire, 1980). This includes 10 percent of fender benders, 20 percent of personal injury accidents, 50 percent of fatalities, and upward of 60 percent of single vehicle fatalities (Ross, 1984).

The risk from drinking and driving is greatest for the youngest and for oldest drivers. Some ten thousand teens and young adults die each year of alcohol-related causes ("Secretary Margaret Heckler," 1983), and perhaps four times as many are permanently crippled or disfigured in accidents (Department of Transportation, 1977). The combination of low tolerance, low body weight, and inexperience combine to make teenage drinkers particularly dangerous drivers (Winter, 1982). Half of the alcohol-related teen accidents involve BACs of .02 or less (Virginia ASAP, 1985), showing that even low levels of alcohol increase the risk associated with inexperience. But inexperience alone does not explain why the risk for young males rises each year until it peaks at nineteen, especially since 54 percent of fifteen to twenty-four-year-old drivers involved in fatalities had BACs above .10 (Lowman, 1982). Alcohol is a major contributor to accidents for young drivers. Likewise, the old are at risk, especially as drunk pedestrians (who compose 19 percent of crash fatalities). The older driver uses experience and judgment to compensate for losses in sensory acuity and reaction time (Winter, 1982). Precisely because it impairs judgment, alcohol compounds driving risks.

I ask my clients how much of an increased risk of accident they will accept for the privilege of driving home drunk. I then present the accident curve (figure 5–1). This was developed from research in the urban environment of Grand Rapids, Michigan (Borkenstein, Crawther, Shumate, Ziel, and Zylman, 1964) and confirmed in more rural Vermont (Perrine, Waller,

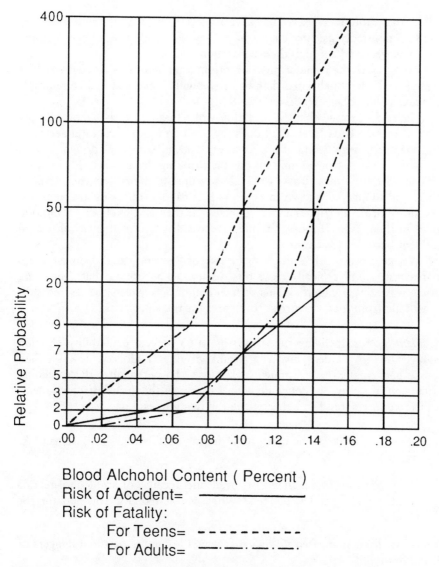

**Figure 5–1. Accident Curves: Risk of Involvement in an Accident or Fatality with Increasing BAC Levels** (adapted from Simpson, 1985)

& Harris, 1971). Although the experienced drinker is safer at any specified blood level, the risk becomes astronomical at the BAC levels of .15 and above that typify my clients. It is high-tolerance drinkers who are involved in most fatal automobile accidents, and half of them experienced prior alcohol-related incidents (usually traffic offenses or accidents, with 4.4 percent having

DWIs) that should have served as a warning (Department of Transportation, 1983). I pointedly ask my clients how they will make use of the warning they have received through their conviction.

Contrary to the popular misconception, a person faces twice the risk of being killed when inebriated than he or she will if involved in a comparable accident while sober (Waller et al., 1986).

Figure 5–1 shows that the probability of a fatal crash rises more sharply with increasing BAC levels than does the probability of a nonfatal accident. In 1985 there were 2.3 fatalities for every 100 million miles driven. This is a baseline risk of 1 in 40 million. For the drinking driver, the odds increase to 1 in 330,000 miles (Ross, 1985). I may update the risk at each level of BAC, and by age, as shown in table 5–1. Although the odds are small for any single drunken trip, clients recognize that they will likely drive 330,000 miles in their lives. If they continue to drive drunk, the chances of a fatal accident become significant.

We have previously estimated the risk of "getting caught" in reference to rearrest. I will typically close this discussion by noting that "there are worse ways to get caught." This shift in emphasis suggests the desired shift in attitude from fear of rearrest to respect for the safety risks.

*Accident Stories.* If the average driver has a 65 percent probability of being involved in an accident involving drunk driving (Podolsky, 1985a), then course participants have a much higher risk. To personalize the foregoing discussion of safety, we conclude with a circuit of the group in which members share in response to either of the following questions:

What was it like to be in a drunk driving accident? As a passenger? As the driver?

Have you ever lost a friend or loved one because of an alcohol-related accident? How did it happen? What was it like for you and for the family?

A moving discussion often follows that drives home the personal dangers of drunk driving.

**Table 5–1**
**Risks of a Fatal Accident by Age, BAC, and Miles Driven**

| | Teens | | Adults | |
|---|---|---|---|---|
| BAC | Risk (%) | Odds/Mile | Risk (%) | Odds/Mile |
| .015–.05 | 300 | 1:13 mil. | 100 | 1:40 million (mil.) |
| .05–.08 | 900 | 1:4.4 mil. | 200 | 1:20 mil. |
| .10–.15 | 10,000 | 1:400,000 | 1,200 | 1:3.3 mil. |
| >.15 | 40,000 | 1:100,000 | 10,000 | 1:400,000 |

**Variations.** I feel free to combine elements of this exercise with the one that follows. Depending on the needs of the group, from one to three sessions may be spent on the direct effort to alter attitudes and behavior in order to stop any driving while intoxicated.

# Attitudes toward Drinking and Driving

*This discussion usually takes thirty minutes. The stimulus movie will require an additional thirty minutes. Only one of the two movies described below would be used in any session.*

**Rationale.** The traditional sympathy for the driver arrested for DWI is based on the mistaken belief that all of us occasionally drive drunk. In fact, 75–90 percent of American adults rarely if ever have driven under the influence. Even when they feel drunk 50 percent have a BAC of less than .055. Only 11 percent are above a .10 BAC when they estimate that they have become illegal (Orr & Lizotte, 1986). The person arrested for drunk driving is not a typical drinker. Instead, this is someone taking exceptional risks. This awareness needs to be fostered.

In this discussion, clients are specifically invited to notice any changes that have occurred since their arrest in their attitudes about drunk driving. Again, personal sharing is preceded by the opportunity to observe others model a range of different attitudes. The opportunity to publicly acknowledge changes in perspective becomes a powerful incentive to proceed with behavior change.

In the overall program flow, the issue of drunk driving is the first to be the focus of problem solving. From this perspective, the preceding exercise provided the new learning needed to set an appropriate goal, the next specifies the strategies for successful change, and the current exercise reinforces attitude change and heightens motivation for sustained effort.

**Content.**

*So Long Pal.* This movie is dated in style (the car models are long out of vogue) but fresh in theme. It can be introduced as an opportunity to examine the source of the attitudes we may have developed that support drunk driving. The movie follows a young businessman through a series of reveries about the history of drinking in America in which alcohol use is consistently reinforced (by association with celebration, risk taking, romance, and courage). This contrasts sharply with the humiliation and sanctions experienced when the protagonist is arrested and convicted of drunk driving. The opportunity to learn new attitudes through involvement in a drunk driver education project is downplayed relative to the influence of friends who commiserate (while drinking) and offer to help him "forget the whole thing." After a day of boating (and drinking), the young man and his family have relaxed enough to ignore the pain caused by drunk driving. He then proceeds to take the wheel, only to drive off a cliff and almost certainly kill his entire family.

The group discussion notes the warning signs missed, the danger of the protagonist's bad attitude, the difficulties in changing attitudes, the negative influence of defenses and the drinking friends that support them, and anger at his jeopardizing the well-being of his children. The anger may be displaced onto the wife, who failed to stop his drunk driving. But more often the drinker is seen as having failed to take advantage of the opportunity to use his DWI conviction to change. In comparison with the fatal crash, assignment to alcohol education classes is hardly punishment. The movie effectively models an altered perspective on treatment: to see it as an opportunity and not punishment.

*Until I Get Caught.* This excellent movie shares relevant information about the safety risks of driving under the influence. But its greatest contribution is to examine systematically the varying attitudes toward drinking and driving through interviews with drinkers, drivers convicted of DWI, law enforcement representatives, safety experts, a sample of Swedes (who have internalized attitudes against drunk driving after years of exposure to tough penalties for violations), and families of victims of DWI crashes. The film ends with a young man, obviously in trouble with his drinking, vowing to continue driving under the influence "until I get caught." Group members usually identify their own prearrest attitude with this model but then feel impelled to point out the risks he is taking and so to acknowledge the need for a changed attitude. We may discuss the role of fear of the law in motivating altered behavior. But the strongest contextual message is the pain caused by drunk driving accidents.

*An Accident Fantasy.* After the movie has been fully processed, I invite the group to join me on a guided fantasy. Participants may loosen collars, remove glasses, lean back against the walls for head support, and then close their eyes. They visualize themselves driving home from group, thinking about the class, and coping with the temptation to stop off for a few drinks with friends. I pause to allow them time to picture their own resolution to this situation. They are guided back to the conclusion of their drive home. With heightened urgency in my voice, I underscore the sudden anxiety they feel (the cold hands, the increased heart rate, the perspiration on the forehead) when they see a police cruiser sitting in their driveway. The officer tells them that there has been an accident; that they are to come with him to the hospital. They visualize the emergency room, the examination cubicle, and the blood-stained gurney on which their loved one lies—either unconscious or dead. They access their feelings, first about their loved one, and then about the person in the next cubicle, identified from his or her drunken mutterings as the person responsible for the accident. I may develop this confrontation, by having group members imagine peeking out of the examining room and seeing the perpetrator. If the group is particularly resistant, I may even have them suddenly recognize the drunk as another member of the group who they know has been lying. I leave them with a vague directive to be aware of the different feelings that they are experiencing so strongly.

This is a private experience, so sharing is invited but not demanded. It is typically easy to talk about the rage toward the drunk driver. But seldom is there discussion of the grief about the loved one. Nor is there mention of whether or not group members drank on the way home. I then dismiss the group, purposely permitting participants to continue thinking about the fantasy. This is covert aversive therapy (Cautela, 1973; Meichenbaum, 1977). Clients are led to punish themselves in fantasy for any renewed thoughts of drinking and driving. By fully personalizing the safety risks, clients are motivated to make the changes discussed in the next exercise.

**Variations.** The elements of this exercise are potent motivators for change or reminders of the need for continued effort. They may be used in problem-solving step 8. They may also be introduced just prior to holidays or events that represent increased opportunity and temptation to drink.

Clients who avoid drunken driving out of respect for the safety risks involved will show appropriate concern about any DWI behavior. Attitude change can be tested in the responses to either of the following discussion topics:

1. Is it ever appropriate to call the police to turn in someone who is driving drunk? Because of the strong values against "ratting" on others, I do not expect a blanket promise to report the offender to police. But the changed attitude should make it possible for clients to consider that arrest might be a favor rather than a curse. I often share the situation encountered by one of my clients: A man drives into a gas station, hitting the curb on

his way in. As he fills up, he is barely able to stand erect. In the car are a woman and three small children, none of them in safety belts. As he drives away, again bouncing over the curb as he misses the driveway, my client realizes how unsafe this man is. He ponders whether to call the police with a description of the car. There is seldom universal agreement within the group as to how to handle such a situation. But a thoughtful discussion is a good sign of improved attitude.

2. Is it acceptable to ride with someone who is intoxicated? I may sarcastically enact the argument between two drunks. One argues, "I'm wasted. You drive." The other counters, "Yeah, but I've already gotten a DWI, and you haven't." The group members may want to discuss how to take a stand so that they do not ride with other drunk drivers. At a minimum, they can use this situation to test the extent to which any change is made out of fear as opposed to respect for the law.

# Strategies for Avoiding Driving while Intoxicated

*This planned discussion lasts about sixty minutes. A chalkboard is helpful.*

**Rationale.** This exercise concludes the education about drunk driving by having each participant develop a strategy for avoiding driving under the influence from among a set of alternatives developed by the group. Any drunk driving from this point forward must be seen as indicating a poor attitude or a severe drinking problem.

This exercise continues the problem-solving process for the issue of drunk driving; it represents the planning stage (step 7). Time must be allotted to reviewing successes and failures in subsequent sessions, so that problem solving can be seen through to its conclusion. But the required changes are so clear-cut that no other sessions need be exclusively devoted to DWI behavior.

For clients without further evidence of a drinking problem and for whom there has been consistent success at avoiding driving under the influence since arrest, this may be all the problem-solving that is required. Having in previous exercises reviewed the risks of drunk driving and having here clarified the change strategy required to maintain the gains, it is now time to think about discharging some clients. In contrast, this exercise removes the last excuse—ignorance—for clients who continue to drive drunk. Having publicly committed themselves to avoid drunk driving, participants who again drive while intoxicated are likely to experience a crisis. It is this crisis that may lead to a change in attitude in which the drunk driving problem is reframed as a drinking problem. These clients will become more responsive to the thorough examination of alcohol-related problems which follows. For all clients, this point in treatment is a moment of truth.

Having developed and tested plans to avoid driving under the influence, group members complete the first application of the problem-solving process with this exercise. Although it is not yet time to teach this underlying change strategy directly, its use with the specific issue of drunk driving prepares clients for its later application with other problems.

**Content.** There are two parts to this exercise. In the first, various plans for avoiding drunk driving are identified and critically evaluated. In the second, each group member identifies the strategy or combination of strategies that they believe they can use with consistent success.

The discussion of different plans can be handled in either of two ways. If the group has demonstrated its maturity or if the leader is trying to encourage more member-to-member communication, it is desirable to use what is called a Tavistock approach (Bion, 1961). Here the leader clearly assigns the topic (I write the question on the chalkboard) and then confines him- or herself to reminding the group members when they have strayed off the subject. I will also serve as recorder, keeping a list of the strategies the group feels might succeed. The passive facilitator encourages the group to become active and to assume leadership. Because the discussion topic requires common sense rather than esoteric knowledge, little is lost if the leader does not contribute to the discussion of DWI avoidance plans. If you choose this approach, give the following instructions:

> List as many plans as possible for avoiding drunk driving. Then consider the strengths and limitations of each strategy. Which are likely to fail in time? Eliminate them. Try to identify the strategy or combination of strategies that will work consistently so that you will never again drive drunk and be subject to arrest for DWI.

The leader should then keep quiet and enjoy watching the group work.

The alternative approach to generating and evaluating plans is to have a conventional group discussion. Here, the leader can be active, usually by sharing stories and ideas from other groups or by playing devil's advocate if the group seems insufficiently critical of weak plans.

Whichever approach is used, the group will generate something like the following list. Some of the strategies are guaranteed to *fail:*

1. *Don't drive if you feel drunk.* Since your judgment will be impaired

and your tolerance is high, you will certainly drive illegally if this is your plan.

2. *Sleep it off in the car, or wait before driving.* The cold or the acetaldehyde agitation will awaken you long before you are legal. You will drive too soon. Also, you may be subject to arrest if your key is in the ignition or if the police officer believes that you have been driving.

Some strategies are certain to work, if you can follow them:

3. *Don't drink.* Someone usually contends that this is the only option that will really work. For those who believe it, this is certainly the best. But it should not end the conversation. Too many abstainers go back to drinking. There is a need for a backup strategy.

4. *Don't drive.* If this restriction in freedom is acceptable (remember, the laws also apply to intoxicated operation of mopeds and bicycles), it will be effective. But some participants will admit to unintended driving if they become unusually drunk or if there is an emergency.

5. *Control drinking so that you are never illegal.* Practically this means counting and spacing drinks. It will only work for nonalcoholics with good impulse control. But it is a worthy aspect of a strategy for anyone who is willing to give up the prospect of heavy drinking.

Some plans carry significant weaknesses but will reduce the risk of DWI if used in combination:

6. *Have someone else drive if you will be drinking heavily.* Will the other person put up with you and still stay sober? If a drinking buddy does the driving but is also intoxicated, then you will be riding in the "suicide seat." Anyone with respect for the safety risks will avoid this arrangement. The risk with having a designated driver (one who abstains from alcohol for the evening) or a light-drinking sweetheart as a chauffeur is that this person may get disgusted with you and leave. Then what? If you arrange to have someone drop you off and then return after a designated interval, can you avoid the temptation to change plans, and can you rely on that person?

7. *Call a taxi.* This may get expensive, but it is cheaper than a DWI.

8. *Leave the car where it is.* One client had a flash of insight and told the group that henceforth he would take his keys and lock them in the car right after he ordered his sixth drink. He was offended when the group howled with laughter. Another participant explained: "I can see it now. You're drunk and ready to leave. You just want to check out the car to make sure it will be safe overnight. Then you notice that the passenger-side window is rolled down and say, 'Hot damn! I can drive home.' " This strategy can work, but there are caveats: Will you pick the lock, or dig out the spare key? And the problem of how to get home remains.

9. *Move within walking distance of the bar.* We review the risks for drunk pedestrians: one of three hit by a car was drunk. Those in the group

who get an overwhelming urge to drive (colloquially known as "gas ass") or like to check out different parties will have to limit their range.

10. *Make arrangements to stay overnight or camp for the weekend.* This will work if you do stay long enough. It is not unusual for clients to report having to leave unexpectedly, however, if, for example, the host and his wife begin arguing. Other risks include sleeping it off for too short a time or resuming drinking the next day.

11. *Drink at home.* This works as long as there are no emergencies, no impulsive decision is made to leave, and the client has an adequate supply of alcohol or has made a commitment to stop when the stock gives out.

There are many more approaches the group can explore. All diminish the risk of driving under the influence, despite their limitations. All require that the drinker plan in advance and make appropriate arrangements while still sober. All demand that the person stick to the plan, even at the most intoxicated moments. As the group members become cognizant of these requirements, their awareness grows that there must be changes in drinking style. Usually someone expresses this by saying, "Any of these will work for a while. But if you keep drinking, sooner or later you are going to slip."

Once the discussion has reached a satisfactory conclusion, I ask that we circle the group, with each participant in turn stating the combination of plans that he or she intends to use. If the plans have already been in use, I ask that there also be sharing of the challenges, including the successes and failures, encountered in practice. The exercise ends when each person has had a chance to state publicly the plan he or she has adopted.

# Alcohol and Anxiety

*This twenty-minute presentation requires a chalkboard.*

**Rationale.** An important obstacle to appropriate concern about a drinking problem is what is alternatively called "a drinker's" attitude or a "don't give a damn" attitude. Alcohol is a tranquilizing chemical. Taken in quantity or with regularity, it reduces alertness and responsiveness to emotional pain. The heavy drinker may be unable to change, despite being chastened by a DWI conviction, because the chemical undermines the motivation to change its use.

This short lecture provides education about the effects of drinking on attitude. It provides a psychopharmacological perspective, in which inadequate efforts at change are explained in terms of the drug effects of alcohol, as opposed to the more common attribution of a weak will. In this sense the lecture is destigmatizing. It is also challenging. Telling clients that their pattern of use will make it difficult for them to make adequate changes is a tacit request for exceptional effort. In essence, the message is that "you can't see clearly the dangers around you, so be more alert than usual." If taken seriously, this admonition will make clients more attentive to the pain in their lives that may signify a drinking problem.

**Content.** There is a paradox about pain. It is a powerful motivator of change. Yet the change desired is the end of the pain, not the resolution of the problem that led to the discomfort. So stress-induced stomach problems will get people to the doctor and assure that they will take the Tagamet that is prescribed. But once the pain is eliminated, such people will lack any motivation to reduce the stress in their lives. The destructive life-style that caused the problem will continue as long as there is no discomfort that cannot be hidden with medication.

Drinkers can readily understand that similar vicious cycles get set up with alcohol. Intoxicated behavior causes problems—arguments, embarrassing scenes, loss of money, or damage to self-esteem—that causes pain. Yet alcohol is one of the most powerful drugs known for blocking anxiety. So the drinker is tempted to "drink to forget" or to get drunk enough so that "it just doesn't matter." Such relief drinking means that alcohol is relied on to mask the problems in living caused by drinking. I may allude to the scene from *So Long Pal* in which the bartender commiserates with a customer who has been arrested for drunk driving by offering him a free drink. When asked, someone in the group will usually volunteer a personal story about using drinking to solve alcohol-related problems. The pattern is obviously destructive, yet it is readily seen to be seductive and common.

Change requires awareness of a problem and motivation. Alcohol interferes with both. Figure 5–2 is drawn on the board and described.

A degree of anxiety that is insufficient to attract conscious attention (A), may create a type of general tension without motivating change. An example would be the nagging feeling that there is something that you forgot to do. As a problem rises to consciousness, it is acknowledged without motivating effort to change as long as the pain is tolerable (B). So the smoker who awakens with a cough will have no intention of following through when he says, "I really have to do something about these cigarettes." Only when the pain becomes difficult to tolerate (C) are plans made to change. And often the problem must be all but overwhelming before the effort is initiated (D).

The group can readily understand that you feel less pain when drinking. This is most evident in the physical injury that is not recognized until the morning after. It applies as well with psychological pain from fright or embarrassment. Alcohol may make it difficult to recognize pain, raising the

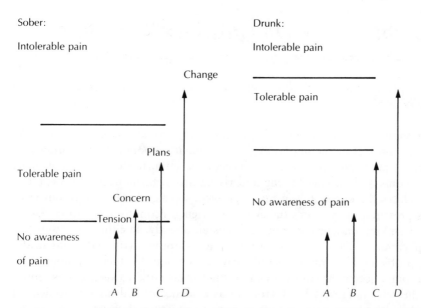

**Figure 5–2. Alcohol Use Reduces Motivation to Change by Raising Pain Thresholds**

threshold of awareness. It also reduces the responsiveness to anxiety. By undercutting the motivating pain, it raises the threshold at which we plan and execute change. Last of all, by making it difficult to plan effectively, alcohol increases the time before we can take effective action even when there is the intention to act. So the drinker may remain oblivious to stages *B* and *C*, and may dismiss *D* as unimportant. When sobriety returns, the drinker may be overwhelmed by the accumulated tension and so, to escape anxiety as quickly as possible, may again drink to "solve" the problems.

The group can use this diagram to visualize how drinking interferes with efforts to change. It helps them to be told that anxiety is something to learn from rather than avoid. An absense of concern may be more of an indication of toxicity than proof that "everything is fine." For this last message to be personalized, the group members must realize that the alteration in attitude can become habitual enough that it persists even when they are not currently drunk. Someone will generally share that the "don't give a damn" attitude disappeared only after months of abstinence.

**Variations.** This discussion parallels that found in the "self-esteem trap" (see chapter 11) and in Father Martin's movie, *Chalk Talk, part 1.* I may well show the movie at this point to underscore further the learning that alcohol abuse makes it difficult to respond rationally to problems.

# Symptoms → Diagnosis → Treatment

*This presentation and discussion takes forty-five minutes and uses a chalkboard.*

**Rationale.** This analogy uses the treatment of a common disease as a model for demonstrating the importance of attitude in responding appropriately to a problem. In the process it emphasizes the importance of acknowledging symptoms and looking for the underlying problem. Indirectly, this exercise introduces the essential elements of problem solving. At an unconscious level, this presentation prepares the group for seeing alcoholism as a disease.

Drinking may or may not be discussed directly. In either case, the clear implication is that a DWI arrest is but one symptom of an underlying drinking problem. The importance of early recognition of other symptoms, and of prompt acceptance of treatment, is the message of the exercise. It is central to the reframing of a DWI problem as evidence of a drinking problem. It models the appropriate attitude of honest concern and effort.

**Content.** Begin by dividing the board into three columns respectively labeled "Symptoms," "Diagnosis," and "Treatment." Note that the information from each is the basis for decisions made in the subsequent area. If you are examined by a doctor, the first question (after establishing how you will pay) is: "Where does it hurt?" Once the symptoms are detailed, the most likely diagnosis is made. Diagnosis determines the appropriate treatment. If the correct treatment is prescribed and followed, the symptoms will subside, the doctor will pronounce a cure, and everyone will be satisfied. If the symptoms remain, a reevaluation of the diagnosis and treatment will be made. There may be further tests to confirm the diagnosis. Alternative therapies may be initiated, and there will be admonitions to follow through on prescribed treatment exactly. This process will continue until the symptoms disappear. This is the logic of treating an illness.

We demonstrate that the reality is more complex. One complication is that symptoms are often elusive or unacknowledged. Another is that there may be several possible diagnoses for a given set of symptoms. Although I may wake up a sleepy group by using venereal disease, I typically use indications of a respiratory infection for the analogy. Under symptoms, I list morning cough, congestion, slight sore throat. With the group's help, I make several discoveries:

1. Multiple diagnoses are possible: excess smoking, tuberculosis (TB), flu, and cancer are all options.

2. Treatment will be very different, depending on the diagnosis. Re-

sponses to excess smoking would include cutting down, quitting, or switching to a low-tar brand. None of these would be considered sufficient if the diagnosis was cancer.

3. Attitude affects the response to symptoms. I ask the group who would go to a doctor with the symptoms mentioned. The predictable differences are discussed and the underlying attitudes clarified. Some people ignore symptoms. Others worry. Many will wait and expect time to take care of things. Some rely on expert advice, while others distrust doctors or worry about the cost of treatment. Some are fatalists who passively observe as things take their course. The wrong attitude can effectively preclude problem solving.

4. Attitude affects diagnosis. Many self-diagnose and self-medicate using home remedies. Many will not diagnose at all. Others will resist any diagnosis that is threatening or that requires a life-style change as part of the cure. We note that denial, minimizing, or the false pride that leads one to resist help are all contributors to an unproductive attitude. The group can usually discover the core message that it is important to have an attitude that allows one to face the symptoms or seek expert help. After all, doctors have special tests that can readily distinguish TB from a virus. (I emphasize this if the group will shortly be completing the alcoholism questionnaires from chapter 7).

5. Attitudes affect treatment. Those who do not trust their doctor may do nothing or may seek a second opinion before commencing treatment. The group usually includes many who comply with the prescribed therapy only when it is convenient. Expensive medicines may be omitted; advice to quit smoking may be ignored. There are many obstacles to complying with a treatment regimen.

I usually develop the analogy to demonstrate the risk of improper or inadequate treatment, especially for a chronic disease. Symptoms will persist or get worse as the underlying disease progresses. Suppose the self-diagnosis is a mild cold that can be safely ignored. A week later the initial symptoms are worse and are supplemented by a loss of energy and blood in the phlegm. Most of the group would now become worried enough to go to a doctor and comply with treatment. Anxiety can change attitudes (confirming the discussion from the preceding exercise). With a resistant group I may fully develop a scenario of a man with lung cancer who ignores initial symptoms, refuses to quit smoking, and delays seeing a doctor until the disease is life threatening. The goal is to foster recognition that it is more foolish than macho to be "hardheaded."

**Variations.** I often resist the temptation to state the optimal attitude. There is less resistance if someone in the group volunteers the importance of facing symptoms, seeking help if symptoms recur or persist, and complying with treatment. Likewise, I will often let the power of the context and the analogy be enough to get clients to relate the discussion to their alcohol use. Ideally clients will experience a dawning inner awareness of previous problems and recurrent concerns, despite halfhearted attempts to change drinking patterns. But the exercise is flexible. These extensions may be useful, especially for a defensive or less intelligent group.

If I proceed, I may ask the group to describe the optimal attitude for facing a problem. The ensuing discussion will bring to the surface the desired responses. Alternatively, I may invite volunteers to share how their attitude affected their handling of major illnesses. This often leads to someone's contrasting a previous resistant stance with a better attitude developed in the course of dealing with a serious disease. With luck, the sharing may be about alcoholism.

I may erase the symptoms from the analogy and insert "DWI." Having tacitly identified the offense as a symptom, I then ask the group to identify "other symptoms of a drinking problem." The resulting list can be used to generate possible diagnoses (when, for example, are the symptoms regarded as varying from social drinking, or when do they collectively indicate alcoholism?). This extension of the exercise enables the group to see the DWI conviction as one among a set of possible symptoms of an underlying drinking problem.

# Changing Attitudes through Rational Self-Talk

*This presentation takes sixty minutes and requires a chalkboard. It may be planned, but it is most powerful when initiated in response to a client who is unable to manage a current, strong emotion appropriately. Most often this emotion is anger.*

**Rationale.** This exercise teaches clients how they can intentionally alter attitudes and feelings. Albert Ellis and other cognitive-behaviorists have convincingly shown that people are capable of talking themselves into and out of depression, social phobias, resentments, and temper problems (Beck, Rush, Shaw, & Emery, 1979; Ellis, 1973; Ellis & Grieger, 1977; Ellis & Harper, 1975; Meichenbaum, 1977). Such issues are obviously pertinent to attitude change and to recovery. I introduce the basic ideas from rational emotive therapy (RET) during a group session, with specific focus on defusing unproductive attitudes toward treatment. Positive reactions to this exercise may lead to referrals of individual clients for more intensive work with RET.

The exercise is likely to be initiated in response to a client's ventilating, usually fulminating in an irrational manner against "the system." It may be seen as a technique for handling the persistence of step 1 resentment at later stages of problem solving.

**Content.** I divide the chalkboard into three columns, label the first column "Situation," and write down the essentials of the external situation that has provoked the client. Examples include: "appointment with case officer, threatening return to court," or "required to go to AA." In the third column, titled "Feelings," I list emotions labeled by the client ("mad as hell" or "outraged") and specific actions threatened that convey emotion (for example, "bust his face"). If I am initiating the discussion, I pose a situation ("You get a letter from your probation officer calling you in for an unexpected appointment") and ask what the likely feeling would be.

I ask the group whether the situation causes the feeling. Most people believe it does: "Anyone would be angry in a situation like that." In fact, there is a range of possible feelings in any situation. Some people are more scared than angry. I ask, "Would everyone in situation A feel C?" and "What other feelings might one have in response to A?" We readily establish that feelings are not an automatic reaction and that persistent feelings require something beyond the situation to keep them alive.

Internal dialogue is the intervening variable. The middle column on the board I label "Self-Talk." If the exercise is prompted by a participant's ventilating, I enter some of the pithiest comments. For an angry client, these might include: "He has no right to treat me this way. I won't put up with it." If I am providing the situation, I will ask the group what they might tell themselves in response to it and what feelings would result. It is easy to see that guilt or fear would result from "What did I do wrong?" The self-talk may be so practiced and automatic as to be almost unconscious. But the group can see that a bit of self-scrutiny will surface internal dialogue that matches the tone of whatever emotion is being experienced.

If self-talk generates feelings, then the statements we give ourselves can be used to control our emotions. Both the type and the intensity of feeling can be managed. I will demonstrate this to the group by asking them what they could say that would keep themselves from becoming emotional, and contrasting this with samples of self-talk that would give rise to several different feelings. For example, the illustrative situation could be faced more calmly if the inner dialogue consisted of thoughts like this: "It's no use trying to guess what the appointment is about; I might as well relax as I wait to see."

One expression of this self-control is to challenge the habitual self-talk that generates troublesome feelings. I will routinely review the type of statements that lead to overly emotional reactions. They will be variations on: "I can't stand this," "No one *should* have to put up with this," or "No one has *ever* had to deal with anything like this." Absolutes (*always, never*) and judgmental imperatives (*must, have to, should*) are linguistic tools that artificially intensify emotion. Such statements are factually inaccurate, hence the designation "irrational ideas." In truth, we *can* stand many situations that are unpleasant or undesirable. To ferret out and challenge the irrational habits is a mental activity that will distract one from and ultimately replace the exaggerated self-talk that maintains excessive emotionality.

I will typically review the irrational ideas behind whatever emotion is most disruptive to the group. Most often it is anger or resentment. The self-talk to be challenged includes absolutism ("he must not . . ."), entitlement ("I am owed an explanation . . ." or "I deserve better . . ."), and confusing rights and survival needs for preferences ("I have to . . ." or "I'll die if I go back to court"). On close examination, each of these stems is untrue. The interested client is referred to the venerable *New Guide to Rational Living* (Ellis & Harper, 1975) for a more thorough discussion of the irrational ideas to be challenged.

My groups practice substituting calming and affirming self-talk. AA is an excellent source of catchphrases that can be used: "Easy does it," "Live and let live," "This too shall pass," and so forth. Rational ideas that replace the anger-generating inner commentary include "I would prefer . . ." (instead of "I must") and "It would be nice if . . ." (rather than "I need . . ."). Anger will diminish if these slogans are used. Actively substituting new habits is perhaps the best way to escape the unproductive self-talk that maintains bad attitudes.

The obvious limit to this discussion is the counselor's familiarity with cognitive behavioral techniques. This session can review only the most basic principles from this approach. But the group generally finds the ideas intriguing, controversial, and useful. A demonstration tends to evolve, in which the leader is challenged to develop appropriate self-talk to handle situations or emotions suggested by the group. A conversant leader can provide a number of very practical phrases. At some point, the burden must be shared. The group is then invited to challenge irrational ideas and to find replacement dialogue that leads to more desired emotions.

The presentation ends with the challenge to participants to identify and change the self-talk underlying unproductive attitudes. My experience suggests that most members must have follow-up exposure to rational emotive therapy to alter self-talk successfully on a continuing basis. This ultimate goal is beyond the reach of most group members, who have been given only a session's familiarity with the technique. But a more limited goal exists that is realistic. The clear awareness that attitude can be changed and that attitudes are chosen rather than dictated by the situation is a powerful invitation to let go of residual resistance and adapt the best of the attitudes modeled by other participants in the group.

**Variations.** The counselor presenting these ideas should have developed expertise in the therapeutic technique employed. This exercise is derived from cognitive behavioral therapy and emphasizes the verbal mediators of emotion. Other approaches emphasize the kinesthetic and visual contributors to feelings. We have all had the experience of withdrawing from a person who looks like someone we dislike or whose touch triggers an uncomfortable feeling. The multimodal therapy of Lazarus (1976, 1977) and Neuro-Linguistic Programming (Bandler & Grinder, 1979; Grinder & Bandler, 1982) represent particularly appropriate alternative strategies for changing attitudes. Counselors experienced in using these approaches are urged to develop strategies to teach these powerful techniques for changing attitudes to their clients.

Alcoholics in the first months of recovery experience emotional hypersensitivity. They are irritable. Any provocation may lead to a major eruption. Whether this is a physiological response to the loss of the depressant drug (the "emotional augmentation" described by Milam & Ketcham, 1981) or whether it is caused by the lack of alternative coping strategies for handling normal stress, it is a major contributor to relapse or misery. I will often defer this exercise until the concluding stage of treatment (see chapter 12). The focus shifts from attitude change to self-management of emotion. Clients suffering from irritability are particularly receptive to any strategy for self-control. If I introduce it for this purpose, when the change in drinking is in place, I will spend more time on using RET as a specific therapeutic technique. Clients are instructed to keep a written record of their feelings and self-talk. As described above, the first objective is to identify the self-talk that leads to undesirable emotionality. Two additional steps need to be taken:

1. Identifying the desired or appropriate emotion.
2. Generating a range of internal comments that will create and maintain this emotion. Again, the process of writing down these phrases is helpful. The client should practice substituting this new self-talk whenever the undesirable feeling starts to surface.

# *Tolerance*

*This discussion takes fifteen minutes and requires a chalkboard.*

**Rationale.** A high tolerance to alcohol is an underlying symptom common to almost all participants in treatment. The twin goals of this presentation are to provide the group with an accurate definition of tolerance and to alter the attitudes toward it.

**Content.** Tolerance is the top end of what an individual can handle. It is the greatest quantity of alcohol that a person can drink without feeling uncomfortable. When the tolerance limit is exceeded, vomiting, passing out, or gross drunkenness will occur.

There are individual differences in tolerance. Some people retain a low tolerance. Every participant knows someone who gets goofy after one drink and sick after two. Many Orientals metabolize alcohol (more accurately acetaldehyde) in such a manner that they will become flushed and uncomfortable after drinking quantities that would not even affect most Caucasians (NIAAA, 1985). Some people are born with a high tolerance and can handle higher quantities of alcohol than their friends from the first drinking occasion. Most people develop their tolerance over time, gradually increasing in their capacity until well into their forties or fifties. The high-tolerance drinker is the one who drinks the most at a party and still feels in the best shape to drive the guests home. This is why so many people are arrested for drunk driving, despite awareness. They truly believe that they are safe to drive.

I then present figure 5–3.

Tolerance, the greatest amount an individual can handle, is to be contrasted with the euphoria point (often called the "high" or the "sporting buzz" in my groups), which represents the amount of alcohol an individual needs to feel pleasantly drug-affected. The low-tolerance drinker will usually also require less alcohol to feel high. But the crucial difference is that there is a physical barrier to excessive drinking: too much alcohol and low-tolerance drinkers know they will be sick or have a horrendous hangover. Quite naturally they stop, usually before consuming four standard drinks. This is not a matter of willpower, since they are just following their feelings.

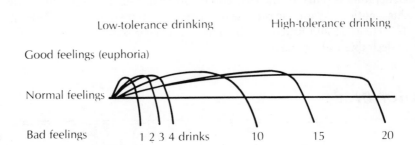

**Figure 5–3. Contrast between Drinkers with Low and High Tolerance in Reaction to Alcohol**

*The Apple-eating Analogy.* Milam (personal communication, October 29, 1982) illustrates this with an analogy. If I brought a bushel of apples into group, I could probably get everyone to eat one willingly. With a little arm twisting ("What's the matter, lightweight?"), I might be able to get everyone to eat a second and maybe a third. Before long, my offer of another apple would be turned down flat. If I then carried on about the tremendous will-power of the group, they would think I was crazy. Why? Because there is no willpower involved if you simply follow your body's signals. That is how drinking is limited in the low-tolerance drinker.

The high-tolerance drinker is the one who is showing willpower by lim-iting alcohol intake to three drinks when the capacity is above a dozen. So control of drinking is different for those with a high tolerance in that it relies on conscious intention rather than on physical sensations. Anything that compromises mental alertness and the will to restrict intake makes it likely that the high-tolerance drinker will consume large quantities. Of course, the drug effects of alcohol cause precisely these changes.

High tolerance is forever. The euphoria point may drop with abstinence or prolonged limited consumption, just as it varies with health and with mood. It is common for a guy who easily handles a six-pack to feel high after two beers if he has not been drinking for two months. But the top end capacity remains high. It is common to hear drinkers report relapsing and quickly returning to levels of consumption that are as high or higher than ever. So the only means of limiting consumption once high tolerance devel-ops is to abstain or use willpower to limit intake. Only aging, liver or brain injury, or the general deterioration in health caused by chronic alcoholism or illness lead to loss of tolerance.

Most people grew up thinking that a high tolerance for alcohol is en-viable. Perhaps it is for the woman intent on defending her honor after matching drinks with a guy twice her size. Perhaps it is for the TV cop who drinks all night and still has the judgment and hair-trigger reflexes to gun down the bad guy without injuring the hostage. Most of us were socialized to believe that a high tolerance is a good thing.

But there is another side to this, namely, the effect of alcohol on health. Medical science still adheres to Sir Francis Anstie's (1864) dictum that any more than three standard drinks may harm the health. Alcohol in excessive quantity is toxic. Most people have heard of someone who chugged a quart of vodka and then died of cardiac arrest or respiratory collapse because of the alcohol overdose. The body does have protection against consuming poisons. I ask the group members what would happen if they ate some rotten meat. They note that the vomiting and diarrhea that are the body's defenses are similar to the response that occurs when they outdrink their tolerance. Additionally, and ingeniously, passing out is an effective way to end the intake of a toxic chemical. However unpleasant it is to be sick, they should regard this as their bodies' signal that they are poisoning themselves.

*The Smoke Detector Analogy.* The unpleasant signal from the body is similar to the operation of a smoke detector, which uses an irritating beep to raise the alarm about the more dangerous risk of smoke and fire. People readily identify with someone who feels the irritation when startled by the alarm. But they would consider it foolish to remove the battery or destroy the wiring of the detector so as to sleep undisturbed but unprotected. Yet that is precisely what the typical drinker does when stretching his or her tolerance. This applies especially to those who pause to vomit, or wake from having passed out, only to drink more. In time they succeed in overriding the body's defenses. They can then consume large quantities of alcohol without feeling ill. But the body then has to cope with toxic amounts of the drug. Such people may feel unaffected. But they are no more safe than the person who returns to sleep after disabling a buzzing smoke detector.

# Models of Alcoholism

*This presentation and discussion takes about forty-five minutes and uses a chalkboard.*

**Rationale.** Over the long history of human inebriation, many theories have been devised to explain why some people become involved in a destructive relationship with alcohol. These theories have entered the popular consciousness as attitudes. Because they have been learned in early childhood, these beliefs about what alcoholism is and how it should be handled are accepted as articles of faith. Yet they are likely to be wrong. They omit much of the new understanding that has developed in the last two decades. Outmoded models make it more difficult for people to accept the possibility of being alcoholic, and they set up obstacles to effective treatment. For these reasons it is helpful to review common models with clients and to help them identify any to which they adhere. More specifically, clients can be confronted with how they use their models of alcoholism to avoid taking effective action to resolve their drinking problems.

The first chapter reviewed some of the history leading to the split between punishment and treatment as the preferred response to alcohol problems. It should be recognized that this controversy occurs on the individual level just as it does at the public policy level. The most common reason given for not admitting alcoholism is the shame it implies to someone who sees the syndrome as a moral failure. As one client expressed it, "After being called a 'goddamned alcoholic' long enough, I thought it was another swear word."

This discussion may be initiated when a client's adherence to a model jeopardizes self-evaluation or treatment. Such timing will almost certainly make the client defensive. It may be preferable to do a planned presentation, such as the one outlined below, prior to self-diagnosis or alcoholism education.

**Content.** Rogers and McMillin (1984) provide a survey of some of the most prevalent models of alcoholism. These can be summarized as follows:

1. *Congenital impairment.* Symbolized by the hapless "town drunk," this model assumes that some people are predestined to alcoholism. Such people are considered hopeless and unable to respond to treatment. Alcoholics are seen as bums, unable to work or sustain family responsibilities. There is often an attitude of condescension and moral disapproval toward them, as is evident in a label applied early this century: "Constitutional Psychopathic Inferiors."

This model is prevalent among those who grew up with an alcoholic relative or who have "burned out" from frequent involvement with the late-stage alcoholics who most resemble the description.

The flaw in the model is that it treats the condition as hopeless. Treatment does work for many. Regular AA attendance is a good corrective for adherents of this model precisely because they will hear so many testify to having recovered from a desolate "bottom."

This model makes it almost impossible for anyone to admit alcoholism, because the diagnosis is tantamount to a death sentence and because extreme symptoms must be apparent before the drinker qualifies. This model underlies many complaints such as "I can't be an alcoholic since I hold a good job."

Occasionally someone admits to alcoholism and passively resists doing anything about it. Having bought the hopelessness of the situation, he or she can disclaim "I'll drink until I die." The model must be challenged before the client can become a participant in the recovery process.

2. *Moral model, dry version.* Since alcohol is the "devil's tool," it is sinful or unwise for anyone to mess with "demon rum." The drinker has slipped from the standards of the community and must be controlled by the family until such time as he or she repents. Social sanctions are administered to create guilt and to motivate a return to abstinence.

The obvious flaw in the model is that alcohol is only selectively addicting. Far from being doomed by the first drink, about 75 percent of the drinking population enjoys a lifetime of use without incurring serious problems. For those with problems, abstinence is an appropriate goal. But the punishment used to achieve it will make recovery difficult since emotional stress becomes an incentive to drink to escape. Moreover, since alcohol is the responsible agent, there is no impetus to keep working on life style change once abstinence is achieved.

This model is evident in comments such as "Anyone who drinks is an alcoholic," and in attempts to use guilt as a means to stop using or to avoid relapsing.

3. *Moral model, wet version.* Drinking remains a moral issue, but it is permitted so long as it is adequately controlled. Problem drinking is regarded as evidence of the weakness or immaturity of the user's character. This is the most common model for Americans today, with good reason. It describes the experience of the majority of drinkers who are not addicted and for whom use is a matter of volition.

The flaw in the model is that it encourages controlled drinking and makes it a test of character. This makes it tremendously attractive even to alcoholics, who would like to prove themselves no different from anyone else. Yet current research suggests they are different: in inheritance, in metabolism, and in neurotransmitters. Experience shows that control strategies are seldom successful and consume most of the alcoholic's energy. Finally, abstinence should be seen as treatment, not as an admission of defeat.

Adherence to this model is immediately evident when a client hopes to use treatment to learn to control drinking. Its persistence is found when the client who is progressing well avers, "I'm so much more mature now, I know I can drink without it's getting out of hand." It should be suspected when drinking is discussed primarily in moral or evaluative terms, as always right or wrong. This is the model that makes willpower such a constant subject.

4. *Stress model.* Drinking is presented as a symptom of an underlying problem. If that problem can be identified and changed, drinking will moderate and all will be well. This is also a very popular model, since most of us have had the experience of using alcohol to handle pressures in living, if only to relax after a hard day or to ease the strain at a cocktail party. The model has been widely promulgated by mental health professionals. There are several different versions of this model currently in vogue. The psychodynamic version makes the culprit the traumas or the unresolved developmental issues of childhood, which must be resolved through insight and a corrective relationship in an extended course of psychotherapy. The family interaction version correctly notes that the drinking may come to stabilize the family by giving prescribed roles, by offering an outlet for affection and hostility, and by stereotyping communication. In this approach, the change must be in the interaction among all family members. The social pressures version correctly notes that there is a correspondence between membership in social groups experiencing unusual stress (for example, combat veterans,

police, the impoverished) and heavy drinking. The suggested solution is to reduce the stress in living.

As with each model, there is some underlying truth. Stress does seem to precipitate excessive drinking. But these accounts do not satisfactorily explain why some people are more susceptible than others, why some become alcoholic with no evident pressures and others withstand extreme stress without continued abusive drinking. But this model does real damage through encouraging use of externalizing defenses. Drinking is attributed to the noxious influence of the past, the spouse, the social pressures, even to an addictive personality. But alcoholics are left with no way to own responsibility for change, since they see themselves as victims of a process outside of themselves. The search for the "why" becomes a distraction from the more important "what are you going to do about it now."

Expect adherence to this model among those who have been in therapy or have read the self-improvement literature. It will be evident in their preoccupation with the "why" of excessive drinking and in the insight into life stresses. It will show itself in the expectation of effortless control over drinking once the problems have been resolved. It may be evident in willingness to depend on psychotherapeutic experts, including the counselor, who are to provide the insights and the answers that explain the "real" problem.

5. *Medical model.* Alcoholism is seen as a disease caused by excessive drinking and is evident in deteriorated organ function. The disease is correctly seen as progressive, with symptoms that get worse the longer drinking continues. But it is not seen as chronic and incurable. This model holds that when drinking stops and the patient is medically detoxified, the alcoholism ends as the organs heal. Once the liver is functioning normally, there is no reason why the drinker should not be able to resume drinking uneventfully. If there has been permanent damage, as with cirrhosis, the drinker should give up using out of fear of an untimely death.

The benefit from the model is that treatment is offered, if only for the physical health problems. But there is no understanding of the need for continuing abstinence, and so no training for the patient in how to maintain it. Not surprisingly, this model contributes to relapse. If the alcoholic returns to the same detox site often enough, he will convince the attending physician, nurse, and himself that the Impaired Model is the one that best describes his condition. This model makes it difficult for the alcoholic to achieve lasting recovery.

Because excessive drinking is the cause of alcoholism in this view, it will be difficult for someone to admit alcoholism so long as drinking is not extreme or daily.

Adherents of this model refuse to admit alcoholism in the absence of physical health problems. They will ignore evidence of problems in the psychological and social domains. They will often cite medical authority as a reason to drink: "The doctor told me to drink a couple of beers a day to flush out my kidneys." And they will be convinced that they can go back to drinking once they have "laid off long enough for the old body to heal up."

Once these models have been presented, group members are invited to identify which describe the attitudes they were raised with and which still are evident in their manner of explaining and dealing with their own drinking problems. Feedback from the leader and from the other members helps them acknowledge the model underlying their attitude. With this goes the recognition of how the model makes it difficult for them to resolve their own problem effectively.

**Variations.** This exercise is effective in changing attitudes toward alcoholism by challenging the outmoded models. But there needs to be an alternative model. I will present this lecture and discussion only after there has been some education about current views of alcoholism (such as the discussion of metabolism in chapter 4). I may precede this discussion with an introduction to the disease model of alcoholism, as presented in the next exercise.

# The Disease Concept of Alcoholism

*This presentation takes sixty minutes and requires a blackboard. It was developed by Michael Borash, M.S.*

**Rationale.** This exercise presents the disease model of alcoholism. Having previously challenged many of the prevailing popular models, the leader presents this model as an alternative. There is an attempt to change attitudes, with the goal being to destigmatize alcoholism.

Once they have accepted alcoholism as a physical disease rather than as a moral or mental failing, clients can then learn the facts about the disease without the need to distance themselves defensively from the information. This presentation leads naturally to the new learning outlined in chapter 6.

**Content.** One of the biggest obstacles to factual discussions of alcoholism is the stigma attached to the condition. To help participants get past any attitude problems, the lecture will focus on diabetes, an illness that is universally accepted as a physical disease and carries no stigma.

Diabetes is defined, with the group's help, and key concepts (italicized) are listed on the board in a column. Diabetes is the third leading cause of death in the United States. It is caused by the body's inability to metabolize sugar normally, with excess glucose circulating in the system and eventually causing organ damage, particularly to the kidney, heart, circulatory system, and eyes. The fault lies in the failure of the *pancreas* to produce adequate supplies of the hormone, *insulin,* to control glucose levels adequately. The disease may result from direct damage to the pancreas, as happens in some cases from chronic alcoholism. But in adult onset or noninsulin dependent diabetes—the most common form—there is an interaction of two elements leading to the disease: an *inherited susceptibility* and consumption of *sugar.* There will be no illness if only one of the preconditions is present, and everyone knows someone who consumes a massive number of calories without developing the illness. The disease often is not evident until late in life, when chronic overeating has led to obesity. In some particularly susceptible people, however, symptoms begin to appear in young adulthood. Group members usually share the experiences of family members, often demonstrating the seriousness of the illness with stories of repeated surgical amputation of gangrenous extremities.

The disease is contrasted with the normal metabolism of sugar. If we left group and ate a candy bar, our blood sugar level would rise above the normal levels of 70–100 milligrams percent (which I translate to .07 to .10 for comparison with BAC levels). It might peak at .18 in perhaps one hour and then gradually drop as insulin is released to help store the glucose. I stress to the group that this is entirely automatic, that there is no will power involved. At some point, the blood sugar level would dip to slightly below the optimal level, insulin production would stop, and glucose levels would stabilize in the normal range.

Diabetes is an example of the type of disease that is *chronic* and *progressive.* Chronic means that there is no cure, that the condition will last as long as the patient remains alive. The group names other chronic illnesses such as brain damage due to stroke, degenerative heart and kidney conditions, AIDS, Parkinson's disease, and so on. Cancer is not chronic since it can often be cured through surgery or chemotherapy. But cancer is a good example of a progressive disease: one in which the symptoms will increase in number and seriousness as long as the disease is untreated. Other progressive diseases include syphilis, TB, and some forms of arthritis. Progressive diseases proceed in stages, which the group identifies as early, middle, late, and death. The symptoms may be so subtle as to be unnoticed at first (the excessive thirst of an early stage diabetic). Adequate treatment is much less drastic if the disease is caught before it has progressed (for example, a colon cancer polyp is easily removed before other tissue is invaded by cancer cells). So the goal in treating any chronic, progressive disease is early detection and treatment. When this is done, the likelihood is good of a person's living to a ripe old age without impaired functioning, despite the potentially fatal illness.

We demonstrate this by discussing the case of an imaginary person named by the group, here called Mike. Mike is a young man at high risk for diabetes because there is diabetes on both sides of his family. His maternal Aunt Claire is adequately controlling hers with twice daily insulin injections. But his paternal grandfather is dying from his, having lost a leg and suffering circulatory inadequacy as his enlarged and weakened heart fails to pump adequate blood supplies to the extremities. Because of education, Mike knows he has to be alert to symptoms of diabetes. But in the meantime he lives, like so many of us, on a diet high in calories and fats.

After noticing an increase in thirst and in frequency of urination and a loss of energy, Mike sees a specialist to be evaluated for diabetes. He is given a test in which he is to fast and then consume a sugary solution, after which his blood is sampled at intervals for five hours. The group can usually name the procedure, as a glucose *tolerance* ("Have we heard that word before?") test. I chart the results that the doctor presents, showing a fasting blood sugar level of .14, an elevated peak tolerance of .22, and a delayed recovery to normal blood levels (see figure 5–4). The doctor reports to Mike that he is an early stage diabetic, that the symptoms are minor, but that it is time to initiate treatment. At this point, the required changes are avoiding sugars, helping the heart through regular exercise, and losing a few pounds.

I ask the group what it would be like to give up all sugar. They readily identify the sense of sacrifice involved, the temptations to cheat at holiday feasts, and the determination required to follow through on the regimen. Complying with treatment is indeed the biggest problem with early intervention in a chronic, progressive disease.

When we don't want to face a difficult problem, defense mechanisms may come into play. Mike used *denial and rationalization*. He compared his relatives' obvious symptoms and use of insulin with his own situation and concluded that "the doctor must be wrong. I can't have diabetes." After a couple of weeks of halfhearted attempts to change, he dropped his diet and *resumed his old life-style*.

I ask the group what will happen in the next months. As with any progressive illness, the disease will get worse and the symptoms will intensify. Indeed, Mike feels less energetic and alert. He notices that cuts take longer to heal. When he returns to the doctor, he faces a dilemma about how candid to be. To save face, he *lies* and claims to have been sticking to a sugar-free diet. After examining him, the doctor confronts him:

> You cannot lie to your disease. It is getting worse, moving into the middle stage. You must follow the treatment prescribed or face permanent physical damage. That treatment will now be more stringent, since the disease has

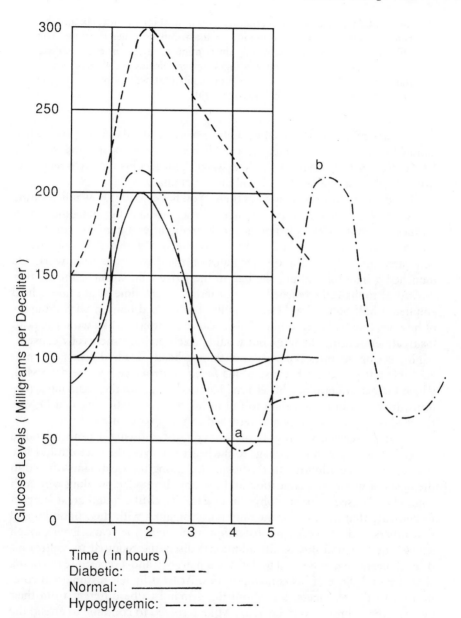

**Figure 5–4.** Results of the Glucose Tolerance Test among Normal, Diabetic, and Hypoglycemic Groups

advanced. Here is a diet book, outlining each meal for the next six months. You may substitute a baked potato for toast, but no other cheating. You will lose thirty pounds. You will do thirty minutes of aerobic exercise three times a week. Above all, you will ingest fewer calories and sweets. Is that understood? Here is a prescription for a pill that will help your insulin work. You will take these before each meal.

Chastened, Mike does change. Out of fear, he avoids sugars, even when tempted by a friend's gourmet deserts. He begins to tell people that he *can't handle the stuff*. As he begins to lose weight and feel his resolve strengthen, Mike develops a new pride in his ability to change.

But the temptations are always there. You have no idea how much eating is a part of our lives: desert or snacks when socializing, doughnuts at a business meeting, the candy bar as a pick-me-up after a hard day, the soothing ice cream before bedtime. Mike *craved* sugar at times. And one Friday, he treated himself to a bag of chocolates on the drive home from work. He munched a handful and put the bag in the glove compartment for another day. At a stoplight, he reached over for more. By the time he got home, he'd emptied a half-pound bag. He felt guilty but calmed himself with thoughts of how well he had been doing. This became a pattern. Mike would stick to his treatment during the week but would "celebrate" his success by consuming increasing quantities of sweets on the weekends. He had become a "binger." He felt powerless because of his *failed control*. He became depressed, which further undermined his efforts. He tried to ignore the recurring symptoms. It wasn't until he began to fail in his sexual functioning that he was shocked out of his self-pity and returned to the physician.

After presenting the results of further tests, showing a peak tolerance above .50, with potential damage to the heart and eyes, the doctor told Mike that he would be admitted to the hospital. Among the treatments offered in the hospital was group education and therapy. It may be puzzling why such counseling is used to treat a physical disease. But Mike found great support in knowing that he was not the only one struggling with this condition and that others had succeeded in *abstaining* from sugar for years. Even though it was not a mental illness, the additional discipline required to control his disease meant that Mike had to develop a maturity and a repertoire of coping skills beyond those of his contemporaries. At least he felt fortunate in comparison to the teenagers, for whom the demand to be different from their peers seemed almost overwhelming. Mike resolved to continue to attend the *support group* even after he was taught to inject his insulin and was discharged from the hospital.

At this point we leave Mike. I ask the group if this story reminds them of anything. The comparison of diabetes and alcoholism, summarized in table 5–2, is evident to all. The group notes the required changes. For al-

Table 5–2
The Disease Model: Comparison of Diabetes and Alcoholism

|  | *Diabetes* | *Alcoholism* |
|---|---|---|
| Metabolic flaw: | Pancreas<br>Insulin | Liver<br>ALDH |
| Preconditions: | Sugar consumption<br>Inherited<br>    susceptibility | Alcohol consumption<br>Inherited<br>    susceptibility |
| Type of disease: | Chronic<br>Progressive | Chronic<br>Progressive |

coholism, the liver replaces the pancreas, acetaldehyde dehydrogenase (ALDH) replaces insulin as the implicated enzyme, and alcohol is inserted for sugar. Inheritance is still a factor, since most alcoholics have blood relatives with the disease. The chronic and progressive nature of the illness is evident to all. I will review the metabolism (see chapter 3) or inheritance (chapter 7) factors as needed, respond to any questions raised by the exercise, and then conclude by asking the group members whether the presentation has altered their attitude toward alcoholism as a disease. Most find the analogy compelling and persuasively destigmatizing: "It has given me a lot to think about."

**Variations.** The analogy developed here is extensive and perhaps overly obvious. With brighter groups, I will be a bit more brief and subtle. In some cases, the entire presentation can be replaced by a brief discussion of allergic reactions. While there are not the clear metabolic parallels that can be developed with diabetes, allergies share the crucial features of being nonstigmatized, often chronic, and avoidable through abstinence. Allergies are common and familiar, so they successfully defuse emotionality. Some, such as allergies to bee stings, are progressive and potentially fatal. Groups can also see the behavioral impact of allergic conditions such as the hyperactivity that some children experience in response to red dye or sugar. Lastly, allergic sensitivity is the model first used by Alcoholics Anonymous. It still is found in meetings and writings. Familiarity with the allergy analogy may help clients use AA.

*Hypoglycemia.* Many alcoholics develop hypoglycemia, a metabolic disorder in which overactive insulin production causes the blood sugar level to plunge below normal. Figure 5–4 can be adapted for a digression about the diagnosis and treatment of hypoglycemia.

When blood sugar levels dip too low, the body literally runs out of fuel. There may be feelings of weakness and nausea. Often there is anxiety or even panic. There will be difficulties in maintaining alertness, attention, or in memory. The condition can be diagnosed with the glucose tolerance test. But self-diagnosis may be appropriate if the symptoms fit, since 85 percent of all alcoholics have been reported to be hypoglycemic (Milam & Ketcham, 1981).

The symptoms are readily reversible when calories are introduced into the system. But this may perpetuate the problem. The sudden rise in blood glucose levels spurs the dumping of more insulin, with a resulting plummet in sugar levels and recurrence of the symptoms. This roller coaster ride may account for part of the mood instability found in newly recovering alcoholics. It represents a clear threat to continued abstinence. Since the alcoholic has long since discovered that drinking, with its readily available calories, is a good source of energy, a hypoglycemic attack may well precipitate a craving for alcohol. The standard AA advice, to eat some sweets, will temporarily handle the craving but will continue the roller coaster ride of rising and falling blood sugar levels.

Increasing attention is being paid to the role of nutrition in lasting recovery from alcoholism (Ketcham & Mueller, 1983). Diet counseling is beyond the scope of the program. But clients can be referred to the literature, to knowledgeable physicians or dieticians, or to the seminars aimed at helping alcoholics with nutritional advice. Additionally, the standard treatment for hypoglycemia can be presented. The key elements are to reduce sugar intake, to substitute fructose or organic sugars in the place of processed sugars, to eat high-protein snacks between meals, and to eat in small quantities up to five or six times a day.

# 6
# Learning the Facts

New perspectives are built on new information. Clients who have successfully completed the first three stages of problem solving will have begun to question attitudes and assumptions that made drinking look benign. They will be receptive to an informed presentation of the risks associated with drinking. Their interest will not be limited to understanding impaired driving. The class must move on to examine the effects of drinking throughout the totality of the user's life. The goal of this section is to provide comprehensive information about alcohol-related problems and alcoholism, giving the client a guidebook with which to examine the degree of alcohol-related damage currently present or potentially to come.

Education is an effective approach to attitude change. Pointing out the areas in which problems are likely to occur makes the risks more immediate. Where there is recognition that some of the problems are already present—where the presentations "step on the toes" of the participants—there is a growing acknowledgment of an existing problem that requires corrective effort. As long as the clients are not too defensive to listen or to identify, learning the facts will consolidate previous efforts at attitude change and will lead readily into the self-diagnosis that follows.

Education has been a major component of the preceding activities, in which facts about drunk driving and about alcohol as a drug, and even some information about alcoholism as a disease have all been covered. In this section there is a shift to applications that are as close to home as the family and finances. This learning is intrinsically more threatening but also more powerful in prompting a total review of the role of drinking. New learning should be paced so that it remains provocative and challenging, and yet acceptable. I gauge the group's readiness for more learning by the self-disclosure of participants in response to the topics raised. When responsive sharing takes place, proceed to the next subject. When the group becomes silent or begins to introduce distractions, it is time to return to less threatening material or to challenge the prevailing attitude. This chapter is organized in a progression from the least to the most threatening topics.

The exception to this graded presentation is the material on alcoholism and withdrawal. I will present these lectures at any point in the program when they seem relevant. It is perhaps preferable to wait until self-diagnosis is complete before discussing the risks of withdrawal. But it is common for individuals to emerge from the attitude change section with an attempt to abstain. These people should know what to expect; I have often seen the relief when a client is told that his vivid and troubling dreams are symptoms of mild withdrawal when "I thought I was going crazy." The needs of the few who are ready to change take priority over the needs of those who are proceeding more slowly. The whole group benefits when serious alcohol-related problems are addressed directly in response to the sharing of a concerned participant.

I am always willing to enhance group sharing or discussion by teaching, as long as the information presented is pertinent to the group's topic and at least one member is ready to relate to what is taught. At this stage of problem solving, the leader needs to be active, to be an authority and a reliable source of information. Only later is it advisable for the leader to become more passive and to allow the group members to rely on their collective resources. At this stage of treatment, education is more useful than a focus on group process.

Education need not, however, imply a passive group. This is a risk only if there are too many lectures. The following activities attempt to combine teaching and discussion in a way that invites active involvement. Encourage identification and sharing. Use role plays and simulations to drive home the ideas. It makes sense to use expertise from within the group, such as asking a diabetic client to do the first part of the disease concept presentation.

Remember that education continues outside of group. I routinely begin by asking for any personal sharing, specifically inviting clients to react to television shows and relevant local events. It helps to have a bulletin board, on which can be posted newspaper clippings brought in by clients as well as a listing of self-help group meetings and upcoming events. It is also helpful to have a bibliography to provide to clients interested in doing outside reading on the topic of discussion. Outpatient treatment relies on the leader to provide the introduction to facts, but even more it relies on the initiative of the group to think about, expand on, and apply the information provided.

# Types and Stages of Alcoholism

*This lecture and discussion last for about thirty minutes.*

**Rationale.** Alcoholism, like cancer, is not a single entity. Rather, it is a family of related disease processes. No one variant will have the same symptoms or course that is shown by a different type. The number of distinct variants is not now known. The types presented are for illustrative purposes and will likely prove to be incomplete in light of future research.

The diversity of alcoholism presents an obstacle to self-evaluation. No matter how many symptoms a client has, there is always someone with more or different ones. So the other person is the alcoholic, and the client is convinced that he or she is still a "social drinker." Most of my clients, predominantly weekend drinkers, are convinced that daily drunkenness is a prerequisite for addiction. Conversely, any period of abstinence or any episode of successful control is presented as proof that they are not alcoholics. The diversity makes it possible to "compare out"—to avoid self-diagnosis by finding all the ways in which one's drinking differs from some mental model of alcoholism. Only 3–5 percent of alcoholics are on skid row, and yet this is the image most often used.

This obstacle to self-diagnosis is best overcome by education about the diverse types of alcoholism. This lecture presents such information and then encourages clients to "compare in" by asking them with which type they most identify.

**Content.** The group is asked, "What is an alcoholic? How does an alcoholic drink? What are the symptoms or problems that show that a drinker has become an alcoholic?" Responses are written on the board. The group becomes appropriately curious and puzzled when the leader successively agrees with contradictory comments, such as "someone who has to drink every day" and "someone who has problems because of drinking, even if he or she only drinks once in a while."

The confusion is resolved with the presentation of the types and stages of alcoholism. Alcoholism is a family of related diseases that will be typified by different symptoms at various stages of progression. The group understands the analogy to cancer: a skin cancer is very different from leukemia, and a single tumor will likely cause fewer problems than one that has metastasized. The leader can then present a brief description of five distinct types of alcoholism:

1. *Progressive alcoholism.* This is the most common pattern in the United States, the one described at every AA meeting. Jellinek (1960) called it the gamma type; Cloninger calls it the milieu-limited type (Cloninger, Bohman, & Sigvardsson, 1981). It is the type whose progression most closely parallels that of diabetes (see chapter 5). An inherited predisposition exists in most cases. The disease becomes evident after excessive drinking (whether from social custom or psychological distress). It is characterized by progressive loss of control, increasing symptoms and problems, tolerance, and potential for physical dependence. This disease process will look different as it progresses.

a. *Early stage*. The loss of control is occasional and easily rationalized as a choice to get drunk. If properly motivated, the alcoholic could stop after three drinks most of the time. But at least once in ten times there is a slip, despite promises and best efforts. The drinker is likely to ignore the initial symptoms because alcohol is enhancing life by providing energy, relaxation, and ease at socializing. Symptoms include tolerance, preoccupation with alcohol, developing a drinking life-style, gulping first drinks to get high quickly, and occasional guilt about drunken behavior. There may be blackouts. There may be arguments, but there are not likely to be severe problems with family life or work. There will seldom be signs of withdrawal. In fact, it is likely that drinking is not a daily activity. Heavy drinking may well be restricted to weekends. Perhaps 75–80 percent of progressive alcoholics are in the early stage of the disease (Mulford, 1980).

b. *Middle stage*. The loss of control is regular, although control strategies (no drinking before 6:00 P.M. or switching from liquor to beer) may be developed to convince concerned parties that there is no drinking problem. Despite this, it is common for the drinker to acknowledge that "one leads to another" and "once I start, I don't stop." Alcohol is regularly used to relieve pressure, including that resulting from prior drinking. There may be unpredictable changes in personality. Family conflict is likely, and there will be clear problems in other areas of living (legal, financial, psychological). There will be pathological organ changes, such as fatty liver, high blood pressure, or stomach pain (gastritis, ulcers). There will likely be minor withdrawal when heavy drinking is followed by abstinence. The withdrawal symptoms might include irritability, shakiness, and insomnia. As a natural consequence there will be absenteeism or lost productivity at work and a growing physical imperative to drink for self-medication.

c. *Late stage*. The loss of control is pervasive, and drinking may become a routine throughout the day. There may be binges, with drinking cycling into periods of constant and debilitating consumption. Problems will be everywhere and overwhelming. Withdrawal will become severe as the physical addiction becomes obvious. Medical complications from drinking may become life threatening. Yet personality deterioration may have proceeded to the point that change seems impossible and help is spurned. This is the image of alcoholism that most often comes to mind. It should be seen as the end result of a process that has been going on for years, that could have been recognized and more readily treated long ago.

2. *Antisocial Drinking*. Heavy drinking is likely to have begun in the teens, with an immediate onset of problems. Personality changes, violence, and legal problems are characteristic of this type. Drinking is often considered to be secondary to a psychiatric disorder (antisocial personality). Indeed, there were often problems with school, family, peers, and the juvenile

courts before drinking began. But there is evidence that this may be an inherited form of alcoholism (Cloninger, Bohman, and Sigvardsson, 1981), passed from severely alcoholic father to son, but showing up even when the son has been raised in a benign adoptive environment. Younger drinkers in my groups often identify with this type, especially if their fathers also have a history of alcohol-related legal problems. It is said to occur at about one-fourth the rate of classic progressive alcoholism.

3. *Binge drinking (Jellinek's epsilon type).* A binge is defined as two or more days of constant drinking. While a weekend or holiday drunk may be part of the experimenting of a hard-partying adolescent, repeated episodes of continuous drunkenness lasting for days is evidence of alcoholism. During the drinking cycle there will be heavy consumption, gross changes in personality, risk of injury, and neglect of physical needs. Binges may terminate in physical problems as a result of poor nutrition and disrupted sleep. Between binges there may be weeks or months of abstinence or nonproblem drinking. Binges may result from psychological stress or may appear unpredictably, although the drinker can retrospectively recognize that "one was coming on." There is some controversy as to whether this is a distinct type or a phase in progressive alcoholism.

A variant on this type is the "weekend warrior." Many drinkers do not drink to any significant degree during the workweek. But they may drink in tremendous quantity during vacations and time off. As a result, they will not be alcohol-free between Friday and Monday. Many of my clients identify with this type, although they would "compare out" when examining late-stage alcoholism since they hold jobs and do not drink every day.

4. *Maintenance drinking (Jellinek's delta type).* This person may drink in small quantities throughout the day. Because of gradual intake and high tolerance and because he or she is never seen sober, the drinker may never appear drunk to others. Such a drinker will fail to identify with stories of loss of control. But the alcoholism is evident in the withdrawal that follows abstinence. This pattern may evolve into progressive alcoholism, with loss of control occurring once the amount of drinking required to self-medicate exceeds the limits of the drinker's tolerance (Rogers & McMillin, 1984).

5. *Stress drinking (Jellinek's alpha type).* Episodes of heavy drinking may alternate with periods of adequate control or easy abstinence. The drinking is a response to a crisis (for example, a divorce) or to an underlying psychological problem. This pattern is reported more frequently for women, with depression as a significant contributor. But research also shows that men exposed to excessive stress, such as soldiers in combat and police officers, are at high risk for alcoholism (Branchey, Davis, & Lieber, 1984). Again, it is unclear whether the stress-induced drinking is a distinct type of

alcoholism, a precipitant for progressive alcoholism, or perhaps a transient form of alcohol abuse that should not be considered part of a disease process.

Once these variants have been presented and discussed, clients are asked with which type they most closely identify. This is not a request for admitting alcoholism. But it is an exercise in reversing the usual tendency by practicing "comparing in." There may well be discussion as different individuals relate experiences in their attempt to personalize the learning. There is often a comment that the session alters the understanding of and attitude toward alcoholism, which is usually now seen as much more common and less repugnant than it was previously.

**Variations.** The material in this discussion can be incorporated in other exercises, most particularly in the self-diagnosis exercises (chapter 7) or in the discussion that follows, "Three Types of Drinkers."

# Alcohol Withdrawal Symptoms

*This presentation and discussion takes approximately thirty minutes.*

**Rationale.** Intensive use of alcohol can result in physical dependency. Sudden abstinence or reduction in consumption is a physiological stress that can show up as withdrawal symptoms. Major withdrawal is a medical emergency: it can be fatal and should be handled in a hospital. In contrast, minor withdrawal can be managed effectively on an outpatient basis using the combination of reassurance and education that is provided in this discussion.

The withdrawing client needs the information presented to know the likely course of the experienced symptoms.

The nonaddicted drinker needs the education to make an informed decision about whether continued patterns of use are sufficiently pleasurable to warrant the health risks described here.

The leader and the addicted drinker need to have a good understanding of the symptoms and course of the alcohol withdrawal syndrome so as to be able to make the correct decision about whether a client needs inpatient detoxification. Fortunately, the outpatient treatment format forces clients to be sober at least once a week. The type of withdrawal that constitutes a medical emergency is rare in this population and is evident at the beginning of treatment.

**Content.** Alcohol has a pronounced sedating effect that lasts for about two hours per dose. What is less often recognized is that alcohol also has a less intense but longer-lasting stimulant effect (Gitlow, 1982). Any drinker who has overindulged, whether a social drinker or an alcoholic, has experienced the edginess and nausea of that excess stimulation. It is called a hangover. This can be a particular problem for the high-tolerance drinker who imbibes to the limits of his or her excessive capacity. Shakiness and early awakening following heavy drinking are further evidence of the delayed stimulant effect of alcohol.

The body adjusts to alcohol's depressant effects by speeding up. This can be explained chemically in terms of catecholamine levels or cell membrane lipids (Sellers & Kalant, 1982). But it is best understood by my clients through the analogy with a heating system. The thermostat is set to maintain a constant temperature. If the temperature drops, the furnace kicks in and produces heat. If a poorly sealed window allows a draft on the resident, he or she may turn up the thermostat, and then the heater may run at full blast, warming up the drafty room but overheating the rest of the house. Analogously, the body adapts to the sedating effects of alcohol by speeding up. If the alcohol is suddenly removed or reduced, the nervous system is left with the "thermostat" turned up too high. Hyperactivity is the result. It is the core of the various symptoms that constitute withdrawal.

Any lasting withdrawal is a sign of physical dependence and addiction to alcohol. It should be used to help the client self-diagnose as alcoholic.

Most people think that physical dependence requires years of heavy drinking. This is usually the case. But withdrawal also results from intense drinking over a short period of time. Minor withdrawal may occur after five days and major withdrawal after forty-five days of continued excessive consumption (Sellers & Kalant, 1982). This is why withdrawal is a particular threat to the binge drinker.

*Major Withdrawal.* Depending on the degree of physical addiction, withdrawal symptoms will appear after cessation or drastic reduction of alcohol intake. Major withdrawal is usually evident within twenty-four hours and is over by the end of one week. It begins with tremulousness and sweating. These also occur in minor withdrawal but would be expected to diminish after the second day. In major withdrawal they intensify and are supplemented by more severe problems.

1. *Alcoholic hallucinosis.* This includes illusions, misperceptions, or frank hallucinations. There may be intese nightmares as dream sleep rebounds after having been suppressed during drinking. In fact, the hallucinosis may represent a continuation of dreaming into a waking state. The person is oriented—able to report who and where he or she is. But there are intruding images, sometimes amusing but often frightening. These are the pink ele-

phants of lore. Dr. Murray Bowen (1984) shares the anecdote about a client summoning him to witness a troop of tiny men marching in formation at the foot of his bed. When queried, the patient smiled and said they were doing no harm. So Bowen instructed him to "let them keep on marching." The hallucinations are not always so enjoyable. One of my clients watched a small hole appear in a dark room as a mouse chewed through the wall. But then the mouse emerged and changed, first into a bat, then into a cat, and then into a mountain lion poised to leap onto the terrified observer. My client ran out of the room screaming and slept next door for the night. The hallucinations are most often visual. But it is common to hear familiar voices discussing the alcoholic in a derogatory manner. About 25 percent of those who are severely tremulous will experience some form of hallucinosis. It may recur intermittently for several days (Kinney & Leaton, 1978).

2. *Seizures (rum fits).* Within twelve to forty-eight hours after a reduction in drinking there may be one or two convulsions. These will be grand mal seizures. They are a harbinger of more severe withdrawal to come. One in three will go on to develop DTs, and 97 percent of those with DTs will have had a prior convulsion (Sellers & Kalant, 1982).

3. *Delirium tremens (DTs).* Usually occuring three to four days into withdrawal and lasting for about twenty-four hours, the DTs are terrifying. Raised temperature and blood pressure and increased heartbeat accompany massive anxiety. There is disorientation and confusion about identity. Hallucinations occur that are terrifyingly real, with both visual and tactile components. I ask my clients to identify with the experience of one patient I evaluated. He was in such a panic that he did not register my presence, even though I was holding his head with both of my hands and staring at him, nose to nose. When I released the restraints that bound his arms, he began to pick frantically at his gown and skin. He then was able to communicate that he could see and feel thousands of roaches as they crawled over him and began to gnaw and burrow under his skin. This man recovered, lapsing into a deep sleep and awakening with partial amnesia regarding the preceding events (as is typical). But DTs are life threatening. Respiratory and cardiac collapse used to kill from 8 percent to 20 percent of those who developed DTs. With prompt medical attention the mortality rate is now lower. Small amounts of alcohol can delay the onset, and the medically supervised administration of tranquilizers can manage withdrawal without most of the major symptoms' occurring.

*Minor Withdrawal.* Those who do not develop the full withdrawal syndrome can be reassured that their symptoms are temporary and not life threatening. Shakiness, anxiety, and loss of appetite will peak on the second day and then gradually disappear. More persistent is the nervous system's hyperactivity. Although gross tremor may be gone by three or four days, the inner shakes may last for two weeks. During this time clients can expect to be restless, to have trouble with concentration and memory, and to be irritable and emotional. Frustrations that once would have been easily ignored may now seem intolerable. The excess emotionality often declines over the first month. Sleep problems are also resolved after a few weeks, although normal patterns may not become stable for months. Hartmann reports, "Withdrawal is associated with insomnia, delayed sleep onset, and multiple awakenings, as well as frightening dreams and hallucinations" (1982, p. 183). Once they are reassured that they are not going crazy, clients accept the transient sleep disorder. The brain needs dream sleep to keep itself in optimal shape. Since depressant drugs (including sleeping pills) reduce dreaming, it is a good sign of recovery when vivid dreams occur. In most cases the quality of rest is better from the outset than during the drinking period, even though there may be fewer hours of sleep.

Minor withdrawal is a matter of allowing time for healing. Families are urged to be patient and to avoid emotional intensity during the beginning period when they are celebrating abstinence. (The suggestion of the positive attitude is intentional). I urge clients to distract themselves from irritating symptoms by keeping busy and physically active. Clients are reminded that the symptoms are transient and can be permanently avoided if there is no more drinking. The sleep problem can be managed best by avoiding daytime naps, engaging in regular exercise, performing some relaxing activity before bedtime, and perhaps getting tryptophan from a health food store (Hartmann, 1982). The most obvious advice is to avoid using other stimulants. Many clients replace the alcohol with excessive intake of coffee or soft drinks. They should carefully avoid the caffeinated varieties.

*Protracted Withdrawal.* Research evidence substantiating the existence of a protracted withdrawal syndrome is unclear. But clinically savvy commentators have found it a useful way to explain the impulsive decision making and emotional reactivity that may be found in the first months of recovery (Milam & Ketcham, 1981; Vaughn, 1982). In turn, this syndrome explains the frequency of cravings and the risk of early relapse (Gorski & Miller, 1979; Milam, 1974). This subacute withdrawal reaction can be expected to peak at about two months and then to taper off for the duration of the first year of abstinence, although it may recur intermittently at times of stress (Gorski, 1986a).

There are several physical mechanisms that could account for a gradual readjustment of the nervous system after abstinence. The lasting disruption in the sleep cycle suggests that alcohol itself has a prolonged impact on the nervous system. Damage to the brain is evident with chronic drinking. Cell regeneration or assumption of functions by uninjured cells would predictably be a gradual process (Milam, 1974). Indeed, memory and abstract thinking continue to improve for months and even years after abstinence is achieved (Goldman, 1983). Neurotransmitter depletion could account for irritability. In addition, there are two enduring sequelae of the alcoholic's inadequate diet. Malnutrition may lead to vitamin and mineral deficiencies. Hypoglycemia, and the resulting irritability and weakness, may be a lasting consequence of addiction for the majority of alcoholics (Milam & Ketcham, 1981; Vaughn, 1982).

The end result is that the nervous system remains hypersensitive. There will be what Milam calls "emotional augmentation" of any stimulus. The newly recovering alcoholic is likely to take everything personally, to be overreactive, and to experience mood swings. Anxiety, depression, and cravings for escape are expectable. There is a temporary but significant oversensitivity to stress. These continuing reactions will occur in 15–30 percent of alcoholics (Jaffe & Ciraulo, 1985). These symptoms are often seen by alcoholics and the people who monitor their progress as signs of psychological disturbance or immaturity. The anxious self-scrutiny thus engendered will lead to further augmentation, creating a vicious circle. But the symptoms are quite possibly physical in origin and not psychological.

The management of protracted withdrawal becomes a goal for the first months of recovery. First, minimize stress. Avoid major decisions, take "first things first" "one day at a time," and get accepting support. (Vaughn's *Addictive Drinking* is an excellent resource here, as is AA's *Living Sober*). Second, develop a program for enhancing physical health through regular exercise and good nutrition. Third, recognize that there is a physical basis for the hypersensitivity that may bedevil early recovery. This should help the client remain patient with limited progress. It will minimize discouragement or preoccupation with imagined psychological failings. It will remind the client that recovery is a process and not an event.

**Variations.** I will often deliver a shortened version of this presentation, focusing on whatever aspect is most relevant. Since the discussion of minor withdrawal is most immediately pertinent, this is the piece that is most frequently reviewed.

The material lends itself to dialogue. I usually conduct this session so as to invite sharing of experiences with withdrawal. Stories about friends and relatives are also appropriate since they tend to deepen the appreciation of the risks of withdrawal. Each group and every leader has a stock of anecdotes that will add richness to the presentation.

The discussion may turn to questions of managing recovery. It may be appropriate to jump to some of the activities described in chapters 10 and 12. Conversely, it may be appropriate to delay the education about withdrawal until clients are adequately motivated to change and to withstand the rigors of early abstinence so clearly documented above. The timing of this presentation depends on the group. I delay it until after self-diagnosis is complete, if possible. But I will share it as soon as it becomes clear that a member of the group is or likely will go through some of the withdrawal symptoms.

# Three Types of Drinkers

*This lecture and discussion takes sixty minutes and requires a chalkboard.*

**Rationale.** This presentation anticipates the self-diagnosis phase of problem solving. Clients are implicitly or explicitly asked to compare themselves to various patterns of problem and nonproblem drinking. Yet the goal at this point is more limited than to expect the alcoholics in the group to accept this diagnosis; it is sufficient if the alcohol abusers drop the fiction that they are "social drinkers." They will then be alerted that their drinking pattern can be expected to lead to some of the life problems outlined throughout the rest of this chapter.

The primary purpose of this exercise is education about the different types of drinking patterns. It reviews or introduces some crucial ideas about tolerance, control, and pathological drinking practices and outcomes. In the process, the presentation continues the demystification of alcoholism while it sharpens the distinctions among social drinking, heavy drinking, and alcoholism.

**Content.** I begin with a few comments about abstaining. Among adult Americans, about one third has not had a drink in the last year (NIAAA, 1981). Some of these are recovering alcoholics. But the majority avoid alcohol because of dislike of the taste or the effect, because of religious belief, or because they have never acquired the habit. Clients are often skeptical, finding it hard to conceive of socializing without drinking. Yet when challenged, most recall relatives or acquaintances who do not drink. Abstainers are more likely to be female (40 percent of women do not drink) and older adults.

Of those who do drink, the vast majority drink moderately. National surveys have repeatedly suggested that another third drinks fewer than three standard drinks a week, while another quarter drinks between three and fourteen drinks each week. Only about 10 percent report consuming more than two drinks a day (Malin, Wilson, Williams, & Aitken, 1985; NIAAA, 1981). Males outnumber females by about three or four to one among these heavy drinkers. Although Chafetz (1982) reports that up to three drinks a day is considered moderate and unlikely to damage the health of the imbiber, in fact the average consumption is well below that level.

Three headings are drawn on the chalkboard: "Social," "Heavy," and "Alcoholic." I share my frustration with these labels. For example, some of the most sociable people I know are extremely heavy imbibers. The label "social drinker" invites them to ignore an extreme drinking problem as long as they remain popular at the bar. I would prefer to substitute "low tolerance" in place of "social" drinker. It is similarly difficult to label the intermediate type. "Alcohol abuser," "prealcoholic," and "problem drinker" have all been applied, but they belie the fact that this drinking type need not progress to alcoholism and may represent a transitional phase before more moderate drinking is routine. Even the label "heavy drinker" may miss the point, since the person who gets drunk on infrequent occasions may consume less total alcohol than average despite clear abuse during the drinking episodes.

The remainder of the presentation involves a discussion back and forth with the group about what the distinctions are among the different types. Group members are asked to volunteer their understandings and stories that define each type considered in turn. The group can do most of the work. The leader should be sure that the central characteristics of each type are understood and listed on the board. It is these defining features that I have included below.

*Social (Low-Tolerance) Drinker.* This type of drinker is characterized by the following:

1. *Low intake:* an average of no more than a six-pack of beer or a half-pint of liquor a week. (I may play "fill in the blank" with the group, which may volunteer "per day" or even "per hour.")

2. *Low tolerance:* fewer than five drinks are consumed even during a prolonged party. The blood alcohol content (BAC) is usually below .07 (New York State Division of Alcoholism and Alcohol Abuse, 1979). These drinkers become uncomfortably intoxicated by .10 (Mendelson, Stein, & McGuire, 1966) and are vomiting or passing out by approximately a .14 BAC. It will be difficult to be arrested for driving while intoxicated (DWI).

3. *Control is natural:* no will power or conscious effort is required to limit consumption when one's body makes it uncomfortable for one to consume more.

4. *Drinking is not important:* although these drinkers will cite the same reasons for drinking as will heavier users (to relax, to be sociable), drinking remains a dispensable activity. Abstinence is easy if there is a reason (such as when given a prescription that is not to be combined with alcohol). Drinking is restricted to special occasions (holidays, celebrations). Alcohol is used for beverage or convivial purposes; its drug effects are not important to the social drinker.

5. *Lack of enjoyment of being intoxicated:* these drinkers are uncomfortable when they are above .05. They do not like the loose-tongued, inadequately self-controlled feelings that go with drunkenness.

6. *Problems are not expected or tolerated:* drinking is expected to be a moderately pleasant activity. Because it is not important, it is not worth paying much of any price to enjoy. Alcohol-related problems would be unacceptable. Although any drinker can create a problem while intoxicated, the social drinker would be embarrassed and upset enough to take corrective action to assure that it would never happen again. This is why blackouts can be used to indicate alcoholism. A blackout is the inability to remember part of a drinking occasion, despite the fact that the drinker was awake and alert. It differs from passing out. It indicates alcohol-induced impairment in the part of the brain responsible for encoding memories. A nonalcoholic may have a blackout, especially during an episode of heavy consumption early in the drinking career. But should this happen, fear and concern will lead the social drinker to make alterations in drinking to prevent a recurrence. Repeated blackouts tolerated without concern are pathognomonic of alcoholism.

Perhaps 70 percent of drinkers are low-tolerance drinkers. This figure is often disputed in the group, since participants are likely to have few light-drinking friends. They can be helped to appreciate why this is so by noting that it would not be much fun for them to party with someone who wanted to leave the bar after an hour and two drinks. If they still doubt that social drinkers exist, they can go to a gathering and stay sober, observing how many other people either abstain or switch away from alcohol. This is often a revelation to drinkers who assumed that everyone else routinely drank as heavily as they did. Perhaps the greatest understanding of this type comes when they remember how easily they became intoxicated at the beginning of their drinking careers. Many of them were once low-tolerance drinkers. Indeed, they often had to work hard (for example, drinking after vomiting or passing out) to overcome their body's defenses against excessive alcohol consumption. With this awareness comes the clear realization that almost no one in the treatment group can claim to be a true social drinker.

*Heavy (High-Tolerance) Drinker.* This type of drinker is characterized by the following:

1. *Higher intake and higher tolerance:* people in this category would prefer to drink a minimum of five or six drinks. When asked, group members will state that their preferred BAC (the "sporting buzz" or "cruising level") would be between .14 and .18. (When someone volunteers that it would be above .20, I tell him or her that we will describe their type later, alluding to the discussion of alcoholism.) They may well feel comfortable and unimpaired above .10, which is why they are so prone to arrest for DWI.

2. *Control is possible:* people in this category can remain below a .07 BAC if the situation requires it. But control will require willpower, since their tolerance would permit much greater consumption. This is why it is likely that they will overconsume when they are celebrating, because their "guard is down." Many will never have become sufficiently concerned about their drinking to have attempted control. The DWI should provide the incentive to check it out (see the control test in chapter 8). It is a clear indication of alcoholism, the third type, for someone to continue to drink in an uncontrolled fashion after having encountered personally unacceptable problems.

3. *Drinking is important:* a life-style develops around drinking. Socializing involves alcohol, drinking friends, and drinking places. There may be a lot of drinking paraphernalia—the favorite big mug, the wide selection of mixers, or a special mallet for crushing ice. Most tellingly, drinking itself becomes a special occasion. In the absence of a suitable celebration, it is enough to say "let's get together for a few drinks." Clients laughingly volunteer the situations that call for celebrating: winning or losing the game, rainy weather or clear weather, birthdays or unbirthdays, Fridays, Saturdays, Sundays, Mondays, and so on. I may underscore the contrast with social drinking by alluding to a poker party. If the beer runs out halfway through, the social drinker would want to continue playing cards: "We're having a good time, who needs the beer." The group usually identifies with the heavy drinkers who would "take a break" for a beer run, even at the risk that the poker game would break up. Although the card game is the public reason for the get-together, it is really the drinking that is of central importance to the heavy drinker. (Thanks to Glenn Paule-Carres for the anecdote).

4. *Positive expectations of drinking:* alcohol is seen as integral to many of the pleasures of life. It makes people in this category relax and feel sociable and confident; it may be needed for them to find the courage to dance, to fight, or to make love. There is a sense that life would be less fun without alcohol. Although they might dispute liking to be drunk (if they translate that as "sloppy"), they certainly enjoy being above .10 BAC. A person qualifies as a heavy drinker if he or she is legally drunk more than four times a year (again, the point can be underscored by having the group guess the interval).

5. *Problems are tolerated:* there is a willingness to pay a price for the pleasure. Heavy drinkers do come to expect negative outcomes of drinking (Rozien, 1983), although they see these outcomes as less noxious than would light drinkers and as less clearly linked to the drinking (Critchlow, 1986). Problems are most likely attributed to the areas of time, energy, and money. Bar drinking with a high tolerance is an expensive proposition (and participants will volunteer the cost). Drinking does detract from the time and energy available for other tasks and pastimes in life. So hobbies are gradually

displaced, and loved ones may complain of insufficient attention if they cannot be included in drinking activities.

6. *There may be a variable drinking pattern:* for some, heavy drinking is a routine. For others, it is a response to a crisis such as an unwanted divorce or to psychological pain. Heavy drinkers are more likely to need psychological assistance than either social drinkers or sober alcoholics. Alcohol is used for its drug effects. Heavy drinking may be a way to fill the time for those who are unclear about roles, responsibilities, and identities. Young men in particular are likely to drink heavily. Schuckit (1985) reports 30–40 percent of young men will demonstrate isolated alcohol problems. This figure is close to the results of a 1983 survey by the National Center for Health Statistics that indicated an increase to 37.7 percent of respondents who reported at least one day of consuming five or more drinks. It is fairly normal for there to be a period of excessive using during the late teens and early twenties in conjunction with college, service, or single life-styles. While some remain heavy drinkers and may proceed into alcoholism, it is also fairly common for these drinkers to return to more moderate drinking as other life goals assume priority (see the values exercise in chapter 10). Cahalan (1970) found that 20 percent of those reporting alcohol-related difficulties are problem-free three years later. Jessor (1985) found one of four males and one of six females to be drinking abusively in high school, and yet the majority report no problems when surveyed as adults seven years later.

Perhaps 20 percent of drinkers have had a period in which they drank heavily and developed a high tolerance. Those who become concerned and make an effort to change can return to more moderate consumption. To all appearances they will be social drinkers. But there is an important exception. They will retain a high tolerance, and with it a lifetime risk of suddenly resumed heavy drinking should they ever lose the incentive to control their consumption.

*Alcoholic Drinker.* This type of drinker is characterized by the following:

1. *Very high tolerance:* the drinker in this category may require and can operate with a BAC above .20. The National Council on Alcoholism (1972a) reports there is no doubt about the alcoholic diagnosis if the individual can handle a BAC above .15 without gross evidence of intoxication, if more than eighteen standard drinks are consumed for more than one day in a row, or if the person has ever been above a .30 BAC. For clients arrested above .20, little additional evidence may be needed to self-diagnose as alcoholic.

2. *In the process of losing control of drinking:* drinking is done either in inappropriate quantity or at inappropriate times. This is not to say that there is never a capacity for control. Most alcoholics can limit themselves at times. In fact, the existence of control strategies—most particularly, switching from liquor to beer to avoid getting carried away—is evidence of alco-

holism. An early stage alcoholic may lose control only occasionally. But there is still the unpredictability, the sense that "once I start, I can't tell what will happen," that shows that limiting consumption is no longer a matter of willpower. Such clients often report that "I can stop after two or three, but give me one more and I know I'll keep at it." The loss of control is evident in an attempt to cut down, followed by a perhaps gradual but inexorable return to troublesome levels of consumption. Middle-stage alcoholics generally lose control. So there is a recognition that "once I get started, I don't want to stop" and that "one leads to another." A late-stage alcoholic may have to drink to avoid withdrawal symptoms. Even when it is obviously against their interests to drink, such as just before coming to alcohol treatment, they may not be able to refrain. Clients who convince themselves they are not alcoholic because they can abstain for a period of time or can control their drinking on a given occasion are missing the point. It is not the absolute loss of control but rather the process of losing control over drinking that indicates alcoholism.

3. *Serious, recurrent problems:* others express concern because problems are clearly evident. The problems may be at the job (absenteeism, tardiness, accidents) or medical (drinking despite a doctor's directive not to). More often the problem is with friends and family. If others are concerned about the use of alcohol, or if drinking has led to arguments or tension, then there are serious problems. At times even the drinker recognizes the problems, only to break promises to avoid risking their recurrence. So I ask clients if they ever promised themselves that they would not again drink and drive, perhaps after a previous arrest. If they have continued to do so, they understand how drinking can lead to repeated problems despite their honest intention to change.

4. *Defenses:* these protect the alcoholic's self-esteem by masking the alcohol problem (see chapter 4). As a result, the alcoholic typically does not acknowledge the drinking problem until seven years after others have noticed it (Kinney & Leaton, 1978).

5. *Pathological drinking patterns:* binges, getting drunk alone, hiding bottles or protecting the supply, gulping or sneaking drinks, or morning drinking (to control incipient withdrawal) are all indicative of alcoholic drinking.

6. *Alcoholics are like heavy drinkers, only more so:* drinking is even more important (they need it), positive expectations are more desperately clung to, and drinking continues in the face of more troublesome problems. The description of the heavy drinker may seem to fit quite well; it is the addition of any of the previous five features that indicates that alcoholism had developed.

Alcoholics compose about 10 percent of all drinkers (for example, Mulford, 1980). At this point, the progression has led onto a one-way street;

alcoholics cannot reliably return to social drinking. So abstinence becomes the only realistic option for them to avoid further problems. The extent of the problems varies depending on how far the disease process has developed. During the early stages, it is typical for symptoms to come and go, and for nonproblem drinking to alternate with periods of loss of control (Schuckit, 1985).

The presentation ends with each client's identifying the type of drinking that best describes his or her pattern of use, with evidence adduced to back up this self-diagnosis.

**Variations.** It may be possible to continue with a description of the types and stages of alcoholism. Clients are often overwhelmed by the material already presented. In fact, if there is confusion evident in the concluding self-diagnosis phase, it may be desirable to give a stripped-down summary: low tolerance identifies social drinkers, while loss of control and recurrent problems distinguish the alcoholic from the heavy drinker.

This exercise can be used as part of the self-diagnosis phase of problem solving, although other exercises are more powerful in confronting alcoholics with their status. This exercise seems better suited to disabuse most of my clients of the false conviction that they are social drinkers. But some participants will self-identify for the first time at this stage. The goal of the exercise will have been attained if clients are alert to the prospect that their drinking pattern has or could likely lead to some of the problems outlined in subsequent exercises.

# I/E + D: *Discussion of Father Martin's* Chalk Talk, *Part 1*

*This presentation consists of the movie,* Chalk Talk on Alcohol, *part 1, lasting forty-five minutes, followed by a fifteen- to thirty-minute discussion of the key concepts. A chalkboard or flipchart will aid the review.*

This venerable movie remains a highly effective teaching tool. There is a revised and shortened version of the movie, which combines parts 1 and 2 (the discussion of alcohol's drug effects and the description of alcoholism, respectively) onto one reel. I prefer to use the original film, feeling that there is so much critical information to be mastered that separate presentations are warranted. Further, part 1 is applicable to all drinkers—not just alcoholics—and is less likely to be ignored by prealcoholics or those in denial if it is not presented with the discussion of alcoholism.

**Rationale.** Because it is meaningful to all problem drinkers, this movie, discussion, and the sharing that follow reinforce the sense of commonality and group identity. This session is a useful bridge between problem-solving stages: attitude changes are consolidated, while important lessons are learned about the effects of alcohol.

The content of the movie demonstrates convincingly that alcohol is a drug and that its effect is the often unrecognized element explaining deviant feelings and actions. This presentation becomes a relatively nonthreatening opportunity for beginning to acknowledge alcohol-related problems. It helps to destigmatize intoxicated behavior so that self-esteem is restored.

**Content.** The movie is given a short but strong buildup. I may begin, rhetorically, by asking: "Have you ever done something really stupid while drinking? Something so out of character you wonder 'was that really me who did it?' Something that left you surprised and feeling guilty?" Knowing that each person in the group has had the experience, I tell them that the movie will explain why they acted as they did. To add the exclamation point, I often continue, "The most important thing you will learn in this program is the idea that $I/E + d = E/I$." Without explaining the formula, I screen the movie.

In a humorous but pointed way, Fr. Joseph Martin discusses the drug effects of alcohol. Two main points are made in the movie that clients must remember. First, there is the comparison of the effects of alcohol to ether, highlighting the essential similarity of alcohol to all other sedative drugs. Second, there is a simple explanation of how sedation affects brain functioning. Even before there are clear signs of drunkenness, the higher cortical functions have been disrupted so that judgment and self-control are progressively sacrificed and drug-affected emotions begin to determine how we act. It becomes likely that the relaxation of inhibitions sought by many drinkers will be followed by a loss of inhibition that permits buried and primitive impulses to surface. The sober person, guided by his rationality and intellect $(I)$, is able to channel his emotions $(E)$ so that they can be satisfied in an appropriate way. As alcohol selectively affects judgment, that control is lost. As Father Martin points out, it makes no more sense to believe you understand a person from his drunken ramblings than from his mutterings when under general anesthesia.

After general reactions to the movie, the group is asked to repeat and define the formula: "*I* over *E* plus *d* equals *E* over *I*." Synonyms for intellect, *I,* are judgment, self-control, self-awareness, and common sense. Synonyms for emotion, *E,* include feelings, desires, instincts, and impulses. We note that *d* is used because other sedative drugs in addition to alcohol are mind altering. It is important to discuss that emotional expression is normal and necessary—that intellect without emotion would make for a very disturbed human being, an unlovable version of Mr. Spock. But unguided impulse is equally sick. I sometimes borrow from a George Carlin routine and pantomime the shock and embarrassment of a society matron caught on the same leash as a dog unconcernedly relieving itself on a neighbor's lawn. The dog operates on impulse; it takes human judgment to be embarrassed because of other's reactions. While the group is still chuckling I share the story of an outraged former client who complained that he would never have been arrested for DWI driving if he hadn't stopped so that a drunk passenger could urinate . . . at noon, in the fire lane outside a major department store. When we function *E/I*, humans too can act just like animals.

I typically extend the formula to emphasize the special challenge facing the high-tolerance drinker. If asked how many drinks it takes for the emotions to start to take over, the group accurately notes that as few as two or three will do the trick. What impulse surfaces? To keep drinking, of course. When "Big *D*" drinking commences, the vestiges of rational control are lost (*i*) and the emotions that surface may be grossly distorted and crazy:

$$I/E + d \rightarrow E/I; + D \rightarrow E/i$$

The stage is set to invite sharing, sometimes cathartic purging, of the types of inappropriate impulsive behavior that may occur after heavy drinking. If prompting is needed, the group is invited to explore the fantasy of a high school class reunion. Perhaps it is tempting to pass up a dance with the wife to savor that extra drink. What might you feel while watching her dance with an old boyfriend? The jealousy that is easily dismissed after two drinks might well lead to angry and paranoid preoccupation after ten. What might happen then? What would she say after a scene? What might you feel? Discussion and sharing usually flow easily at this point.

**Variations.** The process just described is seldom completed because the movie is stimulating enough that discussion focuses on other of Father Martin's pointed comments or on a member's spontaneous sharing. As always, I let the group process take precedence over my presentation. But I encourage the group to remember the *I/E* concept and to incorporate it in their vocabulary.

Brief discussion of the formula may be followed directly by a go-round in which each member shares a "war story." The self-disclosure confirms attitude change by developing a norm of nondefensive sharing and cooperation with treatment. There tend to be about equal parts guilty recollection and humor.

*Chalk Talk* and the *I/E* discussion may be used at other points in the problem-solving cycle. I will often return to the central concepts while discussing the mental/emotional health costs of drinking during the "eight areas" presentation (see chapter 7). I may also do a more in-depth treatment of how the *I/E* concept relates to changes in self-esteem during drinking and recovery. This discussion is outlined in detail in chapter 11. It is an important tool for helping clients understand the obstacles to implementing a successful program of recovery.

# Financial Costs

*This structured sharing takes thirty minutes and uses a chalkboard.*

**Rationale.** This exercise helps clients indentify the financial costs of drinking, as they are incurred by society and in their own lives.

**Content.** There are some alarming statistics about the costs of drinking. The annual cost in the United States is estimated at $120 billion (Schifrin, Hartzog, & Brand, 1980), with up to $60 billion more attributable to the abuse of other drugs. This figure includes more than $10 billion from alcohol-related car crashes (Voas, 1985), part of a national insurance bill for substance abuse totaling more than $45 billion (Krizay & Carels, 1986).

Alcohol abuse accounts for at least 15 percent of the massive national outlay for health care costs (Saxe, Dougherty, & Esty, 1983). Between 38 percent and 50 percent of all admissions to community hospitals, and up to 60 percent of emergency room visits, can be linked to alcohol or drugs (Quayle, 1983).

Most of the costs are buried in the prices of products and services we buy, since half of the total expense is due to lost productivity in the work force. The output of the alcohol-impaired worker decreases between 25 percent and almost 50 percent. Although alcoholics compose less than 10 percent of the labor force, they account for 47 percent of the injuries and 40 percent of the fatalities on the job. Alcohol abusers have four times the accident rate, make five times as many compensation claims, use 33 percent more sickness benefits, and have sixteen times the rate of absenteeism (Quayle, 1983). It is awareness of this drain that is causing government and business to turn to drug screening and disciplinary action against those found to be under the influence.

The tax revenue from the alcohol industry, despite being a hefty $6.7 billion in 1980 (Luks, 1983), totals less than one-quarter of the direct government outlay to alcoholics (Hammer, 1978). Contrary to the opinion of

1. How much is spent to buy beer, wine, or liquor?                                    $870
   (How often do you buy it? Where? In what quantity?
   Here, he claims $2 each weekday to split a six-pack after work, plus
   two six-packs for the weekend and a monthly bottle of whiskey.)

2. How much is your bar tab?                                                           600
   (How often do you go to bars? "Every other week." What is your
   typical tab? "About $25.")

3. Expenses related to drinking and socializing at bars:
   Tips for the bartender or waiter: ("Included.")                                      —
   Buying rounds for friends and acquaintances: ("Included.")                           —
   Buying drinks for the girl at the end of the bar:                                    —
   Dinner, present, motel room for the girl: ("I'm cheap.")                             —
   Extra meals or munchies that would have been skipped if sober:                     180
   Extra smoking because of drinking:                                                  24
   Gambling losses (tip jar, bar bets, extra on games):                               900
   Other drugs that would not have been bought sober:                                   —
   Other: ("Had some money stolen at a bar.")                                         100

4. Transportation expenses:
   Mileage:                                                                            100
   (Do you like to drive around while drinking?
   Do you go to parties or barhop? What proportion of your total
   mileage involves such driving? *Note:* I usually figure 10 cents a mile,
   but may use a percentage of overall expenses if the mileage is
   considerable. "No way! I take a cab. Maybe I'd drive a thousand
   miles a year, before my arrest.")
   Taxi charges:                                                                       240
   Commuting costs (if lost license because of the DWI):                              520
   Increase in car insurance: ("From $400 to $1,300")                                 900
   Car repairs or property replacement because of accidents: ("I hit a                 25
   fencepost last winter.")

5. Health expenses (for illnesses or injuries tied to drinking; doctor's               —
   bills, prescriptions, and so on):

6. Work expenses:                                                                     550
   (Have you missed time because of alcohol-related injury, hangovers,
   legal proceedings, and so forth? Have you been laid off or fired, or
   have you resigned because of drinking? What were you taking home
   a day at the time? "I missed four days because of jail, and three half-
   days because of court and appointments. I was clearing $100 a
   day.")

7. Legal expenses:
   Lawyer fees:                                                                        500
   Court fines and costs:                                                              500
   Admission to the Alcohol Safety Action Project:                                     280

8. Treatment expenses (counseling, rehabilitation):                                    600

9. Other expenses: ("Could there be any more?")                                         —
   Subtotal                                                                         $6,889

   Uncle Sam takes his cut for taxes and Social Security before the                 $1,378
   money is there to spend. Estimate the additional cost.
   (What do you think your tax rate is? "Twenty percent.")
   *Total Estimated Annual Cost of Drinking*                                        $8,267

**Figure 6–1. Cost of a Year's Drinking**

some cynical clients, the government loses money on alcohol since costs far exceed tax revenue.

Because statistics seem abstract, I try to make their personal meaning concrete. If the annual bill of $120 billion is apportioned among the 240 million people in the United States, then each of us pays $500 a year for the social costs of drinking. I will often ask a family man if he could use an additional $3,000 to support his wife and four children.

The costs are higher than this average for the alcohol abusers who are my clients. I dramatize this by asking whether they would quit for a year if someone were to offer them $5,000 to abstain. While I decline the chorus of offers to seal the deal with my personal check, I suggest that they can write a check to themselves and collect it after one year of sobriety. For $5,000 is the average total of alcohol-related expenses for my clients.

This is demonstrated by tracing the direct and indirect costs of a year's worth of drinking. I invite volunteers to share, often including both an admitted big spender and someone who is minimizing the problem. Remaining group members are asked to keep a personal tally and to suggest unmentioned areas in which costs are incurred. In the example on page 117 (figure 6–1), I include the numbers volunteered by a client who downplays his drinking. I prefer not to challenge the distortion directly. Instead, the drama builds as the exercise confronts him with the mounting tally of indirect costs. The areas covered and some of the trigger questions are listed in the figure. The annual costs are recorded, although the questions may be aimed at weekly or monthly costs if this will aid recall.

The client is invited to react to the total, perhaps even being asked, "What else could you do with that kind of money?" The group, which has been commenting throughout, will probably share further reactions at this point. Someone else may share his or her tally. The poorer may comment that they wish they earned that kind of money. Usually there is a powerful immediacy to the presentation that fuels further discussion about costs and testimonials about the need to change. I may end with the promise that those who make the requisite changes in drinking will leave the program, despite its expense, with more money than when they entered. This often elicits agreement from those who have already curtailed their drinking.

# Understanding the Physical Health Risks from Alcohol Abuse

*This combination of a discussion and a movie will take about ninety minutes. A chalkboard and a projector are needed.*

**Rationale.** Most outpatient clients, especially younger ones, do not recognize alcohol as contributing to health problems. In the absense of cirrhosis of the liver, most feel that they are unaffected. Since cirrhosis will develop in only 15 percent of alcoholics (Schuckit, 1985), with the odds against the drinker only after twenty years of heavy daily drinking (Korsten & Lieber, 1985), it is dangerous to use this ailment as the primary indicator of physical damage. The liver is not the only organ affected. Because alcohol reaches all the tissues in the body, all can be damaged and any may show symptoms. High blood pressure or gastrointestinal distress are much more common symptoms of deteriorating health. But the combination of ignorance and denial leads drinkers to downplay the hazards.

This presentation uses education to confront the clients with the personal risks associated with their pattern of using and their unique physiologies. Unless the leader is medically trained, it is advisable to use one of the excellent brief films available. Even if the client is a bit overwhelmed by the vocabulary and the sheer volume of information, the film will leave an indelible impression that alcohol is damaging to all parts of the body. The accompanying discussion supplies facts that are missed in the movie. More important, the discussion helps the client sort out and retain those facts that are most relevant by helping in the identification of personally prominent health risks. If the presentation precedes the movie, it can be framed as an exercise to help the client decide what parts of the film require particular attention. Alternatively, the film can be shown first as a stimulus to more informed discussion of the current and potential health consequences of continued drinking.

**Content.** Not all drinking is going to result in health problems. In 1864, Sir Francis Anstie proposed that it is safe to consume up to three standard drinks (1.5 ounces of absolute alcohol) a day. This guideline is still touted today (see, for example, Chafetz, 1982), although adjustments in dose clearly need to be made because of differences in weight (Segal & Sisson, 1985). Surveys suggest that moderate drinkers are healthier than either heavy users or abstainers, presumably because they are also moderate in diet, exercise, and other features of their life-styles. It is important to acknowledge that not all drinking is going to cause health problems.

Heavy drinking, however, is a major health hazard. The bottom line is that an alcoholic can expect to live ten to sixteen years less than average (Milam, 1974; Saxe, Dougherty, & Esty, 1983; Schuckit, 1985). Although it is listed on seven percent of death certificates (Kinney & Leaton, 1978), alcoholism is underestimated as a cause of death. Alcohol-related incidents kill more than 200,000 Americans a year, making them the fourth leading cause of death (Quayle, 1983). Alcohol-related traffic accidents are the leading cause of death for those under age twenty-five. Drinking contributes substantially to homicides and suicides, respectively the second and third leading contributors to mortality in this age group. So alcohol is a major threat to health, whether through the accidents that are a particular threat to the younger drinker or through the deterioration in organ function among long-term drinkers.

Clients can be helped to recognize or anticipate the consequences of continued alcohol abuse by a review of the following areas:

1. *History of health problems.* There are two types of experience that clients can be invited to share. First, has alcohol directly contributed to any health problem? If prompting is needed, ask whether a doctor has ever told a client that drinking caused any condition or that abstinence was needed to permit the healing of any disorder. Stories about ulcers or diabetes are often volunteered. Second, are there symptoms that are linked to episodes of drinking? Clients often recognize that heartburn or bloody vomit is evidence of drinking's affecting the stomach, even though a doctor was never consulted. Similarly, pounding headaches during a hangover are seen as signs of problems in blood flow to the brain. Direct experiences can be more fully acknowledged when they are publically shared.

2. *Evidence of organ weakness.* Every person has certain organ systems that are vulnerable, perhaps because of inherited weaknesses or old injuries. Susceptibility differs from one person to another, which is why one responds to stress with hives and another gets an ulcer. Since alcohol irritates all of the organs of the body, damage is likely to appear wherever there is special vulnerability. Clients can anticipate which organ systems will likely be affected by chronic alcohol abuse. First they should examine personal history. Did they have chronic respiratory infections as children? Were they prone to soft tissue and joint injuries? Have they always had a sensitive stomach? The affected organs are at risk from continued heavy drinking. If there was a severe concussion from an old accident, a lasting susceptibility for neurological damage may exist. Vulnerable organs may "wear out" early, even though they show no deficit in function through early adulthood. So the second step is to look at the diseases that seem to run in the family. If heart disease or liver cancer seem to be particularly prevalent among older relatives, then it makes sense to be particularly aware of the impact of alcohol on these organs. If there is a family history of diabetes, clients should study the damage done to the pancreas by chronic drinking. By becoming aware of potentially vulnerable organ systems, the client can anticipate where alcohol is most likely to cause health problems.

The pattern of use will affect the health consequences:

3. *Type of drinking.* Binge drinking that continues until physical exhaustion is the most dangerous, both in terms of accidental injury and physical deterioration. The combination of excess alcohol and inadequate nutrition will drain the body by leaching nutrients and preventing the liver from per-

forming its digestive and detoxification functions. This discussion should be addressed to the weekend minibingers in the group, who are likely to minimize the risks of their pattern even though they are regularly drinking instead of eating. Daily maintenance drinking is the next most damaging pattern. Since the liver preferentially metabolizes alcohol, other vital functions will be impaired if some alcohol is always present. Although many of the health consequences will not become evident until middle age, the continued presence of alcohol contributes to eventual deterioration.

4. *Overdose.* Alcohol itself is toxic. Everyone has heard stories of some kid chugging a fifth of vodka and then dropping dead from cardiac collapse. While tolerance and gradual consumption offer some protection, clients should be aware that people start dying with a BAC of .35 and that half the population would be dead by .50 (Favazza, 1982; Rogers & McMillin, 1984). Such BACs can be achieved by fast consumption of a case of beer or a quart of 80° liquor. The real risk is in combining alcohol with other sedative drugs. The combination of alcohol and barbiturates is the third leading cause of accidental death and suicide (see the section on using in this chapter). The presence of alcohol "primes" the metabolic system in the liver, leading to more rapid processing of other sedative drugs used *later.* The resulting tolerance may lead to disastrous results when alcohol is used *at the same time* as the other depressant medication. Alcohol will be selectively detoxified, leaving the other drug to build up to potentially lethal levels.

Accidental death or injury may result from drinking long before health deteriorates. Where alcohol is used in combination with other drugs or where there is an overlapping psychological illness, drunkenness may lead to impulsive risk taking. There is danger in being in the wrong place at the wrong time. As I was detailing the life-style risks that go with heavy drinking, a small man jumped up, removed his set of false teeth, and mumbled: "I was just sitting there, enjoying my beer, when some fool jumped up on the bar and kicked me in the mouth." I try to detail the risks from accidental injury that are not covered in the movies:

5. *Violence.* Do any of the clients get into fights when drinking? Or are any of them big enough that they are likely to be challenged by some who would be "macho man"? Half of all homicides and two-thirds of all assaults are committed under the influence (Kinney & Leaton, 1978). Half or more of all victims of assault or murder are themselves drunk. Alcohol is involved in approximately 45 percent of incidents of marital violence (NIAAA, 1981).

6. *Suicide.* Do any of the group members become more depressed when drinking? Is there a proneness to mood swings? Alcohol contributes to one of three suicides (Kinney & Leaton, 1978; NIAAA, 1981). Alcoholics attempt suicide at fifty-five times the normal rate (Kinney & Leaton, 1978). Where 1 percent of the general public take their own lives, 6–29 percent of alcoholics commit suicide (Goodwin, 1982; Schuckit, 1986). A quarter of

them had alcohol present in their blood when they succeeded in their attempt. Perhaps more alarming, more than half of those attempting were in blackouts at the time (Goodwin, 1982). The suicide may be impulsive.

7. *Accidents.* How many participants smoke? Not only is there fifteen times the risk of facial cancer (Podolsky, 1986), but also there is the immediate danger from passing out with a lit cigarette. Alcoholics cause one in four fires resulting in injuries. An alcoholic runs ten times the risk of dying in a fire, and five to thirteen times the likelihood of a fatal fall (Podolsky, 1985b). Alcohol contributes to 40 percent of falls, 10–20 percent of aviation and rail accidents, and 69 percent of recreational boating incidents (Trumble & Walsh, 1985). Automobile accidents are covered elsewhere (see chapter 5). It is sufficient to remind the participants that drivers had BACs above .10 in from 45 percent to 50 percent of fatal accidents, and combined other drugs with alcohol in 5–15 percent of the lethal episodes (Podolsky, 1985a). Lest they move close to the bar to avoid driving, I remind clients that 42 percent of pedestrians killed after being hit by a car had a BAC above .10 (Kinney & Leaton, 1978).

Gender also alters the health risks:

8. *Women are more prone to physical damage than men.* Their lower body weight and proportionally reduced fluid levels result in higher BACs per dose. Even though their total consumption is less than that of men and heavy drinking tends to begin later in life, women have comparable rates of alcohol-related illness (Ashley et al., 1977; Blume, 1986). The interval between initial drinking and the beginning of physical damage seems to be telescoped. This is particularly true for liver disease, apparent in an average of fourteen years for women as compared with twenty years for men (Wilkinson, 1980). The health risks are general for women. Research suggests that drinking increases the frequency of breast cancer, especially among younger and thinner women who would otherwise be at low risk (Schatzkin et al., 1987; Willett et al., 1987.)

9. *Fetal alcohol syndrome (FAS).* Perhaps the greatest health risk is to unborn children. There is evidence that alcohol may contribute to birth defects by damaging sperm. Additionally, I tell my predominantly male audiences that it is their obligation to educate and support their wives, girlfriends, or daughters in avoiding all drinking during pregnancy and nursing. Alcohol crosses the placental barrier and pools in the fetus because the immature liver cannot detoxify it. There is clear risk to the baby. Half of the children of chronically alcoholic women show some brain damage (Rosett & Weiner, 1982). Birth defects occur in 37 percent of the offspring of heavy-drinking women, 14 percent of moderate drinkers' babies, and 9 percent of light drinkers' children (Ovellette, Rosett, Rosman, & Weiner, 1977). Up to 10 percent of the population may be affected, primarily with residual hyperactivity or minimal brain dysfunction ("FAS Facts," 1980). Maternal

alcohol abuse is the leading preventable cause of mental retardation (Clarren & Smith, 1978).

FAS refers to the combination of growth deficits, malformed faces, major organ dysfunction, and brain damage that is evident in the most severely affected children of drinking women. Of one thousand babies, one to three will show the full syndrome. There will be heart defects in 30–40 percent of these (Warren, 1985), and 5 percent will require heart surgery. Mild to moderate mental retardation will occur in 45 percent, 52.5 percent will need special educational assistance because of learning disabilities, 33 percent will need hearing aids, and 12.5 percent will have a cleft palate. The annual medical, educational, custodial, and lost productivity costs have been estimated at $2.4 billion in the United States (Harwood & Napolitano, 1985). This is the toll among the most severely affected.

There is the additional risk of the baby's being born addicted. The child enters the world in withdrawal. Irritable and inconsolable, the child may form an inadequate bond with the mother. There is an increased likelihood of behavior problems and child abuse. Ultimately, there is a heightened risk of alcoholism. At age thirteen or fourteen, the child will join peers in experimenting with alcohol. While the friends are having their first taste, this child may be having the first relapse. Milam and Ketcham (1981) suggest that those "instant alcoholics" who drink with tolerance and dependence from the beginning may well be showing the continued effects of the exposure to alcohol before birth.

I readily admit to climbing on my soapbox when it comes to preventing FAS or related prenatal exposure to alcohol. We know that these tremendous problems are preventable. We also know enough to state that there is no safe level of drinking during pregnancy. My clients are asked to carry the message about this health risk associated with drinking to all of the women in their lives.

The film *Alcohol and Human Physiology* presents a good overview of the medical complications from excessive drinking. Its strength is in the graphic portrayals of diseased organs and in the interviews with patients suffering adverse consequences. Its explicit warnings may lead some to experience it as propaganda, although it is factual in content.

The set of films *Medical Aspects of Alcohol,* parts 1 and 2, by Dr. Max Schneider, remains a useful survey of the health effects of drinking. The first part excludes the central nervous system but still provides an exhaustive account of the medical complications. Because it is a lecture, with many technical names included, clients are often confused about specifics. But they are inevitably impressed with the range of possible consequences: "I never knew it could effect your body in so many ways." The second part provides a good discussion of hypoglycemia and of delayed agitation following drinking. The discussion of psychological dependence and drug abuse seems to me to be oversimplified. There will be a need for follow-up discussion of these aspects of the film. I will often use the first part by itself.

**Variations.** There is general interest in health effects of alcohol. I may alternate movies or stagger the movie and the foregoing presentation at twenty-week intervals so that the awareness remains fresh. Clients are seldom defensive as health risks are defined. There is usually a willingness to share histories of alcohol-related illnesses or accidents. If there is extensive discussion of personal experiences, it is common to delay the showing of the movie until a subsequent session. Because it is interesting and yet not experienced as threatening, I would recommend that this topic be used to introduce clients to discussion of alcohol-related problems in their lives.

# Family Costs

*This presentation and demonstration takes forty-five to seventy-five minutes. It was developed by Ann Smith, M.A., and the staff of Caron Foundation, influenced by the ideas of Sharon Wegscheider-Cruse (1981, 1985).*

**Rationale.** Nowhere else is the impact of alcoholism more damaging than on family relationships. This is because of both the prevalence and intensity of the problems created. A Gallup survey shows that one of three families has had to cope with a drinking problem. Between 28 and 35 million Americans grew up in an alcoholic home; 12–15 million children still live with a practicing alcoholic (Black, 1981). Each of these is directly affected.

In some cases the damage is obvious. The alcoholic and his or her partner likely come to interact in a negative way or to withdraw from meaningful contact. Sexual relationships suffer because of anger, anxiety, and alcohol's toxic effects (Renshaw, 1975). Among alcoholic women, 75 percent report gynecological problems; among hospitalized alcoholic men, 50 percent have potency problems (Karacan & Hanusa, 1982). Although alcoholics marry as often as others, they separate or divorce at four to eight times the normal frequency (McCrady, 1982). Even if physically present in the home, the alcoholic is often peripheral and excluded from day-to-day decision making in the family (Dulfano, 1982; Jackson, 1954). The spouse is overburdened. Stress leads to psychopathology among 65 percent of the wives of active alcoholic men, as contrasted with a 43 percent incidence for wives of men who have been sober for more than six months (Bailey, Haberman, & Alksne,

1962). The overburdened partner turns to the offspring for support. "What is seen most commonly is a family system where the nonalcoholic parent has made a cross-generational coalition with a child, generally of the opposite sex, which excludes, alienates, and infantilizes the alcoholic" (Kaufman & Pattison, 1982, p. 669). The parental child prematurely exchanges youth for overwhelming and often inappropriate adult roles. Half of the victims of incest come from alcoholic homes. Physical violence occurs in 60 percent of these families (Black, 1981). Alcohol is a factor in 40 percent of the cases heard in family courts (Saxe, Dougherty, & Esty, 1983).

The damage from abusive drinking persists and repeats for generations. There is increased risk of addiction. Between 32 percent and 60 percent of alcoholics have an alcoholic parent (Black, 1981; Cotton, 1979; Penick et al., 1987). When these second-generation addicts manage to abstain, unresolved emotions from childhood contribute to increased rates of dry drunks, cravings, and relapse. Those who do not become addicted suffer from a high incidence of workaholism, eating disorders, stress-related illness, depression, and other psychopathology (Wegscheider-Cruse, 1985). Half of the women from alcoholic families go on to marry problem drinkers (Black, 1981), while others become involved in unhealthy relationships. According to one therapist, "By struggling with their addictive mates, these partners were unconsciously recreating and reliving significant aspects of their childhood" (Norwood, 1985, p. 2). Following the unhealthy pattern of their parents' marriage, with all the best intentions of mastering the problem, the adult children of alcoholics (ACOAs) form families in which they continue to pursue an unavailable spouse and emotionally deprive another generation of children:

> People surrounding the rigidly focused person (food addict, alcoholic, workaholic) become preoccupied with trying to get into the addict's life in a meaningful way. In many respects, the frantic and unremitting efforts to reach the addict become as compulsive as the behavior of the lost person. We refer to this state as Co-Dependency. (Wegscheider-Cruse, 1985, p. v. From *Choicemaking*. Pompano Beach, FL: Health Communications. Reprinted with permission).

"Initially, co-dependency is the normal response to an abnormal situation. However, it is also progressive, chronic, and characterized by denial, compulsive behavior, and emotional repression" (p. 30). The features of alcoholism that most damage the capacity for relationships become part of the family system, even if addictive drinking never again intrudes. Codependency is an often unrecognized consequence of alcoholism, especially for those who escape addiction or are two generations removed from the drinking. Yet its persistence and pervasiveness makes it perhaps the greatest cost of alcoholic drinking.

Not all ACOAs are damaged. Children may develop normally if they find surrogate parents, ways to get positive attention, or achievement orientation. Yet 25–40 percent will show coping problems during their teens, and more will discover identity or intimacy problems as young adults (Black, 1981; Jacob & Leonard, 1986; Werner, 1986).

This exercise attempts to educate drinkers about family costs and codependency for two related reasons. First, raising consciousness about the damage to family members provides drinkers with the opportunity to make informed choices about continued drinking. One of the most common reasons for ending a destructive drinking pattern is the realization that "I can't keep doing this to my family." This exercise makes the damage clear but with a light touch so that clients are not overburdened with guilt. Second, many of the group members are themselves codependents. It can be freeing to discover the basis of troubling feelings and patterns of interaction; it can be helpful to recognize that treatment is available for this problem as well.

**Content.** I share as much of the foregoing as possible without overburdening the group with statistics or with guilt. Participants are seldom willing to admit to physical violence or sexual abuse in the context of the outpatient group. But I watch for reactions that indicate a willingness to share.

What is disclosed is more often an identification with the children who have been victimized in the alcoholic family. Emotional neglect is remembered much more than active abuse. In fact, between the alcoholic's preoccupation with drinking and the spouse's preoccupation with the alcoholic, neither parent is adequately available to respond to the emotional needs of the offspring. As a result most children of alcoholics become prematurely self-sufficient as they experience the futility of reaching out. As one researcher concluded, "The single greatest problem area which I have identified for adult children is their inability to ask others for what they need or for help" (Black, 1981, p. 107). Following the direct injunctions or the modeling of their parents, they learn to keep drinking a family secret and to avoid conscious attention to or sharing about the pain and fear engendered by the unhealthy family situation. This is the basis of the pathological rules that ACOAs adhere to throughout their lives: *Don't Talk, Don't Trust, Don't Feel* (Black, 1981). These "survival tactics" are successful in avoiding vulnerability and pain in childhood. They are usually supplemented by roles that provide an identity within the family system, but that preclude effective relationships later in life and block the unfolding of unique individuality.

It is these roles that are discussed and enacted in the exercise. First, it is important to make some clarifications. Roles are acted. The longer they are played, the more rigid they may become until they may be adopted as a personal identity. But the roles need not constitute the identity: *roles need not be permanent*. There is hope for change with effort. Black (1981) found that it was natural to play two or more of the following roles during the course of growing up in the alcoholic family. Roles evolve because they meet the needs of the relationship system, typically one in which there is insufficient available energy to accept and encourage the uniqueness of each member. *Similar roles may evolve in any dysfunctional family.* Clients who did not have an alcoholic parent may well find that they can identify with one or more of the characteristics, although they are likely to have been developed more rigidly if addiction and codependency dominated the parents' resources. Lastly, the roles may not be distributed according to the birth order outlined below. There is the creative potential in each person to resist or modify the assigned position in the family constellation. Each role provides the room to develop some competencies. But I try to get my clients to realize that *each role also exacts costs,* no matter how subtle and easily denied.

The *Dependent's* role is characterized by preoccupation with some drug or behavior pattern (gambling, sexual conquest) to the degree that he or she ignores responsibilities. The guilt over this failure is repressed and then projected as blame. So the alcoholic husband comes home late from the bar (irresponsibility) and excuses it by complaining that the wife is demanding and unfriendly (blaming).

I get someone to role-play the Dependent, usually promising that he or she has the easy job since the role involves sitting in a chair and focusing as much attention as possible on alcohol (symbolized by a pop can). The group usually helps me draft a "volunteer." Their humorous encouragement helps to undercut the tension created by the enactment.

Every Dependent requires an *Enabler* who will accommodate irresponsibility by becoming overadequate. This is often the "superwoman" who works (to pay the bills), raises the kids single-handedly, and still is active in the church. To the outside world, this role appears commendable. Codependents thrive on comments like, "You're amazing, I don't know how you do it." The role does offer the opportunity to be competent and to appear in control. There is a strong undercurrent of martyrdom that may be further gratifying, especially for ACOAs who have made an art of self-deprivation. Self-sacrifice is the key to the act. It eventually leads to exhaustion and/or resentment. As the Enabler tries to discover why she is getting so little support and so much abuse, there will be episodes of anger (the "bitchy wife" that alcoholic men love to complain about), followed by guilt and vows to try harder to better support the family (more enabling). This guilt dovetails with the Dependent's blaming. In essence, there is a tacit agreement that the Enabler is strong enough to assume and contain the negative feelings for both partners.

The group sees that the roles fit together so that the "blame game" can be played endlessly, even though both parties are in pain. Someone is then drafted to play the Enabler (usually as the wife, since my groups are substantially composed of male Dependents). She is coached to circle busily around the Dependent while complaining about all of her responsibilities and periodically remonstrating about how he could help more. The actors are then allowed to improvise for a couple of minutes until they are "in role." The action is then stopped, midgesture, and the group queries them about how they feel and what they want.

I may provide some of the history, suggesting that she was attracted to his sociable and easygoing ways as an antidote for her stiffness. He, in turn, liked her obvious competence and the way she accepted him without making demands. When they met, his drinking was probably excessive but not yet a clear problem. He may even have fantasized that she would help him become more responsible. I may note the continuation of her role as parental child, overlearned in her family of origin. Alternatively, I may suggest that his apparent confidence gave her faith that he could help her escape from a threatening or cold parent. I will develop the characterizations using my understanding of the alcoholic family, the spontaneous elaborations of the role by the actors, and any sharing from the group.

When the first child is born to this family, it comes into the world carrying the hopes and expectations of the parents and their families. Looking at the father, the in-laws may think, "Now he'll have to shape up." If the wife is beginning to be frustrated in the marriage, she may secretly believe, "Now I'll have someone I can love unreservedly." Even before it is born, before its own personality can make a claim to uniqueness, the baby is given the role of healing the family's pain. The *Hero* tries to fit the expectations by doing well. Academic or athletic achievement, church or community service, competence as a little lady or gentleman all persuade the outside world that "our family is OK." The Hero may baby-sit for younger siblings from a tender age or help out the overburdened Enabler by cooking dinner or cleaning house. The Hero is the Enabler's ally, and in fact is an "enabler-in-training." The payoffs from the role are obvious. There is sincere family pride in the many accomplishments: Heroes do develop managerial and problem-solving skills, and they can graduate into the real world with apparent confidence in dealing with adults. But there are costs. Heros can *do* but not *be*. They are driven, compulsive, prone to stress, and unable to relax or ask for assistance. Having forfeited their chance to be children, they are unable to play or be at ease with peers. They are likely to become compulsive overachievers or to marry someone who becomes a Dependent, at which point they will have graduated to the Enabler role. Despite the apparent successes, the Hero feels like a failure because assuming the responsibility for rescuing the family from the pain of addiction is an impossible task. Inwardly, Heroes feel guilty or bitter. These feelings are repressed, with the loss of emotional spontaneity, and the energy is directed into compulsive work or enabling.

In the enactment, the Hero walks beside the Enabler, promising to help her, cheering up both parents with stories of accomplishments, and periodically joining her in criticizing the Dependent. The Hero is to move fast, stepping out of the family for a few seconds to role-play frantically completing homework or joining in some worthwhile project, and then anxiously returning to get in between the feuding parents. After a few minutes, the action is stopped and each of the role-players is asked how his or her feelings and actions are affected by the presence of the Hero. The Enabler usually experiences relief to a degree comparable to which the Hero is burdened, and the Dependent feels overmatched.

The second child arrives to find that the Hero has already monopolized the positive attention available in the overburdened family. The search for uniqueness leads to an alliance with the Dependent and a decision to seek negative attention. This is the role of the *Scapegoat,* the "black sheep" who acts out the frustration of the family. Outwardly tough and cynical but inwardly hurt and bitter about the felt rejection, the Scapegoat turns early to the streets and to peers for the missing attention. Delinquency, promiscuity and unwanted pregnancy, risk taking and accidents, and alcohol or drug abuse are likely consequences. The rebellion against authority and the punk role assure that rejection remains a continuing theme as long as the role is maintained, which may well be forever. This is the role that gets helpers (counselors, probation officers, and others) involved with the family, although they seldom can see beyond the flagrant pathology of the Scapegoat to the general pain in the family. Scapegoats do have assets that can be used to escape the role. They are independent, energetic, street smart, and skilled with peers. If the underlying lack of self-esteem can be surfaced and challenged, Scapegoats may learn to channel these assets and become successful. The early pregnancy, for example, may prove to be the turning point that allows the teenager to shift away from partying and to assume responsibility. The discipline needed to complete school, support the child, and try to provide the nurturance so lacking in the Scapegoat's own youth may set the stage for success in the middle years. Similarly, the Scapegoat role provides both the risk of active addiction and the will to recover successfully—as so often heard at AA meetings.

When the Scapegoat enters the enactment, the other roles change. The heat is off the Dependent as the Enabler and Hero try vainly to reform the second child through finger pointing, cajoling, threatening, or pleading. The Dependent can either join in the general attack on the Scapegoat or create a secret alliance that may even extend to drinking together. The person playing the Scapegoat begins the role with the permission to swear and to skewer participants with accurate depictions of the dark side of family reality. Many of my clients are Scapegoats. They enter the role with delight at the sanctioned opportunity to rebel. But they quickly begin to retreat into sullen hurt in the face of unremitting rejection from the family. There is often animated discussion of feelings after this stage of the enactment.

The *Lost Child* enters this chaotic scene and quickly withdraws into a world of fantasy to avoid the acrimony. Lacking the aggressiveness to compete for attention, the child becomes skilled at disappearing and renounces any desire for recognition. The enactment is to have the Lost Child stare out the window or draw on the blackboard. The cost of the role is in loneliness, low self-esteem, and the social ineptness that results from never having practiced relationships. This is the passive child who is always on the outside at school, ignored or victimized, and always the last picked for team games. The parents, grateful not to have another demanding child, may ignore the pain. The Lost Child may stay in role and become an ineffectual adult. Alternatively, he or she may become hypochondriacal, having discovered that it is possible to gain attention through asthma, bedwetting, or obesity. In adulthood, gratification is sought through food or possessions rather than in relationships. There is risk of chemical dependence, in this instance from prescription sedatives and painkillers. There may be the opportunity to move into the Hero/Enabler role by staying home to care for the increasingly invalided Dependent. Otherwise the legacy is likely to be one of isolation and futility in living. The hope for the Lost Child is that he or she will become sufficiently depressed and desperate that counseling will help him or her learn to face the pain and loneliness, to reach out, and to learn to make friends. The asset here is the creativity and patience that Lost Children bring to their projects.

The youngest child is particularly likely to become the family *Mascot*. Dismissed and misled about the family disease, this child remains confused and immature. Demanding attention out of anxiety and fear of being ignored, the Mascot will be irritatingly hyperactive or a skilled humorist. Either way the child cannot risk being taken seriously and so never develops the range of potential skills or gets validation for the underlying emotions. Fear develops into doubts about sanity. Clowning becomes a cover for insecurity and inadequacy. Untreated, the role may lead to major mental illness or suicide. With the problem mistreated as hyperactivity, the child may be medicated into quiescence and launched on a career of substance abuse. But correctly treated, the Mascot may learn to take him- or herself seriously, balancing developing skills in assertiveness with natural humor and insightfulness.

The enactment of the role requires energy. The Mascot is to intrude everywhere, pulling on skirts or climbing into laps. No antic is too wild if it distracts from anger or adds life to the dead routine of family interaction.

The discussion of the role-play may lead to switching actors or to developing alternative scenarios. (For example, the group may role-play the attempts to become an active parent by a Dependent who has achieved sobriety, or the plight of the Hero who tries to remain active in the family after acquiring a depressed husband). Be creative. The role-playing makes it possible for clients to express their own childhood experience directly without having to acknowledge it publicly. So select people to play their predominant role and encourage them to improvise.

End with a discussion or an enactment (perhaps of a counseling session) of the family recovery process. It is not enough to stop the active addiction. The family must commit itself to acknowledge and respect feelings, to recognize and drop roles, and to develop new skills at communication and nurturing the tentative emergence of new identities and patterns of relationship. This may be particularly hard for dominant Enablers and Heroes, who may feel disenfranchised and devalued. But all members of the family must confront the pain of the past and the fear of relinquishing familiar roles. The enactment is likely to have mobilized these feelings in the group. They need to be told that the recognition of these difficult emotions is the first step in recovery, to help them avoid the temptation to repress the whole experience. They also need to be told of the local resources—including AlAnon, Alateen, and ACOA meetings—that can help them pursue recovery for the entire family.

The session has achieved its objective, even if there is not yet a commitment to family recovery, if members are sensitized to the potential damage drinking can do to their spouses and children. The enactment usually accomplishes this. Additionally, participants often discover the impact of their own ACOA past. The recognition that they continue to struggle with issues from childhood should be discussed and confirmed. Ironically, most clients are relieved to be told that they have two syndromes to address: ACOA concerns as well as alcohol abuse. The identification of a problem is empowering, as is the demystification of the source of pain. I stress the need to focus first on the drinking problem, but note that the ultimate resolution of ACOA issues will contribute to a fuller recovery, with more enjoyment of life and less risk of relapse.

**Variations.** The costs of addiction for the family can be approached from different directions and are important enough to merit being addressed repeatedly. A few of the many options are suggested below.

Go to meetings of AlAnon or Adult Children of Alcoholics groups when they overlap with treatment sessions. I often follow up the session just described by planning such an outing. I first confirm with contacts from the self-help fellowship that they can handle the influx of six to eight new participants. I then ask my group who would be interested in attending and lead the volunteers to the session. Those who do not choose to attend remain behind to view and discuss a film showing the effects of drinking on the family (*If You Loved Me, The Secret Life of Sandra Blain,* or commercial productions such as *Shattered Spirits* or *Under the Influence*). My clients are usually impressed with the meetings and participate effectively. I encourage follow-up attendance by permitting them to use such groups for outside involvement in lieu of requiring weekly AA attendance.

Review the characteristics of ACOAs. Claudia Black details the lasting impact of the "Don't Talk, Don't Trust, Don't Feel" rules in her film, *Children of Denial. Repeat After Me* (1985), a workbook for recovery, can be used as a source of projects. Janet Woititz's (1983) excellent presentation of thirteen typical behavior patterns can be shared and discussed. See chapter 12 for a further treatment of ACOA issues.

*A Slight Drinking Problem.* This 1977 film, starring Patty Duke Aston and Jimmy Hampton, is my preferred vehicle for raising the issue of the pathology in alcoholic marriages. The first half of the film shows the wife's enabling and denial of his drinking problem. It also portrays the many levels of the struggle for control in an alcoholic marriage. He subverts her authority by missing meals, by moments of threatening anger, and by emotional unpredictability—all the time maintaining the pose of being the innocent and victimized party. She alternates between placating and being angry as she tries to manage his drinking. The succinct portrayal of these typical patterns can stimulate useful discussion, especially if there are visiting Enablers accompanying any of the group members. When I ask the group what will be the likely outcome of the interaction pattern, it is easy to recognize the availability of excuses for continued drinking and the endlessness of the struggle. The second half of the film portrays an AlAnon approach to forcing the drinker to assume responsibility for the negative affects of his drinking as the Enabler learns to detach herself from the problem. The presentation is persuasive. Clients often come to see AlAnon as a support rather than as a threat to their autonomy. It is possible to end with a discussion of how the Dependent can help the Enabler to seek recovery.

*The Blame Game.* I will sometimes detail the central dynamic in conflictual alcoholic marriages, especially if a client and his or her spouse are arguing in the group. Even though the description is pointed, it is acceptable to most clients because it removes the onus of responsibility from either party. The key issue is that neither partner can tolerate or acknowledge negative feelings, so each tries to evoke those feelings and then to manage them in the partner. Because the causation is circular, either spouse's contribution can be described first. I usually begin with the Dependent. A drinking-related transgression triggers renewed feelings of guilt and a drop in self-esteem. The response is to shore up the self-confidence by mobilizing defenses. If projection is used, then the drinker will focus attention on some shortcoming in the partner (the messy house, the nagging, and so forth). The Dependent's blaming and criticizing will create feelings of confusion in the spouse, provoking an internal review of feelings. One of two things will happen for the Enabler. Most likely, the blame will provoke feelings of guilt and penitence, which are then acknowledged. The drinker has succeeded in getting the spouse to assume what were initially the Dependent's uncomfortable feelings. The Dependent responds with caring reassurance or advice—leaving the drinker feeling important and competent—but probably leaving the partner feeling patronized. Alternatively, the Enabler may respond to the initial blaming or the subsequent patronizing with resentment and anger, amplified by a long "laundry list" of past grievances. This results in renewed guilt in the drinker and begins a new cycle of the pattern. The game is summarized in figure 6–2 as it is drawn on the chalkboard in group.

The resolution of the game occurs when the partners are able to assume responsibility for evaluating their actions and for internally handling negative feelings. An example would be for the Dependent to admit guilt feelings but still hold on to self-esteem and so to respond positively to the spouse. Or the Enabler could hear the blame but attribute it to a drinking attitude and not take it personally, obviating the need to respond with either guilt or anger. Such detachment is taught in AlAnon. It helps if both partners are able to identify the game and then to block it by changing their own transactions. Optimally this includes replacing accusatory statements beginning with "you" (as in "If you hadn't done . . .") with "I" statements that describe current feelings and actions. Even if it is necessary to counter an insistently angry partner, it can be done by calmly stating, "I don't want to keep on with this, so I am going for a walk."

*Soft Is the Heart of a Child.* This 1979 movie is a moving depiction of the children's experience of the alcoholic family. It clearly shows the emotional

**Figure 6–2. The Blame Game: Reciprocal Induction of Negative Feelings in the Partner**

neglect by the alcoholic father and the overburdened, codependent mother. Clients are often as critical of her, and particularly of her attempts to hold onto her man by drinking with him, as of the drinker. So they need not feel exclusive responsibility for the pain as they identify with the Dependent. The Hero, Scapegoat, and Lost Child roles are clearly drawn. The movie also illustrates the intervention into the system by a sensitive school counselor, provoking hopeful discussion of what can be done to help the dysfunctional family. But perhaps the most important impact is that the audience is drawn into emotional identification with the pain of the children. The movie shatters denial and clearly shows the painful effects of drinking on the family.

# Using: Combining Alcohol and Drug Use

*This lecture and discussion takes from fifteen to sixty minutes. It is usually initiated in response to questions or when a group member attends under the influence of a drug other than alcohol.*

**Rationale.** Especially for those under age forty, alcohol abuse is likely to be only one facet of the use of many different drugs (Carroll & Schnoll, 1982). This discussion is designed to answer questions and explain the key concepts that must be understood by polydrug users. One goal of this discussion is specifically to invite clients who are engaged in addictive behavior (gambling, sexual addiction, and so on) or in abuse of a drug other than alcohol to apply concepts learned in treatment to all addictive behavior.

My clients are court referred. They are understandably reticent about discussing use of illegal substances. I have to develop a specific contract of confidentiality. Since they were referred because of alcohol, my reports to the judicial system will pertain to alcohol use. I will not specify any other drug use.

**Content.** There are five key concepts to be shared.

The first has to do with abuse of *nonbeverage alcohol*. It is routine for someone in each group to attend with a positive BAC because he or she is using a nonprescription cold remedy that contains from 20 percent to 25 percent alcohol. Because the alleged intent is to suppress a cough, the client will ignore the fact that the proof is equivalent to that found in fortified wines. The body doesn't make such refined distinctions. Alcohol is alcohol.

The addict will tend to maximize the dose. So instead of the recommended capful, clients report drinking half of a bottle at a time. One client with a strong AA program denied drinking and yet swallowed a thirty-two ounce bottle of Scope mouthwash each day. That is the equivalent of a pint of 80° whiskey.

Any client who is trying to abstain should carefully avoid alcohol that may be found in cough syrups, mouthwashes, or food flavorings such as wine and vanilla. Unless it is boiled off in preparation, the alcohol will remain in foods. Although the doses may be small, the practice is irresponsible. For the medicines, a pharmacist can suggest alternatives that are alcohol free and yet equally effective in relieving symptoms.

The discussion of other drugs may begin with reference to a TV program, a government initiative, or a local bust. I continue the dialogue with a few stimulus questions about the use of psychoactive drugs other than alcohol. I may make a list of the responses to the query, "If you could have only one drug to get high on, what would it be?" With nurturing, the discussion of drug experiences usually develops easily. The defiant youth will often compete with stories about risks taken or quantities consumed. They are surprised to discover that some grizzled veteran discovered "whacky weed" twenty years before their birth. In time, someone shares concern about a friend who has gotten "burned out" or has ODed, and the talk begins to shift to expressions of concern about the risks of drug use. Even if there is no direct admission of a problem, questions are asked and an openness to new learning is evident.

The second and third concepts are *cross-tolerance* and *cross-addiction*. Alcohol is part of a family of sedative-hypnotic drugs that all act to depress the activity of the central nervous system and all carry the potential for addiction. The sedative-hypnotics are among the most prescribed and abused drugs nationally. They include minor tranquilizers (Valium, Librium, Miltown), sleeping pills (Dalmane, Placidyl, Quaalude, and so on), and barbiturates (Seconal, Nembutal, Tuinal). Because they are chemical relatives, any of these can be considered "alcohol in a pill form." Tolerance means that with continued use, increasing doses of the drug will be required to achieve the same effect. Cross-tolerance means that the tolerance developed to any of the substances will generalize to all other related drugs. So the habituated user of prescription Valium will discover an increased capacity to handle alcohol. Conversely, the heavy drinker is prone to abusing sleeping pills or tranquilizers. Cross-addiction explains this phenomenon in which addiction to any one drug of the family is tantamount to addiction to all of the related substances. An alcoholic cannot safely use any of the sedative-hypnotics (Gitlow, 1982).

The potential for cross-addiction between alcohol and other depressant drugs has many practical consequences. It may help clients understand the etiology of their alcoholism. Many of these drugs, Quaaludes, for example, are more rapidly addicting than alcohol. Those who used "downers" may have become alcoholic before they began to drink regularly. Cross-addiction has implications for recovery. All sedative-hypnotics should be avoided. Those who use sedatives, ranging from PCP to sleeping pills, need to stop using and consider the possibility that the alcohol problem may be only the tip of the iceberg. It is unsafe for those with alcohol problems to use any street drugs with depressant effects. Alcoholics must also avoid rationalizing the legitimacy of prescription use. It is not necessarily safe just because a doctor prescribed it, especially since the physician's ignorance about the risks of cross-addiction may be compounded by the patient's being less than candid about the drinking problem. Part of the responsibility for continued recovery is to inform doctors about the alcohol addiction and to question actively the prescription of any tranquilizing drug. There are cases in which the use is still indicated, as when major tranquilizers are used to manage hallucinations in the mentally ill alcoholic or when minor tranquilizers are prescribed temporarily during detoxification. Specifically, clients should be alert to the prescription of sedative drugs that are used to treat digestive tract irritability or as muscle relaxants.

The fourth concept is *interaction*. Drugs used in combination may have unpredictable and surprisingly powerful effects. These are known as interaction effects. When alcohol is used in combination with other sedative-hypnotics, the impact of the doses multiply. The equivalent of three standard drinks of Valium plus four shots of whiskey may have the impact of twelve drinks. Metabolically, the liver is tied up in processing the alcohol, allowing the other sedatives to circulate freely. There is a major risk of overdose, with death from respiratory or cardiac collapse. This risk is increased because the overdose can occur at levels of the two drugs that could easily have been tolerated separately. The user may not have considered the dose at all excessive.

Because alcohol is mind altering, it readily becomes part of a pattern of pathological use in combination with other drugs, even if there is no direct risk of overdose or cross-addiction. The fifth concept is *psychological dependence*. When a drug or a combination of drugs is used to regulate mood, fill time, or provide a focus for identity or socializing, then there is a clear *need* to use it that extends far beyond the enjoyment that may accompany recreational drug use. Alcohol is almost always involved, not only as a gateway drug with which to experiment initially, but also as a reliable adjunct to other substance abuse.

Those who are using cocaine, amphetamines, other types of speed, or any "uppers" will note that the drug effects seem to cancel out the impact of alcohol. In fact the effects on judgment are additive with combined use. And the ability to keep drinking all night without passing out means that the body must contend with enormous doses of alcohol. Extreme tolerance develops rapidly. In this way, use of "uppers" hastens the development of physical dependence on alcohol. Psychological dependence also develops, as alcohol is used to ease the edginess or cushion the withdrawal that accompanies the prolonged use of "uppers."

Alcohol is often used in quantity by those whose primary drug of choice is heroin or another opiate. Alcohol is not directly cross-addicting with narcotic depressants, and the interaction effects are additive rather than multiplicative. So the risk would appear minimal. It is not. Any additional depressant can lead to overdose for the narcotics addict whose tolerance means that the effective dose is already perilously close to a lethal dose. Additionally, there is the likelihood of parallel dependence on alcohol as a readily available depressant that is used until a new supply of the preferred opiate is available (Kaufman, 1982). Cohen (1980) reports that 20 percent of New York City heroin addicts show liver damage indicative of chronic alcoholism. Every straight heroin addict who has come to me after a DWI is also alcoholic. In most cases the abuse of alcohol began late (midtwenties), was minimized in importance because of the preference for opiates, and was difficult to address because the ability to beat the heroin addiction made the person overconfident that he or she could handle alcohol easily.

Those who perfer hallucinogens need not worry about interaction effects or cross-addiction with alcohol. They do need to worry about psychological dependence. Many of these are true polydrug abusers, the "junkmen" who will take whatever is available. For them, alcohol is the most readily available stand-in. Even among those who restrict themselves to marijuana, there is a common pattern in which alcohol and pot are used together on a daily basis that betokens a strong psychological dependence and an inability to function comfortably when straight. Even in the absence of physical addiction, it is clear that polydrug abusers need to curtail their use if they are to learn to cope in drug-free consciousness.

I challenge all clients who are coping with an alcohol problem to avoid all mind-altering chemicals for at least a test period of two months. Quitting drinking requires new coping skills and an attitude of mastery that are incompatible with continued use of other chemicals. Marijuana smokers especially question how their pattern can jeopardize their efforts to deal with drinking. There are several clear answers. There is the risk of drug substitution, with increases in smoking to compensate for decreased drinking. There is the heightened risk of relapse that goes with getting high with friends who continue to drink and in the presence of all the old cues for partying. There is the general risk that goes with any drug use that alters judgment (see the earlier *I/E* discussion), and the immediate risk that there will be less resistance to temptation or pressure to drink once one is high on another chemical. Most of all, the continued use of any mind-altering chemical allows the user to hide from a possibility that needs to be faced directly: the likelihood that he or she has become psychologically dependent on a generalized need to be high on something as a way of coping with life. Alcohol abusers need to abstain from all drugs as they adjust to a new style of drinking. I agree with most treatment programs and with the self-help groups that alcoholics must maintain lifelong abstinence from all psychoactive substances.

The film *Alcohol, Pills, and Recovery*, by Joseph Pursch, is my preferred vehicle for educating clients about the risks of "sedativism," the generalized addiction to any and all of the sedative-hypnotic drugs. With clarity and dry humor, Pursch shows the risks of cross-addiction and the dangerous alliance between the uninformed physician and the demanding patient which leads to sedatives' being among the most prescribed pills in the world. Psychological treatment and involvement with self-help groups is presented as the appropriate path to full recovery. This film will effectively reinforce the discussion of the dangers of addiction to prescription pills.

A variety of films are now available to explore the abuse of specific illicit drugs. I urge you to review any that pertain to psychoactive drugs commonly used by the treatment population with which you are working.

**Variations.** This presentation can be effectively dovetailed with the variant on the metabolism discussion (see chapter 4) that discusses neurotransmitters. You will remember that endorphins, derived from the breakdown of acetaldehyde, and opiates are hypothesized to have a common site of action in the brain. Similar chemicals have been reported to occur naturally in opium, marijuana, and hallucinogenic plants. While it is premature to speculate about a common pathway for addiction among the various drugs, clients may be interested to note that there is a link suggested among such diverse types of abusable drugs as narcotics, marijuana, hallucinogens, and sedative-hypnotics.

# The Progression of Drinking: Like It, Love It, Need It

*This presentation lasts 15 minutes. With the structured sharing that is usually a part of it, the exercise takes from 60 to 150 minutes. A chalkboard is needed. The presentation is derived from Johnson's classic book,* I'll Quit Tomorrow *(1973).*

**Rationale.** This exercise helps clients examine the change over the years in the role alcohol has played in their lives. (This discussion is equally applicable to other drugs, and this may need to be stated specifically in group so that polydrug users realize that they can track the changing effects from whatever chemicals are involved). It shows how psychological dependence develops.

There are three variants on the exercise. The first two are usually woven together and include a brief lecture and group sharing of milestones in the progression of drinking. The sharing is a good antidote to the passivity that may occur during the learning phase of problem-solving. The exercise is also helpful in setting norms for sharing of alcohol-related problems. Because much of what is shared is well in the past, it can be discussed with humor or acceptance. Problems can be acknowledged without there being excessive threat. The third variant is to have selected group members conduct a year-by-year review of their drinking careers. This approach helps them personalize the learning about the changing role of alcohol in their lives; it makes the exercise an effective bridge to the self-diagnosis stage that follows.

**Content.** Johnson presents "the feeling chart," a continuum of feelings that runs from pain, through normal mood, to euphoria (see figure 6–3). Individuals vary in what is their predominant mood, with some beginning from a point of chronic dysphoria. But it is important to understand that problem drinkers typically begin in the normal range; they do not usually start drinking to escape pain. Drinking begins in a cultural context in which alcohol is expected to lead in the direction of euphoria. I may ask clients to remember attitudes held before their first drink. The answers listed on the board usually are predominantly positive. They reflect the power of advertising (see chapter 4) and family modeling. Even those who came to expect unpredictable and angry behavior, what would seem to be negative expectations, usually report having been aware that the problems were not normal and were not to be blamed on the alcohol.

The initial experiences with drinking confirm that alcohol does lead to pleasant feelings in a dependable and dose-related manner. Once limits of tolerance are learned, the more alcohol that is drunk, the greater the sense

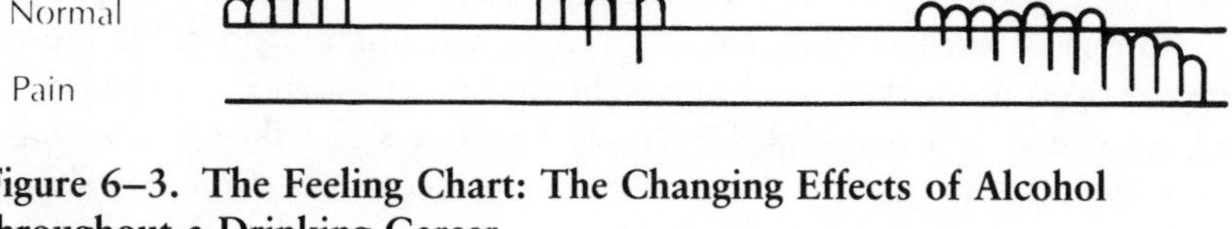

**Figure 6–3. The Feeling Chart: The Changing Effects of Alcohol throughout a Drinking Career.**

of euphoria achieved. There are no prices to be paid; the next day the feelings are again normal (stage 1 in figure 6–3, with each drinking occasion symbolized by an arc with an upswing in mood followed by a return to the baseline). This is the basis of a trusting and positive relationship with alcohol, and it sets expectations of euphoria that last long after drinking has become a problem. It is common to hear an alcoholic who is well aware of the many negative consequences of his or her drinking still to hold on to the hope that somehow "I'll learn to drink so I can have the good times like I used to." Psychlogical dependence is based on actual, repeated, positive outcomes associated with drinking.

The group personalizes the developing relationship with alcohol by sharing memories about the "first time you drank enough to get high" and then about "what drinking did for you when you first began to drink regularly." I usually get four or five volunteers to share in response to each stimulus question, being sure that everyone has made some comment by the end of the exercise. When initial experiences were negative (for example, "I threw up all over the couch and got a whipping from my old man"), follow up with questions about feelings then, feelings now upon looking back, and how long before drinking was resumed. Having been socialized in a culture that glorifies drinking, clients typically blame early problems on their own naiveté about how to imbibe. When we examine the long list of things that drinking did for them (giving them courage, helping in partying, making them more talkative, helping them with sex, giving them confidence, making them less anxious, and more relaxed, and so on), it is understandable how each learned to "like it" and then "love it." They had laid the groundwork for psychological dependency by making a contract for euphoria.

Abusive drinking begins when the search for more euphoria, combined with increasing tolerance, leads to the consumption of greater quantities with increased frequency. At some point there will be negative consequences. The drinker will awaken in pain because of a hangover or with regrets about some action taken while drunk. The implicit contract with alcohol has been altered. The drinking that was to lead to positive feelings has now resulted in negative emotions. A change has occurred, even though the pain will be infrequent at first and interspersed with the familiar enjoyable occasions (stage 2 of figure 6–3). As in a love relationship that has begun to sour (Cruse, 1985), there is insecurity and a need to rethink expectations. Instead, problem drinkers and alcoholics tacitly accept the altered terms of the contract. Negative outcomes are recognized, but are overshadowed by positive expectations (Rozien, 1983). Pain is seen as a legitimate price for the euphoria. At this point there is clear psychological dependence: "I need it."

I ask clients to exclude the DWI and hangovers and then to remember the first time that drinking really caused them problems. As stories are shared, follow-up questions assess the degree of concern, any thoughts about or actions taken in changing drinking, how long it was before regular drinking was resumed, and how long it was before additional problems appeared. This could be an opportunity for recognizing and acknowledging a drinking problem. More often, however, the humorous tone taken shows that the pain has been fended off and the opportunity for learning missed.

Harmful dependence is evident in unchanged consumption in the face of increasing pain. The result is the mobilization of psychological defenses that mask the pain. Rationalization, repression, and projection succeed in making the drinker consciously unaware of the pain. Memory is distorted by blackouts and the selective recollection of the good times (Johnson's "euphoric recall") so that the drinker is blinded to the actual consequences of drinking. Realistic self-appraisal is progressively lost, and the drinker is alienated from family and friends who would force acknowledgment of the damage done (Bacon, 1973). This process creates an unconscious load of anxiety, guilt, and lost self-esteem. The normal, undrugged mood now shifts toward pain on the continuum. The dependence on alcohol becomes more pronounced precisely because the alcoholic is in such need of something to move toward more positive feelings (stage 3 of figure 6–3). In time the psychological dependence combines with physical dependence. The drinker "has to have it" to feel normal.

I ask the group members to remember the circumstances leading to their first concerted effort to change drinking. There is less voluntary participation, in part because some have not yet reached this stage of pathological dependence and those who have are probably in pain because of the presentation. But someone begins, usually someone who is already in recovery. The sharing is now more serious as real losses and failed attempts at control are detailed. In the process, the group gets a fuller appreciation of the strength of psychological dependence.

If there has been open sharing, I may invite volunteers to label how far they have progressed within figure 6–3. This may set up some public self-diagnosis and some dialogue between those at different stages.

When I ask when drinking would change if decisions were made rationally, the group will label stage two as the time to cut back and the beginning of stage three as the time to quit. In fact, most alcoholics hang on to their drinking until the end of stage three, when they are unable to feel normal even when drinking. The presentation may end abruptly at this point, leaving clients to ponder whether the time for change has come.

**Variations.** The exercise is a good vehicle to begin self-diagnosis and to lend urgency to the decision to change. It is possible to follow up the presentation with exercises from these phases of the problem-solving process.

At times it is appropriate to ask several members of the group to trace their drinking histories individually. The selection may be based on the need to encourage sharing by a withdrawn member, to model openness for the group using a candid participant, or to assess the progress of someone who seems to be emerging from defensiveness. I will use this variant to understand more fully the meaning of drinking for someone who appears in need of special services (for example, to see if the addicted child of an alcoholic family is aware that he has always drunk as a way of avoiding chronic pain). Perhaps the most effective use of this variant is to help people recognize that they have changed to a different stage of drinking. Lost in euphoric recall, holding on to the past good times with fond possessiveness, they may have failed to realize that it has been years since the contract with drinking switched to one of predominant pain.

The personal story begins with instructions to discuss changes in drinking on a year-by-year basis. Disclose changes in tolerance, in frequency of using, and particularly in the effects of drinking. The milestones used in group sharing should be covered in detail. The group is encouraged to help the client tell his or her story, by asking questions or sharing similar experiences. The leader will likely keep the story flowing, prompting more detail if the history is too cursory, and keeping track of the chronology ("What was happening in 1968 through 1970?") so that the sharing does not become disjointed. I do little evaluating of the content. The benefit seems to come from the opportunity to review the past and emerge with an updated understanding of the changes in drinking and in dependence on it.

# 7
# Self-Diagnosis

Effective problem solving requires that the underlying problem be correctly identified and targeted for change by the client. The work to this point has helped the client prepare for this step. Active involvement in the change process, education about alcohol-related problems, and destigmatizing alcoholism are all part of the groundwork that enables the client to decide the degree of the underlying drinking problem.

The challenge in accurate problem identification is that the drunk driver already sees the DWI as the issue, when it is often a red herring. A minority may have no significant alcohol abuse pattern. Malfetti and Winter (1980) contend that up to a third of all drinking drivers need make no change beyond avoiding driving during their occasional episodes of imbibing. My experience differs. More than 95 percent of my clients will not be able to avoid other alcohol-related incidents, either recurrent driving under the influence or damage in other areas of living, until they come to recognize that the DWI is a symptom of the real, underlying drinking problem.

The big question is whether the client is alcoholic. The goals for change will be very different depending on the answer. High-tolerance nonalcoholics can hope to continue drinking if they will change their pattern and learn to control their consumption. Alcoholics need to abstain. By stating this, I am staking out a position in a controversial area, since many contend that controlled drinking for alcoholics is a feasible goal (Armor, Polich, & Stambul, 1978; Marlatt, 1983; Miller, 1983; Polich, Armor, & Braiker, 1981; Sobell & Sobell, 1978). The techniques derived from this work are helpful for non-alcoholics learning control. However, with the limited contact afforded during outpatient group therapy, I have not had success in helping alcoholics continue to drink. Even those who seemed most sincere in their efforts have been rearrested in disproportionate numbers. Abstinence is clearly the most appropriate and reliably satisfactory goal for alcoholic clients treated in outpatient groups. The focus of this step in problem solving, self-diagnosis, helps clients face the divergent goals by personalizing the distinction between alcoholic and nonalcoholic drinking.

Self-diagnosis continues to draw more fine-grained distinctions: if drinking is a response to specific emotions; are there are certain friends or situations that evoke cravings and inadequately controlled consumption; and so on. The awareness generated by the exercises in this chapter can help in this more individualized self-assessment. But it is not until later, when specific goal setting begins, that the more fine-grained analysis becomes the focus of work. For many clients, it is enough for now that they admit to themselves and to the group that they are alcoholic—especially since this means that they will have to stop drinking.

The primary objective of this stage of problem solving is for each client to be able to identify whether he or she is alcoholic.

The counselor's role is to provide the facts and the supportive environment in which to personalize them. It is up to the client to draw the conclusions. When the client makes the self-diagnosis, there is a clear assumption of responsibility to make the requisite change, to acknowledge helplessness to avert the likely consequences of unchanged drinking, or to acknowledge the defensive or resistant unwillingness to face the implications of self-diagnosis. The counselor responds to the stance assumed by the client: supporting change, encouraging more intensive therapy or inpatient rehabilitation for the helpless client, or confronting the inadequate attitude of the resistant client. Any of these positions fosters growth and eventual change in drinking. In contrast, the counselor who makes the diagnosis before extending that opportunity to the client is encouraging passivity, avoidance of involvement in problem solving, and assumption of the "victim" role (see chapter 4). When clients say, "You think we are all alcoholics," they are discrediting the counselor's judgment in the same way that they may have dismissed the concerns of friends and family members. My general statement is that "I will be glad to give my professional opinion for any who ask it, but it is up to each of you to make your own self-diagnosis."

The clients' active involvement is critical. Self-diagnosis does more than mobilize initial efforts: it is crucial to continuing efforts to maintain the changes once they are made. Chronic diseases must be treated throughout the course of the lifetime; life-style illnesses require lasting changes in habits. The alcoholic client must continue to remind him- or herself of the self-diagnosis long after treatment has been completed (Rogers & McMillin, 1984). Failure to do this is evident in the common experience of alcoholics who use a period of abstinence to convince themselves that they have been "cured" or misdiagnosed, only to resume drinking and predictably lapse into another cycle of alcohol abuse. The nonalcoholic will also need to continue self-monitoring; continued drinking requires a responsibility to be alert for the appearance of additional symptoms that would indicate alcoholism has developed. To give clients the opportunity for self-diagnosis during the course of treatment is to provide a competency that the client will continue to need long after therapy has ended.

Allowing clients to take responsibility need not mean allowing self-diagnosis to be postponed indefinitely. The counselor provides and reviews the working diagnoses of alcoholism, and then sets the opportunities for the clients to apply them. The activities in this chapter approach self-diagnosis from a range of perspectives, with the expectation that one will speak with particular power to each client. In my program, I increase opportunities for self-assessment by returning to the exercises at regular intervals (twice during the course of tréatment, at six-month intervals). In this way the counselor guides the clients toward taking the critical step of identifying the type of drinking problem underlying the drunk driving.

# Eight Areas of Life: Problems from Drinking

*This exercise lasts from fifteen minutes, with homework to be completed independently, to ninety minutes, if there is writing or sharing in class. A chalkboard is helpful. Pens, paper, and clipboards or other writing surfaces are needed.*

**Rationale.** There are many definitions of alcoholism. One of the core characteristics is the continuation of drinking despite repeated or multiple serious problems as a consequence of alcohol use (Mulford, 1980; Operation Cork, 1982). The goal of this exercise is to enable clients to identify the problems that have resulted from their drinking, or, conversely, to recognize that drinking and drugging may be the common thread running through a number of apparently unrelated difficulties in living.

This exercise is a logical continuation of the presentations from the last chapter. The "Progression of Drinking" provides an opportunity to review one's drinking history. The present activity can be used to organize the recollections of problems into a total picture that makes the costs of drinking more evident. The various alcohol-related problems (for example family, health, or money), previously discussed in the abstract, can now be personally acknowledged.

If there are multiple, recurrent, persistent, or severe personal problems resulting from drinking, then a self-diagnosis of alcoholism is warranted. This self-assessment is private. But the fact that there is no request for public admission of alcoholism does not make the potential impact any less powerful. It is not unusual for a client to tell me: "When I sat down, I didn't think my drinking was really that big of an issue. But after my list of problems was three pages long, I realized that drinking was involved just about every time I ever got into trouble. That's a problem!"

The exercise produces a written record of the various negative consequences of drinking. The document can be used as evidence in self-diagnosis. Additionally, it can be reread during periods of temptation to heighten resolve against further abusive drinking.

Clients often see a similarity between this exercise and the personal inventory completed during the fourth step of the Alcoholics Anonymous program. Both involve acknowledging shortcomings. But there is a different focus. This exercise is not interested in character defects. Rather, the central issue is to acknowledge when alcohol has caused problems. The goal is more in line with AA's first step: facing the unmanageability of life when drinking.

**Content.** The group is asked to guess the major life areas in which alcohol-related problems are likely to appear. With encouragement, the following eight column headings are identified, listed on the board, and defined: Money, Legal, Family, Friends/Reputation, Job, Physical Health, Spiritual Health (including values and a sense of meaning as well as religion or belief in a deity), and Psychological Health.

The group is asked in which area there has been most damage from the DWI. The sharing makes it immediately clear that the arrest and conviction represent a major problem to participants. Financial and legal problems are obvious. Others are more affected by shame or loss of face before family and friends. Those who need a license to drive note the threat to their jobs. Even the jeopardy to physical health may be discussed by those arrested after having had an accident. The review of the consequences of the DWI gives practice at admitting problems. It is a short step to consider other alcohol-related problems.

There are several options as to how to proceed at this point. Most typically, I instruct clients to make a point of sitting down and writing a list of all the alcohol-related problems that fit into each of the eight areas in turn. (Committing the list to writing is important; compared with a period of reflection, it is more tangible, lasting, and powerful). I suggest that the list be retained for review. In some cases clients have posted it on the liquor cabinet (to be considered before pouring a drink), or on the visor of the car (as a reminder not to drink and drive). The class is then dismissed, with the request to bring the completed list to the next session. During the following meeting, volunteers are asked to share some significant portion of their lists with the group. Self-disclosure is encouraged but not required. It is helpful to state that the list may be kept private, that it is for their own use, and that it is intended to be an honest and personal document.

**Variations.** I often allot twenty minutes in group for writing the initial draft of the problem list. Clients are urged to select the most important area and list all elements of the alcohol-related damage to that part of life that can be recalled. The next most important area is then addressed. The process continues until all eight areas have been considered.

In many cases the recollections are unavailable, even if there have been problems. The mental file does not have a category entitled "Problems Because of Drinking." In this case it is helpful to have clients review their drinking career chronologically, beginning with the first drink. Each alcohol-related problem is then listed, and the areas of life affected are appended in parentheses after each entry. If this still fails to elicit memories, the client may be instructed to remember each of the significant problems in life since the age at which drinking began. Each memory is then examined to see if drinking was involved.

The exercise lends itself to immediate group sharing. After reviewing the areas affected by the DWI, the group may be asked to search for examples of drinking-related problems in each area. After a moment, someone is asked to volunteer an instance. After the story concludes, the volunteer selects one of the eight areas and picks another member (for example, "Bill, tell us about a family problem"). That person shares a story about a problem in the selected area, or in another area if no problem had been recognized in the one suggested. The process repeats until all group members have shared some incident. This variant is an excellent way to stimulate memories. It also serves to reinforce the norm of sharing problems; by stimulating self-disclosure, it functions very much like a call for sharing "war stories" (see chapter 8).

This exercise is a chance to review and complete the examination of the likely costs of excessive drinking, which were detailed in the preceding chapter. Additional coverage is provided for legal (DWI laws in chapter 3), spiritual ("Life Values" in chapter 9), and psychological areas ("Defenses" in chapter 4 and the "Self-Esteem Trap" in chapter 11). At times I will have participants complete this exercise before the depth review of each topic. Lists would then be updated weekly to incorporate insights from the detailed review of each of the eight areas.

# *Alcoholism Screening Tests*

*The questionnaires take sixty minutes to administer, score, and discuss. Pens, clipboards or writing surfaces, and copies of the tests are suggested, although*

*oral administration is possible. Use of either of the suggested movies takes
an additional thirty minutes.*

**Rationale.** Alcoholism is often diagnosed based on pathological use of alcohol or on characteristic symptoms. Questionnaires have been developed that survey these signs and symptoms. This exercise involves administering several questionnaires. The ensuing discussion of the items helps clients clarify their understanding of alcoholism. Presentation of cutoff scores aids clients in differentiating whether or not they test as alcoholics. The posting of results facilitates the use of the group as a forum in which to admit alcoholism when it is present.

Each group will have members representing a range of drinking problems, from temporary patterns of abuse to severe and chronic alcoholism. The use of screening tests helps the group understand the range of problems present. This may help counteract denial. To receive a score identical to that of another member seen as worse off is a challenge: "Is the other guy conning? Should I confront him? Is my own problem worse than I suspected?" Clients with similar scores can form useful subgroups, since they are likely to share similar treatment challenges. Clients with dissimilar scores can often learn from one another. It may be shocking but important information for the client who tests as prealcoholic to be reminded by someone testing out as early stage alcoholic that their scores would have matched had the alcoholic been tested three years previously. Knowing the test results for each member enriches the give and take. For this reason it is desirable to make the results public within the group.

There are fewer drawbacks than might be expected from sharing the results in group. There may be conscious distortion of scores to minimize the apparent drinking problem. But this problem occurs in private as well. In fact, having a range of scores within the group may make it safer to acknowledge a problem since others have also done so. Group veterans will often note that their scores have risen since an earlier administration of the tests, in part because of more education and more honesty. This comment makes honest self-assessment easier for all.

The difficulty with group administration is that the choice of tests is limited to those that can be easily scored, which are not the best available. The three that are used share the convenient feature that the total is simply the number of yes answers. But psychologists warn that test takers have response sets—habitual patterns of preferring one option in responding. A "nay saying" response set may lead to a possibly false rating as nonalcoholic, while "yea saying" will lead to a higher score than would be warranted by the drinking problem. Since the attitude of the client will affect the meaning of any score obtained, the cutoff must float down for the self-excusing and up for the self-critical. A single cutoff score is too arbitrary.

Clients will often dispute the results from any single test: "You could get three yes answers after a single good drunk." This argument can be countered readily if light-drinking significant others attending group are willing to share their scores. But the most common tactic for handling skepticism is to pull out another test. If three different tests give the same results, most clients reach a grudging acceptance that there must be some validity to the diagnosis. The third test can also serve as a tiebreaker in instances where there are discrepant outcomes. It is generally advisable to administer several of the screening instruments.

Test results are not expected to generate acceptance of a diagnosis of alcoholism, even when the scores are clearly and consistently above the cutoff levels. Acceptance is a process. But to receive a diagnosis based on personally acknowledged symptoms is the first step toward an internal admission of a problem.

It is useful to repeat the questionnaires at intervals. Clients will regularly report having higher scores on readministration if they are moving to a nondefensive acceptance of a drinking problem. The two movies discussed below may be alternated, to avoid repetition, with each repeat of the self-diagnosis cycle.

The movie *Alcohol Abuse: The Early Warning Signs* portrays a number of drinking patterns associated with alcoholism. It does not relate to any of the questionnaires covered in class, so it will not influence scores directly by giving prior exposure. It does sensitize clients to the importance of recognizing problems with drinking and it raises the issue of self-diagnosis. It can be shown with minimal discussion. The group can then proceed to take the tests discussed later.

The movie *Alcoholism: The Twenty Questions* provides a vignette associated with each of the items on the Johns Hopkins Alcoholism Screening Test. One, in which a woman describes losing her child while in a blackout, is especially memorable. The film can be used to sensitize clients. Alternatively, clients can be asked to take the test by keeping track of the number of yes answers as each of the twenty questions is covered. I stop the movie long enough to post each group member's total before the cutoff scores are presented. This avoids the possibility that clients will distort their results.

**Content.** Clients are told that they will be given several self-screening tests. Those who have significantly changed their drinking while in the group are to answer in terms of their drinking at the time of arrest. Questions should be listened to carefully. Especially if the item begins with "have you ever . . ." the answer should be yes even if the symptom has not been present in years. The rationale for this is that the tests are for symptoms of alcoholism, which is a lifelong disease process. Although symptoms may remit, they can be expected to recur in time if the disease progresses. Questions should be answered as honestly as possible. There are cutoff scores that will be shared. But it is the attitude with which the test is taken that determines the true criterion for differentiating alcoholic from nonalcoholic scores.

The Johns Hopkins Alcoholism Self-Screening Test (figure 7–1) is administered first. After the items are discussed, the score obtained by each group member is listed on the chalkboard and the cutoffs are given. Because many participants will be confronted with unexpected alcoholic diagnoses, there is often a lively discussion. I defend the test by noting that my experience indicates it is generally accurate. But I do not directly challenge the clients' arguments. There are several points that can be made about the test. Since it was designed for preliminary screening of patients coming for med-

Johns Hopkins Alcoholism Screening Test

Yes  No

1. Do you lose time from work due to drinking?
2. Is drinking making your home life unhappy?
3. Do you drink because you are shy with other people?
4. Is drinking affecting your reputation?
5. Have you ever felt remorse after drinking?
6. Have you gotten into financial difficulties as a result of drinking?
7. Do you turn to lower companions and an inferior environment when drinking?
8. Does your drinking make you careless of your family's welfare?
9. Has your ambition decreased since drinking?
10. Do you crave a drink at a definite time daily?
11. Do you want a drink the next morning?
12. Does drinking cause you to have difficulty in sleeping?
13. Has your efficiency decreased since drinking?
14. Is drinking jeopardizing your job or business?
15. Do you drink to escape from worries or trouble?
16. Do you drink alone?
17. Have you ever had a complete memory loss as a result of drinking?
18. Has your physician ever treated you for drinking?
19. Do you drink to build up your self-confidence?
20. Have you ever been to a hospital or institution on account of drinking?

Scoring: If you have answered yes to any one of the questions, there is a definite warning that *you may be an alcoholic.* If you have answered yes to any two, the chances are that *you are an alcoholic.* If you have answered yes to three or more, *you are definitely an alcoholic.*

*Source:* These are the questions used by the Johns Hopkins University Hospital, Baltimore, Maryland, in deciding whether or not a patient is an alcoholic.

**Figure 7–1. Johns Hopkins Alcoholism Screening Test**

ical treatment, norms were set for people with less opportunity to be sensitized to their drinking than the group members. If the greater awareness is translated into elevated scores, then the cutoff is too low. Conversely, if there is heightened defensiveness, then the cutoff is too high. I have seen alcoholics score as low as 1 and nonalcoholics with 4 or 5. Any score above 5 is unambiguous. Clients will also notice that the test omits some obvious characteristics of alcoholism: there is no question about having cirrhosis, for example. The test focuses on the early stages of the disease, the period when there are only subtle and easily overlooked differences between alcoholism and "heavy social drinking" (figure 7–2 illustrates this). It is an important warning if the test suggests more of a problem than the drinker had perceived.

The Alcoholics Anonymous screening questions (figure 7–3) are then administered, scored, and listed. Based on the practical experience of AA members, they represent a different perspective from scientifically derived questionnaires. But just as some early stage alcoholics can not identify with the more severe problems of AA participants, so some early stage alcoholics may test below the cutoff. In my experience, this test errs in the direction of excluding alcoholics, of having too high a cutoff.

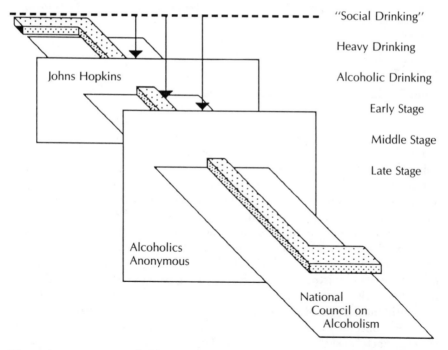

**Figure 7–2.** Portion of the Disease Curve Covered by Various Screening Tests for Alcoholism

Alcoholics Anonymous' Twelve Questions

Yes   No

1. Have you ever decided to stop drinking for a week or so, but only lasted for a couple of days?
2. Do you wish people would mind their own business about your drinking—stop telling you what to do?
3. Have you ever switched from one kind of a drink to another in the hope that this would keep you from getting drunk?
4. Have you had to have an eye-opener upon awakening during the past year?
5. Do you envy people who can drink without getting into trouble?
6. Have you had problems connected with drinking during the past year?
7. Has your drinking caused trouble at home?
8. Do you try to get "extra" drinks at a party because you do not get enough?
9. Do you tell yourself you can stop drinking anytime you want to, even though you keep getting drunk when you don't mean to?
10. Have you missed days of work or school because of drinking?
11. Do you have "blackouts?"
12. Have you ever felt that your life would be better if you did not drink?

Scoring: If you have answered yes to one to three questions, consider it a warning that *you may be alcoholic.* Four or more yes answers indicates that *you are an alcoholic.*

*Source:* Twelve questions from *Is AA for You?* with permission of Alcoholics Anonymous World Services, Inc.

**Figure 7–3. Alcoholics Anonymous' Twelve Questions**

The third questionnaire administered was developed by the National Council on Alcoholism (figure 7–4). Based on Jellinek's (1952) work, it follows the progression of symptoms from the warning signs through the symptoms of full and obvious addiction. It covers the territory of the previous tests and offers the additional benefit of distinguishing the likely stage of the disease based on the total score. While each of the items covers a symptom of alcoholism, and it is possible to be an alcoholic and only have a single yes answer, my experience suggests that a cutoff of 3 or 4 represents the upper bound attained by nonalcoholics. Again, the group repeats the cycle of test administration, item discussion, posting of scores, and sharing of cutoff levels.

With the results of the three questionnaires in front of them, group members conclude the exercise with each persons sharing what he or she has learned. Each is asked to self-diagnose. The leader and the group get a good opportunity to see how nondefensively the information is handled. There may be spontaneous confrontation of alcoholics who remain entrenched in

National Council on Alcoholism Screening Test

Yes   No

1.  Do you occasionally drink heavily after a disappointment, a quarrel, or when the boss gives you a hard time?
2.  When you have trouble or feel under pressure, do you always drink more heavily than usual?
3.  Have you noticed that you are able to handle more liquor than you did when you were first drinking?
4.  Did you ever wake up on the "morning after" and discover that you could not remember part of the evening before, even though your friends tell you that you did not "pass out?"
5.  When drinking with other people, do you try to have a few extra drinks when others will not know it?
6.  Are there certain occasions when you feel uncomfortable if alcohol is not available?
7.  Have you recently noticed that when you begin drinking you are in more of a hurry to get the first drink than you used to be?
8.  Do you sometimes feel a little guilty about your drinking?
9.  Are you secretly irritated when your family or friends discuss your drinking?
10. Have you recently noticed an increase in the frequency of your "memory blackouts?"
11. Do you often find that you wish to continue drinking after your friends say they have had enough?
12. Do you usually have a reason for the occasions when you drink heavily?
13. When you are sober, do you often regret things you have done or said while drinking?
14. Have you tried switching brands or following different plans for controlling your drinking?
15. Have you often failed to keep the promises you have made to yourself about controlling or cutting down on your drinking?
16. Have you ever tried to control your drinking by making a change in jobs, or moving to a new location?
17. Do you try to avoid family or close friends while you are drinking?
18. Are you having an increasing number of financial and work problems?
19. Do more people seem to be treating you unfairly without good reason?
20. Do you eat very little or irregularly when you are drinking?
21. Do you sometimes have the "shakes" in the morning and find that it helps to have a little drink?
22. Have you recently noticed that you cannot drink as much as you once did?
23. Do you sometimes stay drunk for several days at a time?
24. Do you sometimes feel very depressed and wonder whether life is worth living?
25. Sometimes after periods of drinking, do you see or hear things that aren't there?
26. Do you get terribly frightened after you have been drinking heavily?

Scoring: If you have answered yes to any of the questions, you have some of the symptoms that may indicate alcoholism. Yes answers to several questions indicate the following stages of alcoholism: questions 1–8—early stage, questions 9–21—middle stage, questions 22–26—the beginning of the final stage.

*Source:* From *What Are the Signs of Alcoholism?* Reproduced with permission of the National Council on Alcoholism.

## Figure 7–4. National Council on Alcoholism Screening Test

denial. There are often congratulations and suggestions of early release from treatment for those who test as nonalcoholic. There is a heightened awareness that a range of drinking problems is evident in the group.

**Variations.** The movies, with their vivid illustrations, help sensitize clients to the importance of the warning signs. They balance the artifically objective tone set by tests and numbers. But they also take time away from discussion. With verbal groups, the movies may be omitted or postponed.

It may be desirable to use other questionnaires. Tests may be taken one session and scored by staff for discussion the following meeting. This permits use of more psychometrically sophisticated instruments. The Michigan Alcohol Screening Test has documented reliability and validity (Bernadt, Mumford, & Murray, 1984; Knox, 1976; Selzer, 1971). It has been revised for self-administration and is widely used in DWI schools (Malfetti & Winter, 1980). The test, along with keys and cutoff scores, is included in figure 7–5 (page 155). Mayer and Filstead's (1979) Adolescent Alcohol Involvement Scale can be self-administered. Its utility with the adolescent population warrants its inclusion (figure 7–6). These tests can be given to the entire group, or they can be administered as needed to clarify a particular diagnostic question. In the latter case, the individual can complete the appropriate questionnaire in five minutes after the conclusion of the session in which the other scales have been administered and discussed.

# The Disease Curve

*This presentation takes ninety minutes. Pens, writing surfaces, and copies of the disease curve are needed.*

**Rationale.** Jellinek (1952) interviewed two thousand recovering alcoholics about the type and timing of the onset of the symptoms of their disease. The result is a chart—colloquially known as the disease curve or the dip curve— of the typical course of progressive alcoholism and of recovery with abstinence (figure 7–7). It is the most comprehensive of the instruments that lend themselves to self-diagnosis. It covers signs and symptoms, pathological drinking practices, and predictable life problems. It summarizes in one document the material covered in chapter 6 and in the preceding exercises in this chapter. A review of the disease curve consolidates education about alcoholism while it permits self-evaluation. The diagnosis goes beyond the

## Michigan Alcoholism Screening Test

| | Yes | No |
|---|---|---|
| 1. Do you feel you are a normal drinker? | | * |
| 2. Have you ever awakened the morning after some drinking the night before and found that you could not remember a part of the evening before? | * | |
| 3. Does your wife, husband, parent, or other near relative ever worry or complain about your drinking? | * | |
| 4. Can you stop drinking without a struggle after one or two drinks? | | * |
| 5. Do you ever feel bad about your drinking? | * | |
| 6. Do your friends or relatives think you are a normal drinker? | | * |
| 7. Do you ever try to limit your drinking to certain times of the day or to certain places? | * | |
| 8. Are you always able to stop drinking when you want to? | | * |
| 9. Have you ever attended a meeting of Alcoholics Anonymous? | * | |
| 10. Have you gotten into fights when drinking? | * | |
| 11. Has drinking ever created problems between you and your wife, husband, parent, or other near relative? | * | |
| 12. Has your wife, husband, parent, or other near relative ever gone to anyone for help about your drinking? | * | |
| 13. Have you ever lost friends because of drinking? | * | |
| 14. Have you ever gotten in trouble at work because of drinking? | * | |
| 15. Have you ever lost a job because of drinking? | * | |
| 16. Have you ever neglected your obligations, your family, or your work for two or more days in a row because you were drinking? | * | |
| 17. Do you drink before noon fairly often? | * | |
| 18. Have you ever been told you have liver trouble? Cirrhosis? | * | |
| 19. After heavy drinking, have you ever had delirium tremens (DTs) or severe shaking? | * | |
| 20. After heavy drinking, have you ever heard voices or seen things that weren't really there? | * | |
| 21. Have you ever gone to anyone for help about your drinking? | * | |
| 23. Have you ever been a patient in a psychiatric hospital or on a psychiatric ward of a general hospital? | * | |
| 24. Have you ever been in a hospital to be "dried out" (detoxified) because of drinking? | * | |
| 25. Have you ever been in jail, even for a few hours, because of drunk behavior? | * | |

Scoring: Asterisks represent the scored responses. A score of 0–3 loosely translates as *no drinking problem*, 4–6 as a *potential problem*, and 7 or above as an *evident problem* with alcoholism.

*Source:* From Malfetti, J.L., & Winter, D.J. (1980). *Counseling Manual for Educational and Rehabilitative Programs for Persons Convicted of Driving While Intoxicated.* Falls Church, Va.: AAA Foundation for Traffic Safety. Reprinted with permission.

**Figure 7–5. Michigan Alcoholism Screening Test**

### Adolescent Alcohol Involvement Scale

1. How often do you drink?
   a. Never (0)
   b. Once or twice a year (2)
   c. Once or twice a month (3)
   d. Every weekend (4)
   e. Several times a week (5)
   f. Every day (6)

2. When did you have your last drink?
   a. Never drank (0)
   b. Not for over a year (2)
   c. Between six months and one year ago (3)
   d. Several weeks ago (4)
   e. Last week (5)
   f. Yesterday (6)
   g. Today (7)

3. I usually start to drink because:
   a. I like the taste (1)
   b. To be like my friends (2)
   c. To feel like an adult (3)
   d. I feel nervous, tense, full of worries or problems (4)
   e. I feel sad, lonely, sorry for myself (5)

4. What do you drink?
   a. Wine (1)
   b. Beer (2)
   c. Mixed drinks (3)
   d. Hard liquor (4)
   e. Substitute for alcohol—paint thinner, sterno, cough medicine, mouthwash, hair tonic, etc. (5)

5. How do you get your drinks?
   a. Supervised by parents (1)
   b. From brothers or sisters (2)
   c. From home without parents' knowledge (3)
   d. From friends (4)
   e. Buy it with false identification (5)

6. When did you take your first drink?
   a. Never (0)
   b. Recently (2)
   c. After age fifteen (3)
   d. At age fourteen or fifteen (4)
   e. Between ages ten and thirteen (5)
   f. Before age ten (6)

7. What time of day do you usually drink?
   a. With meals (1)
   b. At night (2)
   c. Afternoons (3)
   d. Mostly in the morning or when I first awake (4)
   e. I often get up during my sleep and drink (5)

8. Why did you take your first drink?
   a. Curiosity (1)
   b. Parents or relatives offered (2)
   c. Friends encouraged me (3)
   d. To feel more like an adult (4)
   e. To get drunk or high (5)

9. How much do you drink, when you do drink?
   a. One drink (1)
   b. Two drinks (2)
   c. Three to six drinks (3)
   d. Six or more drinks (4)
   e. Until high or drunk (5)

10. Whom do you drink with?
    a. Parents or relatives only (1)
    b. With brothers or sisters only (2)
    c. With friends your own age (3)
    d. With older friends (4)
    e. Alone (5)

11. What is the greatest effect you have had from alcohol?
    a. Loose, easy feeling (1)
    b. Moderately high (2)
    c. Drunk (3)
    d. Became ill (4)
    e. Passed out (5)
    f. Was drinking heavily and the next day didn't remember what happened (6)

12. What is the greatest effect drinking has had on your life?
    a. None—no effect (0)
    b. Has interfered with talking to someone (2)
    c. Has prevented me from having a good time (3)
    d. Has interfered with my schoolwork (4)
    e. Have lost friends because of drinking (5)
    f. Has gotten me into trouble at home (6)
    g. Was in a fight or destroyed property (7)
    h. Has resulted in an accident, an injury, an arrest or being punished at school for drinking (8)

13. How do you feel about your drinking?
    a. No problem at all (0)
    b. I can control it and set limits on myself (2)
    c. I can control myself, but my friends easily influence me (3)
    d. I often feel bad about my drinking (4)
    e. I need help to control myself (5)
    f. I have had professional help to control my drinking (6)

14. How do others see you?
    a. Can't say, or a normal drinker for my age (0)
    b. When I drink, I tend to neglect my family or friends (2)
    c. My family or friends advise me to control or cut down on my drinking (3)
    d. My family or friends tell me to get help for my drinking (4)
    e. My family or friends have already gone for help for my drinking (5)

Scoring: If the highest score from each item is summed, a total score of 0–41 suggests *nonproblem drinking,* 42–53 indicates *alcohol misuse,* and 54 or above applies to *"alcoholic-like" drinkers* (Moberg, 1983).

*Source:* From Mayer, J.E., & Filstead, W.J. (1979). The Adolescent Alcohol Involvement Scale: An Instrument for Measuring Adolescents' Use and Misuse of Alcohol. Reprinted by permission, from *Journal of Studies on Alcohol, 40;* 291–300. Copyright by Journal of Studies on Alcohol, Inc., Rutgers Center of Alcohol Studies, New Brunswick, NJ 08903.

**Figure 7–6. Adolescent Alcohol Involvement Scale**

binary distinction between alcoholic and nonalcoholic to a differentiation of the different stages of the disease progression.

The film of a lecture by Fr. Joseph Martin, *Chalk Talk, part 2,* is a useful adjunct when presented before the disease curve is filled out. First, the movie contains a review of a number of the predominant symptoms. Second, it provides a compelling presentation of a definition of alcoholism-based life problems. If it is accepted that "anything that causes a problem is a problem," then the self-diagnosis process may be very much simplified. By way of illustration, Father Martin describes a young man whose three drunks had cost him his arm, his family, and his freedom. In discussing this, most of my clients initially deny that this is alcoholism. But they also pointedly decide that they would keep their distance while he was on his fourth drunk. After stopping the movie to permit this discussion, I let them view the rest of the film and then invite any comments about the signs and symptoms of alcoholism. This general review anticipates the personal review follows.

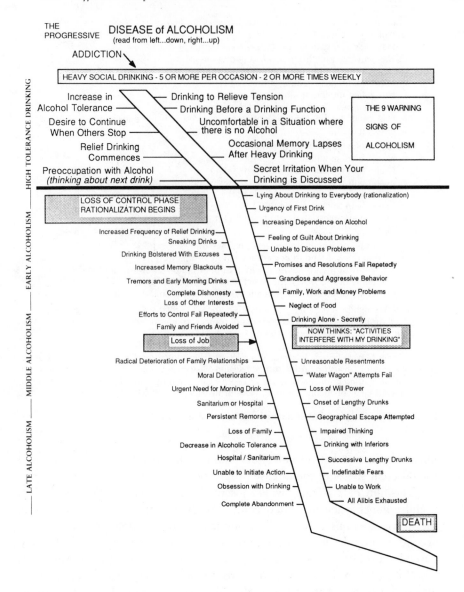

THE PROGRESSIVE ADDICTION

DISEASE of ALCOHOLISM
(read from left...down, right...up)

**HIGH TOLERANCE DRINKING**

HEAVY SOCIAL DRINKING - 5 OR MORE PER OCCASION - 2 OR MORE TIMES WEEKLY

Increase in Alcohol Tolerance ——— Drinking to Relieve Tension
——— Drinking Before a Drinking Function
Desire to Continue When Others Stop ——— Uncomfortable in a Situation where there is no Alcohol
Relief Drinking Commences ——— Occasional Memory Lapses After Heavy Drinking
Preoccupation with Alcohol *(thinking about next drink)* ——— Secret Irritation When Your Drinking is Discussed

THE 9 WARNING SIGNS OF ALCOHOLISM

**EARLY ALCOHOLISM**

LOSS OF CONTROL PHASE RATIONALIZATION BEGINS

——— Lying About Drinking to Everybody (rationalization)
——— Urgency of First Drink
——— Increasing Dependence on Alcohol
Increased Frequency of Relief Drinking ———
Sneaking Drinks ——— ——— Feeling of Guilt About Drinking
Drinking Bolstered With Excuses ——— ——— Unable to Discuss Problems
Increased Memory Blackouts ——— ——— Promises and Resolutions Fail Repetedly
Tremors and Early Morning Drinks ——— ——— Grandiose and Aggressive Behavior
Complete Dishonesty ——— ——— Family, Work and Money Problems
Loss of Other Interests ——— ——— Neglect of Food
Efforts to Control Fail Repeatedly ——— ——— Drinking Alone - Secretly
Family and Friends Avoided ———

NOW THINKS: "ACTIVITIES INTERFERE WITH MY DRINKING"

**MIDDLE ALCOHOLISM**

Loss of Job ➔

Radical Deterioration of Family Relationships ——— ——— Unreasonable Resentments
Moral Deterioration ——— ——— "Water Wagon" Attempts Fail
Urgent Need for Morning Drink ——— ——— Loss of Will Power
Sanitarium or Hospital ——— ——— Onset of Lengthy Drunks
Persistent Remorse ——— ——— Geographical Escape Attempted
Loss of Family ——— ——— Impaired Thinking
Decrease in Alcoholic Tolerance ——— ——— Drinking with Inferiors

**LATE ALCOHOLISM**

Hospital / Sanitarium ——— ——— Successive Lengthy Drunks
Unable to Initiate Action ——— ——— Indefinable Fears
Obsession with Drinking ——— ——— Unable to Work
Complete Abandonment ——— ——— All Alibis Exhausted

DEATH

**Content.** Alcoholism is a progressive disease. Yet great variability exists in the onset and duration of problems. There are likely to be periods when remission in the symptoms takes place, leading to the false conviction that the drinking problem has been resolved. But the symptoms typically recur and intensify in time.

There are two practical implications of this understanding of alcoholism

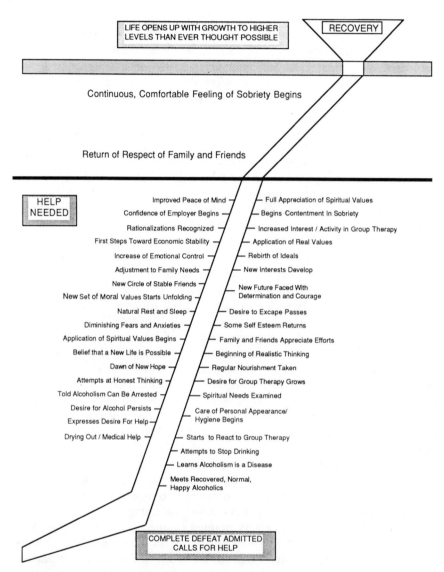

LIFE OPENS UP WITH GROWTH TO HIGHER
LEVELS THAN EVER THOUGHT POSSIBLE

RECOVERY

Continuous, Comfortable Feeling of Sobriety Begins

Return of Respect of Family and Friends

HELP
NEEDED

Improved Peace of Mind —    — Full Appreciation of Spiritual Values
Confidence of Employer Begins —    — Begins Contentment In Sobriety
Rationalizations Recognized —    — Increased Interest / Activity in Group Therapy
First Steps Toward Economic Stability —    — Application of Real Values
Increase of Emotional Control —    — Rebirth of Ideals
Adjustment to Family Needs —    — New Interests Develop
New Circle of Stable Friends —
New Set of Moral Values Starts Unfolding —    New Future Faced With Determination and Courage
Natural Rest and Sleep —    — Desire to Excape Passes
Diminishing Fears and Anxieties —    — Some Self Esteem Returns
Application of Spiritual Values Begins —    — Family and Friends Appreciate Efforts
Belief that a New Life is Possible —    — Beginning of Realistic Thinking
Dawn of New Hope —    — Regular Nourishment Taken
Attempts at Honest Thinking —    — Desire for Group Therapy Grows
Told Alcoholism Can Be Arrested —    — Spiritual Needs Examined
Desire for Alcohol Persists —    Care of Personal Appearance/ Hygiene Begins
Expresses Desire For Help —
Drying Out / Medical Help —    — Starts to React to Group Therapy
— Attempts to Stop Drinking
— Learns Alcoholism is a Disease
Meets Recovered, Normal, Happy Alcoholics

COMPLETE DEFEAT ADMITTED
CALLS FOR HELP

**Figure 7–7. The Disease Curve: The Progressive Symptoms of Alcoholism**

as a progressive disease. First is that the disease can be diagnosed at any time. The worst symptoms need never be experienced if the process is recognized and abstinence is achieved early on. An analogy to a train can be used: each symptom represents a station at which the passenger can disembark, but if the rider fails to see his location, he will eventually end up a long way from where he wanted to go. Second, there is the recognition that no two alcoholics will have identical symptoms at any stage of their drinking careers, although they will become increasingly similar as the disease gradually strips away their individuality. I tell the apocryphal story of trying to overcome the massive denial of a severely alcoholic client by administering a version of the disease curve. After he had checked off all but two of the possible symptoms I was smugly confident that he would recognize his problem when I asked him what he had learned. He responded, "Gee, Doc, I'm glad I don't have those two symptoms, or I guess I'd be an alcoholic." The group usually laughs and gets the message: you do not have to have every conceivable symptom to diagnose and treat a disease. If necessary, I will ask how many of the seven warning signs of cancer would my clients have to have before they would seek expert help. One or two will usually suffice. No one has ever felt that it would require all seven if they knew what to look for.

The disease curve tells them what to look for. Clients can be reassured that the curve is for themselves, that they need not turn in the filled-out sheet, and that the results may be kept private. Participants are, however, invited to review the curve with friends and family to see whether their close associates have a different perspective on which symptoms have been present. Each person is asked to be completely candid and is told that if that proves impossible there is a symptom called "complete dishonesty" that should be checked off. As in the last exercise, problems that were present at some point in the past should be counted as evidence that the disease had progressed to that point, even if they were not present during recent periods of drinking. Getting fired from a job five years ago still counts, despite success in finding employment where drinking has been tolerated in the years since.

With this introduction, clients are each given a copy of the disease curve. Each item is reviewed in turn. Participants are to circle or check off all that have applied to them. There are three variants to how the discussion proceeds. First, the leader can present a definition and illustrative story for each. I tend to use humor to balance very pointed examples. ("Sneaking drinks" is an opportunity to suggest that pouring six ounces of whiskey topped with a dash of cola is abnormal drinking. But I will also tell of the suave partier who appears to help the host by making drinks for four people, only to place one on the mantle and one by the stereo and one on the counter to be personally consumed—to reduce the number of trips to the bar). Second, the group can be asked to volunteer illustrations of each item. The drawback to this approach is that a few clients are likely to share while the others remain silent. My preference is the third approach: to circle the group, asking each in turn to illustrate succeeding items with personal anecdotes. In lieu of sharing personal experience, sharing about a friend's is acceptable. If this too fails, the client can ask for assistance from the rest of the group. In this way each person is active and practicing self-disclosure. I will typically have the group share until all have commented or until middle-stage symptoms have been covered. Few of my clients in outpatient treatment will talk personally about late-stage symptoms. I will revert to a lecture/discussion format for the most severe symptoms on the disease curve.

The group pauses to review the status of a hypothetical person who has checked off the majority of the symptoms up to certain key points. (1) Stop after reviewing the warning signs of alcoholism. It is important to note that not everyone checking off an item is alcoholic. Further, it helps to highlight that relief drinking, a blackout, or irritation at others' concern about one's drinking are all indicators of a need to change lest alcoholism result. (2) When midstage alcoholism is examined, pause to review. The earlier symptoms may have been overlooked because they are not obviously associated with alcoholism. Yet the damage to family communication and problem solving, the narrowing of interests as nondrinking activities are abandoned, and the loss of confidence as increasingly desperate measures are taken to control drinking all indicate an undeniable problem. (I illustrate the progression for a man who loves to fish. At one point drinking would not be allowed to interfere with the concentration on finding the right spot and the right lure. Later there will always be beer present. For some a time will come when fishing is really an excuse to go drinking—and the bait on the hook will go unchecked lest catching fish interfere with drinking. Finally, it is too much of a hassle to get up early and go. Instead the man stays home, drinks, and tells stories about past fishing exploits.) (3) Stop after discussing the symptoms that are immediately recognized by the man in the street as alcoholic. I get clients to note the location on the paper at which physical deterioration appears, commenting that they are "two-thirds of the way to death" before this symptom is reached. The contextual message is, again, that group members need not wait that long now that they have a fuller understanding of the disease progression.

When all the symptoms have been reviewed, I ask each client to identify the last *cluster* of symptoms that have been checked off. There will be some skipped previously, and there may be one or two solitary items checked farther down. But this cluster may be seen as the point to which they have progressed. A horizontal line across the page here will intersect on the right with the recovery issues that are likely to be the first to be faced (the closer to the top, the less involved the recovery). On the left the line will intersect with a stage in the disease progression. This latter is the tool for self-diagnosis.

Clients are then asked to share the self-diagnosis indicated by their listing of symptoms. The circuit of the group usually indicates that the exercise has had a powerful effect, perhaps cumulatively with the preceding exercises in this chapter. More people self-assess as alcoholic, more see themselves as mid- and late-stage, and there is a more confident differentiation between those who see themselves as nonalcoholic and those who recognize a progressive disease process operating in their lives.

# Inheritance and Ethnicity

*This presentation consists of two related discussions, each taking about thirty minutes. It requires a blackboard or flipchart.*

**Rationale.** The younger drinkers, especially, may be more conscious of the existence of familial alcoholism than of their own incipient symptoms. Instead of using the comparison with a relative's gross, late-stage symptoms to convince themselves that they are not alcoholic, these drinkers begin to recognize through this presentation that they may well be following in precisely the footsteps they promised to avoid.

By the end of the discussion, each person in the group should be able at least to approximate roughly the lifelong odds of becoming alcoholic. Because clients do not feel responsible for their ethnic background and familial inheritance, this exercise is a relatively nonthreatening—yet interesting and powerful—way to get clients to estimate the personal likelihood of becoming alcoholic.

**Content.** About half of the alcoholics in the United States come from alcoholic families (Goodwin, 1985). They are likely to have several blood relatives who are alcoholic, to have developed symptoms earlier, and to progress to severe symptoms more quickly. Children who experience parental alcoholism directly may be sufficiently frightened that they abstain. But those who do drink are at particularly high risk for developing problems (Black, 1981). They are likely to develop psychological dependence as they use alcohol to medicate chronic feelings of low self-esteem. But even when they drink cautiously or imitate nonabusive models, their inherited vulnerability may lead them into the disease process (Cadoret, O'Gorman, Troughton, & Haywood, 1985; Cadoret, Troughton, & O'Gorman, 1987). Schuckit and Rayses (1979) discovered that even the moderate drinking sons of alcoholics break down alcohol in a different manner than do sons of nonalcoholics. Because they develop higher concentrations of the stimulant by-product, acetaldehyde, they are typically less drug-affected and more likely to develop tolerance.

A brief digression clarifies the various ways in which alcoholism develops. Not all alcoholism results from inheritance. Murray and Stabeman (1982) conclude that there is "a modest but significant genetic influence" (p. 142). Most people contract the disease "the old-fashioned way": they "earn it" through prolonged heavy drinking. Others lay the groundwork through involvement with more rapidly addicting sedative drugs, including prescription tranquilizers and narcotics (see chapter 6). A minority of the "instant alcoholics" may well have developed their addiction prior to birth, having been exposed to toxic amounts of alcohol by a heavy-drinking mother (see chapter 6).

I often compare alcoholic drinking with learning to high jump. Being able to clear the bar at five feet is analogous to contracting the disease. With enough practice, many people would eventually achieve the feat. Looking dubiously at my squat body and short legs, I sometimes question my potential—to the group's amusement. There is no doubt that the inherited ability makes the job easier, whether it is because of long legs or speed of foot. With the right combination of genetic attributes, very little practice will be required before high jumping five feet is routine. There is no doubt that some people are similarly equipped to become alcoholic.

Goodwin (1979) tried to identify the inherited risk, apart from the risk that goes with being raised by alcoholic parents, through studying identical twins. In each case, one son of an alcoholic parent was adopted early and raised in a nonalcoholic home, while the other continued to live in a heavy-drinking environment. The similar and high rates of alcoholism (40 percent were heavy drinkers by an average age of thirty) suggest that inheritance is a crucial contributor to the disease process. Sons of alcoholics are four times more likely to become alcoholic than are sons of nonalcoholics. This finding could not be applied to daughters, perhaps because it is typical for women to begin problem drinking in the third and fourth decades of life (NIAAA, 1981), too late for this study to catch the rise in their alcoholism rate.

To be conservative, and simple, I suggest that clients assume they have a 30 percent risk of becoming alcoholic if one parent has a drinking problem (Bohman, 1978; Goodwin, 1979). The risk rises to 50 percent, or five times baseline, if both parents are alcoholic. The mathematically minded are invited to interpolate—for example, there is a 40 percent risk if both father and one of mother's brothers show problems.

In group, two or three participants are invited to share their family trees. I start with the siblings, although I may add the caution that alcoholism may be underestimated for the current generation because it may not show up before age forty. I then list parents and aunts and uncles. If there is enough knowledge of family history, I am interested in grandparents and their siblings. I label each as "A" for alcoholic, "S" for the nonproblem social drinking pattern, "N" for nondrinkers, and "?" for those whose pattern is unknown. Clearly, "N" and "?" drinkers can carry the genetic vulnerability for alcoholism, even though they are not known to have developed the disease.

We then collaboratively estimate the risk, looking for alcoholism on both sides of the family and contrasting the total number of heavy drinkers among those listed with the 10 percent prevalence estimate for whole population. Different patterns emerge. Usually one volunteer has a family filled with alcoholic drinkers for generations, perhaps where every man develops the disease and every woman abstains. We then digress into talking about the expected role in the family as well as inherited risk. Others have little heavy drinking in the family tree and tend to feel the imperative to explain the (typically psychological) reasons why they drink or drug more heavily than did their predecessors. Others become aware that they know little about family drinking. This may be evidence of family denial. It is at least a prod to have them interview a relative about the family drinking history. Conversely, the factual sharing of family alcoholism by others can provide the first opportunity for some members to admit painfully suppressed information about drinking by relatives.

Each person is asked to estimate their odds, based on frequency of alcoholism in their family, relative to the 10 percent odds for the aggregated citizens of the United States. My clients usually run two to four times the usual risk.

This information is supplemented by the second means of analysis, a consideration of ethnic background. This presentation is borrowed from the influential work of James Milam (Milam, 1974; Milam & Ketcham 1981). It is admittedly theoretical but is important enough to deserve consideration by group members. Milam's contention is that the 10 percent odds are meaningless for individuals because of the wide variation in risk for different ethnic groups. While other environmental and cultural factors may be involved, much of the variability can be attributed to differences in susceptibility that are inherited.

Milam suggests that natural selection will gradually eliminate alcoholism from the population once society can provide regular access to enough alcohol for the disease to appear. All societies have fermented some alcoholic beverage, but many effectively restricted its use (for ceremonial purposes or celebrations). The longer the society has had routine access to alcohol, the lower the rates of alcoholism. For example, even though Italians drink more per capita than the French, they have had a much longer cultural exposure to alcohol and now suffer a much lower rate of alcoholism.

With participants suggesting ethnic groups, I complete the alcoholism risk and the length of contact with alcoholism. The epidemiological research remains muddled (Mulford, 1982), so the prevalence rates are subject to change. But the current best estimates are included in table 7–1.

Clients are then invited to use the modified baseline representing their

Table 7–1
**Ethnicity and the Inherited Risk of Alcoholism**

| Group | Risk | Length of Time with Routine Access | References |
|---|---|---|---|
| Orientals | Low | Long | NIAAA, 1985 |
| Greeks and Mediterraneans | Low | Long | Milam, 1974 |
| Jews | 1% | 7000 + | Milam & Ketcham, 1981 |
| Italians | 1% | 7000 + | Milan & Ketcham, 1981 |
| Middle and Northern Europeans | 10% | Moderate | Milam, 1974 |
| Blacks | 15–20% | Moderate | Bailey, Haberman, & Alksne, 1965; Barchha, Stewart, & Guze, 1968; Bourne & Light, 1979; Lex, 1985 |
| Hispanics | 20% | Short | Lex, 1985 |
| Irish | 30% | 1,500 | Milam, personal communication, October 29, 1982 |
| Indians | 80% | 300 | Milam, 1974 |

own ethnic heritage in calculating their personal risk. The Shenandoah Valley, where I work, was settled by successive migrations of Scotch-Irish and Germans. There is considerable Indian blood as well. The baseline rate for many of my clients is well above 10 percent.

When family data is combined with the ethnic predictors, a much more specific estimate is possible for each member. One client, the Irish/Indian descendant of a long chain of alcoholic drinkers correctly predicted he was almost certain to develop the disease: "My chance is 250 percent!" Others show little inherited vulnerability.

After each member estimates his or her risk, we conclude by discussing whether group members would to share this information with their children. Most would. The discussion drives home the point that the inherited vulnerability may be passed on even if clients were to quit drinking. I typically ask whether they would be comfortable having their child drink if there was a 25 percent likelihood of that child's developing alcoholism. Most would not. The cognitive dissonance is evident when I ask group members, many of whom have much higher odds, why they continue to drink.

**Variations.** This exercise often develops spontaneously and is delivered in condensed form (fifteen minutes) in response to questions about alcoholism as an inherited, physical disease. The discussion may be interrupted by extended discussion of clients' family of origin's attitudes and experiences with drinking. This often leads to follow-up discussion of the characteristics and treatment of children of alcoholics (see chapter 12). Alternatively, clients without high inherited potential often raise questions about the other ways one becomes alcoholic, which leads to discussion of fetal alcohol syndrome (chapter 6), cross-addiction (chapter 6), and psychological factors contributing to addiction (see the drinking progression discussion in this chapter and in the section, "Self-Esteem Trap" in chapter 11).

# The Controlled Drinking Test

*This discussion takes thirty minutes. It will be necessary to check in with the clients taking the "control test" for five minutes a session for the next four months.*

**Rationale.** There has been considerable controversy about whether alcoholics can resume asymptomatic drinking (Sobell & Sobell, 1973; Pendery, Maltzman, & West, 1982). Between 5 percent and 20 percent of patients treated in abstinence-oriented programs are found to be drinking without immediate problems at follow-up (Armor, Polich, & Stambul, 1978; Heather & Robertson, 1981; Miller & Hester, 1980). Programs designed explicitly to teach moderate drinking as a goal report success rates averaging 65 percent (Miller, 1983). There is an important controversy about the quality of the controlled drinking. For example, Vaillant (1983) argues that the apparent success is not because of successful moderation of intake but is a result of more sustained abstinence. When they do drink, the controlled drinkers are likely to consume heavily or to have to employ stringent external restrictions that limit intake at the cost of removing most of the potential pleasure from drinking. Moreover, profiles of those who do return to asymptomatic drinking suggest that they do not accept the disease concept or see themselves as alcoholic (Polich, Armor, & Braiker, 1981), that they have few problems from drinking, that they have been using heavily for a short time, and that the increased intake is a transient response to a traumatic loss (Vaillant, 1983). In sum, many of those who return to aymptomatic drinking would be better classified as nonaddicted alcohol abusers, the heavy drinkers from our discussion of the three types of drinkers (see chapter 6).

It is inappropriate to encourage abstinent alcoholics to resume drinking. Similarly, those who are clearly dependent on alcohol (those with middle- and late-stage symptoms) should set a goal of abstinence. But it would be naive and inappropriate to view abstinence as the only option for the less problematic drinkers who compose a significant proportion of the clients in an outpatient treatment program. To the extent that those who return to asymptomatic drinking can be identified, clients who resemble them and desire to learn to moderate their drinking should be given the opportunity to demonstrate that they can do so. This exercise has those two objectives: to identify those who have a prospect of learning asymptomatic drinking, and to set a realistic test of their ability to do so.

This experiment allows clients to determine their self-diagnosis behaviorally. A sincere attempt to control that fails will be much more convincing evidence of alcoholism than a discussion of loss of control or the results of a paper-and-pencil test. Those who succeed in temporary control will have first-hand experience with the discipline needed to continue to drink while avoiding recurrence of destructive habits. There are secondary goals related to the fact that the "control test" begins with a requirement of two months of abstinence. Clients are less likely to distort their self-diagnosis simply to preserve their drinking if they know that nonalcoholics hoping to continue drinking will have to achieve temporary abstinence. This break from drinking, with its proof positive that it is possible to quit, often provides the opportunity for a client to reconsider whether abstinence might not be a desired objective. The dry period also forces the drinker to face withdrawal, cravings, or other evidence that controlled drinking is not an option.

This is not a group exercise, but rather an individual assignment that may be appropriate for up to half of the clients. By undertaking the control test together, they can support one another and compare experiences, maximizing the learning. But abstainers and those for whom control is not a realistic goal should not be deluded into believing controlled drinking is an option for everyone in the group. The last thing they need is an additional rationalization ("I'm going to try to control it, like the doc told me to") to buttress their underlying desire to resume drinking. At times I have simply invited everyone who self-diagnoses as alcoholic to take a fifteen-minute break while controlled drinking is discussed with those who remain behind. More effectively, the discussion of control is preceded by a self-assessment step that indicates for whom it is *not* an option. Having been informed of the characteristics for whom controlled drinking is inappropriate, similar clients may be that much more aware of the need to aim for abstinence.

**Content.**

*Control Questions.* There is considerable agreement among researchers as to the characteristics of clients who may succeed in moderating their alcohol consumption. Clients can be asked to see if they meet the following eight criteria. If they fail more than three, they have poor prospects for changing their drinking and should seek to abstain. My experience indicates that only those who violate one or none have a good chance of succeeding, while those with two or three misses will have a continuing struggle to maintain asymptomatic drinking. The criteria are:

1. The person should be under forty years of age. Older drinkers do better with an abstinence goal, while younger drinkers may have less relapse if they aim to moderate their drinking (Miller, 1983; Polich, Armor, & Braiker, 1981).

2. The person should have fewer than five years of heavy or problem drinking (Vaillant, 1983; Vogler & Bartz, 1982). Others have suggested that ten years of high-tolerance drinking is acceptable (Miller, 1983; Polich, Armor, & Braiker, 1981). But if problems have been recurring for that long, there is likely to be alcoholism or insufficient problem-solving energy.

3. Evidence of physical dependence should be absent (Marlatt, 1983; Miller, 1983; Polich, Armor, & Braiker, 1981). Even minor withdrawal (see chapter 6) would be evidence that this condition has been violated.

4. Few life problems because of drinking should exist (Miller, 1983; Sobell & Sobell, 1982; Taylor, Helzer, & Robins, 1986; Vogler & Bartz 1982). Vaillant (1983) found that most of those who achieved moderation on their own had two or fewer life problems because of drinking. Any more than four, including the DWI, typifies those who need to abstain.

5. The person should have few alcoholic blood relatives. Although Vaillant (1983) found that this characteristic did not differentiate abstainers from controlled drinkers, the evidence for inherited vulnerability makes it unwise for alcoholism-prone individuals to continue drinking after developing premonitory symptoms such as the tolerance necessary for a drunk driving arrest.

6. The person should have made no prior attempts to moderate drinking. "The more the patient's history reveals past failures at controlled drinking, the more insistently clinicians should support a goal of abstinence rather than of reduced intake" (Vaillant, 1983, p. 225).

7. The person should have incentive to change drinking. Vaillant found that many who changed without treatment did so because of concern about an alcohol-related health problem or because the beginning of a new love relationship changed the pattern of socializing so as to remove the temptation to drink. The educational and motivational components of the treatment program may supply additional incentive. But success requires a clear and sustained commitment on the part of the client.

8. The person should be strong-willed (hardheaded, field independent, and so forth). Some clients readily acknowledge that they are impulsive or easily influenced by peers. These clients are unlikely to maintain any changes. Conversely, willfulness and counterdependence may now be assets for those intent on changing.

Once the criteria have been presented and discussed, most clients can readily identify their score. More important, they can recognize the rationale for the course of action indicated by that score. It is, however, important to emphasize that it is appropriate to decide on abstinence even if the control questions suggest that moderated drinking might be possible.

*Control Test.* There are risks in attempting controlled drinking. I have had clients rearrested during a slip sustained during the test. But the risk may be worthwhile for those who wish to demonstrate to themselves and to the counselor that they can drink in an asymptomatic fashion. They need to be reminded that the future drinking will differ from that of the past, in tone as well as in quantity. Because they will have to "keep their guard up," they can no longer engage in the carefree drinking of their favorite memories. They will need to make major changes in the circumstances and in the frequency of drinking. Bars and other "hot spots" will probably remain off limits. Consumption will have to be carefully observed and ritualized, as was the case with a woman who only drank three glasses of wine, once a week, with dinner, and when her boyfriend was present for support. If control fails, there must be a commitment to acknowledge the slip, openly and without rationalization, and to accept the need for abstinence as a goal.

The control test is then outlined. It consists of two parts. First, there must be two months of abstinence from all alcohol. This is to break the old pattern, to get used to handling former drinking situations without imbibing, to develop confidence in the ability to change, and to allow the body time to recover from the effects of prior drinking. Controlled drinking proponents concur in the need for preliminary abstinence, although Vogler and Bartz (1982) suggest only two weeks, and Marlatt (1983) requires one month. The longer period suggested allows the client time to register protracted withdrawal, to begin to experience the benefits of being dry, and to develop enough of a pattern of abstinence so as to be able to think through the decision about whether resumed drinking is truly desired. Some clients choose to continue abstinence once they have achieved it.

The second part of the test is for the client to resume drinking in a controlled fashion for an additional eight weeks. I suggest a fixed limit of two standard drinks for women and small men, or three drinks for larger men on any day during which they imbibe. This limit is low enough so that adverse consequences are unlikely (for example, there is little risk of rearrest for driving under the influence). Yet the limit is high enough to "tease" their control. After a period of abstinence, the clients will likely feel some effects from this quantity of alcohol. Clients routinely report that it is more difficult to stop after three than after one or two drinks. This level provides a test. While there is no requirement that this amount be consumed on each occasion, and while it is strongly suggested that these clients not drink every day, consuming this amount regularly without continuing is evidence of control. Any excess, even if the fourth drink is put down before it is finished, should be regarded as a slip. This rigid limit prevents any uncertainty or excuses.

This test is more rigorous than the trials of other clinicians. Vogler and Bartz (1982) require that clients achieve control within the two-month period, believing that any learning takes time and that initial failure need not indicate ultimate lack of success. This may be true for clients who voluntarily seek treatment. For the clients with whom I work, who are court-ordered into treatment, clear-cut evidence of motivation to change is needed.

There are, however, two safety valves that give clients a better chance of success in this test. First, I inform them of the difficulty and urge a week or more of consideration before the challenge is accepted. Clients often use this period of preparation to inform friends, to seek support, and to consolidate determination—reducing the risk of early failures. Second, a single slip is permitted. The suggestion is made that it should be used as an opportunity to learn rather than as proof of alcoholism. A slip should be handled by returning to the beginning and repeating the current stage of the test. If the slip occurs in the second week of abstinence, then the entire test should begin again; but if the slip happens in the fourth week of control, then only the eight weeks of limited drinking need be repeated.

Clients who succeed in the test have demonstrated the ability to change and have laid the groundwork for a new and healthier pattern of drinking. Clients who fail have engaged themselves in a powerful process of self-confrontation that is likely to result in fuller acceptance of the self-diagnosis of alcoholism and of the need for abstinence as a goal.

**Variations.** Controlled drinking, with the observation of preset limits for consumption, is a goal as well as a diagnostic test. It may profitably be continued into the next phase of problem solving.

This exercise may be presented outside of group, to an appropriate individual. I do this when the majority of the participants are clearly alcoholic or are poor candidates for controlled drinking. Outlining the test in private avoids the risk of validating the goal of resumed drinking for the remaining clients. Any appropriate person who desires to drink can be coached individually.

If controlled drinking is being pursued as an option, the leader has an obligation to follow through with education about techniques for achieving successful moderation (see chapter 10). This obligation must be fulfilled in private if it is inappropriate to present strategies for successful drinking to the group as a whole. Books such as Vogler and Bartz's *The Better Way to Drink* can be a great help to the client attempting controlled drinking.

*To the Counselor.* Some counselors reject the disease concept of alcoholism and try to make controlled drinkers out of all clients. This is clearly inappropriate. The criteria are evidence that even proponents of controlled drinking recognize as indicating that some clients must seek abstinence. There are other counselors, particularly if they are themselves recovering alcoholics, who reject even the prospect of resumed drinking by problem drinkers. This exercise will be seen as a challenge to their beliefs. It should be. Counselors whose experience is limited to the fully addicted cannot simply translate their techniques to an outpatient population. There is a need for different approaches, and alternative goals may be appropriate—including moderated drinking. Researchers have demonstrated that drinking is not represented by a simple dichotomy between social drinking and alcoholism. Drinking occurs on a continuum (Vaillant, 1983). The earlier exercise contrasting three types of drinkers is intended to introduce the idea that some high-tolerance drinkers need not be addicted. The present exercise is intended to build on that understanding, by supporting selected clients in modified drinking. This goal is well accepted in Europe and in other parts of the world. It remains controversial in the United States. Those counselors who are troubled by the prospect of controlled drinking are strongly urged to review some of the materials referenced in this section before beginning to work with outpatient alcohol abusers.

# 8
# Setting Goals

Once the problem has been identified, the solution must be determined. In this context, the goal is freedom from any negative consequences of drinking. This is not limited to avoiding drunk driving. By this point, clients must be committed to avoiding any of the potential problems that go with heavy drinking or drunkenness.

In practice, there must be a change in drinking: a reduction of consumption when using, a decreased frequency of drinking, or abstinence. The goal set should be appropriate to the diagnosis, as determined in the last chapter.

Goal setting is primarily a prescriptive process. Knowing details about the self-assessment, any rational and informed person would probably agree about the change needed to resolve the problem. Clients will be able to understand what they "should do."

But the rational goal is likely to remain at variance with the desire to continue past drinking practices. What the clients "want to do" may be very different from what they "should do." Zimberg (1978) observed that the typical progression for the alcoholic patient in therapy is from "I can't" drink because of external pressures, to "I won't" drink when there is conscious agreement with the goal of abstinence, to "I don't need to" drink when there is a working through of the psychological issues underlying the desire to use. Clients are often puzzled by the idea that they can quit while they still want to drink. In fact, there is a long period of recovery before most alcoholics are essentially free of cravings. Much like the ex-smoker who knows that the urge for a cigarette will last long after the last one is smoked, the goal of changed drinking can be set, even with the awareness that there are internal conflicts still to be resolved. Much work can and must be done before the desire to drink can be expected to disappear. The client has met the requirements of this stage when he or she is able to identify correctly what "I should do." The exercises in the next chapter will help to consolidate the motivation to act on the goal chosen here.

The desire to continue problem drinking comes from relying on alcohol for social and emotional well-being. The needs are appropriate, but alternative means of achieving them must be found if the unhealthy dependence on alcohol is to be stemmed. Clients are empowered when they recognize substitutes for the activities or paths to need-fulfillment that must be replaced. The concluding exercises in this chapter assist in identifying these needed life-style changes.

There are, then, two foci for goal setting. First, there is the need to identify the appropriate change in drinking to assure that there will be no more life problems because of personal alcohol use. Second, there must be specified goals for a change in life-style, so that the psychological dependence on alcohol is diminished. The activities in this chapter assist the client in setting both types of goals.

# Goal Setting

*The presentation can take as little as ten minutes. The role-play and resulting discussion may take an additional fifty to eighty minutes.*

**Rationale.** This exercise sets the appropriate goal for change in drinking for each type of drinker. If role-play is employed, a role reversal takes place in which the group assumes the counseling perspective and suggests the necessary objectives for change. Not only does this get the group actively involved in goal setting, but the specific suggestions form the basis for subsequently developed personal goals. The exercise also introduces the idea that a change in drinking may well involve altering other aspects of one's life-style.

**Content.** There are general goals for changes in drinking that are appropriate for each type of drinker. The social drinker has the greatest range of choices, while for the high-tolerance drinker and the alcoholic options are increasingly constricted. Figure 8–1 illustrates the global changes in alcohol use appropriate for each type of drinker. When asked, the group will readily identify that these changes are necessary for avoiding future intoxicated driving as well as other major life problems. The loss of control inherent in alcoholic drinking will assure periods of excessive consumption and impaired judgment that will eventually lead to further trouble. Likewise, a heavy drinker will remain at risk until new habits of controlled drinking become well established.

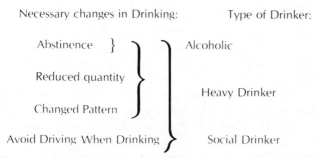

**Figure 8–1. Goals Appropriate for Different Types of Drinkers**

The changes are prescriptive. If the participant knows and accepts his or her diagnosis, then the global change goal is clear. The goal may not be what the participant hoped, but it will be seen as the rational choice.

The goals can be made more acceptable if the group has the opportunity to explain and defend them in the role-reversal situation that follows. The leader explains that the group is going to offer advice and counsel to an acquaintance who asks for help in handling a drinking problem. The counselor then develops a series of roles, describing different types of drinkers. As portrayed in the role-play, the person is concerned and responsive to the group, answering questions about drug and alcohol use openly and nondefensively sharing whatever life circumstances are pertinent. The roles are tailored to resemble those found among the group members, without being obvious or patronizing. Sample roles might include:

1. An addicted alcoholic, afraid of withdrawal symptoms if he abstains and worried about losing face in a managerial/sales job if he must miss work to get help

2. A young, heavy drinker who is probably not yet alcoholic, who is part of a hard-partying social group, but who has future goals (for a family and a better life) that are seen to be inconsistent with continued alcohol abuse

3. A late-thirties single parent with a new pattern of relief drinking in response to depression about a recent and unwanted divorce

Each role presents the group members with several challenges. They must clarify the diagnosis, presumably clarifying distinctions and consolidating self-assessment. They must set the appropriate goal for changes in drinking. If the discussion between members fails to result in a consensus about the appropriate goal, the leader (in role) can elaborate on the drinking problem enough so that the correct goal is endorsed by the group. This is a deliberate attempt to get participants to model effective goal setting. The group must identify treatment resources (such as AA or antabuse). Lastly, additional necessary changes must be specified. Depression must be addressed (through counseling, involvement in a singles group, and so forth); changing friends must be considered for the young drinker; or perhaps a heart-to-heart talk is needed with the boss for the salesman to seek support for inpatient rehabilitation. The group is typically able to get beyond the naive conviction that the drinking is changed through willpower while the rest of the life-style is unchanged. This recognition prepares the way for setting subgoals in later stages of problem solving (see the reframing exercise in this chapter).

The role-plays serve as stimulus for further discussion. If a group member appears to be identifying strongly, he or she can be invited to become the role-player. Remaining members continue to act as advisers. The exercise proceeds, having now become live group therapy. The client engages in goal setting, deriving the benefits of this assistance in problem solving, whether under the guise of role-playing or having directly acknowledged the personal concerns that motivated involvement in the discussion.

**Variations.** The preliminary discussion of appropriate goals for different types of drinkers is often presented by itself. It is useful if it is discussed repeatedly and early on in treatment. It will usually have been part of the discussion of strategies for avoiding drunk driving, for example. It is rare that some participant does not challenge a proposal to use a taxi when drunk: "Hell, when I was arrested, I had people offer to give me a ride home for free. I was too drunk to listen. The only way to avoid drunk driving is to quit getting drunk. For me, that means not taking the first drink." Such an opportunity to talk about global goals should be used, whenever it appears. Prior modeling such as this is what gives the leader confidence that appropriate goals will be suggested when this exercise is presented in the full format outlined in this exercise.

# Personal Problem Solving

*This presentation takes thirty minutes, followed by thirty minutes of individual writing and then by up to twenty minutes apiece over several weeks as the completed problem-solving sheets are reviewed. Copies of the worksheet, pens, and writing surfaces need to be provided.*

**Rationale.** Clients have been engaging in problem solving since before they began treatment. The midstage alcoholic's attempts to avoid drunkenness by switching to beer and the DWI offender's oft-repeated promise not to drive drunk again are examples of informal problem solving. Each client has implicit goals from the outset of counseling. They may be inadequately or only temporarily achieved because of an absence of working knowledge (the kinds covered in the preceding chapters)—but they are there. The first thing this exercise does is to capitalize on whatever the client is doing as an example of goal setting. Then, by applying the progressive and circular process of problem solving, the goals are eventually transformed into realistic and workable ones. No matter how completely the previous steps have been handled, this exercise pulls all the group members into goal setting.

Problem solving is a crucial skill. Though we all do it, few of us are conscious of how we apply the logic of the model. The absense of this awareness means that we often miss crucial steps or get stuck repeating unproductive strategies. For those clients with the capacity to self-observe, this exercise in problem solving provides training so that they can be more effective problem solvers long after they have left group. This is critical since drinking will remain a lifelong issue. An immediate objective of the exercise—to develop an appropriate goal and plans to handle the current drinking problem—is nested within the broader purpose of providing training in the logic of problem solving.

Lastly, the exercise lays out the organizing logic of the program. By explaining how various unrelated activities fit into the steps and by reminding clients of the changing attitudes and efforts that typified their involvement at different stages of the program, this exercise helps the clients organize their experience in the group. As we enter a stage where clients must show more initiative (as their recovery programs will become more individualized and the flow of the group will become correspondingly less definite), this orientation to problem solving helps them be more active partners in planning change.

**Content.** Each client is given a copy of the Problem Solving Worksheet, as shown in figure 8–2. All clients are asked to put their names and the date on the sheet.

Begin with illustrations of the fact that complex changes are made in stages. We would all laugh in disbelief if a judge simply accepted a plaintiff's promise that "I'll never do it again" and dismissed the DWI charges. We would assume that the judge had been conned. Why? Because we know that change requires more than good intentions. Change requires the stepwise mastery of skills. It is like learning to ride a bike. It is often too much to learn simultaneously to steer, pedal, and keep in balance. So we simplify the process by adding training wheels. With practice, steering and pedaling be-

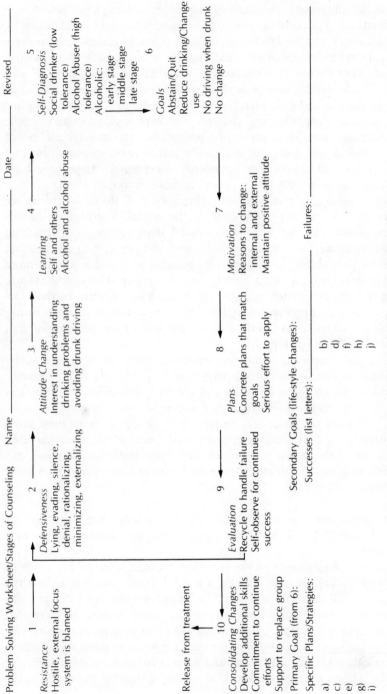

Problem Solving Worksheet/Stages of Counseling    Name _____    Date _____    Revised _____

**1**

*Resistance*
Hostile, external focus
system is blamed

**2**

*Defensiveness*
Lying, evading, silence,
denial, rationalizing,
minimizing, externalizing

**3**

*Attitude Change*
Interest in understanding
drinking problems and
avoiding drunk driving

**4**

*Learning*
Self and others
Alcohol and alcohol abuse

**5**

*Self-Diagnosis*
Social drinker (low
tolerance)
Alcohol Abuser (high
tolerance)
Alcoholic:
early stage
middle stage
late stage

**6**

*Goals*
Abstain/Quit
Reduce drinking/Change
use
No driving when drunk
No change

**7**

*Motivation*
Reasons to change:
internal and external
Maintain positive attitude

**8**

*Plans*
Concrete plans that match
goals
Serious effort to apply

**9**

*Evaluation*
Recycle to handle failure
Self-observe for continued
success

**10**

*Consolidating Changes*
Develop additional skills
Commitment to continue
efforts
Support to replace group

Release from treatment

Secondary Goals (life-style changes): _____

Successes (list letters): _____    Failures: _____

b)
d)
f)
h)
j)

Primary Goal (from 6): _____

Specific Plans/Strategies:

a)
c)
e)
g)
i)

**Figure 8–2. Personal Problem-Solving Worksheet**

come second nature. Then the training wheels are removed and the rider again feels overwhelmed by the challenge. But in time this step too is mastered. A new plateau is reached and with it a sense of competence. Then the rider is ready for new challenges, knowing that the temporary setbacks will be followed by increasing levels of skill. Balancing a friend on the handlebars, then learning to steer with no hands: each successive step is taken until the rider is truly proficient. Looking back, it is hard to conceive that something so overlearned and natural was once seen as an overwhelming task.

The process of dealing with the drinking problem is similar. There are discrete steps to be mastered, and there is the series of sequential challenges that lead through setbacks to greater confidence and accomplishment. Clients are invited to see if they can recognize having experienced the feelings typical at each stage of treatment. If that skill is resolved for the time being, clients can check off the corresponding step number, keeping a running tab on their progress. But they must remember that change is circular (for example, old defenses may recur as new challenges are faced). But, like the bike rider learning a higher level skill, clients can be increasingly confident that they will eventually overcome the obstacles if they continue with the problem-solving process.

The stages are reviewed. For example, the leader might introduce the first step by reminding them,

> Do you remember how angry you were about having to come here at first? You may have promised yourself that no one was going to force you to change. You may have believed that you were being picked on, that you were a victim of an unfair system. This is the initial resentment that is typical in the program. The problem is seen as being outside, in other people, and there is anger about having to come to group. It is hard to listen and harder to talk. Yet those are precisely the things that you saw others doing, and that you were asked to do in your first session. When you did, you had taken your first step toward attitude change.

There is often discussion, as clients recall their experience at earlier phases of problem solving and amplify the description or try to understand what appears to have been an atypical reaction. Clients should be drawn into a sense of the unfolding change process.

When the self-assessment step is reached, the clients are asked to circle the diagnosis that most closely fits their current understanding of their drinking problem (as listed in box 5). They then circle the goal for changed drinking in box 6, and detail it at the bottom of the page in the space provided for "Primary Goal." Under "Secondary Goals" are listed the major life-style changes that will be needed to make the desired change in drinking. After a minute has been provided for listing the goals, the client is asked to note whether the primary goal is consistent with the diagnosis. If not, then an exclamation mark needs to be put in front of box 6, to signify the need to recycle through the problem-solving steps to determine the basis of the lack of match (presumably in unresolved defenses or drinking attitudes). The remaining steps in the ten-stage change model are reviewed. Clients are asked to circle the box that represents the stage of problem solving to which they are currently devoting the most effort.

To this point, participants have been taught about problem solving, drawn into personally identifying with the process, and asked to set goals. I list on the board the additional tasks that they will be writing about in the next thirty minutes. These include:

1. Detailed and specific plans for accomplishing each goal (for example, "staying out of bars entirely" is a step toward the goal of "abstinence")

2. Additional plans. These would include changes that have been thought about but not yet intiated (for example, getting an AA sponsor). Because drinking problems are often minimized, there is a tendency to underestimate the effort that will be needed to make a lasting change. Possible or desirable additional plans should be listed, to be used to strengthen a program of change as needed

3. Prior steps in the problem-solving process that need review. Persistent defenses and difficulty accepting self-diagnosis are frequently listed. This serves as a reminder about the way in which problem-solving recycles until successful change is comfortable.

4. Anything that the counselor or the group can do to help the client make progress in problem solving. This is an opportunity to provide feedback, constructive criticism of the counselor, or to ask for individualized assistance.

Specific plans are written at the bottom of the worksheet. The remaining items are answered on the reverse side. During the time allotted for quiet writing, the counselor can assist any client with writing problems, questions, or requests for assistance in spelling out plans.

The learnings from the worksheets are then shared in the group. This can be as highly structured as asking each to state his or her goals or as individualized as asking participants to pair up and take turns reviewing one another's progress in problem solving. It is important that the worksheets be retained for periodic review and updating as each client progresses through the program.

**Variations.** While suitable at any stage of treatment, this exercise is usually reserved until a number of participants have progressed to the point at which appropriate goals and plans have been developed. This assures that there will be positive models of progress. These people are likely to gain the most from the review of problem solving as a rational basis for planning change.

In some such groups, I make a more detailed effort to review the use of problem solving in coping with any planned change. Ideas from Egan (1982; Egan & Cowan, 1979) and Carkhuff (1973b) are shared, in the more detailed manner covered in chapter 2.

The completed worksheet is a treasurehouse of information that should be used. Most often, I spend some time in each of the succeeding sessions reviewing the progress of individual participants, with the group providing a supportive critique of the goals and plans while the leader completes progress reports (see chapter 11). This is a time-consuming approach if each participant is given twenty minutes. It can become boring for the group. But the review can be alternated with relevant therapy work from succeeding exercises. For instance, a client who reports having to cope with unsupportive drinking buddies may be asked to role-play handling temptation and pressure from friends (chapter 10). The vicarious learning from another member's sharing can be invaluable to some clients. If time permits, this will be the preferred way to use the worksheet. Alternatives include processing the learning in pairs or triads, with participants giving one another feedback; reviewing the ideas in private sessions with the counselor; taking the worksheet home for review with family members; or simply ending the exercise with voluntary sharing of learnings.

Because problem solving is a progressive process, it is recommended that the worksheet be reviewed and updated at intervals of no more than three months.

Because the worksheet will lead to a written detailing of goals and plans, it can be used to form the basis of a contract. In one of its uses, the contract will identify the changes that the client will make and the consequences of failure. For example, a contract to avoid drinking when upset and to learn to moderate use may be backed up by a commitment on the part of the client to abstinence if the goals cannot be achieved within the next month. This exercise also offers an opportunity for the group to contract with the counselor to cover certain topics in the succeeding weeks. Many of the activities in chapters 10 through 12 are discretionary, and they can be selected to support the life-style changes most pertinent to each group. So the leader might offer a time management workshop to one group, assertiveness training to another, and a group trip to a local meeting of the Adult Children of Alcoholic Families (ACOA) fellowship for a third. As the treatment becomes increasingly individualized in the final stages of problem solving, the worksheet generated by this activity becomes indispensable as a statement of the goals for changes in drinking and in life-style that are being sought by each group member.

# Reframing: Finding Alternative Ways to Achieve the Positive Expectations from Drinking

**Rationale.** This section contains a set of four related activities that sharpen the distinction between sober and drunken states for the purpose of appreciating the positive contributions that come from drinking. The goal of this section is to assist clients in identifying the positive expectations and in discovering alternative ways to reach them so that the clients need not continue the previous pattern of drinking.

Clients seeking treatment because of any type of leverage may well not want to change. This matter has been addressed in chapters 3, 4, and 5. Even those who sincerely want to change are likely to have reservations about what will be lost when they alter their drinking. One client had the insight to say this directly: "I am willing to stop drinking if I have to, but then I won't be able to have fun." He had invested his drinking personality with the capacity for enjoyment, leaving his sober personality to be boring and deadly serious. Another client had achieved several years of abstinence before seeking treatment for a chronic subclinical depression. In therapy we discovered (more accurately, *recovered*) an enthusiastic, witty, sociable, and playful side of her that had been repressed. In abandoning her drinking, and with it her promiscuity and manipulations of the people around her, she had also buried many of her most positive qualities.

Not all resistance to change in drinking is based on pathological denial. What is being suggested is that much of what is seen as resistance to changed drinking is really an appropriate attempt to protect important aspects of the personality that have come to be associated with drinking. Those who are desperate enough to abstain will do so, but at the cost of incomplete recovery. Many others will cling to drinking, despite concern about the problems it causes, because that is the only way they know to express certain valued aspects of their personalities.

Goals for change should include discovering alternative ways to accomplish the good things that drinking does. These include facilitating positive experiences and qualities, as in the examples just given. Drinking may also be a way to avoid negative experiences, not the least of which is the felt loss of self-determination that would result from compliantly changing in response to family pressure to quit.

*Reframing* is the word used by Eriksonian hypnotherapists to describe techniques that help clients find positive meaning in negative experiences and behavior patterns (Bandler & Grinder, 1979; Citrenbaum, King, & Cohen, 1985; Grinder & Bandler, 1982). This emphasis on the positive undercuts resistance by allying the counselor with the clients' perspective. At this stage in treatment, it is a good corrective for the consistently negative focus on drinking that has typified the last three chapters. I am not apologizing for the negativism; it provides a necessary corrective for all of the brainwashing provided by advertising and heavy-drinking peers. But there is a need to acknowledge the good that has come from drinking. When the group is encouraged to share positive expectations from using alcohol, they tend to become active, to lower their defenses, and to relax with the counselor.

The key is to remember that acknowledging the positive is just the beginning of reframing. To stop with the good times would be tacitly to encourage continued alcohol abuse. The counselor must aid the clients in moving beyond this point to the recognition that there are other ways to achieve the positive outcomes sought through drinking. I often remind clients of the obvious joy of children at a birthday party. The capacity for uninhibited fun is within each of us. Only through long association of drinking and good times do people come to the common and unfortunate conclusion that they must use alcohol to access these feelings. An appropriate goal for problem solving is to find other avenues that are as immediate and effective as and are more healthy than reaching the positive expectations through drinking.

**Content.**

*Naming the Drinking Personality.* This exercise, developed by John Wallace (1978a), takes ten to fifteen minutes. It is a good vehicle for getting the group talking. It generaly helps clients sharpen the distinction between the sober and drinking aspects of their personality.

Clients are asked to come up with a name for their drinking personality. This may be a nickname that has been in use for years or it may be newly invented for the exercise. After a few moments, clients are asked to share their name and comment on how they feel about it. Other members are invited to respond, by interpreting the meaning they find in the name or by giving feedback as to their sense of its appropriateness.

The names are projective tests, a type of simple Rorschach inkblot. They can be interpreted. Some will hint at important aspects of the personality linked to drinking. "Friendly Sam," "The Mouth," and "Party Animal" are all loaded with meaning. Some may be negative ("Loser" or "The Fool"), while others seem more positive ("Lucky Ducky" and "Loverboy"). The positive names, in particular, can be discussed to ascertain whether these qualities are available when the person is sober. Those that are available only when that person is drinking will need to be subject to further problem solving so that new avenues other than drug use can be used to gain access to the positive characteristics.

*Sharing War Stories.* This common pastime of drinkers can be structured into a useful forty-five-to ninety minutes. The exercise is a good vehicle for heightening group trust and setting a climate of sharing.

Each person is asked to think back to the best time and then the worst time experienced while drinking. Someone is asked to volunteer a story. After the episode is recounted, the first volunteer designates the next person to share, and whether the rendition will be of a positive or a negative experience. While each has the right to pass, there is gentle pressure from the remainder of the group for each client to share something. The cycle continues until each has had the opportunity to tell both experiences. This process may be interrupted as a discussion develops around a particular story, or as one client uses prior sharing as a starting point for spontaneous self-disclosure.

The leader can generally give the group free rein and keep busy listing key words on the board in two columns entitled "Good Times" and "Bad Times." Be alert for clients who are unable (as distinct from unwilling) to recognize either good or bad experiences. This suggests that a major dissociation between the drinking and sober personalities has taken place, with a corresponding schism in available resources. It will be very difficult to alter or quit drinking if important attributes will be unavailable. For example, the overly compliant and generous person may need to be drunk to take an assertive stance. Other ways to be assertive must be found. It will be particularly difficult to do so if one pole is so unavailable that there are no memories of a good time or a bad time. In other words, it is not a good sign when participants can remember no good times; it is not a steadfast commitment to abstinence that is evident, but rather a submerged system of positive expectations that will reemerge and control behavior once a suitable drinking situation is encountered.

When the sharing has been concluded, the group is generally ready to comment on the two columns written on the board. The group readily concludes that drinking leads to both positive and negative feelings. Someone will often observe that the bad times seem less immediate, and so less powerful at the moment when drinking begins (hence the rationale for keeping a reminder such as the list of problems generated during the "Eight Areas" exercise from chapter 7).

This exercise generates heightened awareness of the positive expectations from drinking, without denying the bad times.

*Gestalt Dialogue.* Gestalt therapists (Perls, Hefferline & Goodman, 1951; Polster & Polster, 1973) have developed techniques to help clients recognize and integrate the useful potentials in different and segregated aspects of their personalities. Two chairs are placed in the center of the group. A volunteer works by conducting a dialogue between the sober personality (engaged when sitting in one chair) and the drinking personality (adopted when sitting in the other). Surprising amounts of awareness and emotion can be generated in the dialogue. The objective is to recognize the life-affirming qualities inherent in each of the personalities which can be mutually enhancing. The rational aspect of sobriety can be enriched by the emotionality that is natural for the drinking personality. Self-discipline and spontaneity, restraint and expressiveness, sensitivity and disinhibition are all commonly encountered polarities. Although these pairs of qualities may seem to be incompatible, the need for a balance between both poles comes to be recognized as the interaction continues. By encouraging the dialogue between polarities, the counselor helps the client move to integration (Passons, 1975). It is often adequate to have the sober personality respectfully ask for assistance in making appropriate use of the assets that are more associated with the drinking personality. If integration is not so easily attained, the client nonetheless benefits by becoming aware of a goal—namely, to develop the ability to use that skill without having to drink.

*Reframing.* This hypnotherapeutic technique can be used as an alternative or an extension of Gestalt counseling in gaining access to the assets available to the drinking personality. What follows is not hypnosis, nor is a trance necessary for the exercise to be beneficial. The entire group can work simultaneously, with the process taking about thirty minutes.

Participants are asked to relax, to close their eyes if that is comfortable, and to allow themselves to become aware of the part of the personality that is responsible for their drinking. The degree or nature of the experience that signals access to the drinking personality will be unique to each individual. One may experience nothing consciously, while another becomes aware of a sensation or an image. It is important to be appreciative of that part, because it is trying to accomplish something positive for the person's life. This appreciation will have been fostered by the use of any of the previous activities from this section. There may be aspects of the drinking personality, and certainly of drinking experiences, that will be seen as harmful. But it is important to become aware that this part has positive intentions for the person's well-being. The clients should internally ask that part how it has helped them to get something that they wanted or to avoid something that they feared. The part has remained operative because it has been in some way beneficial, at least in intent. An awareness of its goal may well help in attaining that goal.

The first objective of this exercise will have been accomplished if there is a conscious recognition of different gains from drinking. These may be unique, so the counselor should allow some time for awareness to register.

But there are some predictable payoffs (Citrenbaum, King, & Cohen, 1985). The counselor should continue by suggesting that the person can become aware if the positive intention behind drinking includes any of the following: relaxation or managing stress, relief from boredom, self-assertion (defiance, independence, resisting overcontrol by others), giving pleasure to oneself, having a reliable "friend" in the relationship with alcohol, avoiding feared intimacy, providing an excuse for acting out, belonging to a group, or imitating a loved one. The drinking personality should be thanked for sharing whatever comes to awareness.

Regardless of how much conscious recognition of the contribution of drinking occurs, it should be suggested that there is a creative part of the mind that may now be aware of many alternative and healthy ways to accomplish the intended benefits of drinking. That part may suggest alternatives. If any seem acceptable to the drinking personality, they can be checked out by all aspects of the person. Those that are likely to be immediately effective and those that are likely to carry lasting benefits for the person can become consciously available alternatives to drinking. After a pause here, the clients should then be asked to imagine themselves again in a drinking situation. Instead of taking a drink, they can become aware of which alternative behavior would accomplish what they needed. The clients can then imagine the alternative course of action and check whether it seems to work satisfactorily. If necessary, they can realize that their mind will repeat the process, working even when they are consciously distracted by other activities, until suitable alternative means are found to accomplish whatever are the positive intentions underlying their past drinking. They may want to end by appreciating their own inner wisdom and capacity for growth.

What has been taking place is unconscious problem solving. In some cases there will be a spontaneous recognition of alternative actions that are already available. ("There are many ways I can honor my father's memory without drinking as heavily as he did.") Often, there will be a recognition of skills that will need to be practiced before they are mastered. ("I can learn to dance without drinking first if I can keep reminding myself I don't have to be the best to enjoy myself.") Further problem solving may be necessary if complex skills and information must be mastered. ("I don't know what it will take, but I know I have got to do something about my marriage.") Many of the exercises outlined in chapters 10, 11, and 12 are opportunities to make further progress in mastering skills suggested by this exercise.

The exercise concludes with voluntary sharing by participants. The counselor ends with positive comments, including the suggestion that even those who were aware of little during the activity may well be surprised and pleased by the changes they experience.

These activities should leave the clients in a state of better rapport with their drinking personality. There will be greater recognition of what they sought to accomplish through prior alcohol use. Integration may take place in which resources from the drinking personality become more available when the person sober. Minimally, there will be a recognition that progress toward the goal of changing the pattern of alcohol use will be promoted by efforts to find alternative ways to realize the benefits sought through drinking.

**Variations** These activities can be used in whatever combination and number that seem useful to the group. More trusting and verbal groups may make better use of the Gestalt work, while the internal process of the reframing exercise may be more suited for quiet groups. I will often use war stories early in therapy as a way to encourage greater sharing. Only one of the exercises may be needed to achieve the minimal goal of this section: a clear recognition that alternatives must be found to achieve the positive outcomes associated with drinking. It is a bonus if the exercises go further and accomplish some integration so that the resources of the drinking personality are available when the person is sober. Should this not happen, the development of access to these resources becomes a specific goal for later problem solving.

Both the Gestalt empty chair technique and the reframing exercise are powerful tools. They can be used with reasonable safety as outlined. They are worthy of more development by counselors willing to study the effective approaches to change from which they derive. Gestalt therapy, neurolinguistic programming, and Ericksonian hypnosis have much to offer in treating alcohol problems. The counselor must be able to adopt the techniques and consider the underlying theory openly, since psychological models have much to offer—even to counselors who reject psychological theories of alcoholism.

# The Drinking Diary: Identifying High-Risk Situations

*This exercise is conducted over a three-week period, with clients keeping records between treatment sessions. Explanation of the procedure takes twenty minutes the first session, while review and sharing of results requires sixty minutes of the session two weeks later. A chalkboard will be needed for the presentation. Pocket-sized notepads may be distributed.*

**Rationale.** Goal setting includes assessment of life-style changes that must be made if drinking is to be reduced. The preceding reframing exercises contribute to this by identifying the meaning of alcohol in the abuser's life. Where drinking makes an important contribution, goal setting must specify satisfying alternative means of achieving the same end. But not all drinking has an identifiable purpose. Much of it is simply habitual, a routine acquired by prolonged repetition. Goal setting must identify the contexts that elicit this habitual drinking so that such situations can be avoided or handled with new techniques for coping. The following exercise aids in the identification of high-risk situations for resumed or uncontrolled imbibing.

After years of drinking experience, alcohol abusers develop expectations about the situations in which they will drink and about the subjective effects of alcohol when it is used in these contexts. There will be a conditioned response, like the salivation of Pavlov's dogs in response to the signal bell, which elicits an automatic sequence of behavior. So meeting an old drinking buddy at a bar leads to heavy drinking despite intentions to order soft drinks. There is a directionality (toward alcohol), an impetus (urges), and a sense of powerlessness ("it just happened") that invalidates intentions to change ("I really didn't plan to drink"). Such contexts need to be identified so that the drinker can be forewarned. These situations may include certain times (after work, when watching TV sports, payday, Friday night), certain settings (bars, meetings with specific friends or relatives), or certain emotional states (frustration and anger, boredom, or celebratory moods). The situations will be unique to each individual. So assessment must be individualized. The situations will not necessarily be consciously recognized. So retrospective analysis will be incompletely effective.

The drinking diary is an individualized, real life technique to help drinkers identify the situations in which abuse is a particular risk. Such situations can then be avoided or encountered with clear incentives and plans to avoid excessive drinking.

The drinking diary provides a means of keeping a record of consumption. For some clients, self-monitoring leads to reduced intake. Charting the decline in alcohol used over the weeks may be reinforcing: the client's pride in his or her ability to change may motivate continued efforts.

**Content.** There is ready agreement about the power of old habits. Usually the group can easily identify a number of situations in which there is a high risk of excessive drinking. This sharing may provide an adequate data base for brainstorming coping strategies, in which case one of the variations below can be used.

If individualized record keeping is indicated, there are three different records that may be explained to the group. Complete written accounts of all alcohol use must be kept for the following two weeks. To facilitate timely data entry, it is generally advisable to have clients carry a pocket-sized notepad in which to keep their drinking diary. The records may be kept private if this is necessary for candor. For those who continue to drink at this stage in treatment, the following data should be logged as a summary of each drinking occasion (Marlatt & Gordon, 1985):

1. Time: day of the week, time drinking began, and time drinking ended
2. Setting: people present (specific friends) and place of drinking
3. Mood: feelings or thoughts at the time drinking began; any significant events preceding drinking
4. Amount: the number of standard drinks consumed
5. Consequences: reactions by others, feelings after drinking, noteworthy actions or behaviors

For those who are attempting controlled drinking, a somewhat more detailed version must be kept. The additional goal for these clients is to record reactions after each drink consumed (Vogler & Bartz, 1982):

1. Time: day of the week, then the time each drink is ordered, the time each drink is finished
2. Setting: as above
3. Reason for drinking
4. Mood: feelings and thoughts after each drink (preferably twenty minutes after consumption, when the full effects have been experienced)
5. Consumption: type of drink, amount of drink, estimated blood alcohol content (BAC)
6. Consequences: as above

For those who are abstaining, the focus is to be aware of urges and cravings. These reactions should be presented as temporary responses to the presence of old cues for drinking. As such, they provide significant clues about the feelings, thoughts, and environmental events that correspond to a high risk of relapse. Clients are asked to label and record urges attentively, noting down the following:

1. Time: day of the week, time urge first noticed, duration of urge
2. Setting: as above
3. Mood: feelings or thoughts when the urge was first noted, any significant prior events
4. Intensity of Urge: 1 (passing thought), 2 (definite temptation), 3 (overwhelming desire), or 4 (irresistable, did drink)

5. Actions: what was done to handle the urge; if drinking, amount and duration

Examples can be provided so that drinkers selecting each approach to record keeping are clear about how to use the diary. Commitments to keep records should be solicited. (It is a clinical decision about how to handle those who may decline or fail to follow through).

During the following session, any troubles with record keeping can be covered. The group can be shown how to translate the data into a bar graph of the total amount of alcohol consumed. This voluntary additional task may be motivating to those who want to keep a continuing drinking diary and record of progress. Figure 8–3 records a sample drinking diary and the corresponding bar graph.

Another week later, the results should be discussed. Clients should review their diaries, searching for patterns of association between using and situational elements, checking whether expected "hot spots" were indeed associated with increased consumption, and noting any unexpected patterns that emerge. Records can be reviewed individually with the counselor or in client pairs. More typically, a circuit of the group is made, with each in turn sharing any significant learnings. The exercise ends when there is a clear detailing of times, settings, and emotional states associated with urges or heavy drinking.

**Variations.** For periodic drinkers, the suggested two-week sampling may be inadequate. The drinking diary can be maintained for longer periods. In fact, self-monitoring is an effective tool that may be incorporated into the treatment plans of clients who feel it would be helpful.

If time does not allow keeping a running diary there are alternative activities that can cover the same material. The most direct is to ask those with a history of unsuccessful control or abstinence to describe the situations that led to relapse. Related to this would be to have all members project into the future and imagine the greatest realistic challenge to the type of drinking they have set as a goal. The challenge might be a reunion with a friend last seen during heavy drinking days, or it might be an argument with a spouse. These imagined tests can then be shared and compared. Lastly, research on factors contributing to relapse can be discussed (see the discussion of relapse in chapter 10 for a summary of the factors). Clients can then identify those most likely to pose a challenge for each of them.

The identification of high-risk situations leads naturally into a discussion of how best to handle each of them. Marlatt and Gordon (1985) formalize this by listing the high-risk situations as they are shared, having the clients

| Time | | Setting | Mood | Amount | Consequences |
|---|---|---|---|---|---|
| Thurs. | 5:10–6:30 | Ride from work, Steve drinking | Tired | 5 beers | None |
| Fri. | 5:10–6:30 | " | Good | 6 beers | None |
| | 8:30–1:00 | Bar with friends | Good | 8 mixed dks | Too much $ |
| Sat. | 3:00–5:00 | Alone, watching basketball on TV | OK | 3 beers | None |
| | 8:00–1:00 | Poker, at Steve's | Fun | 12 beers | Hangover |
| Sun. | 1:00–4:00 | Girlfriend's | Good | 4 drinks | None |
| Mon. | 5:00–6:30 | Ride from work | Tired | 4 beers | None |
| Tues. | 5:00–6:30 | Ride from work | OK | 3 beers | None |
| Wed. | 5:00–6:30 | Ride from work | OK | 1 beer | Steve teased about class |

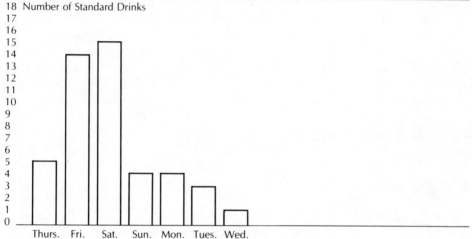

*Note:* Socially influenced weekend abuse is shown. Plans would focus on alternatives for the ride home from work (for example, supply of soft drinks), possible confrontation of Steve or other ride arrangements, and alternative activities for weekend evenings.

**Figure 8–3. Sample of a Hypothetical Drinking Diary**

vote, and then role-playing those identified as the greatest threats. Specific exercises from the planning phase of problem solving (chapter 10) may well be appropriate as a follow-up.

# 9
# Motivation

If you always do what you've always done, you'll always get what you've always gotten.

**M**ost problem-solving models assume that we are intrinsically motivated to pursue the goals we set. But there is considerable resistance to facing drinking problems. Persistent defenses are evident in the conviction that "I really don't have a drinking problem," or that "all I have to do is avoid driving when I've been drinking." There is often an unconscious bargain being struck (with God? with the disease?) when the goal fails to jibe with the self-diagnosis, as when the alcoholic attempts once again to control his drinking. Such outdated attitudes give warning that the previous problem-solving steps have not had the desired effect. The motivation stage may correct these self-defeating assumptions, but only inadvertently. The client will be better served if he is confronted with his failure at a previous step and his need to recycle through the problem-solving process.

The motivation phase is intended to overcome those impediments to effective action that naturally surface when we face a needed but feared change. Most DWI offenders dearly love to drink. Seldom are the problems so frequent or so overwhelming that they truly *want* to change. Education may put them in a position from which they can clearly see that they should change. But that is still a big step away from a sincere desire to alter their patterns of use permanently. Rogers and McMillin (1984) find that physical health problems are the most compelling motivators for their inpatient clients. But only a minority of those I have treated after a DWI arrest recognize any health consequence from imbibing. The typical DWI offender is less likely to be face to face with the problems caused by his or her drinking pattern than those who have admitted themselves to a hospital. Because he or she does not really want to change, the outpatient client may have a greater need for motivators than does the inpatient.

There are other predictable deterrents to implementing realistic plans for changing one's drinking. There is a high probability that pain must be faced before the benefits appear. As one client put it: "It was nice to stop running from problems; but when I did, all the shit caught up with me." The resentful wife now has her partner sober enough finally to hear her litany of complaints. Drinking buddies will tempt or ostracize the client, who deeply fears being isolated. Most clearly, the alcoholic may finally have to face the nausea, irritability, and sleeplessness of minor withdrawal—or worse. Few of us are willing to tolerate immediate pain if the payoffs seem uncertain or months away. Change is also intimidating when it seems, or is in fact, an all-or-none proposition. No wonder the alcoholic wants to try controlled drinking. There is no gradual "shaping of behavior" (as the behaviorists put it) when you quit cold turkey. So it would be naive to expect enthusiasm about forthcoming changes in drinking.

The motivation step has a more limited goal: to get the client to comply with treatment. It may be months or years before the drinker is fully convinced that the change is truly for the better. In the interim, he or she must be willing to follow the program. The motivation step seeks to move the problem drinker from "I should act" to "I will act," and from a commitment to making whatever change is convenient to one based on doing "whatever is necessary." Feelings of hopefulness and enthusiasm may accompany this decision, but they are not necessary. What is necessary is determination, based on the recognition that the drinker cannot continue drinking the way he used to.

This motivation may already exist from the outset of treatment, especially if there has been a prior DWI arrest or a serious accident. It is called *internal motivation* when the client is clear that he or she has made the choice. If that is missing, it is the counselor's responsibility to mobilize the client's will to change. Either external or internal motivation will suffice at the outset, although internal motivation is probably necessary to maintain changes. *External motivation* refers to consequences administered by someone on the outside, such as the spouse who rewards a change in drinking by agreeing to end a separation, the judge who threatens to impose a jail sentence, or the counselor who will drop an uncooperative client from treatment. Of course anyone can assert independence and still avoid trouble by convincing the other person that he or she is obedient, whether or not change really has been made. Drinkers hide bottles from spouses, make promises to judges, and lie to counselors and probation officers. The problem with external motivation is that it lasts only as long as the consequences are administered. Problem drinkers may resume their alcohol abuse once their probation is over. At some point the commitment must become internal if change is to last.

But the KITA (for "kick in the ass"; Herzberg, 1968) technique is excellent for getting some initial movement. The counselor may act as the heavy who "spits in the drink," spoiling it by meaningfully threatening painful consequences. I have had clients swear that they have seen my face in the head on a beer—and I don't think they were hallucinating. A clear form of external motivation is for the counselor to use the real power he or she has over a court-referred client to set explicit and nonnegotiable expectations for change.

**Creating Internal Motivation.** At the core of creating internal motivation is the counselor's ability to heighten the drinkers' awareness of past risks and costs, or of future goals. In this approach, the goal is to have the clients internalize new attitudes about drinking. Motivation is heightened by showing the inconsistency between the clients' drinking and their own values and aspirations. In time, the experience of how life improves when abusive drinking is eliminated becomes the greatest motivator of all. Some sober alcoholics would never resume drinking, even if promised that there was a cure that would protect them from any alcohol-related problems. Not drinking has become a part of their values. Internal motivation must be the basis of compliance with the recovery program if the clients are to maintain gains after leaving treatment. Internal motivation is also an important ingredient in initial attempts to change. The clients must have some clear stake, some clear sense that life will be better because they have altered their drinking, if they are to resist the temptation to run a con job. The exercises used at this stage mobilize the client to make a sincere effort to change his or her drinking.

Developing motivation is an art and a testament to the counselor's skill and sensitivity. Different approaches work for different clients. So the first rule is to be flexible. Nowhere else is that as necessary as when making the switch from limit setting to the supportive exploration of the client's experience, which can lead to internal motivation. The counselor must blend firmness with recognition that lasting change is the client's responsibility and that responsibility may be accepted only after painful failures.

The art of counseling—to provide impetus without preempting responsibility—requires that the helper maintain the balance so that his or her own identity does not get lost in roles or depend on the client's success.

The counselor must take the stand that change is necessary. Part of the power that the counselor has with the court-referred client is to set clear requirements for altered drinking patterns if the client is to complete the program. This can be done without apology and without becoming punitive.

The counselor must be comfortable with power. If he or she is not, there will be a tendency to retreat into a posture of "it's your life; do what you want." This is an echo of the message repeatedly sent by the tired coalcoholic. Any self-respecting drinker will see this (accurately) as an invitation to continue on as usual. We tend to become passive if we are afraid of our authority, or if we want our clients universally to approve of us and like us. These are irrational, unrealistic assumptions (Ellis & Harper, 1975). We do have power because of our role, and clients will routinely resent us for this reason if for no other. If we deny it, we set up this predictable progression:

sensing the counselor's abdication, the clients will become overtly defiant; the counselor will take it until thoroughly angered and will then precipitously use power to punish the clients. Clients will be resistant—and this does not mean they are bad people. The counselor who needs to become angry to be assertive runs the risk of being misread by the client and of becoming aggressive (see some of the good sourcebooks on assertiveness, such as Alberti & Emmons, 1986 or Lange & Jakubowski, 1976). Especially those counselors with a background in nondirective or psychodynamic therapies may need to reevaluate their passivity if they are to be effective with drug-abusing clients.

This need not imply that the counselor is hard. Confrontation is most effective if it is not the primary operating style of the counselor (Egan, 1976). The right to confront is earned through consistently demonstrated concern, empathy, and respect for the client. I find that I can best keep my balance if I acknowledge the power I have vis-à-vis the client without losing the ability to laugh at myself or to learn from my groups. My experience shows me that if I persist in setting clear and consistent limits, clients come to respect me. Then I can help them change. If we succeed, then they become very grateful, and I feel both appreciated and effective. Moreover, clear limits become incorporated in the norms of the treatment group, similarly empowering the group members to give effective feedback.

Internal motivation comes from many different places, most of them outside of group. A doctor's warning about deteriorating health or a near-accident after a resumption of intoxicated driving—either may trigger sincere effort. I try to keep empathically attuned, so that I can hear those experiences. I then remind the client of his own reasons for change while working this problem-solving step.

Some clients will not develop internal motivation. I do not expect much of it early in treatment. If I have time, I will be patient, build trust, and watch for the motivation to develop as the defenses lessen and education proceeds. But there are times when the only motivation evident, even at the end of treatment, is the external pressures added by the court sentence or treatment. I recognize that these clients are not likely to succeed in avoiding future drinking problems. I can at least avoid stigmatizing or condemning them for their failure to learn. To maintain my balance here, I remember that I am not responsible for them. I am not able to be a rescuer, so I won't waste the energy trying. Some clients are very hardheaded (I certainly tell them this). Alcohol abuse is a very powerful teacher, and it will eventually kill them or help them become motivated to change (I share this with them as well). My responsibility is to teach them what they can learn and to convey the interest and power to help them should they become ready to change. If they are not ready, I can accept their failure and still feel all right about myself. In turn, this helps me feel all right about my clients, even those who are trying to con me (and even those who succeed).

Because motivation is so variable in amount and in kind, I must be flexible in my approach with each client. The blend of internal and external motivators used is individualized. This is part of the variety that makes counseling interesting; the flexibility and inventiveness it requires of the therapist is one of the payoffs of this type of work. I think back to working with a late-stage alcoholic who didn't feel he could possibly get sober. Looking for incentive, he asked if I wanted to bet him whether he could stay straight for six weeks. I didn't. (He wouldn't have paid if he had failed, and if he succeeded I wouldn't have wanted to be quite *that* involved in his decision.) But I was able to reframe it so that he bet himself the money. He wrote a check, made out to his probation officer. He cringed at the thought that he might be giving more money to the court system. Conversely, if he abstained he would get to spend it on himself. He really began to work. He attended AA for the first time and became a regular. I was very pleased about my cleverness when he came to fetch his check, looking sober and proud. He must have been sincerely concerned about me, because he made a point of deflating my ego by telling me how much more helpful AA had been to him than I ever was. The cost of success . . .

**Similar Concepts and Exercises.** In its emphasis on personal responsibility to choose, this section resembles the attitude change step. The earlier discussion "Fear versus Respect" for the law can be reviewed and broadened. It now becomes a question of compliance out of fear of punishment as opposed to desire to change from understanding the total impact of alcohol on one's current life and goals. During the attitude change step the responsibility was to learn. Now it is to change. If this shift is made, the exercises from the earlier step can be powerful motivators.

The motivation stage is used to galvanize the drinker into action. But efforts to change are ongoing, beginning at different points in the program for each individual, depending in part on each one's preexisting motivation. In a very real sense, everything that happens in the group can heighten the clients' willingness to work. The counselor's goal is to use everything to enhance motivation.

The ongoing group process is perhaps the most powerful source of motivation. Testimonials from veterans about the improvements in their lives offer powerful models for novices. The sincere concern of a new member, chastened perhaps by the accident that led to his arrest, reminds the group that the motivation to change is already present in their own lives. The most powerful, and most unpredictable, incentive to change comes from the periodic crises brought on by continued drinking. Recently a young man, who sincerely promised himself that he would quit driving if he was drinking at all, painfully admitted to the group that the very next weekend he had a blackout and awoke to find that he had driven to a friend's house to sleep. He had not been rearrested; but he had clearly "gotten caught" in his failure to keep his promise to himself. Such sharing is moving to everyone. The sympathetic concern that arises in the group is based on the spoken or unspoken recognition that the same thing could happen to anyone who is not in control of his or her drinking. Effective treatment capitalizes on such factors, letting the testimonial or group discussion take precedence over whatever exercise has been planned.

# Criteria for Successful Compliance: Clarifying the Minimal Expectations

*This discussion takes thirty minutes.*

**Rationale.** This is the statement of the minimal expectations of the program. It supplies the rationale for the external pressure to change. Because it compromises the clients' sense of freedom, it is likely to surface old resistances. The group process can then be observed. If the group as a whole becomes defensive, this is evidence of the need to recycle to the early stages of problem solving. If the class can accept the rationale given, then the group can be used to support those clients who are later confronted without danger that the group norms will undercut the leverage to change. The presentation of the minimal criteria for successful compliance is a useful prelude to the subsequent confrontation of individual members.

**Content.** After going through the process of determining the type of drinker and the appropriate change for each participant, each member needs at least a trial period of changing to match the goal. For those seeking controlled drinking, this will include a preliminary period of abstinence followed by limited drinking. For those who realize that they need to quit using, it would be foolish not to achieve abstinence while in the supportive environment of the group. At some point during treatment, clients must make a sustained and successful effort to change. "I should" must become "I will" and then "I have" changed.

The program with which I work has a specified purpose: to get the drunk driver off the road. A variety of approaches have been tried in attempting to achieve this goal. As someone in the group will confirm, the policeman's friendly warning to "go home and sleep it off" was never very effective at curtailing drunk driving. More effective are attempts to get the drunk off the highway. The most powerful intervention is to imprison those convicted of DWI. But there are several drawbacks. In addition to the tremendous disruption in the life of the offender, imprisonment is tremendously expensive. Moreover, it works only temporarily. After release, the vast majority go back to drinking and eventually to driving. The most effective solution is to lift the license of the drunk driver (Hagen, 1985; Hagen, Williams, McConnell, & Fleming, 1978; Salsberg & Klingberg, 1981; Waller, 1983). This will immediately reduce the risks, although at a tremendous cost to the offender, who must adjust to life without what has come to be a basic necessity for most people—the driver's license. These approaches make sure the drunk is not a driver.

The third option, and the one underlying the current treatment, has as its goal assuring that the driver is not drunk. Through education and treatment the drinker comes to understand and commit him- or herself to the necessary changes in drinking so that there will be no further drunk driving. Like any change, it means leaving behind something that is familiar, which may be hard. Many clients do not *want* to change but do so because they know they *must* to avoid future troubles. This program is not perfectly effective, and so the change in drinking will not last unless the drinker eventually adopts the goals as his or her own. But the program can at least provide the impetus for temporary change: the chance to experience freedom from the old pattern of drinking. Many who were afraid to change or were skeptical of the need to do so have been pleased to discover that they liked the change once it was achieved. The goal of problem solving is that change will be made and in a manner that the client comes to appreciate.

Progress in the program involves change. Unlike a jail sentence, it is not simply a matter of putting in time. When the counselor releases a client, he or she is pledging to the judge the belief that the client has changed—that there can be reasonable confidence that there will be no more drinking and driving. I will not release anyone as compliant, I will not put my name and reputation on the line, until I have clear evidence that he or she has successfully changed.

What if the attempts to change are unsuccessful? Additional treatment is available for those who want to change: inpatient rehabilitation, antabuse therapy, vocational or personal counseling. If the outpatient group is not enough, more resources will be used. What if there is no willingness to change? Although early resistance is typical, lasting refusal to make adequate change means that the program will be ineffective for that person. Once it becomes clear that the person will not change, then it is the counselor's duty not to waste the program's resources or the client's time and money. The client will be returned to the case officer as noncompliant and will then go back before the judge for sentencing.

In the jurisdiction in which I work, sentences are suspended pending successful completion of counseling. The client has not "beaten the rap" by signing up for treatment. Only after release from treatment are the consequences dropped. Those suspended sentences usually include loss of license and some jail time. Any client who is unwilling to attempt to reach the goals appropriate to resolving the drinking problem can go back to the judge for sentencing. It is the judge who is charged with deciding the consequences. The counselor has a different role: to indicate when the necessary changes in drinking have been made.

Compliant (or successful) release from treatment occurs when the goals are attained. No one will be forced to stay beyond the assigned treatment interval. However, if the change has not been made, the resulting report will be negative. The judge will have to decide whether the effort was adequate; he or she may impose the suspended sentence. Instead of facing the judge, some clients choose to remain in the program until the change is adequate, even though this may mean extending the time of treatment. (My clients are not charged for modest extensions of group involvement, which avoids any appearance that money is behind the decision to retain clients.) Conversely, some clients will be released before the contracted time limit. This will happen because they have met the goals for change and have developed a sufficiently strong system of support and incentive so that it appears likely that they will sustain the change after leaving group. Often this happens with those who have the most severe drinking problems. For them, the goals are clear and the incentive may be the strongest. So length of stay in the program is less related to the severity of the drinking problem and is more a function of speed and effectiveness in meeting the goals for change.

These ideas are discussed until the leader is confident that they are understood. There will likely be some complaints that the limits are unfair. There may be a return to the argument that a person can avoid drinking and driving without making changes in the drinking. The leader should certainly continue to clarify the minimal expectations. But avoid getting into an argument or being maneuvered into the "persecutor" role (see chapter 4). The goal of this exercise is to set clear limits.

**Variations.** Sometimes the minimal expectations for individual clients are spelled out in group. Those aiming to control will be expected to have demonstrated the ability to avoid alcohol by having not fewer than eight weeks of continuous abstinence and eight weeks of successful control since the arrest. Those whose goal should be to stop drinking must have eight weeks of abstinence before being considered potentially compliant. My preference, however, is to set individualized requirements for change in private consultation with the client. In some cases this has included such steps as stopping by the office four times a week to take antabuse in front of a witness. Others have been required to get physical or psychiatric evaluations if concurrent problems are limiting their progress. Some are faced with a requirement of inpatient treatment, particularly if their inability to change their drinking is evident in rearrest, repeated alcohol-related problems, or coming to sessions under the influence. In other cases, there may be unique situations that lead to extending or shortening the period of successful goal attainment. There will be less confusion in these instances if the specific goals are set in consultation with the individual client rather than with the group as a whole. The goal of the activity is to indicate that there are expectations for change, not to specify what those expectations will be in each case.

This exercise stirs up latent resentment. Generally, it is advisable to hear out any complaints and then allow clients to think it over for a week. Typically, by the next session, there will be more acceptance. If hostility or defensiveness persist or generalize throughout the group, one should return to the first three steps of problem solving. Most often this will include exercises reviewing the individual and group attitude, and discussions of necessary changes to avoid future drunk driving (chapter 5). This review should help the group accept the need to change drinking as a necessary precondition for lasting avoidance of any alcohol-related problems.

# Testimonials

*Less an exercise than an attempt to influence or capitalize on group process, this discussion can last from ten minutes to the duration of a session.*

**Rationale.** Influence is more powerful when it comes from respected peers than from a formal authority such as the leader. Group members can become highly motivated to change in response to modeling of attitudes by participants who have internalized the program goals and put them into operation in their own lives. Clients who have achieved successful change are in a position knowingly to describe the differences. They can effectively model hope, gratitude for help, positive feelings about self and the world, and confirmation of the idea that the quality of life generally improves when a drinking problem is resolved. Their sharing helps to establish group norms conducive to change. This exercise seeks to elicit such sharing or to use it when it naturally occurs as part of the group process.

**Content.** Testimonials often occur spontaneously. Perhaps a client, listening to another's problems or poor attitude, comments that he would once have identified but now realizes he has changed. Statements about altered drinking patterns are linked to comments about how much better life has become. As the theme is developed, perhaps in response to questions from the leader or from the group, the client encourages others to change. In such instances, the leader should be as passive as possible—to avoid contaminating the process with any appearance of an "official endorsement"—and yet continue the discussion for as long as the group remains interested. Stimulus questions include: In what ways does life seem different? How have your self-confidence and self-esteem changed? Is there any difference in attitude? Why not go back to the old way of drinking? It may also be useful to backtrack and ask about the decisive elements that motivated the effort to change.

Testimonials can often be prompted. Most directly, those who have maintained abstinence or controlled drinking for three or more months can be asked to contrast their current experience with the quality of life while abusing alcohol. Other opportunities are afforded when a successful client is released from treatment or can be given a progress report (see chapter 11). The leader can initiate the discussion by asking; how is life different now that you are no longer drinking (or drinking heavily)?

Such sharing sets a generally positive tone. It empowers those listening by imparting practical suggestions and by instilling hope (Yalom, 1985). Because change and recovery will be a challenging and incomplete process, there will almost certainly be comments about the downside risks. These will include regrets, frustrations, and continuing temptations. If there is an invitation, the group can help in problem solving aimed at supporting continued growth. But generally, the more negative comments simply confirm that change is hard work. The group benefits by having been "innoculated," and the person sharing is given extra respect for the success to date. The challenges are the backdrop against which determination and accomplishment stand out in contrast.

The 1977 movie *Hollywood and Vine* is a pastiche of clippings from interviews with the celebrities among the first to go public with their addiction and recovery. Dick Van Dyke, Gary Lee Crosby, and Mitchell Ryan are among those who share their experiences. The movie follows the chronology of their developing abuse with successive comments about early drinking, type and extent of problems, hitting bottom, and life in recovery. A very upbeat tone is created by ending with recovery. Images of horseback riding and boating offer a compelling contrast with stories of previous troubles. Recovery becomes a very tangible and attractive prospect.

Clients are urged to retain one or two images or comments that they find moving. These impressions are then shared. Because the movie covers the chronology of the drinking career, some comments about problems are likely. There is usually either an element of identification or a commitment not to get "that bad." Either can motivate change out of a desire to avoid pain. But most often the comments are about the obvious pleasure taken in recovery. The intention is to highlight identification with this recovery, so that change may be motivated by anticipation of a better life. If a client tries to poison this by suggesting that Hollywood stars have too much of the good life to serve as models for "plain folks," it can be noted that the interviews show that these people have suffered as much from their disease as anyone in the group. To the extent that the recovering film stars are accepted as models, their testimony is a powerful motivator for the clients.

**Variations.** There are many other testimonials from public figures. Instead of the movie, the resourceful leader can videotape one of the many talk shows that discuss recovery. Dennis Wholey (1984) has compiled interviews into moving books that clients may enjoy reading.

Recovery generally becomes more stable and more enjoyable with time. Although greater energy and more cash on hand will generally be evident within the first month, many of the more subtle contributors to a sense of being fully alive may not be evident for years. By definition, clients in court-mandated treatment will seldom have as much as a year of change behind them. They can benefit from exposure to those with more time. This is one of the rationales for sending clients to meetings of Alcoholics Anonymous, where heartfelt testimonials about improved life are common. An alternative is to invite several AA members to run a session of the group as a speakers meeting—sharing their stories and inviting responses from the clients. Another option is to have former clients come back to group. At the time of release, I routinely invite clients to return for free follow-up. This invitation is explicitly intended to offer assistance if they slip or encounter difficulties. There has been a pleasant benefit to this policy. Most often it is the successful clients who return to express appreciation and to share their stories. Precisely because it is so easy for current participants to identify with them, the testimonials by former clients are often the most powerful motivation to change. It is a real pleasure that the facilitators who fill in while I am out of town are former group members who have gone on to become alcohol counselors.

# *The Devil's Deal*

*The devil's deal is a planned exercise that takes forty-five to seventy-five minutes. A chalkboard or flipchart is the only material needed.*

**Rationale.** The devil's deal is a powerful tool for confronting group members with the relationship of their drinking to their values. It starts as an abstract and nonthreatening reconsideration of potential losses because of alcohol abuse. It then becomes a vehicle for personalizing. The fantasy of trouble-free drinking is confronted by the reality that each client has cherished aspects of life that are threatened by drinking. Clients usually leave the exercise with an increased appreciation of the importance of their key values and a sense of urgency to change their drinking.

This exercise is also a departure in style. It is playful and teasing in tone. It can be used as a change of pace if the group is getting overly serious or rebellious. It is also an opportunity for the counselor to be theatrical. I often use it when I am bored and am trying to reenergize.

**Content.** The exercise begins with the leader asking the group to brainstorm all the important things that can be lost because of drinking (for example, pride, job, memory, money, freedom, future, sexual functioning, faith in God, family, self-control, and so forth). These are written down as named until the board is filled and all significant areas of life are covered. The leader then asks the members to consider which three things from the list they are least willing to lose. Several members share their rankings and are invited to explain briefly the rationale for their choices.

The leader then digresses, examining the loss list and talking enthusiastically about the value of a "magic pill" that would permit unrestrained drinking without threatening the key areas of life. The leader temporarily becomes a coconspirator with the group, surfacing their secret goal—although the exercise will later reveal the absurdity of this dream. The group is invited to join the fantasy; a mock auction may be held to establish that such a pill would indeed be invaluable (since the core values are of inestimable worth). The leader then reaches into his or her pocket and claims to have the magic pill. Several members playfully volunteer to try it. The leader then acknowledges that none of the members would be able to buy the pill on the open market but expresses interest in an alternative transaction. He offers to trade the pill, with its promise of unlimited trouble-free drinking, in exchange for the loss of one of the three most cherished values on the list. Three or four members are separately drawn into bargaining, while the leader sweetens the deal with rhapsodies about the fun of drinking (personalized for each client) and skepticism about the true importance of the values ("You don't really need your wife and kids. C'mon, you can have a nonstop party with whatever ladies you want"). The rebellion against the high-pressure salesmanship usually guarantees that the deal is ultimately rejected. The leader lampoons his lack of skill and tries with another member. If the deal is cut, the client is congratulated and given some small object (a quarter or piece of chalk) and the self-satisfied leader then proceeds with someone else. The tone remains playful, to mask the serious challenge to the values.

The exercise ends with a discussion, usually initiated by a group member, which surfaces the previously covert message that it would be absurd to sacrifice any key value for drinking and yet this is precisely what has been happening in each of their lives. I will often turn to the list of values and pantomime throwing darts, grimacing as I announce "there goes my job, . . . oh, oh, I lost my self-respect . . ." and so forth. But such dramatics are seldom necessary, since the group usually realizes "it's scary to think what I was willing to risk because of drinking."

**Variations.** (1) Listing potential losses becomes an opportunity to review information about risks (for example, I will often share a story about a patient who never regained his memory after heavy drinking led to Korsakov's psychosis).

(2) Personalizing occasionally leads to a client's testifying about what he has lost because of drinking. This is spontaneous and very powerful. I postpone the exercise until the sharing is complete.

(3) I will solicit value choices from any client I want to engage in subsequent bargaining. I may do this to gain an opportunity to relate playfully with someone who seems intimidated or defensive, but more often the idea is to do values clarification with someone whose lack of values awareness contributes to a "don't give a damn" attitude.

(4) I usually end the exercise by telling the group that it was fun but then explaining that it is also very serious. I share the story of the first time I did the exercise. The man who was too rigid and resentful even to play at bargaining was unable to gain anything and was subsequently rearrested; the man who played along but ultimately refused the deal did indeed get his priorities straight and make a lasting change in his drinking; the young girl who said "take my family, they've caused me nothing but pain" and similarly devalued each of her choices was killed in a drunk driving accident shortly thereafter. This sharing, in part because my pain is genuinely present, drives home the grief to come if drinking continues to overshadow other important priorities in life. I will not share this if the group has already gotten the serious message of the exercise. (Someone will often say, "You want us to refuse the deal because other things are more important than drinking," and I will look pained to be outsmarted). Most important, I do not share the story if someone has seriously made the deal. I may well treat a completed bargain as a therapy issue and attempt to explore the pain and hopelessness that typically underlie this kind of values bankruptcy. We may end up discussing how chronic use of depressant drugs can induce a chemical depression that makes life seem worthless.

(5) I have had people get mad at me for playfully pushing drinking. I

handle the encounter directly, exploring the reaction and expressing my own feelings. This will often develop a group discussion about attitudes toward drinking, toward play as part of recovery, and about the handling of temptation or pressure to drink from buddies.

This exercise is a powerful, if indirect, challenge about the importance of drinking among the clients' life values. The reactive rejection of the importance of drinking leads naturally into the problem-solving step in which plans are implemented. I may also time the exercise to launch some members on the control experiment (see chapter 7).

# Life Values

*This exercise takes forty-five minutes and requires a chalkboard. It is loosely adapted from the work on values clarification by Simon, Howe, and Kirschenbaum (1972).*

**Rationale.** Change is more likely to be lasting if it is directed toward obtaining something of value. Clients change their drinking more willingly if they have a sense of priorities in their lives that will be enhanced by reducing their use of alcohol. This exercise is the flip side of the devil's deal, which focused on avoiding losses. What is being aimed for is the focus here. This is especially important when the positive results of a change in drinking will appear only gradually. This exercise will help give immediacy to the eventual benefits that will result from changing.

**Content.** The group is asked to think about and then to volunteer those things that make life meaningful, that make all the effort worthwhile, or that give the affirming feeling that "this is what it's all about." The leader writes down the suggestions until ten to fifteen items have been listed and important areas of life have been covered. Possibilities include family, love, security, respect, wisdom, possessions, friends, fun, money, dreams, faith, and so on. If drinking or drugging is volunteered, it should be listed without comment.

The participants are asked to rank the three personally most important items on the list. Volunteers are invited to tell the group their choices (and the leader indicates them on the board by placing the initial and rank after the item). The group then discusses the rankings, with the leader assuring that the comments remain nonjudgmental. It will be noted that each person has different values, that the priority is a matter of personal choice rather than objective truth, and that important areas are interconnected. It may be helpful to suggest that values change over time and in response to experience. For example, freedom may seem especially important to those who have been jailed.

The leader suggests that what has been created is a list of life values. Values are what give pattern and meaning to our lives. Whether something is truly a value can be ascertained by checking to see if it meets three conditions (Raths & Simon, 1966). It must be *prized;* there must be a sense of pride and a willingness to state the value publicly in appropriate situations. It must be *chosen,* freely and thoughtfully. Part of the importance of teen rebellion is that it enables the adolescent to be a separate person so that the parents' values can ultimately be chosen without negating that person's sense of uniqueness. Lastly, values are demonstrated in a consistent pattern of behavior. *Actions* speak louder than words. If I claim to be generous and yet refuse to share my time or resources, I will be considered a hypocrite and will be considered not truly to value generosity. Actions become the ultimate demonstration of values.

The leader then adds alcohol to the list on the board. The group is asked where drinking should fit in among the values. Usually the group responds that it belongs at the bottom of the list, or that at least it would be excluded from the top three items. The leader then asks whether alcohol has ever been given such a priority that the ranked values were ignored or jeopardized. Using the criteria of public prizing, choice, and especially action, where would drinking be listed? This confrontation usually provokes a thoughtful silence, followed by rich discussion. Some clients will acknowledge the preeminence of alcohol at some point in their lives. Others will question whether drinking is really a value, in the sense that habits are followed without a sense of pride or choice. Others may note that alcohol has functioned more as an "antivalue," not so much important in itself but as an expression of the lack of other values or as a block against feeling the pain of values being lost or of goals being found to be unattainable. The discussion and sharing should be encouraged.

The group might be asked which values would assume more importance if alcohol use were curtailed. Typically this leads to a concluding discussion of the developing priorities in life.

**Variations.** This exercise leads readily into testimonials about the benefits of sobriety or into a discussion of future plans (see chapter 12).

Especially for those clients whose drinking seems to reflect an absence of clearly defined values, this activity may be the first of a series of corrective exercises aiming at encouraging values exploration. This is particularly likely to be the case for adolescent and young adult alcohol abusers whose drinking seems to be a response to identity diffusion or developmental crisis (Erikson, 1968). Related exercises can be found in the books on values clarification (Simon, Howe, & Kirschenbaum, 1972; Kirshenbaum, 1977).

# 10
# Planned Action

There have been plans to avoid problems caused by drinking—inadequate, to be sure—since before treatment began. When this step has been successfully completed, the plans implemented will be integrated into the problem-solving process. That is, the plans will be clearly linked to the goals they are intended to attain, and the plans can be evaluated and revised until they are consistently successful.

Considerable differences will exist among the plans of clients who are equally successful in achieving similar goals. One may argue vociferously about the need to avoid drinking buddies, while another counters that it is futile to hide from drinking. The variety of plans attempted is an expression of the creativity, the value differences, and the attitude of the clients in the group. The flexibility of the problem-solving model is evident in the range of plans that group members develop.

Clients are urged to be active and creative at this stage of treatment. The leader may be able to be tolerant of even some bad plans; if the client is sufficiently involved, he or she will learn from the predictable failures. Clients can be asked to consider the likely implications of their approach, but they should be given latitude to make their own choices. When it comes to goal setting, the leader needs to be insistent, perhaps requiring unwanted abstinence as a condition for successful completion of the program. But there need be no required uniformity when it comes to plans. In part this is because we know of no single way to alter drinking patterns. For example, only a minority of people seem to respond voluntarily to AA, although it carries the most successful set of plans extant today. Diverse plans are also needed because the strategies for change must match the client's values if he or she is to make a serious effort to implement them. In short, goals can be prescribed but plans cannot.

What, then, are the criteria for successful plans? First, they must be consonant with the goals set. Second, they should be objective and observable enough so that it is possible to discern whether they have been implemented and whether they are succeeding. "I will try to cut down" is a vague intention. In contrast, "I will limit myself to three standard drinks per occasion" is an observable plan. "I will stay home more" will only inadvertently alter drinking. "I will stay out of bars and avoid my drinking buddies when they are using" is goal related and susceptible to evaluation. Third, plans should be defined in such a way that they are related to values whenever possible. It would be better to define enjoyable alternatives rather than simply to deprive oneself by avoiding drinking (as discussed in the "reframing" exercise). Fourth, plans should be realistic, in the sense that the client either has or will be able to attain easily the knowledge and skills needed to execute them. The whole course may be seen as directed toward the development of the requisite working knowledge.

There will be three types of plans. First, there will be strategies to avoid driving drunk (detailed in chapter 5). This chapter addresses the remaining two types. Second, and most important, there will be plans to change drinking patterns. Third, there will be plans to accomplish the life-style changes needed to sustain new and healthier habits related to drinking. These include tactics to increase or maintain the motivation to succeed at goals. The activities in the last chapter provide initial impetus. But continuing efforts must be made if motivation is to continue until the new drinking pattern begins to generate its own rewards. There may be plans to remain aware of the risks of drinking. Continued involvement with AA or with the treatment group may serve as a general reminder of likely problems. More personal risk-awareness will result from plans to make a list of reasons to change, a description of the worst features of being drunk, or a collection of photographs of crashed vehicles or drunken countenances. A similar plan would be to review the list generated during the "eight areas of life" exercise prior to placing oneself in high-risk situations. Plans can be made to heighten motivation by enhancing pleasure in the change process. Asking for praise and support would be an example, as would keeping a chart of reduced drinking levels, or setting aside some of the money saved for rewarding oneself.

The flexibility of problem solving carries a risk. The very diversity of plans that allow for individualized change seems to require that the leader provide a vast array of skills training. To attempt to do so would result in overkill, which might undermine the success of the treatment (Brownell, Marlatt, Lichtenstein, & Wilson, 1986). The group can contract with the leader for some of the particularly pertinent modules presented in chapter 12. Clients can be referred for ancillary counseling if they have unique skills deficits that must be addressed. This chapter is limited to the most basic issues that are likely to be addressed in the plans of all clients.

# Model Plans

*This presentation and discussion consists of two parts, each taking thirty to forty-five minutes. These may be profitably presented in separate sessions to avoid the misleading impression that control and abstinence are interchangeable goals. A chalkboard will help clients follow the discussion.*

**Rationale.** Plans are not prescriptive in the sense that goals are. There is much more room for individualizing, and seldom must certain plans be in place as a requirement for compliant release from treatment.

Certain plans, however, have been found most likely to lead to sustained change. Features of these plans are reviewed in detail in this exercise to give clients a model as they develop their own unique strategies.

**Content.**

*The Cancer Analogy.* This analogy may be useful if the group seems likely to get the contextual message that alcoholism is successfully treatable if caught early. This message will be less likely to be received by participants who believe that a diagnosis of cancer is a death sentence.

I ask the group how a patient would be treated once it was discovered that he or she had an operable, malignant tumor in the lung. There are three stages to recovery from cancer. First, the tumor will be surgically removed. Second, there will be a course of radiation treatment or chemotherapy. Although this may seem to be a source of great discomfort, it serves to protect against any malignancy that was not removed. It may take some prompting for the group to identify the third step. But successful treatment includes life-style changes to remove any threats to health (for example, smoking) and to promote wellness (stress-management training, positive visualization, and so forth).

These same three stages apply in the recovery from alcoholism (see Brown, 1985, and Gorski, 1986b). The first priority is to "cut out" the drinking. Second, a number of possibly painful changes will need to be made to remove any remaining threats to sobriety. The effort to establish a solid AA program or to avoid drinking friends and situations reduces the risk of relapse into active alcoholism. Lastly, there will be a continuing process of developing a healthy life-style. This might involve quitting smoking, developing new interests, establishing an exercise program, or returning to some type of religious practice.

The analogy is completed by asking clients what they would think of a cancer patient who accepted the operation but then refused chemotherapy and continued smoking. How, then, would they evaluate a person who quit drinking but planned to make no other changes in friends, activities, or lifestyle? If the point is not already clear enough, it may be useful to remind the group that alcoholism is a disease of denial. Not only do clients initially minimize the extent of their problems and the need to change, but they may also continue to underestimate the challenge of maintaining abstinence. A client will often self-disclose about a failed prior attempt to quit. Abstaining is only part of the challenge; the goal is to stay off the sauce.

*Issues and Plans for the Recovering Alcoholic.* In AA distinctions are made among admitting, accepting, and surrendering as the alcohol problem is faced. As with cancer, there is a tripartite process of recovery that can be anticipated and planned for. Table 10–1 can be used to organize a discussion of the likely challenges at different stages of recovery, and of the range of appropriate plans that can be made by alcoholics seeking successful change. The discussion usually begins with volunteered comments about plans. It then develops into a dialogue, with the leader presenting typical issues at each stage of recovery while group members suggest effective strategies for handling those issues. Some examples of comments the leader might make are included in the following paragraphs, to illustrate how the ideas in table 10–1 might be amplified.

The first challenge is to quit drinking. This requires overcoming denial and inertia so that a sincere effort is possible. How might this be done? Any exposure to recovering alcoholics or to personal motivators might help. So one person keeps her DWI citation on prominent display, another regularly reviews his "eight areas" list, still another makes a tape in which loved ones remind him of the pain caused by his drinking and the appreciation they feel at his efforts to change. Certainly, going to AA regularly—listening to others contrast old problems with current gratitude, and hearing people publicly discuss their alcoholism—would help the ex-drinker sustain efforts to abstain.

What plans would be needed if an alcoholic knew the disease was damaging his life, knew he could not hope to become a controlled drinker, and yet could not stop? How soon before outside help should be sought? Approaches to abstinence can then be discussed. AA sponsorship, antabuse, detoxification, and inpatient rehabilitation should be reviewed as options.

Many clients who succeed in abstinence fail in recovery. It is not unusual for a client to go four months and then resume drinking, either out of a conviction that alcoholism was an incorrect diagnosis or out of disgust with the poor quality of life while dry. Either explanation illustrates a failure in working toward sobriety. The first month of abstinence may be simply a matter of getting by, especially if withdrawal makes life miserable. By the second month, plans should be developed to move toward a comfortable recovery. This includes accepting the disease and accepting oneself as an

**Table 10–1**
**Plans for Typical Issues in Recovery from Alcoholism**

| Stage/Goal | Symptoms to Resolve | Plans |
|---|---|---|
| *Getting abstinent (first 6 weeks):* | | |
| Admitting problems | Denial | Self-diagnosis by reviewing problems (eight areas list), "comparing in" at AA mtgs. |
| Handling acute withdrawal | Withdrawal symptoms | Support: medical (if severe), educate family and friends |
| Not drinking out of temptation | Temptation, self-pity, preoccupation | Avoid temptation: avoid drinking buddies and "hot spots," no alcohol in house, antabuse, keep busy |
| *Seeking comfort in a drug-free lifestyle (1 to 6 months):* | | |
| Accepting disease concept | Fantasies of controlled drinking | Talk at AA, read/study |
| Getting honest | Defenses, guilt | AA sponsor, AA steps, therapy group, resolve immediate problems |
| Reducing stress | Irritable, isolated, compulsive | Support of family and true friends, relaxation, new interests and activities |
| *Continued growth (from 4 months forward):* | | |
| Handling protracted withdrawal | Cravings, tired, weak, low stress tolerance | Exercise, physical conditioning, nutrition |
| Countering immaturity | Paranoid, self-conscious, can't handle feelings, relationship problems | Social skills training, new relationships, therapy, codependency treatment |
| New meaning | Lack of meaning, stalled recovery, boredom | New goals, meditation, spiritual growth |

alcoholic. It may help to remember that the alcoholic is not responsible for contracting the disease but is responsible for maintaining recovery. Mistakes will have been made and people harmed during the active addiction period. There is little use in guilt. But there is a need to resolve problems. This may include "making amends" as part of working the twelve steps of AA. But early on it will likely be a matter of resolving pressing problems. If there are outstanding bills, it is time to draw up a budget and face creditors to plan a repayment schedule. It is time to acknowledge a shattered marriage, if only to ask directly for time to deepen recovery before deciding about a divorce. Facing such challenges successfully requires a strong support system. AA, friends, and family can be asked to "be there" to lean on or to help maintain a positive attitude. New activities, techniques for relaxation, and means of "re-creation" can be planned to add enjoyment to life.

The commitment to growth and change lasts a lifetime. Without growth, there is the risk of relapse, since the disease is always present even when dormant. Cravings should be seen as an important reminder of the need to keep working. Some of the effort is to counter old "character flaws." The earlier drinking began, and the more all-consuming it was, the more there is likely to be emotional immaturity. Since drinking was always there to help, more adult tools of coping were not developed or practiced. So the dry alcoholic may act in an adolescent fashion, hiding insecurity by trying to control others and throwing tantrums when frustrated. One recovering alcoholic told me, "I'm thirty-eight years old, with an eighteen-year-old's mind, in a fifty-eight-year-old body." The final stage of recovery seeks to create a more integrated person. The integration means to develop and have access to the full range of personal resources. It also means having a new sense of being related to the world. So exercise helps mind and body come together, therapy helps skills catch up with dreams, and spirituality helps in the birth of a new sense of purpose for investing personal talents.

The presentation may conclude in any of a number of different ways. One approach is to lay out a model plan for a hypothetical client. Another is for the leader to role-play a willing candidate for recovery and have the group assist in the development of strategies for whatever issues or stages of recovery are highlighted. Perhaps most commonly, group members can be invited to share their plans for recovery. To enable them to incorporate ideas stimulated by the foregoing discussion, it is useful to ask for current plans, backup plans for periods of adversity, and potential plans for subsequent stages of recovery. Lastly, clients can be shown films about the recovery process. Although both films are somewhat dated, my groups find useful ideas in *The New Life of Sandra Blain* and part two of *The Other Guy*.

*Successful Drinking for the Nonaddicted.* Drinking for the nonaddicted alcohol abuser may be conceptualized as an overlearned habit combined with a permanently elevated tolerance that will permit excessive consumption. The goal, controlled drinking, requires that the old habit be replaced with a new and more healthy pattern of alcohol use. Change may be subdivided into disrupting the old pattern, developing a new habit, and rigidly maintaining the new pattern until it becomes second nature. There are two conflicting forces in this process. The initial adherence to the goal must be more rigid than will be necessary later, precisely because the new habit is weak relative to the old one. Yet learning is a cumulative process, with a greater likelihood of failure early on. Research on controlled drinking shows that there is more success after the first year than in the first months (Marlatt, 1983; Sobell & Sobell, 1978). Clients need to be reminded to learn from their mistakes without feeling defeated, while at the same time they must compensate for the likelihood of failures by having backup plans and especially stringent standards. One aspect of the backup must be to have solid strategies for avoiding drunk driving on those occasions when they will be drinking (see chapter 5).

Note the fail-safe elements in the plan of one drinker, who wanted to be prepared for even emergency situations. He set a limit of three standard drinks; he would use only at home or when his light-drinking wife was with him away from home; and he would drink only when someone else was available to care for his six-month-old child. As Vaillant (1983) notes, this is not a model of carefree drinking. Alcohol use must be cautious and self-conscious if the old habit is to be kept from reasserting itself. Clients are reminded that they must "keep their guard up."

Disrupting the old habit can be accomplished by changing the chain of behaviors in the old pattern. This involves altering the time, the situation, the accompanying activities, and the people involved with the old pattern. For example, one client found it easier to control consumption once he stopped using the favorite mug associated with years of heavy drinking. The most effective means of disrupting the old habit is to abstain temporarily (Marlatt, 1983; Vogler & Bartz, 1982). The control test (chapter 7) can now be seen as part of the model plan as well as a self-diagnostic experiment.

The new habit profits by incorporating the following elements: (1) Set a limit of two or three standard drinks, so that the blood alcohol concentration (BAC) is kept below .05. (Later this may be relaxed to one drink per hour, but the rigidity of a top limit helps initially.) This means the drinker must accept that there will be no more getting drunk, although the interval of abstinence is likely to lower the euphoria point enough that the limited drinking will have a more pronounced effect than would have been the case previously. (2) Slow down drinking by sipping and setting the drink down between tastes. (3) Always use a shot glass for measuring liquor and then weaken drinks by adding extra mixer; or switch to less concentrated drinks. Especially when someone else is preparing the drinks and may be making them strong it is safer to ask for beer or wine. (4) Wait twenty to thirty minutes between drinks, ordering an intervening soft drink if necessary, so that the full effects of the previous drink are felt. (5) Snack while imbibing or drink on a full stomach to slow alcohol absorption. (6) Limit the length of the drinking period to an hour, perhaps by arriving late at drinking occasions. Initially it is important to preserve the freedom to leave an overwhelming situation. It may help to bring a car and have a partner who is willing to escort you home. (7) Drink only to enhance good moods. Avoid all drinking in response to stress, depression, boredom, anger, or whatever other emotions may have been linked to past heavy drinking. (8) Avoid daily drinking so that the new habit includes alcohol-free days and activities. It may be worthwhile to set a limit equivalent to a six-pack of beer or half a pint of liquor a week.

This material can be presented, with key words listed on the chalkboard. It is helpful to invite suggestions or the sharing of additional strategies developed by participants. Any group discussion will help drive home the elements of the model plan for potential controlled drinkers.

# Using All the Levels of the Alcoholics Anonymous Program

*This discussion lasts fifteen to thirty minutes. A "speakers meeting" will take sixty to ninety minutes.*

**Rationale.** All alcohol abusers, whether or not they are alcoholic, should be exposed to AA. Free and widely available, it will become the primary treatment resource for many of them, especially after they complete the group therapy. Alcoholics Anonymous is the best resource for the greatest number of my clients. They need to know how it works so that they can make use of it. Concurrent AA involvement adds to treatment in the following ways: (1) Giving clients contact with long-term sobriety. Court-referred clients seldom have any sustained recovery, and they benefit from realizing the challenges and benefits of continuing sobriety. (2) AA models gratitude about the change in drinking, which is a good corrective to the resistant attitude typical of the client in coerced treatment. (3) In cases where the counselor is not recovering from addiction, AA will offer the perspective of people who have "been there."

My clients are required to attend weekly AA meetings for the duration of their treatment. I would prefer to have clients go voluntarily. But my experience suggests that few will do so. AA works effectively for those who remain involved long enough to feel part of the program, and it often takes ten to twenty meetings before the client feels sufficiently at home and has enough understanding to judge whether AA will be helpful. Required attendance is the most effective way to assure adequate exposure to AA. About 10 percent of my clients voluntarily increase their frequency of meetings, and perhaps 33 percent continue AA involvement after completing treatment.

This exercise works toward the goal of a fuller understanding of AA.

**Content.** Clients are told about the different types of meetings when they are first informed of the AA requirement. Those who want to continue drinking and who do not self-diagnose as alcoholic are encouraged to attend *open* meetings, since interested members of the public are welcome at such sessions. *Closed* meetings are suggested for those who are trying to quit. These meetings tend to be smaller and more intensive, and they tend to encourage greater involvement. Closed meetings will likely be more beneficial for those who qualify for attendance because of "an honest desire to stop drinking."

Clients are encouraged to attend a range of meetings. This is partly to find which groups are most comfortable for them. It also allows exposure to meetings which cover different content. *Speakers* meetings allow clients to witness the detailed sharing of one person's experience with drinking and recovery. *Discussion* meetings allow briefer sharing, by all present who choose to, on a range of selected topics. *Step* meetings review the twelve steps that underlie the Alcoholics Anonymous program. *Big Book* meetings review selected parts of the seminal text of AA. There may well be other meeting formats (beginners, tape, women's, and so on) available locally. It may also be advisable to mix in attendance at meetings of related fellowships such as Narcotics Anonymous (for drug addiction of all types), Adult Children of Alcoholics, AlAnon (for an alcoholic's family and friends), Alateen (for adolescent offspring), Gamblers Anonymous, Overeaters Anonymous, and so forth.

After clients have been attending for several weeks it is profitable to spend some time reviewing and deepening their understanding of the program. This is usually accomplished by a discussion. The first trigger question might be, "How do you like AA?" Some enjoy it from the outset, although I am often confronted with displeasure about required attendance (handled by repeating the rationale stated above). Obstacles to involvement are surfaced and clarified. Particularly for those who feel that religious beliefs are being imposed, there is the need for the group to discuss the difference between spirituality and organized religion. Some clients will complain that the meetings are repetitive and boring. I may tease that I thought they liked repetition, conspicuously bending my elbow. But the discussion is launched by asking those who are bored, "What is it that keeps some people returning to meetings for thirty years? Why don't they get bored?" We may review attitudes, that people seem to benefit more if they go with the intention of learning at least one new thing each meeting. We may discuss the social and peer support needs that can make attendance a continuing pleasure. Eventually we surface the important idea that AA operates on different levels. There are changing goals: switching from an initial focus on staying dry to a lifelong focus on personal and spiritual growth. There are also changing levels of involvement. People can benefit from attending meetings. But most are drawn deeper. Initially there is the socializing and peer counseling that occurs over coffee before or after meetings. This may be followed by developing an advisory relationship with a seasoned veteran at recovery—getting a sponsor. Under the tutelage of the sponsor, the client may accept advice about how to make life-style changes, start reviewing the excellent written resources (starting with the "Big Book," *Alcoholics Anonymous*), and begin to work the twelve steps AA suggests for recovery. There are many more levels of involvement. But the group typically will have enough new ideas to absorb. We may discuss the steps in some detail. More often we end with encouraging clients to try to move one stage deeper into the process.

While the discussion alone can be helpful, it may be more immediate and powerful if it is conducted by a visiting veteran member of Alcoholics Anonymous. This is especially helpful if there are new clients with little previous exposure to AA. The guest could run a simulated speakers meeting, sharing some personal experiences with drinking and recovery before fielding questions from group members. In these instances there is an excellent opportunity to discuss the continuing process of recovery, since personal growth is obviously not completed within the three to twelve months that the treatment program will last. The group is usually respectful, curious, and prone to mirror back the contagious blunt honesty of sharing that typifies AA.

**Variations.** At times an AA member will ask to participate in one of my groups on an ongoing basis, usually out of concern about a friend or relative who is a client. I encourage this. In part, this is payment of a debt of appreciation to AA. But it also aids the group in using AA effectively to have an in-house liaison.

The movie *AA and the Alcoholic* covers much of the content of this discussion.

Individual clients may be required to attend up to seven AA meetings a week. This is particularly useful for clients who feel hopeless, who lack any support system, and whose life-style has long been dominated by drinking. Conversely, I will permit some clients to stop attending AA after twenty sessions if they can convince me that they are better served by investing their energy elsewhere (in counseling, in reading, or through involvement with another self-help fellowship). Clients who have successfully completed the control experiment are no longer required to attend AA, although many continue because the painful testimonials reaffirm their commitment to maintain control over their drinking. My experience makes me confident of the benefit of several months of involvement in AA, since the early vociferous complaints about attendance often result from painful identification with the sharing that lays the groundwork for later willing involvement.

I do not here outline specifics about AA because I assume that the counselor already has developed a personal understanding of the program. Anyone treating clients with alcohol problems has to make a commitment to understand the resources available for treatment. Most people accept this idea when it means reading about new research or going to workshops on new treatment approaches. I am disturbed, however, by the number of mental health professionals who have not made the effort to attend open meetings of AA. It may be because AA members have traditionally been suspicious of counselors and doctors, since many of them were misdiagnosed and mistreated because of professionals' ignorance (Brown, 1985). It may be because AA is misperceived as a religion or a tradition that is incompatible with psychological approaches to treating alcohol problems. Although still widely held among both AA veterans and professionals, these myths are substantially outdated. AA members are generally sophisticated about and receptive to new understandings about alcoholism; after all, it makes sense to develop some expertise about any life-threatening disease you have. Self-confident professionals are not diminished but enhanced when their learning is blended with the personal experience of those who have lived with addiction. To recovering counselors, this will be obvious. The nonaddicted counselor will benefit from regular contact with AA. Not only will the counselor gain a better understanding of a primary treatment resource, but he or she will also gain a new humility when confronted with the power of alcoholism, and a new respect for the strength of commitment that carries some alcoholics into the process of recovery. Attend appropriate AA meetings regularly.

One last variation on this activity is worth mentioning. Near my home is an AA club that offers breakfast and a meeting every Sunday morning. Every once in a while, I will invite interested clients to meet at the office and carpool together "up to the mountain" to join in the session. This has met my need to touch base with AA and to be more of an equal partner with some of my clients. Far from undercutting my professionalism, these Sunday mornings have been a time of sharing that reaffirms our mutual caring and commitment. Besides, the food is excellent!

# Handling Time

*This set of exercises takes between sixty and ninety minutes. A chalkboard, ruled paper, pens, and writing surfaces are required.*

**Rationale.** Heavy drinking takes a lot of time—often, all of the free time available. One of the clients' first challenges upon changing drinking is finding how to fill the extra hours. Most clients have given up the hobbies and activities they used to enjoy. A change in drinking then threatens them with boredom and depression if they isolate themselves without alternative activities or with a workaholic preoccupation with the few remaining involvements. For successful adjustment to life without heavy drinking, especially early on, there is a need to identify the problem of how to fill time, to develop a range of available activities, and to select among them so as to find a satisfying balance. These are the objectives of the following activities.

**Content.** It helps to begin with a demonstration of the need to restructure the use of time. Clients are asked to pick a typical day when they would be drinking. Hour by hour, beginning with the time they arise, they should list what they would be doing along the left border of the paper. They should then review this schedule and see how much discretionary time remained after excluding hours spent in sleep, work, and maintenance tasks (cooking, commuting, and other requirements for daily living). How much of this discretionary time is spent drinking? The discussion that follows tends to confirm that drinking has been the central pastime in their lives.

Clients are then asked to take the same day and list their schedule on the assumption that they have brought their drinking into line with their goals. On the right side of the same sheet of paper they should note how time would be apportioned if drinking were no longer a primary pastime. The contrast between the two columns is then discussed.

Some suggestions about the appropriate use of leisure time can be made. First, clients need alternative ways to use the hours formerly filled with drinking. There is generally a recognition that time management must become an important issue in the change process, and this fuels interest in the remaining exercises in this section. Second, almost anything can be used for recreation. Third, different types of leisure activities can be written on the chalkboard and discussed:

1. *Exercise (E):* physically active time, including sex, sports, walking, or gardening, and so on.

2. *Social interaction (Soc):* time spent involved with other people (and not just having the spouse at home while watching the TV). This interaction would include parties, social clubs, or time spent in conversation with co-workers or neighbors.

3. *Intellectual Stimulation (I):* time spent learning or thinking; for example, reading about an interest area, having a political discussion, or attending a lecture about alcohol abuse.

4. *Creativity (C):* expressing oneself through letter writing, making up a poem or a song, dancing, or planning interesting activities for the coming week.

5. *Spectating (Sp):* watching others, as in going to a movie, observing children at play, or watching television.

6. *Relaxation (R):* taking a long shower, meditating, reading a novel, listening to music, or otherwise taking quiet time for oneself.

Each of these areas will probably be present in a well-balanced schedule of leisure time. Clients can be asked to note how much time is apportioned to each of the six types of activities in the right hand column of their schedule. There will almost certainly be an incomplete representation, which is perfectly appropriate for a single day. But clients can be told that over the course of a week or a month they will feel better if all the areas are allotted time. This is generally accepted well but overshadowed by a more immediate concern. There may be puzzlement about what activities could be used to spend the free time. Clients often suggest tackling unfinished work around the house. (One once reported chopping firewood for the entire neighborhood as a way to handle the irritability and hyperactivity of withdrawal). Next, clients typically pick up on old hobbies and acquaintances. But there is usually a need to develop new interests. Brainstorming these becomes the focus of the next exercise.

Clients are asked to list thirty things that they enjoy doing, consciously attempting to come up with at least five examples of each type of leisure. For some this will prove impossible, and they should be reassured that they can add to their lists ideas suggested by others. For the next step is to go around the group and have clients volunteer any options that have not been previously mentioned.

The list is further developed by asking the clients to put an "A" next to those activities that are readily available, a "P" next to those requiring advanced planning, a "D" next to those that are strongly associated with drinking, a "N" next to those that fulfill a need met by drinking, and a "$" next to those that cost more than five dollars to do. In the discussion that follows, a number of important points will be volunteered or raised. Activities strongly associated with drinking may need to be avoided. Conversely, activities that are readily available and that fulfill needs formerly met by drinking may be very rewarding. There is often a lively discussion of the amount of money to be spent. Many clients approach reduced drinking as a penance. Self-deprivation will likely lead to failure. Plans based on staying at home, avoiding friends, and spending no money will not generally lead to lasting or enjoyable recovery. Since a drinking life-style is almost always expensive (see chapter 6), there is certainly some money that can be spent on alternative activities to enhance the quality of leisure time. The exercise ends with clients asked to rank the ten most desirable activities on their lists, with the suggestion that they may well want to plan to do some of them shortly.

**Variations.** Early recovery often means avoiding many of the familiar social situations associated with drinking. Clients often fear being stuck by themselves at home. This fear can be met head on with the following exercise. Clients are asked to imagine themselves being snowed in at home, alone, with the telephone not working. They have ample supplies and should not attempt to get out. Rather, they have three days to fill with whatever activities they can devise. In the next five minutes, they are to write down as many things as possible that they might do. The lists can then be shared and discussed, in effect using the group to brainstorm even more alternatives.

The change in drinking becomes an invitation to make other life changes. Clients can be asked to think of one thing that they always wanted to do but have never yet attempted. The previous exercises tend to seek more immediately available pastimes, but the sharing that follows this request tends to be of a major undertaking that will require preparation and resources. Parachuting, hiking the Appalachian Trail, living abroad, buying a piece of property, and obtaining a college degree are examples offered in a recent group. Clients are asked to think of the obstacles that have prevented going after the goal and the steps that might be taken to remove these barriers. The implication is that there is a fresh opportunity to pursue long-range goals. This exercise leads readily into a discussion of future plans (see chapter 12).

# Handling Family and Friends: Detractor, Contributor, or Neutral

*This discussion takes fifteen minutes. Role-plays may take up to an additional forty-five minutes.*

**Rationale.** No matter how evident the need for someone to change drinking, family or friends may undermine the effort. The family identity may be based on having a dysfunctional member (Berenson, 1976; Bowen, 1974/1978; Ewing & Fox 1968), or drinking may be the most familiar pathway to intimacy and expressiveness (Steinglas, Davis, & Berenson, 1977). Drinking buddies may be reluctant to let go of their "free ride" or may be threatened by the client's admission of a problem. Clients need to develop tools to handle others' resistance to their change. But countering negative influences is not enough. They also need to develop a support system behind the new goals. Friends and family can be arrayed along a continuum that extends from detracting from efforts, through a neutral stance, to contributing to changes in drinking patterns. This exercise helps clients learn how to move others along the continuum by neutralizing detractors and cultivating contributors.

**Content.** To organize the discussion, write the terms "Detractor," "Neutral," and "Contributor" on the chalkboard. The detractor is the one who tempts, teases, or resents the client's effort to change the drinking pattern; those who are neutral keep a hands-off posture; and contributors may offer praise and advice to maintain efforts to change.

The discussion covers issues about who to tell and how much to tell, about handling pressure to drink, and about getting the needed support from family and friends. The following points should be raised, with the leader suggesting them if the group discussion does not raise them.

Most people do not notice and do not care how much you drink. They require no explanation. Nothing need be said about changes, and there is no need to be self-conscious since they simply will not notice whether you are sipping on a mixed drink or a soft drink. Any questions that do arise are likely to be casual and satisfactorily handled with a nonanswer such as "I don't feel like drinking tonight," "I'm cutting down for a while," or "My doctor said I should lay off." (I always give my clients permission to quit, so the last response is literally true.) Some may find it hard to believe that others are uninterested in their drinking. They should be invited to go to a company party or a reunion and not drink, if only to discover how many others drink little and so how unexceptional they are. Casual acquaintances are particularly unconcerned. Even drinking buddies are likely to respond to the change by happily noting "that means there is that much more for me." The art of handling those who are neutral is to treat the change in drinking as a nonevent.

It helps to have some family or friends who contribute to the effort to change. They may offer praise and support, help with planning how to handle tempting situations, accept calls at times of crisis, or actively remind the client about the reasons for changing. Contributors may attend sessions or review class materials (such as the disease curve or the eight areas list). The more informed they are, the more help they can be.

The key is for the client to recognize that who contributes and how they contribute is up to the client to decide. There are likely to be many who are eager to support the change. But contributors are cultivated by the drinker. Not everyone who volunteers is suited for the role. Those who are so co-dependent or so controlling that they will preempt responsibility for change may best be encouraged to remain uninvolved and neutral. One client told about his wife who counted his antabuse pills after he left for work, anxiously checking to see whether he had taken his daily dose. He ended up hiding his pills because he resented her intrusion. Those who are that over-involved should be asked to remain neutral. Some are too close to help.

Especially if there have been lies or broken promises about changed drinking, some loved ones will remain mistrustful and skeptical at the time the client most needs support for change. The drinker needs to understand and accept their perspective, lest this be a source of resentment and these family and friends end up detracting from recovery. Figure 10–1 illustrates the differences.

Family members will typically see a problem developing earlier and will see it as being more severe than will the drinker (at point *a*). Conversely, they will need time to see that an announced change will really be made. They may not accept recovery until long after it is evident to the changing drinker (point *b*). If they are so involved that they need to protect themselves, they should not attempt to be contributors. With codependency treatment and AlAnon involvement, they may eventually learn enough detachment to accept the drinker as being responsible for the change. In the meantime, they should be asked to remain neutral. Family therapy may be needed if the detracting continues despite this request.

The ideal contributor is someone who is able to avoid judgment and yet is close enough that the praise matters. Such a person can be there for the drinker. Group members need to realize that the only way this person can know how to be most helpful is for the client to tell him or her what to do. One person might be needed for talking out problems and strategies, while another contributes by providing distraction with, perhaps, good-natured teasing. Contributors are made. One objective is to identify potential contributors and to sit down and tell them how to help. These may be new acquaintances, like an AA sponsor. These may be old friends. These may be people who were previously neutral and who are deliberately cultivated to be contributors. It is up to the client to select these people, educate them about alcohol problems, inform them about goals for change, and help them realize the role they can play in supporting the client's efforts.

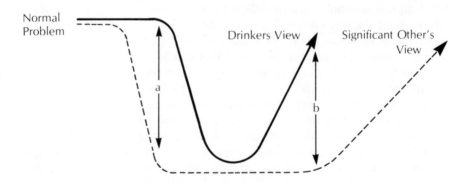

**Figure 10–1. Differences in Perspective on Problem Drinking and Recovery of the Drinker and Significant Others**

Everyone benefits by having contributors, particularly if the change entails giving up some old associates. Clients should be urged to work on developing a network of contributors.

Detractors directly or indirectly discourage change. These may be drinking buddies threatened by the client's efforts. They are really trying to reassure themselves when they say, "You're not that bad, come on and have one." Since one of the leading causes of relapse is pressure from other drinkers (Cummings, Gordon, & Marlatt, 1980), clients must learn to avoid or handle detractors. Many strategies exist for handling them, which are based on two key premises:

1. Talk to detractors. Sometimes pressure is a test of resolve. When friends realize that the effort to change is sincere, they may become quite supportive. "You know you will be drinking within a week" may really be a challenge for the client to show them up. Often there are legitimate reasons behind the pressure. Buddies may be sincerely concerned about losing a friend when they taunt, "Are you too good to drink with us?" An honest discussion may amicably resolve the dispute with an agreement that the client and the drinking buddies can still be friends but that they need to get together at times when there won't be any drinking. The objective is to make detractors neutral or supportive. The technique is to get beneath the pressure to understand the reason behind it. This approach is particularly suited for co-workers and old friends who cannot be easily avoided.

2. Say no and mean it. True friends accept us. If others try to make us do precisely what we have told them we do not want to, they are not being friends (Vogler & Bartz, 1982). There is no need to feel guilty about a strong response, even if they take offense. One client reported complete success at neutralizing pressure with a very direct confrontation: "I'm an alcoholic. What are you trying to do, [expletive deleted] kill me?" It is possible to be less forthright about explaining the reason for the change; after all, detractors have not shown the concern that warrants a full explanation. But there is no replacement for a firm no. The edge of anger that comes from resenting pressure can lend force to rejecting the drink. Clients report more problems with the internal temptation that develops when a friend rhapsodizes about how good a cold beer can taste. Here clients need to rehearse their own reasons for changing before they can effectively confront their acquaintance with the inaproriateness of even subtle pressure. Consistency in saying no will result in drinking buddies' either becoming neutral or disappearing. If the client is unable to resist coercion, drinking friends should be avoided.

Role-playing and rehearsal help clients handle pressure. Group members can be invited to share how they have dealt with detractors. Sharing successes models the skills. Failures should be role-played. When a client reports difficulties or doubts, the group can be invited to play the role of tempters while the client tries to counter the lines. Good humor and shared purpose make the exercise nonthreatening. Clients often respond by surprising themselves with their effectiveness at countering the pressure. If the leader feels the client is about to be overwhelmed or about to give in, another group member can be asked to help out for a moment by contributing support or offering his or her own comebacks to the groups' lines. Role-playing can be managed so that success is maximized.

**Variations.** Saying no to detractors requires assertiveness. If there is a widespread problem with countering pressure, it may be helpful to continue with an assertiveness training module (see chapter 12).

# Relapse Prevention: From "I Can't Drink" or "I Won't Drink" to "I Don't Want to Drink"

*This discussion takes from twenty to sixty minutes and uses a chalkboard.*

**Rationale.** Relapse is a major problem. Even model DWI education programs report about 20 percent rearrest rates within a two-year period (Holden, 1986; Reis, 1983). Across addictions, 50–90 percent resume using (Hunt, Barnett, & Branch, 1971; Marlatt & Gordon, 1985), usually within the first three months after treatment ends. But the situation is not hopeless. Half of those who slip will return to abstinence (Gorski, 1986b; Pickens, Hatsukami, Spicer, & Svikis, 1985). Still, the need for education about relapse is evident.

It helps to distinguish a lapse from a relapse. The former, colloquially known as a slip, can be countered. It can provide motivation for renewed efforts to maintain a recovery program and to build stable abstinence. A slip is a crisis. If it provokes expectations of future failure, or if it is seen as the first step in an inevitable slide back into active addiction, full relapse is likely to follow. It is useful to counter these assumptions. A slip attributed to temporary or situational pressures will lead to less pessimistic expectations than if it is blamed on personal traits (Marlatt & Gordon, 1985). A client educated to see a slip as an emergency calling for activating prearranged contingency plans is likely to be take initiative and feel capable of coping. Invite discussion of slips and identify steps that can be taken so that a lapse does not progress to a relapse. This can be done without giving implicit permission to slip. Preplanning is analogous to receiving an innoculation:

exposure to the risk can be managed so that the result is defenses against the threat and not infection.

The first step of effective relapse prevention is education about the nature of the risk. Ludwig and Stark (1974) found that 78 percent of alcoholics can expect to experience cravings. There are three interacting factors that contribute to cravings and to slips (Brownell et al., 1986). The first is physiological. Most slips occur during the first three months after treatment ends. For many who achieve abstinence late in the program, this period corresponds with protracted withdrawal. This is the discouraging combination of physical unease, heightened emotionality and sensitivity to stress, and cognitive limitations (difficulties with abstract thinking, memory, and concentration) that make problem solving difficult (Gorski, 1986a; Gorski & Miller, 1979). These physical reactions should be described as normal and time limited to assist the client who must cope with them. See chapter 6 for the educational presentation.

Anger, frustration, depression, or other negative emotions are the most common reasons given for slips (Cummings, Gordon, & Marlatt, 1980; Littman, Eiser, Rawson, & Oppenheim, 1977; Marlatt, 1978; and Pickens et al., 1985). Many of the following exercises—from relaxation to fair fighting techniques—are tools for emotional self-management. Such skill training is helpful. Simply educating clients that negative emotions should alert them to be especially vigilant about slips is a powerful initial step.

Slips also occur because of temptation that results from social pressure or exposure to drinking situations. These may be particular threats to recovery for the client who refuses to change his or her life-style or circle of friends.

The following presentation provides a convenient model with which clients can organize the information about factors contributing to relapse. The goals of the discussion are education about relapse and about the optimal attitude for avoiding a slip.

The model is original. The elements were inspired by Zimberg's (1978) discussion of the stages of treatment. He saw a typical progression from compliance with treatment because of external control ("I can't drink"), through internal motivation ("I won't drink"), to conflict resolution and adjustment to a sober life-style ("I don't want to drink"). I find that the typology is useful, but the progression is unreliable. Clients often enter treatment with the commitment to sobriety and the pride of having already expressed this choice to friends and drinking buddies. In some instances the internal motivation lapses into resentful compliance when these clients are asked to make concrete changes such as attending AA meetings. The stages may not progress in the order Zimberg outlines.

The presentation may be initiated earlier in treatment (especially during the motivation stage) to counter the belief that "you have to want to change before you can stop drinking." I will agree that internal motivation is generally necessary to maintain abstinence. But people often achieve sobriety after entering treatment in response to an ultimatum from a boss, judge, or spouse. In short, many people begin from the position that "I want to drink, but I can't."

Most often, the model is presented in response to a client's demonstrating one of the emotions or attitudes associated with increased risk of relapse.

**Content.** I draw a diamond on the board, as in figure 10–2, and label the corners. I then describe some scenarios in which a person who still wants to drink might decide that "I can't." The reasons might include a DWI, or leverage from a boss or a spouse. Life-threatening complications from drinking, such as esophageal varices, might lead to compliance with a doctor's directive to abstain. The bottom line is that the problems have become obvious and serious enough that continued drinking is no longer an option. The desire to drink may well remain. But the person realizes it must be ignored or combated through accepting whatever assistance is available. If instructed to go to AA, the drinker is likely to comply. Prospects for continuing abstinence are improved precisely because the drinker is aware of the power of the disease and of the ineffectiveness of his or her previous attempts to manage it. There is sufficient humility that the client will adhere to a treatment program.

The person who believes that "I can't drink" will still run the risk of relapse. The group will usually identify feelings of helplessness, futility, or

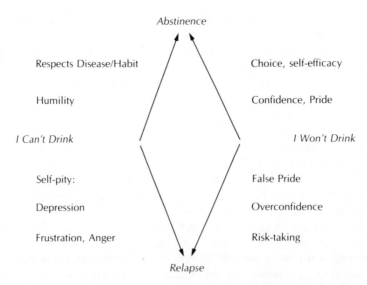

Figure 10–2. Attitudes toward Drinking and the Risk of Relapse

self-pity as the primary obstacles. These are the negative emotions identified by research as being the prime factors in relapse. Anything that contributes to a further loss of self-esteem or self-control could set off a cycle of depressive isolation or resentful rebellion which might precipitate resumed drinking.

I contrast this with the experience of the person who sees abstinence as a challenge, as a test of his willpower. This person would say that "I won't drink" or "I've chosen to quit." From this perspective, every day of abstinence is a victory that further validates growing self-esteem. Marlatt and Gordon (1985) report that exposure to a risky situation without a slip leads to heightened self-efficacy and decreased probabilities of future relapse. Growing confidence confirms the decision to abstain and makes it more likely that the ex-drinker can face the life-style changes required by recovery—such as making new friends and finding new interests to fill the time. The greatest advantage of this position for beginning abstinence is that change becomes a matter of pride.

Relapse remains a risk for the person who says, "I won't drink." The group recognizes that pride can easily turn into false pride, with all the resurgent defensiveness it entails. The challenge of continued sobriety is minimized as the drinker begins to doubt the alcoholic diagnosis: "I don't believe it's a chronic disease. I have got myself so together now I believe I can handle some social drinking." Overconfidence may lead directly to resumed drinking; it accounted for 10 percent of the slips in the survey by Marlatt (1978). It will also support the rationalization that "I can't hide from it forever"; so there will be increased risk taking as drinking situations are no longer avoided and there is exposure to a lot of others' drinking. In time, efforts at recovery and life-style change will lose momentum as the old "drinker's attitude" reasserts itself and using resumes.

When the descriptions are complete and a few of the trigger words have been added to the diagram, clients can be asked how the diagram applies to them. Attitudes, feelings, and behavior patterns can be reviewed. Isolating from people might indicate the "can't" approach, while continued involvement in drinking occasions suggests the "won't" position.

The resulting discussion usually leads to a recognition that successful early recovery usually requires a combination of the best features of each approach. The advantages of one offset the liability of the other. A thorough understanding of the disease concept, with acceptance of the self-diagnosis, will contribute the appropriate respect and caution to temper the client's justifiable pride at having changed. The choice and competence evident in not drinking can be used to counter the self-talk that leads to self-pity. It is possible to be simultaneously humble and proud if there is recognition that powerlessness over drinking coexists with efficacy in managing a solid recovery and enjoying a changed life-style. In such a discussion, the group ends up modeling and rehearsing an appropriate attitude toward recovery.

**Variations.** Clients may rationalize continued drinking because "you can't quit until you want to." This exercise demonstrates that it is indeed possible to begin from other positions. The presentation can be continued with the question, "What is required to reach the point where you can honestly say, 'Even if I could drink, I don't want to'?" There is clear recognition that it takes time to be comfortable with any major change. There may be a fruitful discussion of the elements needed for steady state sobriety. The reframing exercise from chapter 8 may be reviewed to emphasize that it is important to find alternative means of accomplishing what drinking used to offer. There may be an opportunity to identify the need to master skills presented in the subsequent exercises, with a group contract about which of the activities to pursue.

This presentation represents an introduction to relapse and relapse prevention. Marlatt and Gordon (1985) provide a technical but valuable guide that can be used if more detailed relapse prevention training is indicated. Of particular interest is their concept, the abstinence violation effect. At one time, alcoholics were often indoctrinated with the idea that the full force of their disease would overwhelm them if they took a single drink. The intended goal was to emphasize the risks of any drinking. The unintended by-product was that recovery becomes an all-or-none thing, that clients are programmed to see a lapse as inevitably leading to full relapse. This self-defeating belief must be directly countered. The gains of recovery are not lost immediately. One drink need not lead to a drunk; one day's drinking need not lead to relapse. A slip is an emergency. But it can lead to more committed efforts to recover. Half of those who slip resume abstinence (Pickens et al., 1985). This is part of the wisdom contained in the AA slogan, "One day at a time."

*HALT.* Alcoholics Anonymous has developed the acronym HALT to identify situations that can lead readily to relapse. It is often useful to review the four elements with the group. *H* stands for hunger. The risks associated with hypoglycemia as either an acute or chronic condition can be discussed (see the metabolism exercise in chapter 4). *A* is for anger, the most frequently cited reason for relapse (Marlatt, 1978). Everyone attempting abstinence should have plans actively to resolve the problem or distract him- or herself from excessive anger. (Chapter 12 contains exercises on assertiveness and fair fighting that teach how to handle anger effectively.) *L* signifies loneliness, which can lead readily to self-pity and to the risks of relapse discussed earlier. Particularly if the loneliness is a symptom of social isolation, the need for involvement in a support group is critical. *T* is for tired. As with each of the four warning signs, tiredness represents an immediate risk because willpower and a commitment to recovery are at an ebb. Tiredness is also a sign of insufficient attention to needs for rest and recreation. Many alcoholics stop using drugs but maintain the same personality structure by shifting their preoccupation and becoming workaholics. This is not recovery.

A caveat: the foregoing can be adapted for those whose goal is controlled drinking. They too must manage moods and temptations if they are going to succeed. Their tolerance is chronic, even if they are not alcoholic. Those who need to abstain but do not "want to" may benefit from the reminder that recovery can begin before the desire to stay sober has been fully developed. However, a group with a minority made up of those who are abstaining will not be ready to identify with relapse prevention. It may be advantageous to split the group, for at least a session, so that only those committed to sobriety participate in the discussion. If the nonabstinent cannot be involved in a separate discussion or in viewing a more pertinent movie, they can be paired with abstainers whom they are to monitor throughout the discussion and about whose strength of commitment to recovery they can then give feedback. Abstainers are moved into an inner circle and encouraged to join the discussion. Nonabstainers remain silent observers from an outer circle. If they wish to comment, they must step into an empty chair among the abstainers, with all the symbolism of change that is entailed in such a move. I will use this approach if I want to silence a resistant subgroup or highlight the differences between those who have chosen to abstain and those who have not. When using this technique, be sure to allow time for individual feedback to the abstainer from the observer and then for general group comments.

# 11
# Evaluating Progress

E valuation is the critical time for decision in problem solving that determines the direction of future work. An evaluation of success leads to consolidating gains and discharge from treatment; failure leads to a recycling through the previous stages to identify and correct the earlier mistakes that have led to the unfavorable evaluation.

It is self-evaluation that makes problem solving a dynamic process. Drinkers can be given a regimen for recovery based on prescriptive approaches that provide pat solutions for given situations. Many wise counselors can tell a client what should be done; so long as treatment continues, external advice is readily available and the client will not be harmed by depending on others. But the key to sustained change lies in what happens after therapy has been concluded (Gorski & Miller, 1979; Marlatt & Gordon, 1985). A client who has learned to self-monitor progress and update plans as necessary will be able to respond effectively to changing conditions. If the client has learned problem solving, much of the counselor's role has been internalized and will be available to the individual long after treatment is over.

If the client has learned to self-evaluate, the therapist can be flexible. Instead of prescribing an optimal plan to a resistant client, the therapist may be able to develop a compromise approach more attractive to the client. Success builds confidence. Failure can lead to motivation to try more effective strategies—as long as self-evaluation continues assuring that failures are acknowledged and dealt with. Although the counselor can prompt self-evaluation and can function as an auxiliary monitor, the client must eventually assume responsibility for continued self-evaluation.

A number of related questions must be answered during the evaluation phase of problem solving. First, have plans been implemented? Second, do the plans contribute to attaining goals? Third, are the goals being met? Successful problem solving requires that each of these questions be consistently answered in the affirmative.

There are two additional criteria that determine whether the evaluation step has been completed appropriately. First, can the plans be integrated into the client's life-style so that the effort to change can be maintained? Plans need to complement significant values and be practiced enough so as to become habitual if they are to continue after treatment has ended. There will likely be a need to adjust plans adopted early in treatment, even if they once operated effectively, to meet these criteria. For example, initial abstinence accomplished through staying home and avoiding friends may be threatened by increasing boredom as the weeks pass. Plans are often modified so that there is less reliance on avoidance and more emphasis on the search for alternative means of gaining the positive effects previously sought through drinking. If these modified plans are in line with the client's values, the likelihood is greater that they will be maintained. Second, the client should have internalized the ability to evaluate progress. The following exercises give the client practice at self-monitoring and criteria for measuring progress, thus encouraging the development of the skill of self-evaluation.

The evaluation phase of problem solving identifies the need to rework previous steps that were not completed successfully. Resistance, defensiveness, or continued ignorance is implicated if goals are unrealistic or plans have been poorly matched to goals. Motivation needs to be reevaluated if plans are not being implemented. The plans themselves will need modification if a good faith effort fails to lead to consistent attainment of goals.

**To the Counselor.** It is not always appropriate to have a client continue in a problem-solving approach. It is a rational process, and alcohol abusers often fail to act in rational ways. At times this betokens a need to provide problem-solving training. Most behavioral models of intervention with alcohol abusers advocate such training (Gorski & Miller, 1979; Marlatt & Gordon, 1985; Sobell & Sobell, 1978). As with any skill, practice increases the likelihood of mastery. Recycling through earlier stages is clearly appropriate if there is evidence of partial success in changing, if there is an improving attitude, and if there is developing skill at self-evaluation. Initial failures often lay the groundwork for later success. Clients should be encouraged to learn from mistakes (that is, to use problem-solving skills) rather than to become discouraged. Though the prior efforts at goal setting and planning are designed to minimize the experience of failure, failure is still seen as a normal and temporary variant of the problem-solving process. But repeated failure, especially when the client experiences a sense of futility about change or an inability to observe and learn from previous experience, suggests that the client may not be able to use this approach to treatment.

An important part of the evaluation of a client's progress is for the counselor to identify when to make a referral for additional or alternative treatment. The client may be too impaired for outpatient therapy. Inpatient drug and alcohol rehabilitation is required of 3 percent of my clients and is voluntarily sought by perhaps another 5 percent in the interval between the DWI arrest and the conclusion of treatment. This course is particularly appropriate when an alcoholic client is rearrested during treatment, repeatedly attends group intoxicated, or totally fails to maintain trial abstinence. Psychotherapy may be appropriate for those whose emotionality overrides rational decision making or whose lack of social skills precludes productive involvement in the group. Clients who are unable to get beyond negativism and resistance may be unavailable for any treatment. They should be therapeutically discharged and handled judicially (if referred by the court system).

It may be evident that the client will respond to another approach besides problem solving. In this case, the counselor should be flexible enough to change stride to match the client. Group members often respond more to the personal qualities of the counselor than to the information imparted. This process is known as transference, and there is extensive literature on how it can be used in therapy (for example, Kennedy, 1977). Counselor empathy, caring, and involvement may provide the crucial motivation for change to a client who is seeking the counselor's approval. Other clients respond best to clear, authoritative guidance. Many alcoholics who become sober in AA do so by "keeping their mouths shut and following directions." In many cases DWI clients are not desperate enough to surrender their wills so totally to another, whether to an AA sponsor or to an alcohol counselor. Those who are should be treated with a prescriptive approach, usually with the expectation of intensive involvement in the Alcoholics Anonymous program. The problem-solving process is still active in these cases, although the counselor does most of the evaluation of progress. The beauty of the problem-solving model is that it provides maximum flexibility in conducting treatment while offering criteria for judging the adequacy of resulting change.

For the leader, evaluation goes beyond helping the individual clients take a look at their progress. Simultaneously, the leader is evaluating the progress of the group as a whole—by monitoring the success of the majority of members and the quality of the group process. A working group will offer support and advice to a member who is struggling. In short, a functioning group will encourage self-evaluation and will help the faltering client catch up. A group in trouble will avoid evaluating progress. It may be necessary for the counselor to return to exercises from earlier in the program. Evaluation is a recurrent process for each individual and for the group as a whole.

The capacity for honest self-evaluation is an important but elusive skill. It is not surprising that this ability will be atrophied or underdeveloped among clients who have been using a reality-distorting drug. The counselor will predictably find him- or herself in the position of providing for clients what the client cannot provide for themselves: honest evaluation of progress. This is only partially attributable to the counselor's role as authority in the group. I contend there is a further reason that the leader will be forced to judge: the client may not know how to self-evaluate. The counselor's goal is to model the qualities of an effective conscience for internalization by the client.

Guilt is an appropriate feeling; it should signal that change is needed. Many alcohol abusers have a preexisting antisocial personality disorder (Barry, 1982; Bohman, 1978; Pernanen, 1981). For them, the counselor is a parental superego, telling them clearly of the consequences if they do not conform to certain standards of conduct (in this case with regard to their drinking). More often, self-evaluation is evaded because of excessive guilt and a fragile sense of self-esteem. Many clients are rigidly judgmental. This is illustrated in the tough laws most clients would develop to deal with drunk drivers (see chapter 3). Research on moral development shows that there is a stage of immature conscience in which transgressions are punished harshly, without consideration of mitigating circumstances (Kohlberg, 1969). For these clients, the counselor must model the capacity for forgiveness and acceptance. Then judgment can be made with tolerance for human fallibility.

What qualities of conscience does the counselor seek to model for clients? Ideally: (1) Evaluation is a continuing process that is commonplace and not to be avoided. (2) Evaluation should be objective; standards need to conform to reality. (3) Mistakes are an opportunity for learning. Mistakes require change. A colleague, Glenn Paule-Carres, leads a pertinent discussion in which he asks clients whether they will tell their children about their DWI conviction and treatment. It is noted that parents want their children to respect them and so tend to highlight their successes and hide their failures. Yet the discussion concludes with an appreciation that one of the most valuable tools for living is to have one's parents teach one to learn from mistakes so that growth can proceed. From this perspective, real maturity is being able to admit a mistake and take corrective action. Failures are examined rationally to maximize learning, which is then applied in changed behavior. (4) To defuse self-blame and excessive emotionality, failures should be responded to with caring. Behavior can be bad even while the person engaging in it remains good. (5) The counselor expresses belief that clients can learn to use self-evaluation productively in their lives. There is underlying faith in the client's capacity to grow. The counselor makes judgments in the service of helping clients to become better judges of themselves. The exercises in this section provide clients the opportunity to use self-evaluation in a positive way.

**Related Activities.** Since self-evaluation is an ongoing process, any group activity provides an opportunity to measure progress. Articulating goals and plans provides opportunity and challenge to adhere to them. Normative standards become criteria for self-evaluation; the activities in the preceding chapter are a rich source of standards against which clients can measure themselves. The group members can be asked to compare their experience to the stages of recovery, with the elements of the twelve steps of the AA program, or with the relapse warning signs represented by the acronym HALT. In addition, questionnaires are available or can easily be developed which allow clients to check off symptoms of dry drunks or impending relapse. The disease curve (see chapter 7) includes a sequential list of expected signs of recovery which can be reviewed in group.

But most self-evaluation takes place outside of group, as clients anticipate or review their actions in drinking situations. This self-monitoring is brought into the group through responses to the question with which I typically open each session: "Has anything happened this week that you would like—or need—to share with the group?" An accepted invitation to share allows the group to participate in evaluating progress and handling setbacks. Even those who remain silent have, for a moment, reviewed their experience and asked themselves how they are doing.

# Evaluating Plans

*This exercise is a follow-up to the personal problem solving activity from chapter 8. The sheets completed at that time should be distributed for review. Pens and writing surfaces should be available. The group discussion will likely last for forty-five minutes during each of two sessions.*

**Rationale.** The primary goal is to involve each client in a self-evaluation of progress toward the related goals of avoiding drunk driving, altering drinking to prevent occurrence of other problems, and initiating the necessary lifestyle changes so that the alterations in drinking will be continuing and as comfortable as possible. The degree of progress is evaluated with respect to the personalized list of goals and plans—effectively a contract with oneself. Where there have been failures, the exercise supports recycling through the problem-solving process and developing more effective plans. Successes can be celebrated. Either way, there is a public recommitment to goal-directed change.

The individual and the group are central in this exercise, with the leader remaining quiet. It is the individual who presents an account of personal successes and failures, shares current plans, and decides on any alterations in plans. The group supports this work by empathizing with the efforts to change, by sharing similar experiences, and by offering strategies for handling challenging situations. It is also a test of the group's maturity. A functioning group will be interested, active, and willing to confront inadequate plans and effort. The mature group can make and express judgments about an individual's progress in a way that remains supportive. An immature group will avoid the threat of evaluation. The exercise will be eviscerated by the group's blandly praising all plans, no matter how unrealistic, or by changing the subject. The leader can use the quality of group interaction to plan subsequent sessions. Effective evaluation will surface issues that need to be discussed further, perhaps leading to exercises from chapter 12. An ineffective process alerts the leader that it is necessary for the group as a whole to recycle back to earlier stages in the problem-solving process.

When either the group or an individual needs to recycle, the following guidelines are suggested: (1) Return to the handling of hostility and defensiveness if plans are vague or there has been minimal effort to implement them. The failure in motivation usually represents regression to a negative attitude, on the part of the individual or the group, and it must be met by programming directed toward the first three steps in problem solving. (2) Failure when a client has made an effort to implement plans suggests a need to reevaluate the diagnosis and the goals. For example, it is particularly likely that early stage alcoholics will have to experience unintended loss of control while implementing controlled-drinking plans before they can accept the diagnosis. (3) Plans that will eventually be successful may fail at first simply because they are new and unpracticed. If there is evidence that needed skills or information may be lacking, the leader can offer skills training. In the interim, the group can offer encouragement while the individual develops extra support and backup plans to sustain the effort until the core plans become habitual. The recycling will be to selected areas in chapter 6 (for information), to chapter 10 (to refine plans), and to chapter 12 (for additional skills).

The exercise proceeds as a discussion among group members in response to the shared successes and failures of selected individuals in the group. It is typical and appropriate for the group to become immersed in a discussion about how to handle a particular situation or issue. This should proceed to completion. But the leader must eventually help the group return to the individual member, to his or her self-evaluation, and to the group's comments about the progress evident. I find that this discussion may begin to flag or become repetitious after forty-five minutes. It may be desirable to switch to a relevant activity (for example, role-playing handling pressure from friends) or to a movie about efforts to change drinking. If there is a switch, the leader needs to return to this exercise during subsequent sessions until each client has had an opportunity to share progress in achieving change goals.

This exercise is usually begun one to two months after the personal problem solving activity. It can be profitably repeated again three months later.

**Content.** Return the personal problem solving sheets completed previously. Ask clients to review their goals. Are the goals still current? Any changes in the first six stages of problem-solving may be noted. Are the goals (for avoiding drunk driving, for changing drinking, and for related life-style changes) being reached? Then plans should be silently reviewed. Are they succeeding? This implies both that the plans have been implemented and that they are contributing to one or more of the goals. Any new plans can be entered on the sheet, and outdated plans can be scratched off. The first step of the exercise, lasting about ten minutes, is privately to review and update the worksheet.

Each client will successively share personal goals, plans, and an evaluation of successes and failures. After the self-evaluation comes feedback from the group. There may be comments and suggestions about strengthening plans. There should be explicit evaluation about how well the individual appears to be progressing toward attaining the stated goals. The group needs to be reminded to be active and specific in their comments. It may be necessary to have each member in turn offer feedback after the sharing of the first one or two group members. This will clarify the norm and allow for guidance in the skill of offering feedback. (See Egan, 1976 for an excellent review of the "skills of challenge.")

The client should respond to the feedback, if only to confirm that it has been heard. If the group has suggested changes, the client should explicitly state which additional or altered plans he or she is willing to implement. If the group has suggested recycling through problem solving, the confrontation will have begun the process.

**Variation.** It will save time if the group is broken up into subgroups of three or four to conduct the evaluation. I seldom do this, feeling this benefit is outweighed by the loss of the opportunity to monitor group maturity, to keep all participants informed of the progress of each member, and to develop spontaneous discussions about pertinent issues raised during the sharing.

If the leader wants to make extensive recommendations, or wants to probe more deeply into sensitive material that may be unsuitable for group disclosure, the evaluation may be cursory during this exercise. The individual would receive a more detailed and private evaluation through the completion of a progress report, as outlined in the next section.

# Progress Reports

*Progress reports take up to fifteen minutes apiece. They should be done with each individual member at regular intervals throughout treatment.*

**Rationale.** First and foremost, the progress report is a chance for the counselor and the client to evaluate jointly the client's movement through the problem-solving process. The report culminates in written recommendations. These may be administrative, including discharge or release from treatment. The recommendations may also specify goals and plans. To the extent that they are mutually agreed upon, they function as a contract for change. Where there is disagreement, the report forces the client and the counselor to confront the differences in perspective, which clarifies the nature of the upcoming work that will be needed to resolve the conflicting viewpoints. For example, the client who continues to drink when the counselor diagnoses early stage alcoholism may be asked to complete the control test as one condition for successful involvement in the program. The progress report clarifies the mutual expectations of the client and counselor for the steps that must be taken for the client to comply with program goals. The group may be involved in the process. But unlike the situation in the previous exercise, the group is not central. It is the counselor and the client who must engage in dialogue. In the process, the client has the opportunity for self-evaluation and feedback from the counselor.

Second, the progress report can be used to meet the needs of the court or referring agency for information about the client's success in treatment. A report will be completed at the conclusion of treatment. One or more reports will also be done during the course of therapy, alerting both the client and the referring agency to the client's progress in facing and resolving the drinking problem.

**Content.** The progress report may be done privately during a break or at the end of the group session.

The report is written. But it is generated out of a free-flowing dialogue. To highlight the self-evaluative aspect of the task, I will typically begin by asking the client, "How do you think you are progressing in handling the drinking [or drinking/driving] problem?" The ensuing discussion will cover the steps of problem solving, with the counselor asking about any areas that have not been covered. Although the specific format of the written document must be modified to meet the reporting requirements in each setting, the following should be covered:

1. Any evidence of being intoxicated during the group sessions. This is a prime indicator of the degree of availability for therapeutic involvement in treatment. Clients unable to attend "straight" are too hostile or too impaired to succeed in outpatient treatment. Any using during sessions becomes part of the documentation justifying noncompliant return for judicial disposition or required inpatient rehabilitation.
2. Attitude toward treatment, as evident in the quantity and quality of participation in group.
3. Evidence of learning, including the personal application of cognitive information covered in group.
4. Self-diagnosis, with comments about the degree of acceptance, residual defensiveness, and the counselor's sense of the accuracy of the self-assessment.
5. Current drinking and long-term goals for drinking.
6. Evaluation of success and of strategies for avoiding drunk driving.
7. Evaluation of success and of plans to change drinking and to make lifestyle changes so that drinking problems will not recur.
8. Contract for change: the accepted recommendations for change, including further plans or maintaining current strategies.
9. Additional recommendations for change, including requirements for compliant release from treatment.
10. Status in the program, including evaluation of readiness for release, prognosis and degree of improvement at the time of release, remaining problem-solving steps and estimated interval before release, and reasons for any noncompliant termination from treatment.

The progress report gives the client a chance to evaluate progress, both as seen internally and from the perspective of the counselor. It also represents a time for private sharing, for feedback to the counselor, and for confirming the therapeutic alliance. Although there is evaluation, the tone is not always judgmental. Many progress reports become an opportunity to celebrate changes already made.

**Variations.** The progress report may be done in group, with feedback from other members. I often ask the group to interview the client, while I write. The group setting is particularly appropriate if there is successful change to be modeled and celebrated or if the individual must address an issue that is pertinent to several other participants. Group involvement is appropriate if the leader is trying to develop a group norm for feedback and candid evaluation of progress. Lastly, the group may be needed to assist in an intervention. When a client is given the choice of complying with an unwanted recommendation or being dropped from treatment, the group can support the client through the initial hostility at the leader and yet encourage appropriate action.

# Grief Work

*This presentation lasts forty-five minutes and requires a chalkboard.*

**Rationale.** A recovering alcoholic friend tells of the time she ordered tonic water and was instead served a gin and tonic. After a first taste, she had her husband confirm the presence of alcohol and then set the drink aside. When he asked her what she thought, she responded simply: "An old friend."

For most alcohol abusers, alcohol is "an old friend." What is it like to say goodbye permanently, to lose an old friend forever? Especially when the relationship is a central part of living, or when there is a sense of guilt and responsibility for the ending, the person will probably experience prolonged mourning (Bugen, 1977). The alcoholic who must abstain, and even the problem drinker who gives up the drunkenness and the carefree drinking, can be expected to go through a grief process.

To understand the grief process and to be encouraged to express the feelings that typically accompany it enables ex-drinkers to manage early recovery more easily and to reach a stable acceptance more readily. This exercise provides clients with the tools to evaluate their progress in mourning the loss of their old relationship with alcohol. The goal is to reach a stable acceptance of the change.

This presentation may be in response to a client's sharing about other personal losses such as a death in the family or the end of a marriage. Most often, however, the exercise is timed so that it is delivered when clients are grieving the end of the old relationship with alcohol.

**Content.** Elizabeth Kubler-Ross (1969) is credited with raising public awareness about the process of coping with death and dying. If clients are familiar with her work, they can be asked to share their understanding. If not, the group can be told that she interviewed patients and came to understand that there are predictable feelings that come unbidden and automatically which must be dealt with by those who are dying.

The acronym DABDA is written on the board. The group is asked to name the likely feelings represented. With help, the group identifies and illustrates the key stages:

1. *Denial:* "It can't be me. Those must be someone else's test results. It is all a misunderstanding. I'm not that bad." Denial is an initial buffer against a full awareness of unwanted reality. It is a defense. If there is time, the denial will gradually lose some of its power and the reality of death can be acknowledged. Often, denial will recur, so that anticipatory grief work proceeds in starts and stops.

2. *Anger:* Rage, envy, and resentment are displaced on the ones around the dying person. In the hospital this will be the "unfeeling" nurses or the "incompetent" doctor. It may be focused on loved ones, or on an acquaintance who seems to have no purpose for living: "It should have been him and not me." In frustration over the unwanted change, the patient may shake his fist at God, at "the system," or at any outside authority. The person is hard to live with when angry. But it is a sign that death is being acknowledged, that feelings are being expressed, and that the grief work is proceeding.

3. *Bargaining:* There is an attempt to strike a deal with God ("I will never again . . ."), with the doctor ("Can't you operate and take my lung. I promise I'll follow your instructions perfectly"), or with death ("Just give me a few more weeks"). Motivated by guilt over transgressions for which death is seen as the penalty, the patient tries to win a reprieve by promising to change. But the bargaining will continue indefinitely, since it is motivated by the hope of avoiding the ultimate change.

4. *Depression:* When the reality hits home, there will be a sense of loss and preparatory grief. Reassurance is not helpful, since there is need to express the sorrow over the losses.

5. *Acceptance:* When the feelings have been expressed and the reality is fully acknowledged, there will be the peace that comes when the struggle is over. There may be an absence of feelings. There may be little need to talk, and the dying patient may no longer welcome visitors. The patient has let go of the old life.

The process of moving through these feelings is unsteady. It may take different lengths of time, some stages may be skipped or experienced out of sequence, and there will be a tendency to vacillate back and forth so that there will be repeated episodes of denial. A patient may get stuck, especially if he or she cannot face or discuss a stage (Ramsay & Noorbergen, 1981). But eventually there will be a tendency for more and more time to be spent in acceptance.

This process has application beyond those who are dying. Kubler-Ross (1969) found that the families of patients faced the same process, although not at the same pace. The patient might be reaching acceptance, only to have to contend with an angry spouse who promises "to get you out of here to some place where they can help you." Long after the patient has admitted the problem, some relative will be trying to persuade him "not to give up" since "you're not really sick—not compared to Uncle Jack, who had it really bad." The family's grief work is complicated by guilt over imagined responsibility for the illness or past conflicts with the patient. Moreover, the family has to continue after the death, facing life without the lost one. Survivors often develop stress-related physical symptoms, become preoccupied with thoughts of the lost one, or withdraw from the world and lose the initiative to develop a new daily routine (Lindemann, 1944). The mourning continues after the patient's death until the relatives learn to free themselves from the dependence on the lost one, to adjust to a new daily routine, and to form new relationships.

This process is applicable not only to dying patients and their families, but to anyone who has suffered an important loss. This is the grief process. Clients can be asked whether they went through anything like these stages in response to any losses in their lives. Moves, broken relationships, changes in work environments, and changes in habits may be discussed.

If the idea is not suggested by a client, the leader should note that the change in drinking entails a loss of the old pattern of alcohol use. Even for those who are grateful for the opportunity to rid themselves of an injurious habit there is still loss. The stages of grieving apply as well to the person who has attempted to give up the old relationship with alcohol.

There is usually a great deal of identification with the listed stages. The discussion should be encouraged, as should any ventilation of feelings. But the exercise has a self-evaluative purpose as well. The presentation concludes with a go-round in which each participant is asked to identify which stage was the hardest to deal with and which best represents his or her current feelings.

**Variations.** Selected clients can be invited to review the history of their attempts to come to terms with the need to change their drinking.

Clients who see themselves as stuck in bargaining can be asked to do a Gestalt dialogue (Perls, Hefferline, & Goodman, 1951). They can be asked to identify with whom they are bargaining. Most often it is the entity "alcoholism." In the dialogue, they alternately play themselves and alcoholism. This counseling technique can help them clarify the defenses and the fears about change that typically underlie an attempt to hold on to unsafe drinking practices.

# The Self-Esteem Trap

*This discussion lasts from fifteen to forty-five minutes and uses a chalkboard or flipchart.*

**Rationale.** There is a vicious circle in which alcohol-related troubles contribute to growing self-hatred, which is then masked by self-medication with further drinking. This is the self-esteem trap. It must be labeled and understood for "stress drinkers" (Vaughn, 1982) to restore their pride in themselves as competent and loving human beings. This discussion develops a model of the trap, showing the contribution of a negative self-image to continued destructive drinking. Specifically, understanding the model (1) reframes painful drinking experiences so that guilt and self-hatred are relabeled as drug induced; (2) reinforces acceptance of the disease concept; (3) highlights the role of emotions in recovery and relapse; (4) emphasizes the importance of enhancing self-esteem as part of recovery; and (5) warns of the paradoxical danger of overconfidence as self-esteem grows.

This presentation is appropriate for the evaluation stage because it is at this stage of the process, when efforts to change have been initiated, that self-esteem is most pivotal and unstable. Some clients will be blocked from changing by a lack of self-confidence. For them it is useful to understand that their failures may be attributed to their drugged state rather than to intrinsic worthlessness. Others find that initial success leads to renewed defensiveness—the "false pride" that suggests that the drinking problem was not really that bad or that its solution won't really require much effort. If evaluating progress contributes to overconfidence, it is timely to stress the importance of balance between pride and humility. Realistic self-esteem avoids the extremes, whether of self-loathing or conceitedness.

This discussion may result from a client's spontaneous sharing of problems, from processing the disease concept, or from the presentation of the *I/E* idea in Fr. Joseph Martin's movie *Chalk Talk* (see chapter 6).

**Content.** The simplest form of the model shows the vicious circle:

$$\curvearrowright \text{excessive drinking} \ \rightarrow \text{trouble} \rightarrow \text{guilt}$$

Any group member with a history of self-punishing drinking will readily recognize the self-esteem trap.

In a recent session, a young man was sharing a distressing experience that still preoccupied him years after it occurred. He had been drinking heavily and had gotten into an argument with his wife. Impulsively, he tried to throw her from the back of a pickup truck traveling at fifty-five miles per hour. With real pain he said, "I would have succeeded—I had her on the side—if our friends hadn't grabbed me." Parallel sharing from other group members and empathy from the leader enabled him to acknowledge his former drunken desire to see her "bust open on the highway." He did not see himself as a violent person and yet had to accept the evidence of his experience. He felt very guilty.

This contrast of self-image and experience enabled us to discuss the difference between saying about oneself "I do bad things" and "I am a bad person." It is difficult to feel good about yourself if you are saying the latter. In contrast, self-esteem need not be damaged by saying "I do bad things" so long as good efforts and intentions can also be recognized. The group decided that isolated problems could be accepted but that recurring problems must lead to bad feelings about the core self.

At this point another group member shared his growing self-contempt over a seven-month period of heavy drinking, ending with a failed attempt to shoot his girlfriend and himself. The contrast of his former desperation and his pride as he sat newly sober in group provided a powerful contextual message about the instability of self-esteem among alcoholic drinkers.

Repeatedly putting oneself in situations in which emotions—and particularly drugged emotions—control behavior leads to recurring problems and to an eventual deterioration of self-esteem. With enough repetition, trouble is internalized in expectations about oneself:

"Bad things happen to me" becomes "I am bad"

"I have lost important things" in time is translated "I'm a loser"

"I can't control what's happening" finally turns to "I am powerless"

Once this negative identity is accepted, self-confidence is undermined, and the ability to change in positive ways declines. The damage to self-esteem becomes fixed. Abusive drinking continues, in part to dull self-contempt. Previously, problems would have lead to appropriate concern and efforts to change ("I'm getting carried away with my drinking—this has got to stop"). Once the negative expectations are internalized, the effort to change decreases and the drinker gives in to resignation and the "I don't give a damn" attitude. Recurring problems come to be seen as expected and deserved; after all, "I am a loser."

This is a good juncture at which further sharing can be invited. Self-contempt is isolating. Most clients protect their damaged self-esteem by keeping secret those experiences that are most painful. Given a supportive climate and the context set by this presentation, drinkers may unburden themselves of preoccupying memories. The act of sharing is healing, as is the experience of universality that develops when others acknowledge similar experiences and feelings (Yalom, 1985).

The presentation also provides the information with which clients can reinterpret their behavior. Here it is useful to help them assume diminished responsibility for their behavior. Instead of blaming themselves for being intrinsically violent or evil, they can relabel themselves as impaired by a toxic drug. Father Martin's film *Chalk Talk* is an invaluable source of perspective.

In comparing the intoxicating effects of alcohol and its chemical relative ether, Father Martin notes the progressive loss of mental functions with increasing doses of the drug. With intellect ($I$) and common sense mildly inhibited, emotions ($E$) come to the surface. Normally this is the relaxed and expressive state of mild intoxication sought with alcohol. High-tolerance drinkers tend to go well beyond the mild euphoria. The group readily acknowledges that $I$ over $E$ becomes $E$ over $I$ with two to four drinks. One of the most common impulses is then to continue drinking ("let's go for that sporting buzz"). With considerably more imbibing, there is little remaining $I$ to temper the increasingly primitive and drug-affected impulses that surface. Here the analogy to ether is especially useful. Father Martin rhetorically asks his audience what they would think of a psychiatrist who tries to evaluate a patient who is under the influence of ether. The extension is obvious: when grossly under the influence of alcohol, the behavior of the heavy drinker is as remote from his "true personality" as is that of the person coming out from under anesthesia.

The discussion to this point is designed to free up the drinker who has convinced himself that he is evil. It offers diminished responsibility as a strategic maneuver. It does not imply total absense of responsibility. After all, the person chose to drink and so remains accountable. The path out is to acknowledge that he has a habit or disease that periodically eliminates his ability to control his drinking. This is often raised spontaneously in the group discussion. If it is not, the leader may explicitly state that many drinkers found release from guilt and an avenue for productively assuming responsibility for their lives when they were able to accept fully the idea that they have a disease.

The group is asked, "What are the ways to break the vicious cycle?" Typical responses include: (1) A fortuitous lift to the person's self-esteem. Particularly for the person marginally involved in the cycle, a pay raise, a social success, or an empathic encounter reminding him of his resources may be sufficient to break the cycle. In effect, he says, "It's time to get on with my life, and drinking this way won't help." (2) Hitting bottom—some combination of events that leave the drinker too sick or miserable to continue with the cycle. This experience is familiar to those with AA experience, who are often mid- or late-stage alcoholics. But it also occurs among many who are psychologically dependent. One man talked about months of constant drinking after the sudden death of his wife. It ended when his young daughter woke him one day at 8:00 P.M. to ask when he was going to fix dinner. The image of her face and his guilt over ignoring her needs were enough to jolt him out of his self-pity. He was able to resume responsibilities and go back to relatively moderate drinking. (3) Outside intervention—even the crew who insist they can beat their drinking on "willpower" tend to acknowledge the importance of something from the outside putting an end to the drinking. Often this means hospitalization, though we often have people describe the shock of a DWI arrest and subsequent confrontation in outpatient therapy as being adequate to break the drinking cycle. (4) Acceptance that they have the disease of alcoholism—this brings with it a certain release of responsibility; after all, the disease process prevents their willpower from protecting them against intoxication (and the *E/I* state). Guilt can be reduced. Energy is instead devoted to the challenge of adjusting to a sober lifestyle.

This discussion can be profoundly liberating to clients burdened by self-contempt. The model, drawn on the board and shown in figure 11–1, presents a visual schema that explains and allows them to externalize their guilt over being involved in self-destructive cycles of drinking.

There is often enough meaningful discussion to stop the presentation with the focus on how to interrupt the cycle. But I often choose to push further. Particularly if the group is reluctant to accept the disease concept or underestimates the power of alcoholism, I will continue with a discussion of how people fall back into the vicious cycle once they have escaped. My query usually elicits two explanations for relapsing, both linked to an unstable self-image: (1) Some event that leads to a sudden decline in self-esteem—social rejection, a death in the family, or some other important loss—is often enough to precipitate resumed self-destructive drinking. (2) Overconfidence. Paradoxically, feeling too good can be just as great a threat in the early stages of recovery. Many slips occur because overconfident abstainers reimmerse themselves in the drinking situations they carefully avoided during the initial struggle to quit, citing some variation on "I can handle it now that I'm so much more in charge of things."

This last point of discussion has a chastening effect on most groups which may be inconsistent with the previous objective of reducing guilt and fostering acceptance of the disease concept. I use it selectively and only when I believe the group needs to be confronted with the difficulty in avoiding reinvolvement with the vicious circle. This will happen most frequently if the group has adopted a counterdependent stance in which many members are alcoholics who are intent on "beating it on their own." It will also be included if the discussion is initiated in response to a member's slip through overconfidence.

The power of the last addition to the model lies in the dichotomous thinking that has typified many in my groups. They are quite prepared to recognize that "underconfidence" is detrimental but are correspondingly inclined to believe that its opposite must be beneficial. When presented with the idea that overconfidence is equally a risk, most agree but feel dispiritingly hemmed in. This makes them more receptive to further discussion of the need for some kind of emotional balance, often cast in terms of the AA slogans: "One day at a time," "First things first," and "Easy does it." At

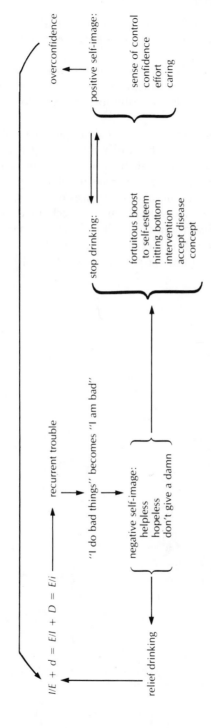

**Figure 11–1. The Self-Esteem Trap: The Vicious Circles of Abusive Drinking and the Avenues of Escape**

other times, the discussion links to more frankly psychotherapeutic topics such as emotional control using rational emotive techniques.

**Variations.** Although typically developed in response to a client's sharing guilt-laden material, the model can be presented in processing the *Chalk Talk* movie or in discussing the contribution of psychological problems to excessive drinking.

Elements of the model may be omitted. Depending on the degree to which the model elicits sharing, the leader may restrict discussion to "the trap" and postpone discussion of abstinence and recovery of self-esteem. Some groups may not need to review the risks of relapse and overconfidence at this point. The leader has a number of choices of emphasis.

The discussion of AA or psychotherapeutic techniques, which is a frequent upshot of this presentation, anticipates the group members' more detailed discussion in the next phase of the problem-solving process—consolidating gains and continuing recovery—which will be the subject of the next chapter.

# 12

# Consolidating Gains for the Continuing Effort

The effective client in a working group will reach the concluding phase of problem solving before completing treatment. This stage of therapy provides the opportunity to make plans and acquire skills for the continuing effort to maintain altered drinking patterns. Goals at this stage include (1) considering plans to keep alive the attitude of concern and effort; (2) greater familiarity with problem solving, so that the model can be used independently; (3) arrangements to find any necessary replacement for the treatment group; and (4) the identification of directions and resources for future growth. In sum, a client will have completed this stage and be ready for discharge after having made an appropriate change in drinking and having developed workable plans to maintain the gains.

Recovery means moving on to a more productive and enjoyable life. The focus broadens beyond drinking to survey essential skills in living. The exercises that follow address some of the most commonly encountered issues for those seeking continued personal growth, and provide tools to counteract the stresses that might undermine their continuing change effort.

There is a risk as the focus broadens; a scattershot approach may prove confusing or overwhelming to the client (Brownell et al., 1986). A superficial exposure to too many new skills may backfire, since there may be reversion to pathological habits in the absense of mastery of any single new alternative. There are two caveats to keep in mind in using the following exercises. First, these exercises are introductory. Their intent is to expose clients to needed information and skills. A referral to additional resources will have to be made before the client can be expected to develop mastery of the skill. It is the counselor's job to be aware of the local resources, although some general suggestions are included in each of the following sections. Second, these exercises are not a routine part of the group curriculum. One or more of these exercises may be sampled with a group—if there is interest on the part of the members and if the counselor feels the topic is important for a significant number of the participants. In chapter 10 are the topics that are likely to be germane to most clients and most groups. The presentations in this chapter are discretionary.

Among the possible topics are the following:

1. *Self-esteem and self-awareness.* The treatment group can heighten self-esteem by systematically reinforcing positive self-statements and expecting this to result in lasting improvements in the drinking pattern (Opei & Jackson, 1984). Referrals for group psychotherapy, particularly if it employs expressive techniques that facilitate recovery of a full range of feelings, are an important treatment option.

2. *Nutrition.* Because hypoglycemia and malnutrition are common results of alcohol abuse, clients may need to alter their diets. Important ideas are addressed in Ketcham and Mueller's *Eating Right to Live Sober.* Local nutritionists, physicians, or holistic healers with experience in treating alcoholics should be identified.

3. *Exercise.* Conditioning programs build self-esteem as well as restore bodies that may have been long neglected. My clients are urged to have a general physical examination before beginning an exercise program. There is now a network of sports physicians, intramural programs, and fitness facilities that can help in planning a well-balanced exercise regimen. The work by Cooper (1977, 1982) may serve as a good introduction for those who want to begin by reading about aerobic conditioning.

4. *Interventions.* Many clients will be involved with friends and family members who are in need of treatment for their own addictions. Both Johnson's book *I'll Quit Tomorrow* and the movie of the same name provide an introduction to this approach to actively confronting a person with the costs of dependency. Local ministers, mental health professionals, employee assistance programs, or substance abuse programs may provide this service. Prior to arranging an intervention, it is important to develop a support network for the concerned family. This is best accomplished through referrals to AlAnon and through reading Drews's (1980–1986) books entitled *Getting Them Sober.*

The alert counselor will soon supplement this list and the activities outlined in this chapter with additional vehicles for helping clients continue their personal development.

# *Addressing ACOA Recovery*

*The presentation and movie take about ninety minutes. Projection or videotape equipment is required.*

**Rationale.** Most clients show significant symptoms of codependency (see chapter 6 for definitions and further discussion). Untreated, codependency undermines recovery efforts by frustrating attempts to live a satisfying sober life. It contributes to dry drunks, to impulsive relapse, or to chronic subclinical depression. Fortunately, it is an eminently treatable condition.

Treatment for the stress of growing up in an alcoholic family is usually delayed until there is a secure change in the drinking pattern (usually including six months of sobriety for alcoholics). This is because the therapy is stressful and likely to provoke intense negative emotions that may distract from or even overwhelm efforts to change. There is no harm in a client's early identification as an adult child of an alcoholic family (ACOA). The additional diagnosis provides an explanation of some of the troubles encountered during the period of initial change in drinking, and, by doing so, reassures the clients that things can be expected to improve if they persevere in treatment.

There may be overriding reasons to treat codependency immediately. Alcohol abuse and ACOA issues should be treated concurrently when there is intoxication to self-medicate emotional pain, emotional explosiveness, excess conflict in primary relationships that distract the person from change efforts, or inability to use help because of pervasive guilt and low self-esteem. To the extent that being an ACOA contributes to these impediments, codependency treatment may be immediately necessary if success in addressing the drinking problem is to be achieved.

There are two goals for this exercise. The first is for those with prominent symptoms of codependency to identify the presence of the syndrome in their lives. The second is for these clients to understand the resources available to assist in the process of recovery from codependency. In many cases, understanding that their chronic emotional pain results from a treatable condition provides these clients with a high level of motivation for therapy.

This exercise is a continuation of the discussion of family costs (see chapter 6). The two activities may be combined. But there are differences that may justify separating the presentations. The family cost role-play focuses on the experience of children in the alcoholic home, with clients invited to consider what their drinking will do to their own children. The current presentation propels clients into a consideration of the effect of their childhood family experiences on their own adult functioning. In this frame, they are the victims rather than the victimizers. If this switch in focus would prove disruptive, the two exercises should be separated.

**Content.** There are several options for helping clients to identify whether they are suffering from codependency. The most powerful is the recognition that they have played one or more of the survival roles (Enabler, Hero, Scapegoat, Lost Child, or Mascot) long enough so that it has influenced their self-identity. Material on these roles may have to be reviewed (from chapter 6).

Alternatively, there can be a discussion of the characteristics of adult children of alcoholic families. At the core is chronic low self-esteem, evident in passivity, extreme dependency or counterdependency, guilt, or depression. In combination with a pervasive mistrust of authority, the low self-esteem makes it difficult for the client to ask for help even when he or she is experiencing significant personal pain. Clients who remain silent in group when they feel they are dying within can identify with this evidence of the operation of the "Don't Talk" and "Don't Trust" rules (Black, 1981). The "Don't Feel" injunction leads the adult child into difficulties managing emotions. Many clients will identify with the typical pattern of being unaware of specific feelings (because of denial or repression) until self-defeating withdrawal or explosiveness occurs. Such mood swings undermine love relationships. Codependents commonly show intimacy problems (Wegscheider-Cruse, 1985; Woititz, 1985). This may be because of avoidance of emotional sharing, especially among men. The women are more likely to show excessive dependence—the type of love addiction in which they remain emotionally attached to the potential in their partner and are oblivious to the frustration they experience in contact with the real person (Norwood, 1985). Additionally, codependents may show difficulties in sustained efforts at problem solving. Conditioned from childhood to seek immediate emotional gratification, since delayed rewards were not reliably provided as promised, these clients have little faith that persistent effort will ever pay off. One client summarized this beautifully, saying, "I get halfway across a bridge and then jump into the river; I know the bridge is going to collapse anyway." If clients have found themselves, during treatment, making plans to change without then following through, they may be seeing further evidence of codependency's undermining their effectiveness in living. Discussion of these characteristics aids in self-diagnosing.

Perhaps the best summary of typical personality patterns found among adult children of alcoholics is derived from Janet Woititz (1983). The group can read and attempt to identify with each of the thirteen characteristics listed in figure 12–1.

A more indirect means of identifying the presence of codependency is through completing a questionnaire designed to determine the presence of parental alcoholism. This approach may block identification if codependent patterns were learned in other types of dysfunctional families. But the questionnaire has the advantage of helping identification by those in denial of parental alcoholism, and it carries the power we ascribe to objective scores. Figure 12–2 reproduces the Children of Alcoholics Screening Test (Jones, 1983).

Identification is the beginning of the recovery process, which continues when the "Don't Talk" rule is broken and help is sought. Next comes the

Adult children of alcoholics characteristically:
1. Guess at what normal is.
2. Have difficulty following a project through from beginning to end.
3. Lie when it would be just as easy to tell the truth.
4. Judge themselves without mercy.
5. Have difficulty having fun.
6. Take themselves very seriously.
7. Have difficulty with intimate relationships.
8. Overreact to changes over which they have no control.
9. Constantly seek approval and affirmation.
10. Feel they are different from other people.
11. Are either superresponsible or superirresponsible.
12. Are extremely loyal, even in the face of evidence that the loyalty is undeserved.
13. Are impulsive. They tend to lock themselves into a course of action without giving serious consideration to alternative behaviors or possible consequences. This impulsivity leads to confusion, self-loathing, and loss of control over their environment. In addition, they spend an excessive amount of energy cleaning up the mess.

*Source:* From Woititz, J. G. (1983). *Adult Children of Alcoholics.* Hollywood, FL: Health Communications. Reprinted with permission.

**Figure 12–1. Characteristics of Adult Children of Alcoholics**

painful process of reacknowledging feelings and reexperiencing the old hurt, with the understanding that it was a by-product of the parental (or grandparental) addiction and not personally deserved. Emotions that are acknowledged and brought into play in relationships eventually become the basis for a developing sense of personal integrity. With this new feeling of self-worth, it is possible to set more appropriate boundaries—in work and in relationships. New skills at self-care make it possible for these clients to relinquish the old survival roles gradually. With support, new patterns of behavior can be integrated. This thumbnail sketch of the recovery process shows that growth out of codependency is a protracted and challenging adventure, one that promises better integration of emotions, enriched relationships, and enhanced self-esteem.

There is a rapidly growing network of supportive services to assist in recovery. Residential treatment for ACOAs is becoming available in workshops lasting from a weekend to a month. There are also an increasing number of therapists who understand codependency. ACOAs can expect such treatment to help them develop insight into the present-day effects of childhood family experiences. The treatment is typically expressive, with insight supplemented by experiential techniques. These allow the corrective reengagement with old feelings and old relationships. But the intensive treatment typically begins after preliminary involvement with two important

C.A.S.T.

Yes  No

1. Have you ever thought that one of your parents had a drinking problem?
2. Have you ever lost sleep because of a parent's drinking?
3. Did you ever encourage one of your parents to quit drinking?
4. Did you ever feel alone, scared, nervous, angry, or frustrated because a parent was not able to stop drinking?
5. Did you ever argue or fight with a parent when he or she was drinking?
6. Did you ever threaten to run away from home because of a parent's drinking?
7. Has a parent ever yelled at or hit you or other family members when drinking?
8. Have you ever heard your parents fight when one of them was drunk?
9. Did you ever protect another family member from a parent who was drinking?
10. Did you ever feel like hiding or emptying a parent's bottle of liquor?
11. Do many of your thoughts revolve around a problem drinking parent or difficulties that arise because of his or her drinking?
12. Did you ever wish that a parent would stop drinking?
13. Did you ever feel responsible for and guilty about a parent's drinking?
14. Did you ever fear that your parents would get divorced due to alcohol misuse?
15. Have you ever withdrawn from and avoided outside activities and friends because of embarrassment and shame over a parent's drinking problem?
16. Did you ever feel caught in the middle of an argument or fight between a problem drinking parent and your other parent?
17. Did you ever feel that you made a parent drink alcohol?
18. Have you ever felt that a problem drinking parent did not really love you?
19. Did you ever resent a parent's drinking?
20. Have you ever worried about a parent's health because of his or her alcohol use?
21. Have you ever been blamed for a parent's drinking?
22. Did you ever think your father was an alcoholic?
23. Did you ever wish your home could be more like the homes of your friends who did not have a parent with a drinking problem?
24. Did a parent ever make promises to you that he or she did not keep because of drinking?
25. Did you ever think your mother was an alcoholic?
26. Did you ever wish that you could talk to someone who could understand and help the alcohol-related problems in your family?
27. Did you ever fight with your brothers and sisters about a parent's drinking?
28. Did you ever stay away from home to avoid the drinking parent or your other parent's reaction to the drinking?
29. Have you ever felt sick, cried, or had a "knot" in your stomach after worrying about a parent's drinking?
30. Did you ever take over any chores and duties at home that were usually done by a parent before he or she developed a drinking problem?

Scoring: Total the number of yes answers. If there are 0 or 1 yes responses, there is *no parental drinking problem;* 2–5 yes answers suggest a *problem drinking parent;* 6 or more yes answers indicate *an alcoholic parent* (Pilat & Jones, 1985).

*Source:* From Jones, J.W., (1983). The Children of Alcoholics Screening Test: Test Manual. Chicago, IL: Camelot Unlimited. Reprinted with permission.

## Figure 12–2. Children of Alcoholics Screening Test

sources of support. The first is a self-help group fellowship, either through AlAnon or a specialty group for ACOAs. The second resource for beginning recovery work is bibliotherapy. There are a number of excellent books available. I particularly recommend the books by Black (1981, 1985), Norwood (1985), Wegscheider-Cruse (1981, 1985), and Woititz (1983, 1985). I refer clients to these wellsprings of recovery with the caution to avoid falling into the classic codependent's trap of trying to do it alone when they need to allow others to be involved in their growth. If there is a solid connection with the reading and the support groups, recovery will proceed.

The 1983 movie *Another Chance*, by Sharon Wegscheider-Cruse, gives an inside look at one person's recapitulation of her life, using family reconstruction as the therapeutic tool. It dramatically documents the anger, hurt, guilt, and low self-esteem arising out of a childhood in a chemically dependent family. But as the role-playing extends to the early experiences of the parents, the persecutors are themselves seen as victims and the ACOA's rage is eclipsed by caring and forgiveness. The emotions are expressed. Then comes behavior change. Again interacting with role-players representing significant family members, the client renegotiates relationships with current intimates.

The movie gives an overview of recovery from codependency in intensive therapy. It provides an opportunity for identifying. It gives clients a sense of the emotions that must be faced and the encounters with loved ones that must be made as recovery unfolds. Because the film captures the intensity of a weekend of advanced work, the depth of sharing can be intimidating for some clients unused to expressive work. But for those whose codependency complicates efforts to change a problem drinking pattern, the film gives a clear message that there is expert support for both aspects of recovery.

# Relaxation Training

*This exercise takes about forty-five minutes and requires no props.*

**Rationale.** A number of productive ways to alter consciousness have been proposed as an alternative to using psychoactive drugs. Self-hypnosis, alpha chambers, biofeedback, prayer, meditation, and progressive relaxation have all been touted as useful alternatives. Despite the differences in instructions (and in the marketing), there is an underlying similarity in the physiological state resulting from any of these approaches (Shapiro, 1982). It has been called the relaxation response (Benson, 1975). It involves a reduction in physical stress in combination with a relaxed mental attentiveness that creates a sense of peace and well-being.

Relaxation training contributes to the continuing change effort in several ways. It reduces stress levels. Regular meditation will make it a routine to take some time for oneself during each day, providing an opportunity for daily growth work. Relaxation is also a specific technique for combating cravings. Not only does it provide an alternative way to achieve stress reduction, but it also provides a focus that distracts from the obsession with drinking.

Because different clients will respond positively to different approaches to relaxation, it is suggested that the experiential presentation include two or more approaches. I tend to use hypnosis, progressive relaxation, and breathing techniques. But that is a matter of personal preference and training. Optimally the counselor will know several techniques and tailor the presentation to the preferences of each group.

**Content.** Begin with a discussion of relaxation. It should be suggested that each client can develop a personal variation on the approach presented, that there will be greater success with regular practice, and that there will be noticeable results with as few as ten minutes a day of meditation—although the suggested routine would involve two daily periods of meditation lasting twenty minutes each. If guided imagery is to be used, the group agrees on a desirable place for a destination.

A modification of Jacobson's (1929) progressive relaxation is used. Clients are invited to loosen tight clothing, remove glasses, set down coffee cups, shift chairs so that they can lean their heads back against the wall, close their eyes, and generally make themselves comfortable. They are asked to be aware of their breathing—its pace, depth, and flow. Often there is a deep, cleansing breath in response to attention to typically constricted respiration. In the same way, awareness of tension can lead to deliberate efforts to let go. Progressive relaxation makes the contrast conscious by deliberately constricting a muscle group to heighten tension, holding it for up to five seconds until it becomes uncomfortable, and then relaxing the muscles and enjoying the difference in feeling. When attention shifts to the next muscle group, clients attempt to retain the relaxation in parts of the body previously worked on. Clients with injuries or knotted muscles should be instructed to omit painful contraction, although they can concentrate on releasing tension in the sensitive areas. The leader illustrates the "tense, hold, release" process by having participants make a fist and then notice the warmth and pleasant limpness they will usually feel when the fingers relax. The process is repeated systematically for other parts of the body:

1. Lift both legs off the ground, pointing the toes away, tightening the legs up through the thighs
2. Lift the legs, pointing the toes back toward the head, tightening the calves
3. Push the knees together, tightening through the buttocks
4. Push the stomach out and the shoulders back into the chair, tensing the back
5. Suck the stomach in, tightening the chest and holding a breath in
6. Hold up the arms and splay the fingers, tensing the arms
7. Lift the arms horizontal to the ground; clench the fists; create an arc of tension running through the arms, shoulders, and neck
8. Push the shoulders back and the shoulder blades together
9. Shrug the shoulders and tense the neck, like a turtle pulling its head into its shell
10. Squint the eyes and stretch the mouth as widely open as possible
11. Clench the teeth together and contract the forehead forward and down
12. Squint the eyes and tense through the cheeks and temples
13. Raise the eyebrows and tense through the scalp

With clients slumped in their chairs with their eyes still closed, invite them to journey through their body to search out and eliminate any remaining tension. Then their attention can be directed back to their breathing. There should be no suggestion to change it; rather, have them simply focus on its rhythm for a moment. They might be invited to repeat mentally a word such as *peace* as a personal autosuggestion (and mantra) with each exhale. This is the beginning of a meditational state that can be maintained for a minute.

Guided imagery begins with an invitation to group members to imagine themselves beginning to float out of the chair, as on a sailboat in a gentle breeze. Clients are invited to develop the sensations suggested by the counselor's words if they wish, or to ignore the voice and go wherever they need to go. The counselor then develops an image of the chosen destination, being sure to invite awareness in all sensory modalities. While the imagery can be very specific, it is helpful to end with deliberate vagueness. Each client will then elaborate the image in a way that is maximally personal and useful. The counselor's voice should be slow, clear, and quiet so as to reinforce the general tone of relaxation and ease.

It might be suggested that group members imagine themselves floating into a tropical beach. They could feel the warmth of the sun matched by a comfortable breeze. They could hear rustling palm fronds or perhaps muted bird calls against the gentle rhythm of the surf on the beach. They might imagine what they could smell or what lingering taste they might have in their mouths. They could be aware of a sense of peace, of timelessness, of limitless freedom. As they imagine their eyes drifting closed, they could take in a last pleasant image of the beach and shoreline. Then their minds could wander to another special time when they had similar feelings of well-being. After a pause to let the clients privately elaborate their own images, the leader might suggest that they gradually begin to float back into the room, slowly becoming aware of sounds and of the pressure of the chair. In a moment they may want to open their eyes and to stretch. I end by suggesting that they be aware that they can bring back the sense of peace with them and can become aware of a sense of pride at their ability to give themselves such a pleasant experience. I then awaken any who have fallen asleep, congratulating them on doing what they most needed to do. The tone is deliberately positive and permissive, encouraging clients to repeat and further personalize the experience of relaxation.

Comments are invited and shared. It is noted that some will prefer the meditation to the imagery, while others gained more from the progressive relaxation. This is normal. Clients are specifically invited to practice whatever components seemed useful to them. They may be asked when they will find it useful to fit this relaxation into their daily schedules. It should be remarked that a few moments of meditation may provide an alternative to drinking.

**Variations.** I will often use group hypnosis to achieve relaxation, doing this exercise in conjunction with hypnotic reframing (chapter 8). In this case, I do not specify the destination for our guided imagery. Instead I invite group members to go to their own special place and time.

There are many alternatives to the three approaches to relaxation sampled in this exercise. Counselors should tap their interests and skills to develop other techniques. Clients are likely to be interested in the meditations suggested by inspirational writings published through AA or Hazelden (for example, see *Each Day a New Beginning*, 1982). Yoga or biofeedback could be used. I have yet to see it applied, but I can imagine a very effective group session in hot tub. The goal is to have the counselor's creativity give license so that each client can identify a uniquely pleasing approach to personal relaxation.

# Communication Skills

*This presentation takes about ninety minutes. A chalkboard is helpful.*

**Rationale.** The ability to communicate clearly is critical in times of change.

Altered drinking alters relationships. There is the need to renegotiate roles (for example, the man who wants to become active in parenting after years of avoiding the responsibility), to clear the air by ventilating old resentments, to establish a new intimacy or acknowledge the death of relationships damaged by alcohol abuse and codependency, and to shed the survival roles and replace them with more authentic patterns of interacting. Such change demands effective communication skills, especially those pertaining to expressing and hearing internal experiences. The following lecture and exercises serve as an introduction to these skills.

**Content.** Communication is a complex process. Even when partners attempt to be direct, there is room for crossed signals. Figure 12–3, which is drawn on the board, illustrates the elements that must be successfully organized if a message is to be sent and accurately understood.

Think of how a message can be distorted. Distracted attention means that the message may not be fully heard. Since we all attach idiosyncratic meaning to words, the message may be decoded in terms very different from those intended by the speaker. The meaning is interpreted in light of past experiences and current motivations that are unique to the receiver. Especially when there has been an ongoing relationship, there are assumptions about the meaning of the communication that may override the content of the message sent. If Person A says, "How are you today?" Person B may assume that the question is prying into private business, while Person C might hear it as a sincere invitation to share, and Person D might experience it as a greeting that requires only ritual response. We are in danger when we assume we understand another's motivation without having checked it. The wit noted that to assume (ASS/U/ME) is to make an ASS out of YOU and ME. Yet there is seldom time to confirm fully the intended import of any message. Add to this the fact that there are often mixed intentions, including a desire to be unclear and indirect. Messages may be modified by unconscious factors (such as the tensed jaw of a person who is unaware of

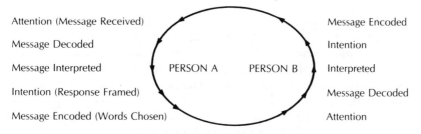

**Figure 12–3. Steps in the Communication Loop**

his underlying anger). Communication relies on a limited vocabulary of words with multiple and sometimes contradictory meanings. Lastly, every communication includes an implicit comment about the relationship between the parties in addition to the content that can be transcribed in words (Watzlawick, Beavin, & Jackson, 1967; Watzlawick, 1976). There are multiple meanings in every message. It is not surprising that in some relationships it is difficult to ask for a glass of water without offending someone.

Satir (1972) notes that there will likely be confusing mixed messages, especially if someone needs to protect a fragile sense of self-esteem. The vulnerability is usually masked behind one of four false communication patterns:

1. *Placating (people pleasing),* in which the person attempts to appease the other by assuming blame or acting ingratiatingly. The implicit message is of worthlessness and helplessness. The voice tone is whining. The archetypical posture would be that of a supplicant: on bended knee, with hands extended upward to beg for help.

2. *Blaming,* in which the person protects his or her self-esteem by attacking and dominating others. Lecture, but do not listen. Be sarcastic or condescending. The voice is loud and grating. The finger is pointed, the chin thrust forward, the eyes are bulging, and the whole posture conveys aggression.

3. *Computing,* in which emotions are buried under an artificially calm, overintellectualized rationality. The style is pedantic. Words are long. Meaning is obscure. All expressiveness is missing from the face and body. The message is, "How could one so reasonable ever be accused of making a mistake?"

4. *Distracting,* in which meaning is lost in a confusing blur of activity. The body is doing at least three things at once, in perpetual hyperactivity. The words are non sequiturs: there can be no discernable connection between any comments made and the ongoing flow of conversation. Conflict is avoided; so is all meaningful communication.

Each of these styles blocks feared assault on a vulnerable self-esteem, at the cost of precluding meaningful sharing of internal experience. All these styles block intimacy and growth. They will prove deadly to communication and attempts to build a new relationship. So it is critically important for clients to recognize whether they characteristically adopt one of these styles of interacting.

A powerful and yet humorous way to get clients to identify their pathological styles is to set up a role-play among four group members, each assuming one of the four patterns. They should exaggerate the roles into caricatures, even adopting the requisite position and body language. They should be assigned a task: to decide on a vacation or to adjust family responsibilities. Then they should interact until it is abundantly clear that there can be no satisfactory problem resolution or relationship building. When each role-player has become completely frustrated, he or she is instructed to switch to a different style of interacting:

5. *Leveling*, in which the intent is to communicate clearly and honestly what the inner experience is. Threats to self-esteem are labeled as such. Personal needs and caring for others is shared openly, and with a congruence of words and body language. The attempt here is to communicate and to foster relationships.

The group should observe how the interaction changes as the role players successively shift to leveling. Then the enactment ends and is discussed. Clients are encouraged to identify which of the pathological styles they adopt when threatened and to compare strategies for leveling when dealing with others who are using unhealthy interaction patterns.

Successful communication requires the intention to communicate clearly—to level with the listener. Additionally it demands a series of discrete skills (Carkhuff, 1969; Egan, 1976). These include self-awareness, so that there is an understanding of the feelings and motivations behind intended messages; self-disclosure skills, which permit clear and specific communications; empathy skills, to check the intended message; and immediacy skills, so that assumptions can be discussed and updated by new sharing about the status of the relationship.

Empathy, or perception checking, is particularly important. It involves a brief restatement of the content and feelings heard. By playing back the message received, the listener can confirm or correct the understanding of the message sent. Empathy closes the feedback loop.

The rudiments of empathy can be practiced in a group exercise. Each client is asked to remember a significant recent experience, one that stirred up feelings. One person shares the experience. At first the group practices summarizing the *content*, with the person sitting beside the discloser checking to see whether he or she could capture the central point of the message to the satisfaction of the person sharing. As subsequent experiences are related, the focus shifts to identifying the most significant *feelings*. Participants listen to the story and then volunteer both the spoken and unspoken feelings that they heard. Again, the speaker is queried about which feelings match the internal experience. Such practice sensitizes the group members to the essentials of a spoken message. The exercise ends with the leader's commenting that feelings are not to be judged as right or wrong, nor are they to be questioned. Each person is the ultimate expert on his or her own inner experience. One basic skill in communication is to be able to delay the tendency to judge or to respond long enough really to hear what is being said.

**Variations.** At times it is helpful to get the group to practice clear expression of feelings. This would be done to enhance skills at self-disclosure or to build up the climate of trust in the group. Each member takes five minutes to record as many feeling words as possible. The lists are then shared and discussed. Clients are invited to notice how extensive their feeling vocabulary is and whether they specialize in either a certain intensity or type of emotion (for example, each group seems to have a depression specialist). A volunteer shares an experience, with the group guessing the underlying feeling. The first discloser then chooses the next person to share, and the feeling to be talked about. For example, "Bill, tell us about a time you felt excited." The sharing continues until all have had a chance to self-disclose. The group can practice checking out any additional feelings heard, again practicing empathy. Alternatively, there can be feedback to each client about the directness and genuineness of the self-disclosure. This variation provides practice of the two crucial skills in effective communication: self-disclosure and empathy.

There are many resources for enhancing communication skills. Satir's (1972) classic, *Peoplemaking,* is effective bibliotherapy. Many couples will seek marital or family therapy during the process of recovery. I would particularly recommend a couples' group, especially if there is one specifically for families affected by chemical dependency. Significant help can be found in workshops aimed at marital enrichment, listening skills, parent or marital effectiveness, or life skills training. Human Relations and Group Dynamics classes offered through local colleges may also be a resource.

# Assertiveness: An Introduction

*This presentation takes seventy-five minutes and uses a chalkboard. It is adapted from the work of Jakubowski-Spector (1973).*

**Rationale.** Confidence in one's ability to cope in challenging situations is the basis for self-esteem. Such expectations of self-efficacy have been empirically demonstrated to reduce the risks of relapse (Chaney, O'Leary, & Marlatt, 1978; Rist & Watzl, 1983). Assertiveness training increases the range and accessibility of coping resources.

Interpersonal effectiveness may be conceptualized as requiring three component communication skills: an awareness of one's own needs and feelings, the ability to express oneself directly, and an awareness of others' rights and desires. The first two are interactive; we often discover more about our preferences as we attempt to explain them to another. This introduction to assertiveness seeks to foster both increased self-awareness and ease in stating preferences. The following module on fair fighting provides the techniques for maintaining alertness to the feelings and goals of one's partner, even in conflictual situations. This module is specifically designed for those who are indirect or incomplete communicators—those who typically respond in a passive and nonassertive manner.

Assertiveness is the practical skill directly associated with the ability to maintain change. When it comes to drinking, assertiveness involves having made a clear personal choice about the extent of alcohol use and conveying that choice firmly to others. Assertiveness is used to counter pressure to drink and to avert affronts to one's rights and feelings that lead to deflated self-esteem and drinking out of disgust. It is by maintaining an active stance in relationships, one in which needs and desires are willingly shared and actively pursued, that a lasting and comfortable alternative is found for problem drinking.

**Content.** Assertiveness occupies the midpoint on a continuum between being passive and aggressive. The first task is to define these terms. Assertiveness may best be described as the ability to communicate one's own rights, needs, feelings, and preferences directly without ignoring or trampling on those of another. Words are backed up by voice tone and body language that convey purpose and confidence through eye contact, firm and fluent voice, appropriate emotional emphasis, and relaxed but erect posture. The message is: "I take myself seriously and would like you to as well." This contrasts with the passive person, whose attempts to avoid conflict result in unmet needs, violated rights, physiological symptoms of stress, and low self-esteem. The message is: "My needs are unimportant; we'll do what you want." The aggressive person communicates: "I'll get my needs met at your expense." Aggression alienates others, who feel dominated, put down, blamed, or discounted. Assertiveness differs in conveying a respect for the other as well as for the self.

The leader clarifies the distinctions by asking for examples of how each of the three types would handle the situation in which a restaurant waiter had to be reminded to refill an empty water glass.

The group members can then be asked which type most accurately represents their own style. During the resulting discussion, it is useful to check specifically to see whether any clients go through personality changes in which they become aggressive when drunk as a compensation for being

passive while sober. For these clients it is particularly important to be assertive in daily life so that there will be less need for "liquid courage."

Assertiveness is more likely to be used when there is a foundation of
beliefs about basic rights. So the group is asked to brainstorm basic interpersonal rights, which are written on the board. Sharing may be prompted
or extended by adding from the following list of rights (adapted from Bloom,
Coburn, & Pearlman, 1975):

Right to your own feelings and opinions

Right to be treated with respect

Right to be taken seriously

Right to make a request without apology

Right to refuse a request without guilt

Right to have promises and contracts honored

Right to set your own priorities

Right to ask for information

Right to make mistakes

The recognition of rights may be fostered by inviting clients to share situations in which it is difficult to be assertive and then searching them for the
unacknowledged rights. Such sharing also fosters the recognition that there
are inevitable conflicts in interpersonal living as rights and needs compete.
One's right to make an honest mistake runs afoul of another's right to have
commitments honored. This gives rise to awareness that there is another
right: to choose not to be assertive in all instances. It is not passivity if one
*knowingly chooses* to postpone or forsake a personal goal in service of those
of another.

The group is then invited to discuss thoughts and feelings that block
assertive behavior. These typically fall in four classes. First, there are blocks
that come from adhering to outdated rules from childhood: always be polite,
others go first, a good host must . . . , and so on. The group can be asked
stimulus questions that probe childhood training about balancing one's own
needs with those of others, about handling conflict (faced or avoided, compromise or victory as goal), about how direct to be in making a request
(including flirting, whining, nagging, or being stoic as indirect approaches
to getting needs met). Anger is the second block to assertive leveling. It is
evident in the desire to hurt or dominate others, or in being passive out of
the fear of becoming aggressive. Anxiety is the third block. Change always
leads to discomfort, especially for the perfectionistic client, since practice is

required before mastery. There are many fears about making an assertive response: will the other be injured, will he or she become aggressive, am I being selfish, will it work? Attending to interpersonal rights or summoning rehearsed images of successful outcomes may help overcome such blocks. The fourth class of impediments is irrational thinking (Ellis & Harper, 1975). Exaggeration, exclusive focus on the worst possible outcome, or assuming responsibility for the other person's emotional state in a way that generates guilt all characterize irrational thinking. As an example, assertive plans will likely be neutralized by an internal dialogue that proceeds thus: "He'll *die* if I ask him to do that; I'd *never forgive myself* if I made him help me against his will." Such thinking needs to be countered with rational self-talk, as in: "He has the right to say no, and I have the right to ask for help."

Identifying blocks has two goals in the present exercise. First, there may be an easily recognized impediment to assertiveness that is obviously outdated and destructive. Recognition will bring liberation. Second, there is the implicit message that more subtle blocks can be overcome with time and effort. Becoming assertive is a process.

The session ends with a role-play. If there is no obvious example from previous discussion, the group may be asked to brainstorm situations in which assertiveness would be an appropriate but challenging response. Alternatively, the leader might suggest a scenario. It might be particularly appropriate to rehearse handling pressure to drink from a "friend." A client is asked to model assertiveness while others in the group role-play the situation. As always, role reversal and assistance from the leader or group members momentarily functioning as an alter ego can be used to aid the client in successfully reaching an assertive resolution to the challenge. The resulting discussion provides feedback to role-players, practice at forming alternative assertive responses, and an opportunity to consider how the new skill can be transferred to the unique situations faced by individual participants.

**Variations.** This presentation may be a natural extension of the discussion of handling friends (chapter 10). It may be enough to deliver a truncated version of this session in which assertiveness is simply defined, presented as an appropriate response, and used in a role-play of handling pressure to drink.

The discussion of irrational thoughts may lead into an extended treatment of how to use corrective "self-talk" (chapter 5) to find more rational and productive alternative attitudes.

Especially if a number of group members tend to respond aggressively, this presentation should be followed by a discussion of "fair fight" techniques, as detailed in the following exercise.

This presentation is an introduction only. Assertiveness is a complex and important skill. Many clients should be referred to the resources that will help them achieve a fuller mastery than is possible in a single session. Assertion training courses are widely available through colleges, mental health centers, personal growth programs, and psychotherapists. Among the good books on the subject are Alberti and Emmons's (1986) *Your Perfect Right,* and Lord and Lord's (1976) *How to Communicate in Sobriety.*

# Fair Fighting: Constructively Handling Anger

*This presentation takes sixty to ninety minutes and requires a chalkboard.*

**Rationale.** Anger, frustration, resentment, and similar uncomfortable emotions are among the most potent stimuli behind relapse. Yet conflict is inevitable if relationships are to change enough to provide support for a pattern of nonproblem drinking. Most clients, like most people in our fight-phobic culture, need to develop new skills for conflict management. George Bach's guidelines for "fair fighting" have been popularized in three books (Bach & Goldberg, 1974; Bach & Wyden, 1968; Nicholson & Torbet, 1980). An introduction to Bach's work is the goal of this activity.

The exercise alternates among presenting ideas, group sharing, and role-playing. Wherever possible, clients should be encouraged to raise and enact their own issues. It is particularly helpful to use a role-play to contrast uncontrolled fighting with that using fair fight guidelines.

**Content.** Mature people do not get angry; a sign of recovery is that it is easy to hold your tongue when frustrated. Right? Wrong!

Anger is a normal, in fact inevitable, experience for people. It is how the anger is experienced and expressed that determines whether it enriches or damages relationships. There is a continuum (drawn on the board) running from undercontrolled to overcontrolled hostility. Obviously there is a problem with the person who flairs up or becomes violent over the slightest provocation. But those who overcontrol their anger are also headed for trouble. Anger that is not expressed contributes to depression (hostility redirected back at the self), to psychosomatic symptoms (for example, ulcers from trying to "swallow" rage), or other stress-related disorders. Suppressed anger leaks out in passive-aggressive behavior that drives others crazy despite the disavowal of harmful intent. (We all have memories of a cashier who dawdles endlessly, to the frustration of the line of waiting customers.) Lastly, denied anger leads to a phony "niceness" that discourages intimacy and may give way to violent explosions. It seems that whenever someone "goes off," the neighbors are always surprised that such violence could come from such a "nice" person. Either end of the anger continuum will present problems. The goal is to move toward the middle of the continuum, to a point where anger can be acknowledged and expressed in a productive way.

This is particularly pertinent for the high percentage of problem drinkers who use alcohol to release accumulated emotions. Many in the group can identify with the pattern of being accommodating, self-sacrificing, overly generous, or deferential when sober. Intoxication then becomes the opportunity or the excuse for venting all of the accumulated frustration in a hostile outburst: "He's a great guy when he's not drinking, but watch out when he's drunk." Such a person needs to develop new ways of channeling anger when sober if recurrent drinking problems are to be avoided.

Effective expression of anger has two key components: *emotional release* and *communicating information*. In the midst of an argument, these components tend to be mutually contradictory. Despite all the words, most combatants remember only who won and how hurt he or she felt. The information was lost and with it the possibility of accommodation and change. A new orientation is needed. At the core is the realization that arguing, especially with family and co-workers with whom one has an ongoing relationship, should not be a win/lose situation. To go for the "knockout" may bring temporary satisfaction to the victor, but it assures that there will be a rematch or an ambush by the vanquished. If one loses, both lose. The goal of fair fighting is for both to win.

Bach and Goldberg (1974) suggest that the fight outcome, for both parties, will be better to the extent that "informative impact" is increased and "hurtful hostility" is decreased.

How can there be emotional release without the hurtful hostility predominating? Perhaps part of the answer is to be found in the experience of those couples who seem to fight all the time and love it. They discover that arguing can be entertaining, invigorating, and a fast way to make intense contact. They find other meaning in the conflict than an attempt to damage one another. *Hostility is not hurtful if it is not taken personally.* For example, there is little discomfort in listening to a friend rage, if it is about the car mechanic or if it is "just blowing off steam." Techniques that allow emotional and physical discharge without a personally directed assault are good releases:

1. The "Vesuvius" (Bach & Wyden 1968): A one-way explosion, lasting a predetermined time (two to five minutes), with witnesses observing without comment, in which the person tries to offload all accumulated frustration and anger in a volcanic eruption.

2. The Virginia Woolf (Bach & Goldberg 1974): A two-way explosion,

again with a time limit, in which partners get face to face and exchange insults and invective. The goal is to be so busy raging that nothing said by the partner is heard. It is understood that nothing is to be taken personally, nothing heard is to be brought up later, and there will be no violence. The baseball manager and umpire in full throat are a good approximation (except, of course, neither partner in a Virginia Woolf is ejected from the game). Instead, the ritual often ends with a hug and a laugh to celebrate the release.

3. Bataca bat or pillow fights: All of the muscular and emotional release of a donnybrook without physical damage. Foam bats and pillows simply do not hurt that much.

4. Temper tantrums: When rage is too great or too threatening to be expressed in front of a partner, it can be purged alone. Some go out in the woods and scream, others retreat to the bedroom to punch pillows or beat the mattress with a tennis racket. The muscular release should be accompanied by a verbal tirade against any and all who have offended.

5. Physical release: Through chopping wood, swimming, or athletics. I used to visualize that it was my boss' head that I was clobbering when I served a racketball.

Clients are then asked to describe and compare the effectiveness of their own outlets for frustration.

There will be less opportunity for anger to accumulate and lead to hurtful hostility if it is recognized early. Clients are asked to identify their own early warning signs. Physical clues include headache, tightened stomach, held breath, flushing, and increased heart rate. Self-talk such as "that's not fair" or "he has no right," mentally replaying scenes to find the right thing to say, or finding oneself cussing suggest angry thoughts. The more promptly the anger is addressed, the less the likelihood that it will amplify or be contaminated by the accumulation of other frustrations.

Once emotional release has been achieved prospects are better for sharing information and negotiating change through honest leveling. The "informative impact" of a fair fight will be increased by:

1. Rehearsing in advance what is to be communicated about the hurtful incident, its impact, the desired change, and any nonnegotiable demands.

2. Having the rule that there will be no change in topic (particularly no rehashing of unrelated past incidents) without the mutual agreement of the fight partners. The real issue may not become clear until the fight is joined. Complaints about money may cover hurt about lack of attention, for example. There must be flexibility to shift. But any change in topic should be identified and justified in a way that is convincing to the partner. Otherwise there needs to be a return to the original fight issue. This prevents the hit-and-run addition of unrelated topics that confuse most arguments.

3. Having an absolute rule that there will be feedback on the partner's last comment before continuing with one's own remarks. This will slow

down the fight so that there will be less emotionality and more thoughtful responses. It assures that there will be momentary pauses so that each participant gets a chance to get a word in edgewise. The rule also guarantees that there will be listening and communication rather than the parallel monologues that typically pass for discussions. To assure understanding, the feedback should be a translation of the partner's comments, not a rote parroting of words. The partner may correct and restate until satisfied of being accurately heard. Only then may new remarks be added.

4. Having an "emergency brake"—an agreed upon signal for an immediate and total stop to the fight. This protects someone who is being overwhelmed and reduces the need for fighting dirty, which happens most often when one party feels cornered. After a pause, the partners can negotiate whether to resume the discussion or to break. If the fight is not concluded, an appointment must be made for a date and time to continue.

A fair fight conducted by these rules permits even touchy topics to be aired with little acrimony and a maximum opportunity for information exchange. The fight ends when interest is lost, when exhaustion sets in, when it is clear that there will be no accommodation, or when an agreement has been made. A follow-up session should be scheduled to evaluate success in complying with any agreements. There is no guarantee of problem resolution. But the separation of information exchange and emotional release makes it likely that fights will not be contaminated by anger. If there is room for agreement, it is more likely to be found. This in turn reduces the sources of frustration in living that breed anger.

A role-play of a domestic quarrel, perhaps about drinking, can be staged. With good-humored pressure from the group, the partners can be goaded into an unproductive argument. Once the issues and fight styles have been illustrated, the process is stopped and then restarted employing the fair fight rules above. This requires that the partners pause to negotiate an "emergency brake." Such fighting about how to fight is itself a contribution to correcting unhealthy patterns of conflict management. Once the argument resumes, it is immediately apparent that the tone has changed and that the emotionality has been reduced. Fair fighting has been demonstrated.

**Variations.** Some clients amplify anger unnecessarily in their mental rehearsing of life events. There are warning signs that anger is being irrationally magnified (Ellis, 1977; Weisenger, 1985) if the internal dialogue is replete with imperative words (must, should), with absolutes (always, never), if preferences are being exaggerated into rights ("they owe me . . . ") or survival needs ("I'll die if they . . ."), or if events are being overgeneralized into global judgments ("All women . . ."). Such self-talk can be handled effectively through techniques drawn from rational emotive therapy, as was discussed earlier in the section changing attitudes through rational self-talk (in chapter 5).

Anger can be reduced through a daily ritual in which others are consciously and intentionally forgiven. Psychotherapists are developing techniques for letting go of old anger (see Fitzgibbons, 1986). Perhaps the best resources are to be found in religious teachings, which offer formalized rituals of forgiveness.

Where more extended exploration of anger is desired, a number of group exercises for experiencing cathartic release through graded expression of anger have been developed by Pesso (1969). One safe introduction is the Bowling Game. One client pantomines rolling a bowling ball. The rest of the group is arrayed as pins, to tumble over at the imaginary moment of impact. The enjoyment and release from this simple enactment, which can be quickly repeated so that as many as want to can have the opportunity to bowl over the group, energizes members to consider the effects of suppressing hostility.

If this introduction spurs interest in further work on appropriate expression of anger, clients should be referred to the works of Bach, to local workshops and courses on communication or conflict management, to marriage enrichment programs, or to therapists who offer such training.

# The Serenity Prayer: When to Use Problem Solving

God grant me the serenity
to accept the things I cannot change,
the courage to change the things I can,
and the wisdom to know the difference.

*This discussion takes fifteen to thirty minutes and requires a chalkboard.*

**Rationale.** There are many ways in which to understand this prayer, written by Reinhold Niebuhr and adopted by Alcoholics Anonymous as the Serenity Prayer. It is a prayer ("God grant me . . ."), a specification of goals (serenity, wisdom), and a statement of personal characteristics to be developed (acceptance, courage). The Serenity Prayer also induces problem solving, providing an opportunity to review this crucial skill.

The goal of the exercise is to have clients commit themselves to use the

Serenity Prayer whenever they feel unsettled and to use the prayer to stimulate problem solving. This routine will enhance efficacy in dealing with life and will reduce the risk of a buildup of the type of emotional distress that would endanger clients' efforts to change their drinking.

This topic usually emerges spontaneously out of a discussion of AA or of how to cope with a troubling situation.

**Content.** The Serenity Prayer should be used when emotional equilibrium has been disrupted. Yet it does not simply request a return to balance. It asks that a discrimination be made between those situations that are susceptible to change and those that are not. In essence this is the first task of problem solving: defining the problem to be addressed. Following the guidance of the prayer will involve the client in a process in which problems are acknowledged and dealt with actively.

The prayer leads into the second step of problem solving: brainstorming workable solutions. Two types of goals are outlined. Situations that are outside individual control can be handled through learning acceptance, while events that are susceptible to change can be faced directly. The chalkboard can be divided into two columns entitled "Accept" and "Courage to Change." If there is a specific situation that has stimulated the discussion, the group can be asked to help the client determine which of the two approaches is most appropriate and then brainstorm potential solutions. For example, a client might complain that "even though I haven't had a drink in two months, my family doesn't trust me." If the problem is determined to be "their trust," it is a situation outside of the individual's control. It may help to realize that there is often a lag of six to twelve months before the family comes to believe that a lasting change in drinking has occurred (see figure 10–2); the client must come to accept this. Facing it may be enough, as may prayer for patience, reassuring self-talk about confidence that "they will come to see in time," or active search for a support group to tide the client over until the family can be more trusting. If the problem is defined as "proving that I am trustworthy," then there are a number of things that can be done. The client might directly communicate the felt lack of trust or deliberately act in ways that show "I have changed." Whatever the choice that is made, there will be an experience of choice and power that can evoke positive emotions.

When the discussion has not been stimulated by a problem volunteered within the group, participants simply brainstorm potential activities that would be suitable for each column. Acceptance may be heightened by meditation, prayer, or other attempts to find meaning in the troubling situation. Problems that must be endured can be faced with more equanimity if there can be a focus on sources of support or on other pleasures in life (a warm bath, relaxation, or a conversation with a good friend, relaxation, and so on). In contrast, courage to change can be heightened by skill training that boosts confidence in the client's ability to handle situations successfully, by assertiveness training that highlights his or her right to seek to have preferences honored, or by rational self-talk that emphasizes that one need not be perfectly competent or successful to try a new approach.

The exercise concludes with a review of the remaining steps in the basic problem-solving model. There are three steps in the basic model: (1) define the problem, (2) consider effective courses of action, (3) implement and evaluate the effectiveness of the chosen course. The Serenity Prayer leads naturally through the first and second steps. Once potential courses of action have been stated, it is necessary to choose the one or the combination that is most likely to match the criteria of being effective, practical, and in line with the client's values and life-style. Choice leads to action. Action leads to a review of success, with either an awareness of problem resolution or a modification of the definition of the challenge and another cycle of problem solving. The Serenity Prayer provides an excellent starting point for ongoing use of the problem-solving strategy in the course of daily living.

**Variations.** The review of problem solving can be brief or extended, depending on the group's interest and familiarity with the steps. This exercise can be used as a prelude to personal problem solving regarding drinking (chapter 8). More often it is a review intended to remind clients to apply the strategy throughout their lives, since problem solving is applicable beyond the handling of the drinking problem.

The brainstorming of solutions—written on the board under the two global headings of "Accept" and "Courage to Change"—highlights the range of possible activities that the group can pursue in the concluding phase of the program. From the "laundry list" of activities listed, the group might decide to have the leader present modules on relaxation and assertiveness. This exercise leads naturally to the activities that help consolidate gains— the goal of this final step in the ten-step problem-solving process for drunk drivers.

# Goals for the Future

*This exercise takes thirty to sixty minutes. A chalkboard is helpful.*

**Rationale.** As the drinking problem is resolved, the change in life-style makes it possible for the client to develop a new sense of mission in life. It is the ability to pursue these long-term objectives and accomplishments that provides the ultimate payoff for the change effort. This exercise invites clients to explore what the new goals might be. Further, the exercise acquaints clients with a previously neglected aspect of problem solving: that large goals can be broken into small and sequential steps that, successively accomplished, can provide short-term rewards and can lead to the attainment of goals that once seemed impossible. This exercise points to a change in attitude that will reach fruition in later recovery when the client has the sense of self-efficacy and internal control of living so that long-term plans can be made with confidence.

**Content.** Clients are invited to review quietly their future goals. It may help to drift back in time and remember earlier dreams and plans. It may help to consult one's sense of values and to identify an effort or accomplishment that would make life worthwhile. The clients are asked to identify two worthy goals—one attainable in three to six months and one that may take several years to approach.

These goals are then shared in a circuit of the group. Discussion allows explanation of the underlying values, comparing of aspirations, and a deepening of the awareness of the personal meaning of the goals. One or more can be adopted as examples with which the group can practice. For instance, one young man hoped to move out of a company bunkhouse and into his own house or apartment. This goal proved eminently attainable once considered realistically—it was reached within a month—even though it had eluded him during several years of heavy drinking.

Next, the group discusses how to handle obstacles to goal attainment. In all likelihood, the goals were previously entertained and then set aside as impossible because of these hurdles. Yet they are probably manageable if three steps can be taken:

1. *Identify each of the obstacles.* Only by looking directly at the enemy can one see how formidable it is. The barriers to moving out of the bunkhouse were identified as money and transportation. Working in an expensive community in a low-paying job, with a revoked license complicating commuting, the client despaired of changing his situation.

2. *Consider how each obstacle can be overcome or skirted.* Military tactics suggest that an enemy can be overwhelmed with firepower or can be outmaneuvered. Similarly, there are many possible ways to deal with each obstacle. Brainstorming alternatives helps clients to escape fixation on only one tactic, freeing them to be more flexible and creative. In the example, the group suggested many possible solutions to financial limitations: changing jobs, living in a low-rent neighborhood, seeking government assistance, housesitting, getting a coachhouse in exchange for managing a property, or getting a roommate. Although the client had assumed he would have to wait the three years until his license was returned, the group pointed out that he

could handle transportation by joining a carpool or rooming with a co-worker, as well as by residing close to work. With this opportunity to free himself from self-limiting assumptions, the young man arranged with a relative to buy an old family property, with expenses shared by a co-worker. In less than a week he had gone from being stuck to implementing a realistic plan.

3. *Break the goal down into a series of manageable steps.* Most long-term accomplishments are the result of much preliminary work. Remaining motivated requires an awareness of how each step fits into the larger picture. Many clients will have to seek additional education or training to realize their vocational potential. But they need not relinquish the dream of the ideal job. They must accept that it may take five years of part-time GED and community college classes to become qualified. One class at a time, the goal can be approached without overwhelming the client. Likewise, writing a book seems a daunting task to most people, as it once did to me. But it is possible and feasible to complete three pages at a time. With sustained effort, a book will have been written. The clearest application of stepwise goal attainment is saving money for a major purchase. Clients who are spending in excess of fifty dollars a week on drinking can save half that amount easily if they abstain. The savings accumulate rapidly: twenty-five dollars per week is one hundred dollars in a month and six hundred dollars in less than half a year. One client made a downpayment on acreage he had been admiring for years with the money saved during treatment. Another reported that her most effective means of handling occasional cravings was to retreat to her bedroom—to admire the new bedroom suite she saw as the product of her efforts during the first months of her sobriety.

**Variations.** Identifying goals can be a challenge. Additional exercises can be used to "set the stage." It often helps to invoke the perspective of the future to clarify the meaning of present efforts, and the sense that life is fleeting can lend appropriate urgency to the pursuit of dreams. Samuel Johnson once said, "When a man knows he is to be hanged in a fortnight, it concentrates his mind wonderfully." The following exercises, adapted from the values clarification approach (Simon, Howe, & Kirschenbaum, 1972) can be used to identify meaningful goals:

1. *Life-Line.* Have clients draw a horizontal line on a piece of paper, with left terminus representing birth (have them enter a zero) and the right end standing for death. Each is to enter the age at which they guess they will die. They are then to mark the line at the proportional spot representing their current age. The awareness of death that results from examining this line can in itself be a powerful stimulus for discussing values and meaning. Clients are then asked to mark the line with diagonal slashes to represent important accomplishments in their lives to date. Marriages, graduations, personally significant accomplishments, and so forth are written on the di-

agonal lines. Future important personal accomplishments and events are then entered on additional diagonals, at whichever points on the lifeline that they are anticipated. Included may be events such as the birth of the first grandchild, the purchase of a house, the shift to a satisfying job, or the beginning of a committed relationship. These represent important values.

2. *Obituaries*. Have clients compose the obituary that they would hope to have printed at the time of their deaths. Include items such as: "He was survived by . . . ," "She will be remembered for . . . ," "At the time of his death, he was working on . . . ," and so on.

3. *"How would your life be different if . . ."* Clients can imagine what would give their lives meaning and focus if the usual constraints were stripped away. The variations I ask them to imagine and then discuss include how life would be different if they had enough wealth that they would never again have to work, or what they would do if they had the power to make one wish to change the world and one wish to change themselves.

This exercise on future goals can be easily attached to previous exercises. The presentation on financial costs (chapter 6) can conclude with a discussion of goals for saving. The devil's deal and life values exercises (chapter 9) highlight personal values central to plans for the future.

There are additional resources for continuing work on planning for the future. An excellent introduction to the importance of the search for meaning is Victor Frankl's *Man's Search for Meaning*. Clark Vaughn's *Addictive Drinking* provides a provocative discussion of options for reordering life in pursuit of meaning which is specifically for the recovering alcoholic. There are life planning workshops and workbooks. While primarily oriented toward career planning, the best include educational and recreational goals as part of a discussion of personal fulfillment. The published works by Bolles, (1981, 1987; Crystal & Bolles 1980) are especially recommended. State vocational rehabilitation offices and local colleges may offer life-planning assistance. The subject is often covered in college courses on the Psychology of Adjustment, and there are workshops and books that more fully describe the self-management skills needed to implement plans for change (Mikulas, 1983; Watson & Tharp, 1985; Williams & Long, 1983). The more spiritual aspects of the search for meaning can be pursued with the support of local clergy and self-help fellowships such as Alcoholics Anonymous and AlAnon.

# *Farewells*

*Elements of this ritual are repeated whenever an individual successfully completes treatment. It takes approximately fifteen minutes of the client's final session.*

**Rationale.** Graduation from treatment is an important transition. Past accomplishments are reviewed and celebrated. Probable future challenges are identified, and appropriate responses are rehearsed. The tone is usually upbeat, in keeping with the intention to send off the client with encouragement.

**Content.** Four areas are covered in the course of the farewell ritual, with the prospect of other themes emerging during the free-flowing interchange among the graduate, the leader, and the rest of the group. First, the farewell provides the final opportunity for a group-supported pass through the problem-solving cycle. Self-diagnosis, goals, and plans are restated. While there may be discussion of initial efforts, the focus is now on the strategies for maintaining gains through the critical first months after the end of formal therapy. So the review focuses on the degree to which there is now internal motivation to sustain the effort, on the degree to which plans are consonant with personal values and integrated comfortably into the client's life-style, and especially on any provisions to replace the support and monitoring function previously played by the group. It is routine for someone to ask whether there are plans for continued involvement in Alcoholics Anonymous.

Second, the ritual always includes a specific invitation to return to group if at some future time there is need for a refresher or additional temporary support. This gesture is a confirmation of continued partnership. While only a minority do return, they have commented that the permission enabled them to reach out for help more readily.

It should be noted that the postdischarge period is a particularly common time for clients to admit themselves for inpatient rehabilitation. When it becomes clear that the current change is inadequate and that there is now no way to sustain the fantasy that someone else will take responsibility for their recovery, some clients finally begin to work. Regularly, if infrequently, a client will signal that he or she is not ready for discharge. This may be communicated directly. More typically, the client will manipulate the counselor into delaying release by expressing doubts about the adequacy of plans to maintain change, by failing to make final payment for treatment, or even by attending the final session with traces of alcohol in the system. The counselor needs to be receptive to such signals and willing to help the client directly explore the reasons why discharge is premature.

The third focus of the farewell ritual is on appreciation of the program. The client is asked what he or she gained through treatment, what some of the decisive points were in developing a positive attitude and effort, and what he or she will remember about group counseling a year hence. Such questions raise the prospect of criticism, which is appropriate and accepted nondefensively. But more often there is an expression of gratitude for caring concern, for confrontation about the seriousness of the problem, and for the education about alcohol and change. It is common for clients to verbalize the wish that they had been exposed to treatment years earlier, or even to note their gratitude that they got arrested before their problem developed further.

Appreciation is not directed exclusively to the counselor. The fourth topic is feedback to and from the group. Often there have been group members who have had a decisive impact. I will ask specifically if there is anyone in the group to whom the graduate would like to make a personal comment. Conversely, the group may need to honor an important participant. The leader may instruct the group to take advantage of this final opportunity to direct comments to the graduate. Once the reticence about personal feedback has been overcome, meaningful advice and encouragement are often exchanged as the farewell concludes.

**Variations.** The feedback appropriate to partings may be fostered by the giving of imaginary gifts. Especially with graduates who are insightful and talkative, I may forewarn them that they will be asked to give each group member a token by which to remember them. The gifts are verbal; no money is spent and no physical presents exchanged. Most often it is psychological qualities that are offered. One client may be offered the self-confidence to appreciate what he or she has to offer, while another will be given fanciful football pads better to withstand the jolt of confrontation within the group. Often the present is simply appreciation and encouragement. In one instance the client prepared cards that were given to everyone in the group, with the present specified. The affirmations on the cards are still being referred to, after two years. While it is the graduate who is instructed to give the gifts, it is common for other participants to offer presents spontaneously. The genuineness of the caring and feedback can vitalize the group process.

At times the farewell must be a time of confrontation. Usually this takes the form of sharing that there are significant reservations about the extent or durability of actual change on the part of a person who will nonetheless be released. It is not unusual for me to share the expectation that it will take more personal pain for the client to be prepared to commit to change. The group tries to help the client set appropriate limits on his or her behavior. An early stage alcoholic who plans to "have a sociable drink once in a while" may be asked about contingencies if more than three drinks are consumed per occasion or challenged to quit and return to group if again guilty of impaired driving. Given the national baseline of 15–30 percent rearrest rates for DWI offenders, reservations will often be expressed at the time of release. At times, the confrontation carries more immediate consequences: some clients are told that to terminate treatment at the current time will result in a recommendation that the judge consider them noncompliant with treatment objectives and reinstate the suspended sentence. Such a confrontation carries a powerful impact, in part because it affronts the anticipated celebration. I will always give such a client forewarning, and most "volunteer" in advance to continue in therapy until they are compliant (usually until they have achieved a two-month period of trial abstinence). In such cases, the group farewell is simply postponed. The confrontation in the final session occurs rarely, only with the most hardheaded of clients, and is done precisely because the power of the intervention usually mobilizes the group to help the client accept a contract for change that will result in eventual compliant release.

# 13

# My Typical Program: A Suggested Sequence of Exercises

I n the setting in which I work, the court system refers suitable DWI offenders to be treated in outpatient group therapy. I do not work for the court; I have a private practice conducted out of my offices. Clients who are referred to me have been prescreened by probation officers. Those regarded as not having an evident drinking problem are diverted to a court-run education program. Only those regarded as being at risk of alcoholism— 63 percent of those convicted of DWIs in the jurisdiction last year—are sent to me for extended treatment. The program outlined below is tailored for this unique population.

## The Typical Treatment Program

The typical program includes forty weekly sessions of two hours each. A client will be in treatment for about ten months. Early release is possible, if the client has demonstrated mastery of the ten steps of problem solving. Discharge may be delayed for those who are slow to make successful changes, although the court would prefer that the entire treatment process be completed within one year. Some 28 percent of those entering the program will be returned as noncompliant, with about 8 percent subsequently returning and successfully concluding their treatment. Many of the noncompliant fail because of nonpayment of court fees, attendance problems, or other reasons that are unrelated to their success in the problem solving. About 3 percent are required to undergo inpatient rehabilitation as part of their treatment.

Figure 13–1 shows the typical treatment cycle. Beginning at the top and proceeding clockwise, the flow is from attitude work (*a*), through a focus on alcohol-related problems (*b*), to a final focus on change and recovery issues (*c*), after which the cycle repeats itself. This process is interrupted so that twice during each cycle there is concentration on drunk driving (1) and

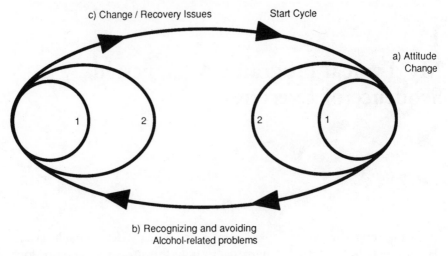

**Figure 13–1. Progression of a Typical Program**

on self-diagnosis (2). In effect, these two critical areas are covered every four to six months. The first loop through the drinking and driving module presents an introduction to problem solving. That is, there is confrontation and education to identify clearly driving under the influence as a problem; there is a discussion of accident risks and legal consequences to motivate change; and then strategies for change are reviewed, selected, applied, and evaluated for effectiveness. Before tackling the more controversial issue of altered drinking, clients are led through the problem-solving process to resolve the initially identified concern with avoiding drunk driving.

The repetition of the DWI avoidance and self-diagnosis cycles has two clear rationales. First and foremost, these are the critical elements of treatment. The first goal of treatment is to get the intoxicated driver off the road. Module 1 gives clients the needed skills to achieve this aim. The second goal of treatment, to prevent further damage in any area of the clients' lives because of alcohol use, requires that the clients know their diagnosis in order to develop an individualized plan for change. This is particularly critical in a setting in which there will be a range of diagnoses—alcohol abuse as well as alcoholism—and diverse goals. Having been exposed to those who seek to continue to drink, albeit in a reduced and controlled fashion, those who are alcoholic will need to have a clear understanding of their own self-diagnosis if they are to stick to abstinence. While it might be desirable to treat clients in homogeneous groups, the population referred includes too many who fall in the gray area between abuse and alcoholism for segregating clients by goal. So the self-diagnosis activities constitute the pivotal step in determining the manner in which problem solving will proceed for each client. Additionally, it is a difficult and protracted process to come to an honest self-assessment about the extent of the drinking problem. The repetition allows clients to update their self-diagnosis, with a corresponding change in goals and plans, once they have had more time to resolve defenses and learn about alcohol-related problems. The repeated exposure supports coming to a deeper acceptance.

The second reason for repetition is that new clients are continually joining an open group. Repetition assures that they will be exposed to these modules early in treatment; new members are helped to "catch up" quickly.

In some cases, clients are inappropriately referred for extended treatment. For example, one client had two DWI arrests within two months after the sudden death of his young wife. With the resolution of the grief process, reinforced by a clear awareness of the painful consequences of drunk driving, this client quickly returned to the prior pattern of infrequent light drinking. He reached an accurate self-diagnosis of transient alcohol abuse and had already taken the appropriate steps to develop alternative sources of support so that he would no longer drink in response to stress or depression. He did not need a full forty-week cycle of treatment. He remained for sixteen weeks, long enough to learn more about drunk driving, to discuss handling emotions, and to demonstrate his control. Having the DWI avoidance and self-diagnosis cycles repeating at intervals permits exposure to these critical parts of the program without unnecessarily prolonging the treatment for those who do not appear to need it.

Table 13–1 provides an outline of the activities that would be planned for a typical forty-week treatment program. The schedule remains flexible, permitting spontaneous sharing by the group or substitution of more immediately appropriate exercises. But I will always have an exercise planned. This organized progression of educational and behavior-change units contrasts with traditional group therapy, in which the group is allowed to flounder until it can select its own topics. Only toward the end of the treatment cycle does the group assume primary responsibility for selecting the topics of discussion.

Flexibility is designed into each session. Meetings start with time allotted for participants to initiate a discussion; for the rituals of introduction (the arrest report in chapter 3); for progress reports (chapter 11); for farewells; for follow-up on success at controlled drinking or results from the drinking diary; and for blood alcohol content (BAC) checks and confrontations of anyone who appears to be attending under the influence. The session is likely to begin with an opportunity for sharing. If I want to remind the group of its primary task, I may begin by asking: "Has anyone been rearrested in the past week? Has anyone been driving when he or she could have been rearrested?" More often the group begins with a go-round that allows all present

## Table 13–1
## Typical Activities Planned during a Forty-Week Treatment Program

| Week | Activities (and Chapter in which They Are Discussed) |
| --- | --- |
| 1 | Introductory Lecture (3) |
| 2 | DWI Laws (3), *So Long Pal* (5) |
| 3 | Standard Drink (4), Tolerance (5) |
| 4 | *Drink, Drive, Rationalize* (4), Alcohol Metabolism (4) |
| 5 | Calculating BACs (4), Strategies for Avoiding DWIs (5) |
| 6 | *Chalk Talk*, part 1 (6), I/E + d (6), Accident Stories (5) |
| 7 | Three Types of Drinkers (6) |
| 8 | Mass Media Myths (4), Progression of Drinking (Personal) (6) |
| 9 | Symptoms → Diagnosis → Treatment (5) |
| 10 | Control Questions (7), Control Test (7) |
| 11 | Disease Concept (5), Alcohol Withdrawal Symptoms (6) |
| 12 | Types of Alcoholics (6), *The Other Guy*, part 1 (6) |
| 13 | Alcoholism Screening Tests (7), *Alcoholism: The Twenty Questions* (7) |
| 14 | Disease Curve (7) |
| 15 | Personal Problem-solving (8), Goal Setting (8) |
| 16 | *The Other Guy*, part 2 (10), Personal Plans (8), Progress Reports (11) |
| 17 | Handling Family and Friends (10) |
| 18 | Understanding Physical Health Risks (6), *Alcohol and Human Physiology* (6) |
| 19 | The Devil's Deal (9) |
| 20 | Identifying Defenses (4), *A Slight Drinking Problem* (6) |
| 21 | Family Costs (Roles) (6), *Soft Is the Heart of a Child* (6) |
| 22 | Reframing (8) |
| 23 | *Under the Influence* (5), Accident Curve (5) |
| 24 | The Eight Areas (7), Financial Costs (6) |
| 25 | *Until I Get Caught* (5), Fear versus Respect for the Law (5) |
| 26 | *Chalk Talk*, part 2 (7), Evaluating Plans (11) |
| 27 | Calculating BACs (4), Metabolism (Neurotransmitters, Antabuse) (4) |
| 28 | Inheritance and Ethnicity (7) |
| 29 | Alcoholism Screening Tests (7), *Alcohol Abuse: The Early Warning Signs* (7) |
| 30 | Using All of the Levels of Alcoholics Anonymous (10), *AA and the Alcoholic* (10) |
| 31 | Goal Setting (8), Criteria for Successful Compliance (8) |
| 32 | Rational Self-Talk (5), Victim, Rescuer, Persecutor (4) |
| 33 | *Hollywood and Vine* (9), Testimonials (9), Model Plans (10) |
| 34 | Grief Work (11), Evaluating Plans (11) |
| 35 | Communication Skills (12) |
| 36 | Serenity Prayer (12) |
| 37 | Relapse Prevention (10) |
| 38 | *Alcohol, Pills, and Recovery* (6), Using (6) |
| 39 | Values (9), Goals for the Future (12) |
| 40 | Farewells (12) |

to say a few words. For this sharing, the participants may be instructed to mention how they are feeling, what happened with their drinking during the preceding week, what they would like to discuss during the session, or how they react to a stimulus question related to the expected topic for the meeting. For example, clients may be asked to share any prior attempts to control their drinking as a prelude to a discussion of goals. Cross-talk between members is encouraged during this go-round. On occasion the whole session will be taken up with the issues that emerge. In these cases, the planned agenda is simply postponed.

The model curriculum from Table 13–1 will be modified freely, with activities selected to maintain a productive group process. Priority is given to exercises that, in order of precedence, counter any negative attitudes being incorporated into the group norms, encourage sharing and active involvement, and set the stage for any needed individual confrontations. For example, the presentation on types of alcoholics (chapter 6) might be moved up to challenge the "comparing out" of a vocal client who "is only a weekend drinker." The format is also varied so that there is an alternation among movies, lectures, role-plays, and discussions. Mature groups, with active and honest participation, can make more productive use of discussions. The schedule will also be altered so that drunk driving is highlighted before the New Year's, Fourth of July, and Labor Day holidays.

What follows is a brief commentary on the program outlined in table 13–1. (1) The introductory lecture will often be done for all new clients before assignment to treatment groups. The requirement for weekly AA involvement will be presented at this time so that all clients will be regularly attending within the first weeks. (2) It should be noted that there is a general progression through the stages of problem solving. But this does not proceed in lockstep. There will be considerable jumping around among levels. There will often be a linkage between different activities presented sequentially. Week six begins with the $I/E + d$ discussion from chapter 6. Its focus on doing the unwise and unintended when under the influence makes it a good prelude to sharing accident stories (an activity from chapter 5). (3) The presentation of the progression of drinking in week eight would be appropriate only for a nondefensive group. Its purpose at this time would be to firm up norms of sharing in a group that had already demonstrated open self-disclosure. Even so, the typical reluctance to admit problems would be normalized by the initial discussion about the mass media myths that distort our perspective on drinking. The placement of these exercises demonstrates the attempt to stretch the group gradually in the direction of self-assessment and behavior change. (4) After the first pass at self-diagnosis and goal setting, the program concentrates on sensitizing clients to the range and types of problems created by alcohol abuse. The eight areas exercise loosely organizes these activities, which are the focus of weeks eighteen, nineteen, twenty, twenty-one, twenty-three, and twenty-four. (5) The inclusion of reframing in week twenty-two is to lend a balance. After all of the negative focus on drinking, it is important that the group be permitted to express the awareness that drinking has also had positive effects in their lives. (6) Clients are typically required to have achieved eight consecutive weeks of abstinence before they will be eligible for compliant release. By week thirty-two this requirement must be accepted if they are to be released on time. The goal setting, motivation, and evaluation stressed in weeks thirty-one, thirty-three, and thirty-four are all intended to support clients who may have been confronted during this part of the program. The reprise on defenses (the roles of victim, rescuer, persecutor) and attitude change (rational self-talk), in session thirty-two, is intended to handle the reactive negativism that may have resulted from confrontation with the criteria for successful compliance during session thirty-one. (7) Had there been evidence of unaddressed cross-addiction, the discussion of using (week thirty-eight) would have occurred earlier in treatment. Its inclusion at this point has a cautionary purpose. It is used here as an extension of the relapse prevention discussion, highlighting the importance of not compromising recovery by naive use of physician-prescribed sedatives or recreational use of other drugs.

Although hypothetical, this schedule of activities can be seen to blend continued awareness of attitudes and process for a unique group with the progression of exercises suggested by the formal problem-solving process. It is the ability to adjust the model to specific settings that will make the use of the problem-solving approach maximally effective.

## Systemic Aspects of DWI Treatment

Treatment does not operate in a vacuum. Rather, there is a system of interacting groups, often with competing interests, that must function collaboratively for there to be effective intervention with the drinking driver. The weakest link will limit the effectiveness of the outcome.

The system relies on an underpinning of public awareness that creates social pressure to discourage drunk driving and to develop effective countermeasures. Arrest rates are highest in states where attitudes opposing alcohol abuse prevail, even though there may be a lower incidence of drinking problems than in states with more permissive attitudes (Linsky, Colby, & Strauss, 1986). The drunk drivers are out there in all states. Public attitude largely determines the reaction. In response to the public outcry, legislation has been passed confirming that drunk driving must be dealt with as a serious offense. Ironically, that pressure has led to a tendency to criminalize the DWI offense so that options for treatment are reduced as punishment is mandated. If punishment becomes excessive, the system will be short-circuited as police avoid arrests, or prosecutors and judges permit guilty pleas on lesser charges. Treatment is a vital cog in the system, but enrollment is likely to decrease if there is no reduction in sentence to provide an incentive for successful involvement. Clients who do participate may undermine treatment if they know that insufficient communication takes place between counselor and judge for there to be consequences for inadequate behavior change. Treatment personnel must also forge contacts with providers of specialized services (for example, medical detoxification, inpatient rehabilitation, or psychotherapy) and aftercare to assure an adequately flexible response to the needs of clients with widely varying degrees of alcohol involvement. Lastly, the same public that has become outraged enough about drunk driving to demand that something must be done has to find the understanding and forgiveness to support the continued efforts of the treated offender to maintain changes.

It may sound like a daunting task to coordinate the elements effectively so that treatment is part of an integrated unit, and it certainly can be. Yet there is a realistic prospect that treatment personnel can contribute to the development of a coherent system if they can become sensitive to the needs of the different groups involved, if they can forge personal relationships with significant parties, and if they use their expertise at fostering consensus to find areas for cooperative effort. The counselor can be active in strengthening the system that seeks to reduce the incidence of drunk driving.

Understanding the elements of the system is the first step toward collaborating. Treatment personnel need to be aware of the areas of potential conflict and potential cooperation.

**Public Awareness.** Public awareness of the DWI problem is the basis of any effective effort to alter laws, encourage enforcement, or provide deterrent education. It is the key to an effective system. If the intervention system is seen as a train, then public awareness is the engine that pulls it. In recent years there has been a ground swell of determination to do something, which has permitted the development of new and potentially effective intervention strategies. Public interest has forced the system to be more effective because it is now accountable to a wider and more passionately involved constituency. Such public awareness is worthy of support.

This awareness must be nurtured. The publicity generated gives an impression of general interest when, in fact, there is little involvement by the person in the street. In part this may be because there is a lack of general awareness of the risk. Most people are unaware that they have a 65 percent chance of being personally involved in an alcohol-related auto accident (Podolsky, 1985a). General support may be restrained by the incorrect perception that "everyone drives drunk." Having had a drink before driving is very different from having had the fifteen drinks typical of those arrested for DWI (Waller, 1982). When people are asked to drink to what they believe is a .10 BAC, 50 percent are really below .055 and only 11 percent exceed .10. In fact, between 75 percent and 90 percent of Americans never or rarely drive under the influence (Orr & Lizotte, 1986). The moderate drinking majority may be mistakenly identifying with the DWI offender who has a very different pattern of alcohol use. The counselor should support public awareness and can do so most effectively through education. Such efforts will pay dividends as the interest in countering drunk driving becomes more widespread.

Most of the momentum behind public awareness comes from advocacy groups. In many cases, there is enough commonality of goals that the counselor can be productively involved. I would recommend a low profile, however, so that the counselor's advocacy does not lead clients to see that counselor as being on the "other side," precluding development of a therapeutic alliance. But the counselor should support organizations that seek to provide preventive education, drug-free alternatives for young people, early intervention for those developing a problem with substance abuse, and advocacy for safer highways.

Some of the vocal advocacy groups have on their agenda removing treatment as an option for the convicted DWI. In some cases their goal is for punishment to be the exclusive and mandatory response to DWI offenders. In other instances the goal is neo-Prohibition, with alcohol again cast as a villain. I have already made my argument that punishment has an important role so long as it does not eliminate the prospect of meaningful treatment. Counselors can support the call for prompt and equitable punishment. But the counselor has a duty to prevent the moral model (see chapter 5) from again becoming the dominant way in which drinking is conceptualized. It disturbs me that the recent report of the Presidential Commission on Drunk Driving deals so little with the contribution of alcoholism to the DWI problem (Foley & Leschuk, 1986). For those who believe alcoholism is a disease, there must be a rehabilitation component available if an effective response is to be made (Bunn, 1983). Not only does the alcoholic offender benefit from such provisions, but the public also benefits from identifying alcoholism as a disease because nonalcoholics are not seduced into believing the myth that all drinking is evil. Historically, temperance movements have fronted for abstinence movements. Although many counselors may have personally chosen abstinence, they should seek to counter social pressures that would stigmatize all drinking and all drinkers. This approach they owe to their clients, whose self-esteem is an important resource if they are to admit and cope with alcohol abuse.

**Legislation.** A great deal of legislative activity has taken place in the attempt to control drunk driving. A developing body of research indicates the likely effects of different sanctions (Ross, 1984). My review leads me to believe that it is the felt likelihood of arrest and the speed and certainty of punishment that most effectively deter drunk driving. Increasingly severe punishments, however, may paradoxically reduce deterrence by reducing the reporting of accidents and the prosecution of offenders. Police, prosecutors, and judges may divert the offender from the normal judicial process in a quiet revolt against excessive punishment. Equitable enforcement is further distorted by the technical ploys of defense attorneys, who are becoming increasingly necessary as the laws stiffen. Enough has been done to increase penalties in most jurisdictions. It would be more profitable to increase the certainty of punishment by simplifying the court process (for example, with per se laws that make for an automatic conviction at a BAC of .10 and by eliminating the prospect of reducing the charge). Deterrence would be further enhanced by legislation increasing the prospects of apprehension and immediate censure. Counselors should support initiatives that explicitly permit randomly checking driver's BACs at roadblocks or immediately lifting the licenses of those with illegal levels of alcohol at the time of arrest. Legislative progress is needed to increase the likelihood of apprehension:

> Research suggests that the driver in the US would have to commit 200 to 2000 DWI violations to be caught, after which he would still stand only a 50-50 chance of being punished—mildly at that. Such a risk is apparently acceptable even to most social drinkers, who are able to control their drinking. (Jones & Joscelyn, 1978, p. 56.)

The counselor can support efforts to increase the probability of arrest and conviction.

**Law Enforcement.** If the probability of getting caught is crucial, then the police officer is on the front lines. Arresting often obnoxious drunk drivers can be unpleasant and time consuming. Enforcement personnel can be easily demoralized if conviction rates are low. Counselors can support enforcement through joining public efforts to streamline arrest procedures, assure prompt judicial disposition, and guarantee appropriate punishment for those convicted. Community support for special patrols and roadblocks will lead to higher arrest rates. Counselors can also capitalize on personal contacts with police. They must make sure that it is understood that diversion to treatment is not a way for drunk drivers to escape consequences. Rigorous treatment will appeal to enforcement groups to the extent that clients make an effort and the program is effective.

**The Judicial System.** Since court personnel are the immediate managers of referrals to and release from treatment, it is indispensable for the counselor to develop a personal relationship with them. This goes beyond an understanding of their responsibilities and a willingness to accommodate their legitimate needs to creating a climate in which there is frequent and warm personal contact. I will adjust my report schedules to facilitate their work, take time to explain treatment decisions to them, and use weekly phone contacts to keep close to their efforts. I will also make direct attempts to influence the way in which they do business so that treatment is more likely to be effective. Judges can be invited to review the treatment approach so that they can be knowledgeable about problem drinking and the treatment it requires. Informal consultations about other cases demonstrate competency—which is important since it is only the counselor's "failures" who are dropped from treatment or rearrested and appear again in front of the judge. The counselor should initiate efforts to heighten the mutual respect and cooperative effort that will enhance treatment effectiveness.

The counselor should have a good understanding of how the judge will handle DWI cases. There are some ideals toward which to work. Optimally the judge will impose stiff penalties and then suspend enough so that there is incentive for involvement in treatment. A client who successfully completes treatment might be rewarded with an early return of a suspended license. Conversely, treatment leverage increases if there will be consequences for a noncompliant return to court. Although twenty-eight days of inpatient rehabilitation may intimidate a client, they may well be preferable to the ninety days of jail time that can be expected by those dropped from treatment. It is the clear understanding of court procedures and the coordination of effort that determine the coercive power of treatment. While the goal is to develop the clients' internal motivation, it is indispensable to have the court's authority to back up demands for changed drinking.

**Treatment.** Since no program can handle all of the treatment needs of the clients, the counselor contributes to the effectively functioning system by developing a network of referral resources. Minimally this includes medical and social setting detoxification sites, inpatient rehabilitation centers, halfway houses, mental health centers, and counselors specializing in substance abuse and codependency. The network can profitably be expanded to include welfare, vocational rehabilitation, educational, Veterans Administration, medical, nutritional, and recreational resources. The counselor must develop contacts and manage referrals for ancillary treatment, serving as the client's advocate and case manager. In the treatment area, as in the wider system, the counselor must move beyond offering a set program to foster cooperative efforts with related resources.

A primary resource used by clients is Alcoholics Anonymous. Because the organization is so decentralized and client involvement so individualized, the counselor cannot make direct referrals to anyone who functions as an intake worker. Instead, a network of individual contacts can and must be developed. The counselor can do some of this work directly, by attending meetings and getting to know some of those active in AA. Inviting interested AA participants to sit in on sessions of the treatment group helps to forge positive relationships. Former clients who become AA members also foster a positive link with the fellowship. This goodwill is important, because there will be strains on the relationship that result from mandating AA involvement for resistant clients. AA has years of experience in handling those attending involuntarily:

> In a very real sense, every single AA member is at first "sentenced" to AA— if not by a court, then by employer, family, friends, doctor, or counselor, or by his own inner suffering. We would not come to AA until we *had* to, in some way (*AA Guidelines: Cooperating with Court, A.S.A.P., and Similar Programs*, 1986, p. 4).

Yet there will still be frustration if disruptive or uninterested clients invade a meeting. Problems can be minimized by sending reluctant participants to open meetings and to speakers meetings. Clients should be told in advance about AA procedures and etiquette. AA contacts are reminded that clients are guests, who can be excluded if they become disruptive. But ultimately, it is the relationships fostered that help manage the inevitable rough spots. In one anecdote, a frustrated AA member pointed to someone leaving the meeting early and complained to his neighbor that court-referred clients shouldn't go to AA since "they don't care and don't contribute like we do." To this, the neighbor—my client—responded by saying simply, "I first came to AA because it was a required part of my treatment for a DWI." The network of veterans from treatment who continue to contribute to AA is the best means of maintaining the cooperative linkage with this primary resource.

**Aftercare.** Since self-diagnosis and change efforts must continue after the end of formal treatment, the counselor must support the client's involvement in aftercare. For my program, there is a standing invitation to return for follow-up contact with the treatment group. But this is a stopgap. The goal is to facilitate client involvement in whatever further growth work is needed. The counselor may again serve as case manager, helping to make connections with any of the resources mentioned above.

Aftercare includes the social support network that mediates the client's recovery. Attempts should be made to involve family or friends during treatment so that they will have the education or referral to needed help so that they can be maximally supportive of the client's change. More globally, the counselor can be active in helping to change public attitudes so that it becomes increasingly acceptable to engage in alcohol-free activities or to identify oneself as a person who used to have a drinking problem. Counselors contribute to creating positive public attitudes by helping clients value their changed drinking patterns enough that they are appropriately open about their altered drinking practices. We have come full circle; the intervention system concludes where it began: with public awareness. But this time, the counselor's contribution is to empower clients to become active in creating an environment in which drunk driving is identified as a problem that must be and can be resolved.

# 14
# Epilogue: Modifying the Model and the Presentations

The problem-solving model is remarkably robust. It can be applied to a wide variety of settings with minimal adaptations. The tone, pace, and content of the presentations will certainly be altered as needed, but the underlying logic of problem solving remains constant. Any successful program will help participants to develop an attitude in which problems are clearly targeted for change, impart relevant information, set appropriate goals for change, support development of realistic plans, and help participants learn to evaluate and modify their efforts until the problem has been resolved.

The ten-step model outlined in this book is specifically adapted for use with resistant clients, such as those mandated for treatment by the court system. Because of the lack of initial investment in change that typifies such clients, the basic problem-solving model was expanded so that appropriate internal motivation could be gradually created. The steps related to resistance, defenses, and motivation successively shape an attitude of appropriate concern and effort so that even the reluctant client can become an active participant in recognizing and changing the pattern of alcohol abuse.

When clients enter treatment already committed to change, as would be the case in a voluntary outpatient alcoholism treatment program, for example, the problem-solving model can be simplified. The attitude change and learning phases can be modified to incorporate relevant information about defensiveness. Motivation can be collapsed into evaluation. The modified problem-solving model for cooperative clients would then include seven stages: attitude change, learning, self-diagnosis, goal setting, planned action, evaluation, and consolidating gains.

When complex or sequential changes must be made, it may be helpful to expand the model by subdividing goal setting into separate steps. Egan (1985) distinguishes mission, major aims, goals, and subgoals. Let us illustrate this expanded model by applying it to the operations of a halfway house. The mission is a broad statement that relates the treatment program's intended effects to the needs of its participants. Here, the mission might be for clients to achieve a productive and enjoyable life based on solid sobriety. One of the major aims would include educational/vocational training so that residents can become productive contributors to society. Goals would be specific, verifiable, and attainable translations of the aims. Two examples would include earning a GED (equivalent to high school graduation) and completing other appropriate training indicated by intellectual and interest testing. These goals could easily be overwhelming unless subdivided into manageable steps. The sustained and complex effort is subdivided into subgoals: developing time management and study skills, mastery of basic academic skills, and then enrollment in a GED program. The specific plans detail the steps in achieving each subgoal. When complex or protracted efforts are indicated, it will be appropriate to expand the problem-solving model.

In the treatment of DWI clients there are three related goals: avoiding driving under the influence of alcohol or drugs, making a change in drinking sufficient that there will be no further significant life problems attributable to alcohol use, and making the necessary life-style changes so that the foregoing goals can be achieved in a comfortable and sustained manner. For any individual, these goals will of course be much more specific. Most of the required changes can be made in short order, with clearly prioritized steps. For this reason the ten-stage model is adequate.

Where there is certain to be modification is in the content and form of the presentations described. The exercises presented are those I have found to be useful and to represent my best understanding of the current findings related to alcohol use and abuse. I presume that the reader will have disagreed with some of what is included. Further, I am sure that advances in research and treatment will soon make some of my comments outdated. That is as it should be. I envision this book's being used as a teaching manual, with notes in the margin and related exercises clipped into each chapter. The current exercises would be supplemented with additional activities and materials, filed in the most appropriate section of the problem-solving sequence. Paragraphs should be replaced as new facts become available. The text is a way of organizing knowledge for sharing. It should not constrain learning by implying that what is included is all that is needed. Rather, it lends a structure so that new activities can be organized and sequenced for delivery in a way that will maximally empower clients to change.

The presentations should be modified to meet the needs of different audiences. In this respect, anyone using elements of the program outlined is a co-creator, along with myself and the many sources of the oral tradition of treatment that lies behind these materials. It is in this spirit that I would welcome comments about modifications, or outlines of additional exercises that you have found useful in helping your clients reach a new understanding of their alcohol involvement.

# References

## Print

*AA guidelines: Cooperating with court, A.S.A.P., and similar programs* (1986 printing). New York: Alcoholics Anonymous World Services.

Alberti, R. E., & Emmons, M. L. (1986). *Your perfect right: A guide to assertive living* (5th ed.). San Luis Obispo, CA: Impact Publishers.

*Alcoholics Anonymous* (3rd ed., 1976). New York: Alcoholics Anonymous World Services.

American Medical Association. (1986). Alcohol advertising, counteradvertising, and depiction in the public media. *Journal of the American Medical Association, 256,* 1485–1488.

Anstie, F. (1864). *Stimulants and narcotics, their mutual relations; with special researches on the action of alcohol, aether, and chloroform on the vital organism.* London: Macmillan.

Armor, D. J., Polich, J. M., & Stambul, H. B. (1978). *Alcoholism and treatment.* New York: Wiley.

Ashley, M. J., Olin, J. S., leRichie, W. H., Kornaczewski, A., Schmidt, W., & Rankin, J. G. (1977). Evidence for accelerated development of physical disease in women. *Archives of Internal Medicine, 137,* 883–887.

Atkin, C., & Block, M. (1981). *Content and effects of alcohol advertising.* Springfield, VA: National Technical Information Service.

Bach, G. R., & Goldberg, H. (1974). *Creative aggression.* Garden City, NY: Doubleday.

Bach, G. R., & Wyden, P. (1968). *The intimate enemy: How to fight fair in love and marriage.* New York: William Morrow.

Bacon, S. (1973). Process of addiction to alcohol: Social aspects. *Quarterly Journal on the Study of Alcohol, 34,* 1–27.

Bailey, M. B., Haberman, P. W., & Alksne, H. (1962). Outcomes of alcoholic marriages: Endurance, termination, or recovery. *Quarterly Journal of Studies on Alcohol, 23,* 610–623.

Bailey, M. B., Haberman, P. W., & Alksne, H. (1965). The epidemiology of alcoholism in an urban residential area. *Quarterly Journal of Studies on Alcohol, 26,* 19–40.

Bandler, R., & Grinder, J. (1979). *Frogs into princes.* Moab, UT: Real People Press.

Barchha, R., Stewart, M. A., & Guze, S. B. (1968). The prevalence of alcoholism among general hospital ward patients. *American Journal of Psychiatry, 125,* 681–684.

Barry H. (1982). A psychological perspective on the development of alcoholism. In E. M. Pattison & E. Kaufman, (Eds.), *Encyclopedic handbook of alcoholism* (pp. 529–539). New York: Gardner.

Beck, A. T., Rush, A. J., Shaw, B. F., & Emery, G. (1979). *Cognitive therapy of depression.* New York: Guilford.

Beitel, G. A., Sharp, M. C., & Glauz, W. D. (1975). Probability of arrest while drivcing under the influence of alcohol. *Journal of Studies on Alcohol, 36,* 109–116.

Bensen, H. (1975). *The relaxation response.* New York: William Morrow.

Berenson, D. (1976). Alcohol and the family system. In P. Guerin, (Ed.), *Family and therapy and practice.* (pp. 284–297). New York: Gardner.

Berger, T., French, E. D., Siggins, G. R., Shier, W. T., & Bloom, F. E. (1982). Ethanol and some tetrahydroisoquinolines alter the discharge of cortical and hippocampal neurons: Relationship to endogenous opiates. *Pharmacology, Biochemistry, and Behavior, 17,* 813–821.

Bernadt, M. W., Mumford, J., & Murray, R. M. (1984). A discriminant function analysis of screening tests for excessive drinking and alcoholism. *Journal of Studies on Alcohol, 45,* 81–86.

Berne, E. (1964). *Games people play.* New York: Grove.

Bion, W. R. (1961). *Experiences in groups* (2nd ed.). New York: Basic Books.

Black, C. (1981). *It will never happen to me.* Denver, CO: M.A.C.

Black, C. (1985). *Repeat after me.* Denver, CO: M.A.C.

Bloom, L. Z., Coburn, K., & Pearlman, J. (1975). *The new assertive woman.* New York: Delacorte.

Blume, S. B. (1986). Women and alcohol. *Journal of the American Medical Association, 256,* 1467–1470.

Bohman, M. (1978). Some genetic aspects of alcoholism and criminality: A population of adoptees. *Archives of General Psychiatry, 35,* 269–276.

Bolles, R. N. (1981). *The three boxes of life.* Berkeley, CA: Ten Speed Press.

Bolles, R. N. (1987). *What color is your parachute, 1987.* Berkeley, CA: Ten Speed Press.

Borkenstein, R. F. (1976). Efficacy of law enforcement procedures. *Problems in Pharmacopsychology, 11,* 1–10.

Borkenstein, R. F., Crawther, R. F., Shumate, R. P., Ziel, W. B., & Zylman, R. (1964). *The role of the drinking driver in traffic accidents.* Bloomington, IN: Indiana University Press.

Bourne, P. G., & Light, E. (1979). Alcohol problems in blacks and women. In J. H. Mendelson, & N. K. Mello (Eds.), *The diagnosis and treatment of alcoholism* (pp. 84–123). New York: McGraw-Hill.

Bowen, M. (1978). Alcoholism and the family. In *Family therapy in clinical practice* (pp. 259–268). New York: Aronson. (Original work published 1974).

Bowen, M. (1984, April). Discussion. In M. Bowen & P. Steinglass (Chairs), *Research and theory: Family systems with alcoholism*. Symposium presented by the Georgetown University Family Center, Washington, DC.

Branchey, L., Davis, W., & Lieber, C. S. (1984). Alcoholism in Vietnam and Korea veterans: A long-term follow-up. *Alcoholism: Clinical and Experimental Research, 8,* 572–575.

Breed, W., & DeFoe, J. R. (1981). The portrayal of the drinking process on prime-time television. *Journal of Communication, 31,* 58–67.

Brown, S. (1985). *Treating the alcoholic: A developmental model of recovery.* New York: Wiley.

Brownell, K. D., Marlatt, G. A., Lichtenstein, E., & Wilson, G. T. (1986). Understanding and preventing relapse. *American Psychologist, 41,* 765–782.

Bugen, L. A. (1977). Human grief: A model for prediction and intervention. *American Journal of Orthopsychiatry, 47,* 196–206.

Bunn, G. (1983). DWI countermeasures as part of a systemic approach dealing with the entire alcohol problem continuum. *Proceedings of the DWI Colloquium: DWI Reeducation and Rehabilitation Programs—Successful Results and the Future* (pp. 62–81). Falls Church, VA: AAA Foundation for Traffic Safety.

Cadoret, R. J., O'Gorman, T. W., Troughton, E., & Haywood, E. (1985). Alcoholism and antisocial personality: Interrelationships, genetic and environmental factors. *Archives of General Psychiatry, 42,* 161–167.

Cadoret, R. J., Troughton, E., & O'Gorman, T. W. (1987). Genetic and environmental factors in alcohol abuse and antisocial personality. *Journal of Studies on Alcohol, 48,* 1–8.

Cahalan, D. (1970). *Problem drinkers: A national survey.* San Francisco: Jossey-Bass.

Carkhuff, R. R. (1969). *Helping and human relations* (vols. 1–2). New York: Holt, Rinehart and Winston.

Carkhuff, R. R. (1973a). *The art of helping: An introduction to life skills.* Amherst, MA: Human Resource Development Press.

Carkhuff, R. R. (1973b). *The art of problem-solving.* Amherst, MA: Human Resource Development Press.

Carroll, J. F. X., & Schnoll, S. H. (1982). Mixed drug and alcohol populations. In E. M. Pattison & E. Kaufman (Eds.), *Encyclopedic handbook of alcoholism* (pp. 742–758). New York: Gardner.

Cautela, J. (1973). Covert processes and behavior modification. *Journal of Nervous and Mental Disease, 157,* 27–35.

Chafetz, M. E. (1982). Safe and healthy drinking. In E. M. Pattison & E. Kaufman (Eds.), *Encyclopedic handbook of alcoholism* (pp. 483–489). New York: Gardner.

Chaney, E. F., O'Leary, M. R., & Marlatt, G. A. (1978). Skill training with alcoholics. *Journal of Clinical and Consulting Psychology, 46,* 1092–1104.

Citrenbaum, C. M., King, M. E., & Cohen, W. I. (1985). *Modern clinical hypnosis for habit control.* New York: Norton.

Clarren, S. K., & Smith, D. W. (1978). The fetal alcohol syndrome. *New England Journal of Medicine, 298,* 1063–1067.

Cloninger, C. R., Bohman, M., & Sigvardsson, S. (1981). Inheritance of alcohol abuse. *Archives of General Psychiatry, 38,* 361–368.

Cohen, S. (1980, September). Alcohol-drug combinations. *DUI Tieline,* pp. 4–6.

Cooper, K. E. (1977). *The aerobic way: New data on the world's most popular exercise program.* New York: Evans.

Cooper, K. E. (1982). *The aerobic program for total well-being.* New York: Evans.

Corey, G., & Corey, M. S. (1982). *Groups: Process and practice* (2nd ed.). Monterey, CA: Brooks/Cole.

Cotton, N. S. (1979). The familial incidence of alcoholism. *Journal of Studies on Alcohol, 40,* 89–115.

Critchlow, B. (1986). Powers of John Barleycorn: Beliefs about the effects of alcohol on social behavior. *American Psychologist, 41,* 751–764.

Cruse, J. R. (1985). *The romance: A story of chemical dependency.* Rapid City, SD: Onsite/Nurturing Networks.

Crystal, J. C., & Bolles, R. N. (1980). *Where do I go from here with my life?* Berkeley, CA: Ten Speed Press.

Cummings, C., Gordon, J. R., & Marlatt, G. A. (1980). Relapse: Strategies of prevention and prediction. In W. R. Miller (Ed.), *The addictive behaviors: Treatment of alcoholism, drug abuse, smoking and obesity* (pp. 291–322). Oxford, UK: Pergamon.

Davis, V. E., & Walsh, M. J. (1970). Alcohol, amines, alkaloids: A possible biochemical basis for alcohol addiction. *Science, 167,* 1005–1007.

Department of Transportation. (1977). *An activist's guide for curbing the drunk driver* (DOT Publication No. HS 802110). Washington, DC: U. S. Government Printing Office.

Department of Transportation. (1983). *Fatal accident reporting system, 1981* (DOT Publication No. MS-806-251). Springfield, VA: NTIS.

Drews, T. R. (1980–1986). *Getting them sober* (Vols. 1–3). South Plainfield, NJ: Bridge Publications.

Dulfano, C. (1982). *Families, alcoholism, and recovery.* Center City, MN: Hazelden.

Duncan, C., & Dietrich, R. A. (1980). A critical evaluation of tetrahydroisoquinoline induced preference in rats. *Pharmacology, Biochemistry, and Behavior, 13,* 265–281.

*Each day a new beginning.* (1982). Center City, MN: Hazelden.

Egan, G. (1976). *Interpersonal living: A skills/contract approach to human-relations training in groups.* Monterey, CA: Brooks/Cole.

Egan, G. (1982). *The skilled helper* (2nd ed.). Monterey, CA: Brooks/Cole.

Egan, G. (1985). *Change agent skills for the helping and human service professions.* Monterey, CA: Brooks/Cole.

Egan, G., & Cowan, M. A. (1979). *People in systems: A model for development in the human service professions and education.* Monterey, CA: Brooks/Cole.

Ellis, A. (1973). *Humanistic psychotherapy: The rational-emotive approach.* New York: Julian.

Ellis, A. (1977). *How to live with and without anger.* New York: Readers Digest Books.

Ellis, A., & Grieger, R. (1977). *Handbook of rational-emotive therapy.* New York: Springer.

Ellis, A., & Harper, R. A. (1975). *The new guide to rational living.* North Hollywood, CA: Wilshire Books.

Erikson, E. H. (1968). *Identity: Youth and crisis.* New York: Norton.

Ewing, J. A. (1982). Disulfiram and other deterrent drugs. In E. M. Pattison & E. Kaufman (Eds.), *Encyclopedic handbook of alcoholism* (pp. 1033–1042). New York: Gardner.

Ewing, J. A., & Fox, R. E. (1968). Family therapy of alcoholism. In J. H. Masserman (Ed.), *Current psychiatric therapies* (Vol. 8, pp. 86–91). New York: Grune and Stratton.

Farber, N. (1985, April 22). Clarence Busch, the drunk driver who inspired a movement, faces prison for another accident. *People,* pp. 151–152.

F. A. S. Facts. (1980). *Professional Alcoholism Counselors Association News, 2,* 14–15.

Favazza, A. R. (1982). The alcohol withdrawal syndrome and medical detoxification. In E. M. Pattison & E. Kaufman (Eds.), *Encyclopedic handbook of alcoholism* (pp. 1068–1075). New York: Gardner.

Fitzgibbons, R. P. (1986). The cognitive and emotive uses of forgiveness in the treatment of anger. *Psychotherapy, 23,* 629–633.

Fluharty, D. G. (1987). *Is alcoholism an inborn error of metabolism?* Manuscript submitted for publication. (Available from Box 1774, Newport News, VA 23601).

Foley, D., & Leschuk, K. (1986). The Presidential Commission on Drunk Driving: An analysis and summary. In D. Foley (Ed.), *Stop DWI: Successful community responses to drunk driving* (pp. 17–31). Lexington, MA: Lexington Books.

Frankl, V. E. (1963). *Man's search for meaning: An introduction to logotherapy.* New York: Washington Square.

Gitlow, S. E. (1982). The clinical pharmacology and drug interactions of ethanol. In E. M. Pattison & E. Kaufman (Eds.), *Encyclopedic handbook of alcoholism* (pp. 354–364). New York: Gardner.

Goldman, M. S. (1983). Cognitive impairment in chronic alcoholics. *American Psychologist, 38,* 1045–1054.

Goodwin, D. W. (1979). Alcoholism and heredity. *Archives of General Psychiatry, 36,* 57–61.

Goodwin, D. W. (1982). Alcoholism and suicide: Association factors. In E. M. Pattison & E. Kaufman (Eds.), *Encyclopedic handbook of alcoholism* (pp. 655–662). New York: Gardner.

Goodwin, D. W. (1985). Genetic determinants of alcoholism. In J. H. Mendelson & N. K. Mello (Eds.), *The diagnosis and treatment of alcoholism* (2nd ed., pp. 65–87). New York: McGraw-Hill.

Gorski, T. T. (1986a). Long term withdrawal: A complicating factor in recovery. *Alcohol Health and Research World, 11,* 63–64.

Gorski, T. T. (1986b). Relapse prevention planning: A new recovery tool. *Alcohol Health and Research World, 11,* pp. 6–11, 63.

Gorski, T. T., & Miller, M. (1979). *Counseling for relapse prevention.* Hazel Crest, IL: Alcoholism Systems Associates.

Grinder, J., & Bandler, R. (1982). *Reframing: Neuro-Linguistic Programming and the transformation of meaning.* Moab, UT: Real People Press.

Hagen, R. E. (1985). Evaluation of the effectiveness of educational and rehabilitative efforts: Opportunities for research. In T. B. Turner, R. F. Borkenstein, R. K. Jones, & P. B. Santora (Eds.), *Alcohol and highway safety: Proceedings of the North American Conference on Alcohol and Highway Safety. Journal of Studies on Alcohol* (Supplement No. 10), 179–183.

Hagen, R. E., Williams, R. L., McConnell, E. J., & Fleming, C. W. (1978). *An evaluation of alcohol abuse treatment as an alternative to drivers license suspension or revocation* (Report No. 68). Sacramento, CA: Department of Motor Vehicles.

Hammer, R. L. (1978). *Almost everything you ever wanted to know about alcohol.* Lansing, MI: Michigan Alcohol and Drug Information Foundation.

Hartmann, E. L. (1982). Alcohol and the sleep disorders. In E. M. Pattison & E. Kaufman (Eds.), *Encyclopedic handbook of alcoholism* (pp. 180–193). New York: Gardner.

Harwood, H. J., & Napolitano, D. M. (1985). Economic implications of fetal alcohol syndrome. *Alcohol Health and Research World, 10,* 38–43.

Heather, N., & Robertson, I. H. (1981). *Controlled drinking.* London: Methuen.

Herzberg, F. (1968, January). One more time: How do you motivate employees? *Harvard Business Review, 46,* 53–62.

Holden, R. T. (1986). Rehabilitative sanctions for drunk driving: An experimental evaluation. In D. Foley (Ed.), *Stop DWI: Successful community responses to drunk driving* (pp. 55–71). Lexington, MA: Lexington Books.

Huber, H., Karlin, R., & Nathan, P. E. (1976). Blood alcohol level discrimination by nonalcoholics: The role of internal and external cues. *Journal of Studies on Alcohol, 37,* 27–39.

Hunt, W. A., Barnett, L. W., & Branch, L. G. (1971). Relapse rates in addiction programs. *Journal of Clinical Psychology, 27,* 455–456.

*Is AA for You?* (1973). New York: Alcoholics Anonymous World Services.

Jackson, J. (1954). The adjustment of the family to the crisis of alcoholism. *Quarterly Journal of Studies on Alcohol, 15,* 562–586.

Jacob, T., & Leonard, K. (1986). Psychosocial function in children of alcoholic fathers, depressed fathers, and controls. *Journal of Studies on Alcohol, 47,* 373–380.

Jacobson, E. (1929). *Progressive relaxation.* Chicago: University of Chicago Press.

Jacobson, M., Macker, G., & Atkins, R. (1983). *The booze merchants: The inebriating of America.* Washington, DC: Center for Science in the Public Interest.

Jaffe, J. H., & Ciraulo, D. (1985). Drugs used in the treatment of alcoholism. In J. H. Mendelson & N. K. Mello (Eds.), *The diagnosis and treatment of alcoholism* (2nd ed., pp. 355–390). New York: McGraw-Hill.

Jakubowski-Spector, P. (1973). *An introduction to assertive training procedures for women.* Washington, DC: American Personnel and Guidance Association.

Jellinek, E. M. (1952). Phases of alcohol addiction. *Quarterly Journal of Studies on Alcohol, 13,* 673–684.

Jellinek, E. M. (1960). *Disease concept of alcoholism.* New Haven, CT: College and University Press.

Jessor, R. (1985). Adolescent problem drinking: Psychosocial aspects and developmental outcomes. In H. Moskowitz (Ed.), *Alcohol, drugs, and driving: Proceedings of the International Symposium on Alcohol, Drugs, and Driving* (pp. 69–96). Los Angeles, CA: University of California Press.

Johnson, V. E. (1973). *I'll quit tomorrow.* New York: Harper & Row.

Jones, J. W. (1983). *The Children of Alcoholics Screening Test: Test manual.* Chicago, IL: Camelot Unlimited. (Available from 5 North Wabash, Suite 1409, Department 18PG1, Chicago, IL 60602).

Jones, R., & Joscelyn, K. (1978). *Alcohol and highway safety: A review of the state of the knowledge* (Tech. Rep. HS803-74). Washington, DC: National Highway Traffic Safety Administration.

Karacan, I., & Hanusa, T. L. (1982). The effects of alcohol relative to sexual dysfunction. In E. M. Pattison & E. Kaufman (Eds.), *Encyclopedic handbook of alcoholism* (pp. 686–695). New York: Gardner.

Kaufman, E. (1982). Alcoholism and the use of other drugs. In E. M. Pattison & E. Kaufman (Eds.), *Encyclopedic handbook of alcoholism* (pp. 696–705). New York: Gardner.

Kaufman, E., & Pattison, E. M. (1982). The family and alcoholism. In E. M. Pattison & E. Kaufman (Eds.), *Encyclopedic handbook of alcoholism* (pp. 663–672). New York: Gardner.

Kelman, D. (1958). Compliance, identification, and internalization: Three processes of attitude change. *Journal of Conflict Resolution, 2,* 51–60.

Kennedy, E. (1977). *On becoming a counselor: A basic guide for nonprofessional counselors.* New York: Seabury.

Ketcham, K., & Mueller, A. (1983). *Eating right to live sober.* Seattle, WA: Madrona Publishers.

Kinney, J., & Leaton, G. (1978). *Loosening the grip: A handbook of alcohol information.* St. Louis, MO: Mosby.

Kirschenbaum, H. (1977). *Advanced values clarification.* La Jolla, CA: University Associates.

Knox, W. J. (1976). Objective psychological measurement and alcoholism: Review of the literature, 1971–1972. *Psychological Reports, 38*(1), 1023–1050.

Kohlberg, L. (1969). Stage and sequence: The cognitive-developmental approach to socialization. In D. A. Goslin (Ed.), *Handbook of socialization theory and research.* (pp. 347–480) Chicago: Rand McNally.

Korsten, M. A., & Lieber, C. S. (1985). Medical complications of alcoholism. In J. H. Mendelson & N. K. Mello (Eds.), *The diagnosis and treatment of alcoholism* (2nd ed., pp. 21–64). New York: McGraw-Hill.

Krizay, J., & Carels, E. J. (1986). *The fifty billion dollar drain.* Irvine, CA: Care Institute.

Kubler-Ross, E. (1969). *On death and dying.* New York: Macmillan.

Lange, A. J., & Jakubowski, P. (1976). *Responsible assertive behavior: Cognitive/ behavioral procedures for trainers*. Champaign, IL: Research Press.

Lazarus, A. (1976). *Multimodal therapy*. New York: Springer.

Lasarus, A. (1977). *In the mind's eye*. New York: Rawson Associates.

Lex, B. W. (1985). Alcohol problems in special populations. In J. H. Mendelson & N. K. Mello (Eds.), *The diagnosis and treatment of alcoholism* (2nd ed., pp. 89–187). New York: McGraw-Hill.

Lieber, C. S. (1976, March). The metabolism of alcohol. *Scientific American, 234,* 25–33.

Lindemann, E. (1944). Symptomatology and management of acute grief. *American Journal of Psychiatry, 101,* 141–148.

Linsky, A. S., Colby, J. P., & Strauss, M. A. (1986). Drinking norms and alcohol-related problems in the United States. *Journal of Studies on Alcohol, 47,* 384–393.

Littman, G. K., Eiser, J. R., Rawson, N. S. B., & Oppenheim, A. N. (1977). Towards a typology of relapse: A preliminary report. *Drug and Alcohol Dependence, 2,* 157–162.

*Living sober*. (1975). New York: Alcoholics Anonymous World Services.

Lord, L., & Lord, E. (1976). *How to communicate in sobriety*. Center City, MN: Hazelden.

Lowman, C. (1982). Drinking and driving among youth. *Alcohol Health and Research World, 7,* 41–49.

Ludwig, A. M. (1986). The mystery of craving. *Alcohol Health and Research World, 11,* pp. 12–17, 69.

Ludwig, A. M., & Stark, L. H. (1974). Alcohol craving: Subjective and situational aspects. *Quarterly Journal of Studies on Alcohol, 35,* 899–905.

Luks, A. (1983, September 4). 'Neo-prohibition': Pouring taxes and stigma on drunks. *Washington Post,* C1–C2.

Malfetti, J. L., & Winter, D. J. (1980). *Counseling manual for educational and rehabilitative programs for persons convicted of driving while intoxicated (DWI)*. Falls Church, VA: AAA Foundation for Traffic Safety.

Malin, H., Wilson, R., Williams, G., & Aitken, S. (1985). 1983 alcohol/health practices supplement. *Alcohol Health and Research World, 10,* 48–51.

Mandell, W. (1982). Preventing alcohol-related problems and dependencies through information and education programs. In E. M. Pattison & E. Kaufman (Eds.), *Encyclopedic handbook of alcoholism* (pp. 468–482). New York: Gardner.

Marlatt, G. A. (1978). Craving for alcohol, loss of control, and relapse. In P. E. Nathan, G. A. Marlatt & T. Loberg (Eds.), *Alcoholism: New directions in behavioral research and treatment* (pp. 271–314). New York: Plenum.

Marlatt, G. A. (1983). The controlled-drinking controversy. *American Psychologist, 38,* 1097–1110.

Marlatt, G. A., & Gordon, J. R. (1985). *Relapse prevention: Maintenance strategies in the treatment of addictive behaviors*. New York: Guilford.

Mayer, J., & Filstead, W. (1979). The Adolescent Alcohol Involvement Scale: An instrument for measuring adolescents use and misuse of alcohol. *Journal of Studies on Alcohol, 40,* 291–300.

McCrady, B. S. (1982). Marital dysfunction: Alcoholism and marriage. In E. M. Pattison & E. Kaufman (Eds.), *Encyclopedic handbook of alcoholism* (pp. 673–685). New York: Gardner.

McCrady, B. S., Noel, N. E., Abrams, D. B., Stout, R. L., Nelson, H. F., & Hay, W. M. (1986). Comparative effectiveness of three types of spouse involvement in outpatient behavioral alcoholism treatment. *Journal of Studies on Alcohol, 47,* 459–467.

McIntire, J. (1980). Defining the alcohol and traffic safety problem—A matter of perspective. *DUI Tieline,* 1–2.

Meichenbaum, D. (1977). *Cognitive behavior modification: An integrative approach.* New York: Plenum.

Mendelson, J. H., Stein, S., & McGuire, M. T. (1966). Comparative psychological studies of alcoholic and nonalcoholic subjects undergoing experimentally induced ethanol intoxication. *Psychosomatic Medicine, 28,* 1–12.

Mikulas, W. L. (1983). *Skills of living: A complete course in you and what you can do about yourself.* New York: University Press of America.

Milam, J. R. (1974). *Emergent comprehensive concept of alcoholism.* Kirkland, WA: ACA Press.

Milam, J. R., & Ketcham, K. (1981). *Under the influence: A guide to the myths and realities of alcoholism.* Seattle, WA: Madrona Publishers.

Miller, W. R. (1983). Controlled drinking: A history and critical review. *Journal of Studies on Alcohol, 44,* 68–83.

Miller, W. R., & Hester, R. K. (1980). Treating the problem drinker: Modern approaches. In W. R. Miller (Ed.), *The addictive behaviors: Treatment of alcoholism, drug abuse, smoking, and obesity* (pp. 11–141). Elmsford, NY: Pergamon.

Moberg, D. P. (1983). Identifying adolescents with alcohol problems: A field test of the Adolescent Alcohol Involvement Scale. *Journal of Studies on Alcohol, 44,* 701–721.

Mulford, H. A. (1980). On the validity of the Iowa Alcoholic Stages Index. *Journal of Studies on Alcohol, 41,* 86–88.

Mulford, H. A. (1982). The epidemiology of alcoholism and its implications. In E. M. Pattison & E. Kaufman (Eds.), *Encyclopedic handbook of alcoholism* (pp. 441–457). New York: Gardner.

Murray, R. M., & Stabeman, J. R. (1982). Genetic factors in alcoholism predisposition. In E. M. Pattison & E. Kaufman (Eds.), *Encyclopedic handbook of alcoholism* (pp. 135–146). New York: Gardner.

Myers, R. D. (1978). Tetrahydroisoquinolines in the brain: The basis of an animal model of alcoholism. *Alcoholism: Clinical and Experimental Research, 2,* 145–154.

Myers, R. D., & Critcher, E. C. (1982). Nalaxone alters alcohol drinking induced in the rat by tetrahydropapaveroline (THP) infused ICV. *Pharmacology, Biochemistry, and Behavior, 16,* 827–836.

Myers, R. D., McCaleb, M. L., & Rowe, W. D. (1982). Alcohol drinking induced in the monkey by tetrahydropapaveroline (THP) infused into the cerebral ventricle. *Pharmacology, Biochemistry, and Behavior, 16,* 995–1000.

Myers, R. D., & Melchior, C. L. (1977). Alcohol drinking: Abnormal intake caused by tetrahydropapaveroline (THP) in the brain. *Science, 196,* 554–556.

Nathan, P. E. (1982). Blood alcohol level discrimination and diagnosis. In E. M. Pattison & E. Kaufman (Eds.), *Encyclopedic handbook of alcoholism* (pp. 64–71). New York: Gardner.

National Council on Alcoholism. (1972a). Criteria for the diagnosis of alcoholism. *American Journal of Psychiatry, 129,* 127–135.

National Council on Alcoholism. (1972b). *What are the signs of alcoholism?*. New York: Author.

National Institute of Alcohol Abuse and Alcoholism. (1981). *First statistical compendium on alcohol and health* (DHHS Publication No. ADM 81-1115). Washington, DC: U. S. Government Printing Office.

National Institute of Alcohol Abuse and Alcoholism. (1985). *Alcoholism: An inherited disease* (DHHS Publication No. ADM 85-1426). Washington, DC: U. S. Government Printing Office.

National Safety Council. (1972). *Alcohol and the impaired driver.* Chicago: American Medical Association.

New York State Division of Alcoholism and Alcohol Abuse. (1979). *Problem drinker-drivers: Evaluation and treatment* (Project No. AL79-002). Albany, NY: Author.

Nicholson, L., & Torbet, L. (1980). *How to fight fair with your kids . . . and win!* New York: Harcourt Brace Jovanovich.

Norwood, R. (1985). *Women who love too much.* Los Angeles: Jeremy Tarcher.

Opei, T. P. S., & Jackson, P. R. (1984). Some effective therapeutic factors in group cognitive-behavioral therapy with problem drinkers. *Journal of Studies on Alcohol, 45,* 119–123.

Operation Cork. (1982). *Alcoholism and the physician.* Dartmouth, NH: Dartmouth Medical School.

Orr, L., & Lizotte, A. (1986). Public information and public tolerance of drunk driving. In D. Foley (Ed.), *Stop DWI: Successful community responses to drunk driving* (pp. 139–149). Lexington, MA: Lexington Books.

Ovellette, E. M., Rosett, H. L., Rosman, N. P., & Weiner, L. (1977). Adverse effects on offspring of maternal alcohol abuse during pregnancy. *New England Journal of Medicine, 297,* 528–530.

Passons, W. R. (1975). *Gestalt approaches in counseling.* New York: Holt, Rinehart and Winston.

Pendery, M. L., Maltzman, I. M., & West, L. J. (1982). Controlled drinking by alcoholics? New findings and a reevaluation of a major affirmative study. *Science, 217,* 169–174.

Penick, E. C., Powell, B. J., Bingham, S. F., Liskow, B. I., Miller, N. S., & Read, M. R. (1987). A comparative study of family alcoholism, *Journal of Studies on Alcohol, 48,* 136–146.

Perls, F., Hefferline, R. F., & Goodman, P. (1951). *Gestalt therapy: Excitement and growth in the human personality.* New York: Delta.

Pernanen, K. (1981). Theoretical aspects of the relationship between alcohol use and crime. In J. Collins (Ed.), *Drinking and crime: Perspectives on the relationship between alcohol consumption and assaultive criminal behavior* (pp. 1–69). New York: Guilford.

Perrine, M. W., Waller, J. A., & Harris, L. S. (1971). *Alcohol and highway safety: Behavioral and medical aspects.* Washington, DC: National Highway Traffic Safety Administration.

Pesso, A. (1969). *Movement in psychotherapy.* New York: New York University Press.

Pickens, R., Hatsukami, D., Spicer, J., & Svikis, D. (1985). Relapse by alcohol abusers. *Alcoholism: Clinical and Experimental Research, 9,* 244–247.

Pilat, J. M., & Jones, J. W. (1985). Identification of children of alcoholics: Two empirical studies. *Alcohol Health and Research World, 9,* 27–33.

Podolsky, D. M. (1985a). Alcohol, other drugs, and traffic safety. *Alcohol Health and Research World, 9,* 16–23.

Podolsky, D. M. (1985b). That not-so-safe refuge: Unintentional injuries in the home and at play. *Alcohol Health and Research World, 9,* 24–27.

Podolsky, D. M. (1986). Alcohol and cancer. *Alcohol Health and Research World, 10,* 3–9.

Polich, J. M., Armor, D. J., & Braiker, H. B. (1981). *The course of alcoholism: Four years after treatment.* New York: Wiley.

Polster, E., & Polster, M. (1973). *Gestalt therapy integrated.* New York: Bruner-Mazel.

Quayle, D. (1983). American productivity: The devastating effect of alcoholism and drug abuse. *American Psychologist, 38,* 454–458.

Ramsay, R. W., & Noorbergen, R. (1981). *Living with loss.* New York: William Morrow.

Raths, L., & Simon, S. (1966). *Values and teaching.* Columbus, OH: Charles E. Merrill.

Reis, R. (1983). Traffic safety impact of DUI education and counseling programs. *Proceedings of the DWI Colloquium: DWI Reeducation and Rehabilitation Programs—Successful Results and the Future* (pp. 38–61). Falls Church, VA: AAA Foundation for Traffic Safety.

Renshaw, D. C. (1975). Sexual problems of alcoholics. *Chicago Medicine, 78,* 433–436.

Richman, A. (1985). Human risk factors in alcohol-related crashes. In T. B. Turner, R. F. Borkenstein, R. K. Jones & P. B. Santora (Eds.), *Alcohol and highway safety: Proceedings of the North American Conference on Alcohol and Highway Safety. Journal of Studies on Alcohol* (Supplement No. 10), 21–31.

Rist, F., & Watzl, H. (1983). Self-assessment of relapse risk and assertiveness in relation to treatment outcome of female alcoholics. *Addictive Behaviors, 8,* 121–127.

Rogers, R., & McMillin, C. (1984). *Don't help: A guide to working with the alcoholic.* West Friendship, MD: Education and Training Institute of Maryland.

Rosett, H. L., & Weiner, L. (1982). Effects of alcohol on the fetus. In E. M. Pattison & E. Kaufman (Eds.), *Encyclopedic handbook of alcoholism* (pp. 301–310). New York: Gardner.

Ross, H. L. (1984). *Deterring the drinking driver.* Lexington, MA: Lexington Books.

Ross, H. L. (1985). Summary of topic C—countermeasures. In T. B. Turner, R. F. Borkenstein, R. K. Jones & P. B. Santora (Eds.), *Alcohol and highway safety: Proceedings of the North American Conference on Alcohol and Highway Saftey. Journal of Studies on Alcohol* (Supplement No. 10), 207–209.

Rozien, R. (1983). Loosening up: General population views of the effects of alcohol. In R. Room & G. Collins (Eds.), *Drinking and disinhibition: Nature and meaning of the link* (NIAAA research monograph No. 12, pp. 236–257). Washington, DC: U. S. Government Printing Office.

Rupp, K. L. (1985, June 8). The week. *Winchester Star,* p. 4.

Salsberg, P. M., & Klingberg, C. L. (1981). *License revocation and alcoholism treatment programs for habitual traffic offenders* (Report No. 049). Olympia, WA: Department of Licensing.

Satir, V. (1972). *Peoplemaking.* Palo Alto, CA: Science and Behavior Books.

Saxe, L., Dougherty, D., & Esty, J. (1983). *The effectiveness and costs of alcoholism treatment* (Congressional Office of Technology Assessment case study, Publication No. 052-003-00902-1). Washington, DC: U. S. Government Printing Office.

Schatzkin, A., Jones, D. Y., Hoover, R. N., Taylor, P. R., Brinton, L. A., Ziegler, R. G., Harvey, E. B., Carter, C. L., Licitra, L. M., Dufour, M. C., & Larson, D. B. (1987, May 7). Alcohol consumption and breast cancer in the epediologic follow-up study of the first national health and nutrition examination survey. *New England Journal of Medicine, 316,* 1169–1173.

Schifrin, L. G., Hartzog, C. E., & Brand, D. H. (1980). Costs of alcoholism and alcohol abuse and their relation to alcohol research. In *Alcoholism and related problems: Opportunities for research* (pp. 165–186). Washington, DC: National Academy of Sciences.

Schuckit, M. (1980). Alcoholism and genetics: Possible biological mediators. *Biological Psychiatry, 15,* 437–447.

Schuckit, M. (1985). Treatment of alcoholism in office and outpatient settings. In J. H. Mendelson & N. K. Mello (Eds.), *The diagnosis and treatment of alcoholism* (2nd ed., pp. 295–324). New York: McGraw-Hill.

Schuckit, M. (1986). Primary men alcoholics with histories of suicide attempts. *Journal of Studies on Alcohol, 47,* 78–81.

Schuckit, M., & Rayses, V. (1979). Ethanol ingestion: Differences in acetaldehyde concentrations in relatives of alcoholics and controls. *Science, 203,* 54–55.

Secretary Margaret Heckler, (1983, August 31). *Alcohol Report, 11,* 1.

Segal, R., & Sisson, B. V. (1985). Medical complications associated with alcohol use and the assessment of risk of physical damage. In T. E. Bratter & G. G. Forrest (Eds.), *Alcoholism and substance abuse: Strategies for clinical intervention* (pp. 137–175). New York: Macmillan.

Sellers, E. M., & Kalant, H. (1982). Alcohol withdrawal and delirium tremens. In E. M. Pattison & E. Kaufman (Eds.), *Encyclopedic handbook of alcoholism* (pp. 147–166). New York: Gardner.

Selzer, M. L. (1971). The Michigan Alcohol Screening Test—The quest for a new diagnostic instrument. *American Journal of Psychiatry, 127,* 1653–1658.

Shapiro, D. H. (1982). Overview: Clinical and physiological comparison of meditation with other self-control strategies. *American Journal of Psychiatry, 139,* 267–274.

Silverstein, S. J., Nathan, P. E., & Taylor, H. A. (1974). Blood alcohol level estimation and controlled drinking by chronic alcoholics. *Behavior Therapy, 5,* 1–15.

Simon, S. B., Howe, L. W., & Kirschenbaum, H. (1972). *Values clarification: A handbook of practical strategies for teachers and students.* New York: Hart Publishing.

Simpson, H. M. (1985). Polydrug effects and traffic safety. In H. Moskowitz (Ed.), *Alcohol, drugs, and driving: Proceedings of the International Symposium on Alcohol, Drugs, and Driving* (pp. 17–44). Los Angeles, CA: University of California Press.

Sobell, M. B., & Sobell, L. C. (1973). Individualized behavior therapy for alcoholics. *Behavior Therapy, 4,* 49–72.

Sobell, M. B., & Sobell, L. C. (1978). *Behavioral treatment of alcohol problems: Individualized therapy and controlled drinking.* New York: Plenum.

Sobell, M. B., & Sobell, L. C. (1982). Controlled drinking: A concept comes of age. In K. R. Blanstein & J. Polivy (Eds.), *Self-control and self-modification of emotional behavior.* New York: Plenum.

Stapleton, J. M., Guthrie, S., & Linnoila, M. (1986). Effects of alcohol and other pychotropic drugs on eye movements: Relevance for traffic safety. *Journal of Studies on Alcohol, 47,* 426–432.

Steinglass, P., Davis, D., & Berensen, D. (1977). Observations of conjointly hospitalized 'alcoholic couples' during sobriety and intoxication: Implications for theory and therapy. *Family Process, 16,* 1–16.

Taylor, J. R., Helzer, J. E., & Robins, L. N. (1986). Moderate drinking in ex-alcoholics: Recent studies. *Journal of Studies on Alcohol, 47,* 115–121.

Tewari, S., & Carson, V. G. (1982). Biochemistry of alcohol and alcohol metabolism. In E. M. Pattison & E. Kaufman (Eds.), *Encyclopedic handbook of alcoholism* (pp. 83–104). New York: Gardner.

Trumble, J. G., & Walsh, J. M. (1985). A new initiative for solving age-old problems. *Alcohol Health and Research World, 9,* 2–5.

*The twelve steps and the twelve traditions.* (1953). New York: Alcoholics Anonymous World Services.

Vaillant, G. E. (1983). *The natural history of alcoholism.* Cambridge, MA: Harvard University Press.

Vaughn, C. (1982). *Addictive drinking.* New York: Viking.

Virginia Alcohol Safety Action Program. (1985). *ASAP education: Curriculum instructor's manual.* Richmond, VA: Author.

Voas, R. B. (1985). *Alcohol and highway safety, 1984: A review of the state of the knowledge.* Washington, DC: National Highway Traffic Safety Administration.

Vogler, R. E., & Bartz, W. R. (1982). *The better way to drink.* New York: Simon and Schuster.

Wallace, J. (1978a). Behavioral-modification methods as adjuncts to psychotherapy.

In S. Zimberg, J. Wallace & S. B. Blume (Eds.), *Practical approaches to alcoholism psychotherapy* (pp. 99–117). New York: Plenum.

Wallace, J. (1978b). Working with the preferred defense structure of the recovering alcoholic. In S. Zimberg, J. Wallace & S. B. Blume (Eds.), *Practical approaches to alcoholism psychotherapy* (pp. 19–29). New York: Plenum.

Wallack, L., Breed, W., & Cruz, J. (1987). Alcohol on prime-time television. *Journal of Studies on Alcohol, 48,* 33–38.

Waller, P. F. (1982). Alcohol and highway safety. In E. M. Pattison & E. Kaufman (Eds.), *Encyclopedic handbook of alcoholism* (pp. 395–405). New York: Gardner.

Waller, P. F. (1983). Spitting in the ocean: Realistic expectations of the impact of driver alcohol education and rehabilitation programs on the problem of drunk driving. *Proceedings of the DWI Colloquium: DWI Reeducation and Rehabilitation Programs—Successful Results and the Future* (pp. 122–136). Falls Church, VA: AAA Foundation for Traffic Safety.

Waller, P. F., Steward, J. R., Hausen, A. R., Stults, J. C., Popkin, C. L., & Rodgman, E. A. (1986, September 19). The potentiating effects of alcohol on driver injury. *Journal of the American Medical Association, 256,* 1461–1466.

Warren, K. (1985). Alcohol-related birth defects: Current trends in research. *Alcohol Health and Research World, 10,* 4–5.

Watson, D. L., & Tharp, R. G. (1985). *Self-directed behavior: Self-modification for personal adjustment* (4th ed.). Monterey, CA: Brooks/Cole.

Watzlawick, P. (1976). *How real is real?* New York: Random House.

Watzlawick, P., Beavin, J. H., & Jackson, D. D. (1967). *Pragmatics of human communication.* New York: Norton.

Wegscheider, S. (1981). *Another chance: Hope and help for the alcoholic family.* Palo Alto, CA: Science and Behavior Books.

Wegscheider-Cruse, S. (1985). *Choicemaking.* Pompano Beach, FL: Health Communications.

Weisenger, H. (1985). *Dr. Weisenger's anger work-out book.* New York: William Morrow.

Werner, E. E. (1986). Resilient offspring of alcoholics: A longitudinal study from birth to age 18. *Journal of Studies on Alcohol, 47,* 34–40.

West, L. J. (1984). *Alcoholism and related problems: Issues for the American public.* Englewood Cliffs, NJ: Prentice-Hall.

Wholey, D. (1984). *The courage to change: Personal conversations about alcoholism.* Boston, MA: Houghton Mifflin.

Wilkinson, P. (1980). Sexual differences in morbidity in alcoholics. In O. J. Kalant (Ed.), *Research advances in alcohol and drug problems in women* (pp. 331–364). New York: Plenum.

Willett, W. C., Stampfer, M. J., Colditz, G. A., Rosner, B. A., Hennekens, C. H., & Speizer, F. E. (1987, May 7). Moderate alcohol consumption and the risk of breast cancer. *New England Journal of Medicine, 316,* 1174–1180.

Williams, R. L., & Long, J. D. (1983). *Toward a self-managed lifestyle* (3rd ed.). Boston: Houghton Mifflin.

Winter, D. (1982). *Senior adults, traffic safety and alcohol.* Falls Church, VA: AAA Foundation for Traffic Safety.

Woititz, J. G. (1983). *Adult children of alcoholics.* Pompano Beach, FL: Health Communications.
Woititz, J. G. (1985). *Struggle for intimacy.* Pompano Beach, FL: Health Communications.
Yalom, I. D. (1985). *The theory and practice of group psychotherapy* (3rd ed.). New York: Basic Books.
Zimberg, S. (1978). Principles of alcoholism psychotherapy. In S. Zimberg, J. Wallace & S. B. Blume (Eds.), *Practical approaches to alcoholism psychotherapy* (pp. 3– 18). New York: Plenum.
Zobeck, T. S., Williams, G. D., & Bertolucci, D. (1986). Trends in alcohol-related fatal traffic accidents. *Alcohol Health and Research World, 11,* 60–62.

## Video

*AA and the alcoholic.* (1981). Miller, M. (Producer, Director), & Miller, J. (Director). Los Angeles, CA: Motivational Media.
*Alcohol abuse: The early warning signs.* (1977). Glendale, CA: Aims Media.
*Alcohol and human physiology.* (1984). Ralmon, J. (Producer). Glendale, CA: Aims Media.
*Alcohol: From use to abuse.* (1979). Marshall, S. (Presenter), & Miller, M. (Producer, Director). Los Angeles, CA: Motivational Media.
*Alcohol, pills, and recovery.* (1978). Pursch, J. A. (Narrator), Frederick, J. (Producer), & Kleiter, P. (Director). Los Angeles, CA: FMS Productions.
*Alcoholism: The twenty questions.* (1980). Miller, M. (Producer, Director). Los Angeles, CA: Motivational Media.
*Another chance.* (1983). Wegschieder, S. (Presenter). Center City, MN: Hazelden.
*Chalk talk on alcohol,* parts 1 and 2. Martin, J. (Presenter), & Navy Human Resources Division (Producer). Washington, DC: General Service Administration.
*Children of denial.* (1982). Black, C. (Presenter), Fahey, J. (Producer), & Tartan, J. (Director). Center City, MN: Hazelden.
*Denial: The inside story.* (1985). Rigolia, S. (Producer), & Swift, P. F. (Director). Center City, MN: Hazelden.
*Drink, drive, rationalize.* (1973). Starbecker, G. (Producer, Director). Falls Church, VA: AAA Foundation for Traffic Safety.
*Hollywood and vine.* (1977). Frederick, J. (Producer), & Miner, R. A. (Director). Los Angeles, CA: FMS Productions.
*How to sabotage your treatment.* (1982). Rogers, G. T. (Producer). Center City, MN: Hazelden.
*If you loved me.* (1977). Rogers, G. T. (Producer, Director). Center City, MN: Hazelden.
*I'll quit tomorrow.* Rogers, G. T. (Producer, Director). Center City, MN: Hazelden.
*Medical aspects of alcoholism,* parts 1 and 2. (1974). Schneider, M. (Presenter), Cromer, G. (Producer), & Medford, L. (Director). Long Beach, CA: Southerby Productions.

*The new life of Sandra Blain.* (1978). Tartan, J. (Producer, Director). Long Beach, CA: Southerby Productions.

*The other guy,* parts 1 and 2. (1970). Kahn, E. C. (Producer), & Skoble, H. (Director). Chicago, IL: Blue Shield.

*The secret love of Sandra Blain.* (1977). Tartan, J. (Producer, Director). Long Beach, CA: Southerby Productions.

*Shattered spirits.* (1985). Greenwald, R. (Producer, Director).

*A slight drinking problem.* (1977). Cooper, H. (Producer, Director). Long Beach, CA: Southerby Productions.

*So long pal.* (1976). Southerby, N. (Producer), & Hoster, D. (Director). Long Beach, CA: Southerby Productions.

*Soft is the heart of a child.* (1978). Rogers, G. T. (Producer, Director). Center City, MN: Hazelden.

*Under the influence.* (1977). Lisciandro, F. J. (Producer), & Tartan, J. (Director). Long Beach, CA: Southerby Productions.

*Under the influence.* (1986). Greene, V. (Producer), & Carter, T. (Director). New York: CBS.

*Until I get caught.* (1980). Cornell University, Department of Psychology (Producer). St. Petersburg, FL: Modern Talking Picture Service.

# Author Index

# Subject Index

# About the Author

**John S. Crandell** is a clinical psychologist in private practice in Winchester, Virginia. He received his Ph.D. from Loyola University of Chicago, an M.S. from Eastern Michigan University, and a B.A. from Kalamazoo College. He was on the faculty in the Department of Psychiatry at Northwestern University Medical School, and there collaborated on scholarly papers about program evaluation and management information systems. His current interests and writing pertain to family therapy, psychomotor psychotherapy, and substance abuse treatment.